T0059789

ESOTERIC HOLLYWOOD

Sex, Cults and Symbols in Film

Jay Dyer

Esoteric Hollywood: Sex, Cults and Symbols
Copyright © 2016 Jay Dyer All Rights Reserved

Published by:
Trine Day LLC
PO Box 577
Walterville, OR 97489
1-800-556-2012
www.TrineDay.com
publisher@TrineDay.net

Library of Congress Control Number: 2016955373

Dyer, Jay
 – 1st ed.
p. cm.
Includes references
Epub (ISBN-13) 978-1-63424-078-9
Mobi (ISBN-13) 978-1-63424-079-6
Print (ISBN-13) 978-1-63424-077-2
1. Motion picture industry -- California -- Los Angeles. 2. Occultism -- Political aspects -- United States. 3. Subliminal projection -- United States. I. Dyer, Jay. II. Title

First Edition
10 9

Printed in the USA
Distribution to the Trade by:
Independent Publishers Group (IPG)
814 North Franklin Street
Chicago, Illinois 60610
312.337.0747
www.ipgbook.com

Hollywood is a place where they'll pay you a thousand dollars for a kiss and fifty cents for your soul. I know, because I turned down the first offer often enough and held out for the fifty cents.

– Marilyn Monroe

Contents

Glossary

Aleatory: Depending on chance.

Aristotle: 4th century B.C. Greek philosopher, student of Plato and tutor to Alexander the Great. Aristotle emphasized study of the natural world through empirical and sensory evidence. Considered the father of both modern science and the founder of formal logic, Aristotle rejected Plato's ideal realm of "forms" and located all "essences" in material objects. By contrast, Plato taught real objects are immaterial and ideal, more akin to mathematics and numbers, rather than the phantasms and impressions of sense-data.

Athame: A black-handled knife in some tales of the Key of Solomon, a grimoire originating in the Middle Ages. The main ritual implement among others used in the religion of Wicca and other neo-pagan traditions.

Da'at: Knowledge. In Kabbalah, Da'at is the location (mystical state) where all ten sepiirot in the Tree of Life are united as one.

Deus absconditus: Hidden God, or God unknowable to the human mind.

Deva: A divine being or god in Buddhism, Hinduism and Jainism.

Eleutherian mysteries: Greek for giving or protecting freedom, as utilized in John Fowles' 1965 novel, The Magus.

Ex nihilo: From nothing.

Fideistic: Reliance on faith for knowledge.

Gematria: An Assyro-Babylonian-Greek system of code and numerology later adopted into Jewish culture that assigns numerical value to a word or phrase in the belief that words or phrases with identical numerical values bear some relation to each other or bear some relation to the number itself as it may apply to nature, a person's age, the calendar year, or the like.

Gnosis: Understanding of spiritual mysteries.

Harpocrates: In late Greek mythology, the god of silence, secrets and confidentiality.

Hegumen: The head of a religious community in the Eastern Church; used also as a title of honor for certain monks who are priests.

Heilsgeschichte: An interpretation of history emphasizing God's saving acts and viewing Jesus Christ as central in redemption.

Hermetica: Alchemical or magical. Also, protected from outside influence.

Hierophant: The chief priest at the Eleusinian Mysteries. An interpreter of sacred mysteries and arcane principles.

Katabasis: A descent to the underworld.

Literary Topos: In classical Greek rhetoric, 'topoi' mean "common places," signifying a standardized method of organizing an argument, or line of reasoning.

Manichaean: A philosophy which sees existence as an apocalyptic struggle between Good, the spiritual world of light, and Evil, the material world of darkness, with no middle ground.

Mystagogical: The spreading of mystical doctrines.

Noumena: Perceived things unexplainable. Unwordable.

Obeah: A Caribbean religion developed among West African slaves, specifically of Igbo origin.

Ouroboros: An ancient symbol, depicting a serpent eating its own tail.

Panspermia: The hypothesis that life exists throughout the Universe, distributed by meteoroids, asteroids, comets, planetoids, and, also, by spacecraft in the form of unintended contamination by micro-organisms.

Pharmakeia: The use or the administering of drugs, poisoning, or sorcery.

Praxis: Performance or application of skill.

Prima Materia: In alchemy, Prima materia, or first matter, is the ubiquitous starting material required for the alchemical magnum opus and the creation of the philosopher's stone.

Psychosphere: Contrasted with the biosphere, the noosphere or psychosphere is the realm of human thought or the psyche. For many thinkers and hermeticists, including Plato and Carl Jung, the realm of the psychosphere of all humans (and gods) is fundamentally connected or conjoined and may identified with, or an aspect of, the spiritual realm.

Sandhyabhasa: Twilight language. A supposed polysemic communication system associated with tantric traditions in Vajrayana Buddhism and

Hinduism. It includes visual, verbal and nonverbal communication: as in Tantric texts, written in "twilight language" that is incomprehensible to the uninitiated reader.

Semiotics: The philosophy or study of signs and symbols and their relations.

Simulacrum: An image or mimicry of a thing, often signifying an inadequate representation.

Techne: Craftsmanship, personal characteristics, the essential thing. [See Kant].

Telos: An end or purpose, in a fairly constrained sense used by philosophers such as Aristotle. It is the root of the term "teleology," roughly the study of purposiveness, or the study of objects with a view to their aims, purposes, or intentions. It is central to nearly all philosophical theories of history, such as those of Hegel and Marx.

Thelemic: Believing that, "Do what thou wilt shall be the whole of the Law. Love is the law, love under will." The law of Thelema was conceived in the early 1900s by Aleister Crowley, who espoused the idea of personal will guided by "magick."

Tesseract: The four-dimensional extension of a cube.

Theophanic: (theophania) A manifestation or appearance of God, or a god, to a person.

Topoi: [See Aristotle].

Toponomy: The study of place names (toponyms), their origins, meanings, use, and typology.

Vesica Piscis: The intersection of two disks with the same radius, intersecting in such a way that the center of each disk lies on the perimeter of the other. "Fish bladder."

ESOTERIC HOLLYWOOD

SEX, CULTS AND SYMBOLS

Introduction

Film as Ritual

Genres are a form of contemporary myth, giving expression to the mean-
ing of everyday life. Genres carry an intrinsic worldview. They become
stylized conventions to portray universal conflicts whereby viewers can
participate ritualistically in the basic beliefs, fears, and anxieties not
only of their age, but of all ages. As Orson Welles once remarked, "The
camera is much more than a recording apparatus; it is a medium via
which messages reach us from another world that is not ours and that
brings us to the heart of a great secret. Here magic begins." Genre films
become iconic. That is, through repetition, a certain imagery, storyline,
and characterization become archetypal.[1]
– Robert K. Johnston, *Reel Spirituality: Theology and Film in Dialogue*

Everyone loves the movies. We've grown up immersed in the Hollywood *mythos* whether we wanted to or not. We swim in a veritable *aether* of perpetual celluloid synthetica, churned out in mass
cookie-cutter fashion and beamed into every corner of our life. And while
I bash and critique it, fashioning myself a critic of a different sort, I simultaneously love film, as I'm sure you probably do, too.

This book represents my own attempt to decode and interpret the images and symbols that scroll across these all-pervasive screens that dominate our daily lives. It seems as if screens are now the paradigmatic lenses
by which we reflect, interpret and reinterpret the external world, as well as
ourselves, and supply our existence with the ruling archetypes of hidden
control ... a chaotic narrative, both sacred and profane. The discipline
of semiotics is the philosophy of interpretation of signs and symbols, so
what the reader can expect in this work is my own attempt to decipher
what enters our mass mind, or more properly the collective unconscious,
a semiotics of mass media.

I invite the reader to consider the existential experience of the various films chosen and how, though it may seem counter-intuitive, fictional
films can present more "reality" than mainstream media. We know, for

example, that cryptography and ciphers have, for millennia, encoded hidden messages in many forms, and so it will be with this book. Think of it as a hidden message that is intended to be understood, but not immediately apparent. However, as I think you will find, the popularity of my film analyses will lend some credence to the fact that I am onto something. Thus, the reader will travel with me on a mental journey into the *psychosphere*, understand the semiotic system I utilize, and in turn be able to interpret film in a deeper, esoteric sense on their own.

This book does not represent another Hollywood scandal rag, as the focus of my analyses and investigations do not center around who had sex with who or what star was whacked. Rather, we will think in terms of metaphysics and the esoteric, looking at what Michael A. Hoffman accurately called "Twilight Language."[2] We will investigate patterns, images, as well as religious, political and historical connections between the films chosen and so-called reality. If you happen to be wondering what "Twilight Language" is, it will be explained in the book.

"The camera is much more than a recording apparatus; it is a medium via which messages reach us from another world that is not ours and that brings us to the heart of a great secret. Here magic begins."

My thesis is that, as the above quote from the great Orson Welles explicates, film and our mass attendance at theaters is fundamentally religious in character. It is a ritual process at work, and I believe many of the "Hollywood insiders," producers and directors have this same mindset. This will also explain why certain films that may seem odd or unexpected have been chosen for analysis. Some were chosen based solely for my own sentimental reasons, while others were chosen for both their symbolism and mass popularity. Some films were chosen because of their iconic status in the history of cinema, while others were left out due to space considerations, and still others are analyses of the novels that form the basis for the film.

Beyond the philosophical and esoteric dimensions of film, I highlight the emergence of the formation of the mass consciousness through mass media from its ritual and cultic connections, paying close attention to the popular context of the symbology. We will travel out of the media circus for a moment to the realm of liturgy, or communal ritual working. Comparative religion luminary Mircea Eliade sheds light on this primal art, much in line with Wells' above comment, in the following section of his *The Sacred and the Profane*:

"[S]ince religious man cannot live except in an atmosphere impregnated with the sacred, we must expect to find [a] large number of techniques for consecrating space. As we saw, the sacred is preeminently the *real*, at once power, efficacy, the source of life and fecundity. The religious man's desire to live in the sacred is in fact his desire to take up abode in objective reality, not to let himself be paralyzed by the never-ceasing relativity of purely subjective experiences, to live in a real and effective world, and not in an illusion.... But we are not to suppose that human work is in question here, that it is through his efforts that man can consecrate a space. In reality the ritual by which he constructs a sacred space is efficacious in the measure in which it reproduces the work of the gods." (pg. 28)[3]

Eliade is invoking the primal urge in man to consecrate sacred space – a space where the gods of old come to communicate meaning, morality and *telos* to mankind, where upon the high places, the heavenly realm of celestial

MIRCEA ELIADE (1907-1986): Romanian philosopher, writer and comparative religion scholar. Eliade's work focused on religious experience and notions of the sacred and the profane, time and eternity, and notably his own version of the Nietzschean concept of "eternal return," where religious initiates actually participate in the eternal mysteries of the classical myths.

intelligences might make a theophanic manifestation to shape earth into the form of the above, imposing order upon unruly chaos. Yet modern man is no longer superstitious, we are told; and with the dawn of the "Age of Reason," he abandoned ritual and liturgy for the reasonably rational life of being an "informed citizen" of his Enlightened Democratic Republic, intimately involved in forming and shaping his local, social-contracted propositional government covenant. However, if we reflect a little further on Eliade's comment, we begin to see that space-age man is just as "religious," if not more so, than ignorant, savage ancient man. The difference emerges as merely one of form and medium, not substance, and his new temple is wherever the television screen or theater feeds him his new narrative by which to read his world.

Most of us do not seek out the village shaman or *hierophant* for messages from the spirit realm, yet, do we not daily gaze into our handheld magical mirrors and screens that transmit the messages of the priests, shamans and ascended media masters, with little, if any, critical perspective? The liturgical icon of old has now become the moving icon of vivacious info-babe, the holy mothers of Channel 5 Monastery. From the towering cathedrals of the major film studios to CNN and Fox, the word of the gods issues forth to guide we supplicant masses with tales of the lives of

5

new civic patron saints and mythologies of Hollywood heroes that subsist in the realm of the unattainable forms.

Unfortunately, our new gods do not always issue messages of hope and salvation. Our *devas* are very much gods of wrath and vengeance, inflicting upon the mass psyche a continual barrage of spells and incantations geared toward confusion and hysteria. Just as the priest's ritual dagger divides the sacrifice, so the priests of our day divide the psyche on the edge of the ritual athame, with endlessly channeled fear and destruction. As the sacrifice is cut in half and "doubled," the mass psyche sacrifice is divided into incoherent Orwellian double-mind and double-think.

Few are those concerned with the virus of programmed liturgical psychodrama their magical mirror screens enchant them with, as they are lulled under the vodoun spell of the zombie. It should never be forgotten that the zombie mythology arises from the shaman's ability to *drug* the unlucky victim, causing the unwitting to become subject to the suggestions of the shaman's new narrative – that he is under the shaman's mind control.

In this regard, the explosion of the zombie phenomenon over the last decade or so is a manifestation of this divine revelation from our rulers on high – you are under the spell, under the thumb of the *obeah*, a doll for the media voodoo worker's nefarious machinations. Shamanic Network, Inc.'s designs are not the mystical unknowns of a *deus absconditus*: the zombie is a parasitical entity that feeds on the living. The designs of the media papacy are to divide and slaughter your *psyche*, transforming you into a zombie who in turn divides and consumes his fellow man. Thus, the zombie is under the spell that death is life, that parasitism will grant power, that sex is death, when in reality zombies *are death* feeding on their own death, the fullest blossoming of the covenant of death, which is self-destruction.

Eliade illustrates this well with an example from African comparative religion:

> Among the Mandja and the Banda of Africa, there is a secret society named Ngakola. According to the myth told to the candidates during their initiation, Ngakola was a monster who had the power of swallowing men and then disgorging them renewed. The candidate is put in a hut that symbolizes the monster's body. There he hears Ngakola's eerie voice, there he is whipped and tortured, for he is told that he is now in Ngakola's belly and is being digested. More ordeals follow; then the master of the initiation proclaims that Ngakola, who had devoured the candidate, has disgorged him. (Ibid. 192)[4]

There is no "Ngakola" – he is the invention of the deviant priest class that sought total mind control over its candidate through the ritual psychodrama of torture, deprivation and (I feel sure) drugging. The "secret society" of priests exercise their control of the tribe through dividing the *psyche* of their supplicants and devotees with the very same ritual psychodrama the mass media mavens of our day utilize, only our ascended Hollywood *hegumen* are more technologically sophisticated. For them, the wires and waves of electrical signals and currents are the medium for their message, and the medium's message is the medium – to further its own existence as the source of meaning through its faithful presentation of its own mystagogical psychodrama. A striking example of this form of psy-op is found in Ian Fleming's *Dr. No*, where the villainous Dr. No constructs a "dragon" out of a tank and flamethrower to scare the local superstitious populace from snooping around his organized crime racket. Fleming's imagery recalls a real-world example mentioned in Victor Marchetti's classic *The CIA and the Cult of Intelligence*, which describes a scenario of manipulation in the Philippines:

IAN FLEMING (1908-1964): English author and Naval Intelligence Officer, Fleming is best known as the creator and author of the James Bond novels. Based in part on his own life, as well as other secret service agents and their real-world exploits (as well as villains based on the likes of Aleister Crowley), the 007 novels offer insights into the shadow government apparatus, psychological warfare, propaganda and aspects of the esoteric. Fleming's Bond would eventually become one of the most recognizable icons in the world, as well as one of the most successful Hollywood franchises of all time.

> When I introduced the practical-joke aspect of psywar to the Philippine Army, it stimulated some imaginative operations that were remarkably effective.... One psywar operation played upon the popular dread of an *asuang*, or vampire.... When a Huk patrol came along the trail, the ambushers silently snatched the last man of the patrol.... They punctured his neck with two holes, vampire-fashion, held the body up by the heels, drained it of blood, and put the corpse back on the trail. When the Huks returned to look for the missing man and found their bloodless comrade, every member of the patrol believed that the *asuang* had got him and that one of them would be next.... When daylight came, the whole Huk squadron moved out of the vicinity.[5]

With that in mind, and the intelligence agencies' associations with media I, and others, have long documented, think now of ritual. Liturgical ritual is the continual 're-presentation' of some primal event of timeless significance, and for this reason mass media is our new liturgy, re-presenting

7

the self-perpetuating *mythos* that it is our source of meaning and *gnosis*. Is it not all one and the same process? The drugs of today's obeah are not the poison of a blowfish, but the tinctures and potions of big pharmaceutical *pharmakeia*. Its saints and monastics, wearing suits and ties, sing the chant of the cinematic serpentine doxological refrain. Its priests are the dramaturgical actors who play the role of incarnating our gods and goddesses.

Michel Foucault (1926-1984): French philosopher, social theorist and critic of modernity. Generally considered postmodern, Foucault stressed the relationship of power in knowledge and institutions, as well as sexuality. Analyzing the history of ideas such as discipline, punishment, and the institutionalization of "madness," Foucault attempted to develop an archaeology of ideas. Foucault believed civilization coincided with madness, yet remained a committed liberal in his advocacy for socialism and homosexuality.

While we gaze into our screens and await the latest download and update from our overlords on what the orthodox consensus reality is, let us not forgot it is a ritual psychodrama that is playing out, lest we be swept up into the religious rapture of the beatific television spell. The iconography of the screen is the crafted narrative and mythology of the establishment's choosing. It is the cacophonous echo chamber of the holy mammon foundation and is under the think-tank theologians' purview. Its ritual is the one in which we daily tithe our time and thoughts and attention, as we await with mystical gaze the new revelations Olympus will dictate from its shiny stellar satellites. Its present soothsaying word from beyond is that of viral doom and zombie programming, a flagellant torture and scourge as it howls the eerie voice of Ngakola.

What is the solution? It is the realization of the real threat: the entrenched belief that for truth and meaning to be obtained, we must gaze at the gods of mass media and kneel as neophyte communicants at the tele-altar techno-theatrical cathedrals, like acolytes or sorcerer's apprentices. Modern man is far from being irreligious, even in our science-driven era. He has, as Michel Foucault said, simply changed his old priests and gods for new ones, and in *Esoteric Hollywood*, I will decipher how this has been done.

Endnotes

1. Johnston, Robert K. *Reel Spirituality: Theology and Film in Dialogue*. Grand Rapids, MI: Baker Academic, 2006, pg. 188.

2. Hoffman, Michael A. *Secret Societies and Psychological Warfare*. Coeur d'Alene, Idaho: Independent History and Research, 2001. pgs. 130-1.

3. Eliade, Mircea. *The Sacred and the Profane: The Nature of Religion*. New York: Harcourt/HBJ, 1959.

4. Ibid.

5. Marchetti, Victor and John Marks. *The CIA and the Cult of Intelligence*. New York: Dell Publishers, 1975. Chapter 4. http://www.statecraft.org/chapter4.html

Part One

Hollywood Babylon and Kubrick

Chapter 1

The Occult Empire

"The earliest gods were invoked by ritual act (dromenon = the thing done) such as a sacrificial dance, commemorating the fact that our life begins and ends when they call upon us. Subsequently the thing was said (legomenon) as well as done, and the dromenon was on its way to becoming the drama. Once speech within the temple precincts has been endowed with the power of word-magic, we have 'the invocation' properly so called."
– Dudley Young, *Origins of the Sacred: The Ecstasies of Love and War*[1]

Hollywood might be understood in the sense of David Lynch's last surrealist nightmare production, *Inland Empire* – a kind of covenantal city-state of its own, with its own religion, including all the trappings of neophytes, acolytes, servants, agents, star saints, hierophants and hierarchs and holy sites. As Kenneth Anger noted:

> Professional do-gooders branded Hollywood The New Babylon, whose evil influence rivaled that of the ancient city: banner headlines and holier-than-thou editorials would equate sex, dope and movie stars. Yet for the vast public out there Hollywood was a magic three syllables invoking the wonder world of make believe. To the faithful it was more than a dream factory where one young hopeful out of a million got a break. It was Dreamland, Somewhere Else; it was the Home of the Heavenly Bodies, the Glamour Galaxy of Planet Hollywood.[2]

The religious verbiage of Anger is accurate: It is a veritable *polis* of initiatory esoterica where the holy sites and rites of Hollywood are not the altars of mainstream religion, but another ancient religion, ultimately summed up in the epithet of the ancient mysteries.[3] The ancient mysteries comprise the competing religious practices of the

DAVID LYNCH: American director, screenwriter, artist, musician and actor. Lynch's films are generally considered surrealist, characterized by his own unique style. Often satirical and dark, Lynch's films focus on dreamscapes, nightmares, sexuality and trauma. David Lynch is known for films such as *Blue Velvet, Dune, Wild at Heart, Twin Peaks, Lost Highway*, and *Mulholland Drive*, as well as popular musical projects with Moby, Lykke Li and Chrysta Bell.

empires of old, but the one empire that seems to have achieved the most appropriate association with Hollywood is Babylon – the "gate of the gods."

Babylon was the ancient pagan empire prominent in biblical prophetic works as an enemy of God's people due to their idolatry. Hollywood is no different, functioning as the propaganda arm of the antichrist media establishment, intent on re-engineering society into its alchemical opposite,

KENNETH ANGER: American underground and experimental filmmaker whose works include themes of occultism, homoeroticism, and surrealism. Anger is an adherent of Crowley's philosophy of Thelema and is known for films such as *Lucifer Rising* (1972) and *Invocation of my Demon Brother* (1969), and the book *Hollywood Babylon* (1965). Anger's works have influenced prominent directors such as David Lynch, Martin Scorsese and John Waters.

unleashing the destructive forces of cultural Marxism and death. This is why stories and narratives continue to emerge of Hollywood scandals, sex and murder rituals and occult crime, with no puzzle pieces ever put together from mindless denizens of talking head puppet-dom. From the dozens of in-depth analyses on my site looking into the esoteric meanings in Hollywood films, it logically follows that this classic thesis of "Hollywood Babylon" is not far off. This title is not new, either: detailed accounts are found in insider researchers like Peter Levenda, and even older than his *Sinister Forces* trilogy, occultist Kenneth Anger's book and documentary, *Hollywood Babylon*.

From its beginnings, Hollywood has been an empire of tragedies, full of lost lives, drugs, and real-life drama, but this troupe lifestyle is nothing new. The stage has long been the site of tragedy and something much darker – ritual invocation, all the way back to the ancient Greeks and Romans. For Greece and, in debased form, Rome, the stage was sacred, where the dramaturgical interactions of the gods were actually a form of magical invocation. The actors donned the costumes of the gods, with the playwright scripting the narrative to inculcate the masses into the appropriate morals of the state. Although the idea of the theater as explicitly sacred is foreign to the modernity, it was not for historic man, nor is modern man's *praxis** any less religious in regard to the theater. Sir James Frazier elaborates the ancient belief in the magical character of dramaturgy and acting in his classic, *The Golden Bough*:

> Here then at the great sanctuary of the goddess in Zela it appears that her myth was regularly translated into action; the story of her love and the death of her divine lover was performed year by year

as a sort of mystery-play by men and women who lived for a season and sometimes died in the character of the visionary beings whom they personated. The intention of these sacred dramas, we may be sure, was neither to amuse nor to instruct an idle audience, and as little were they designed to gratify the actors, to whose baser passions they gave the reins for a time. They were solemn rites which mimicked the doings of divine beings, because man fancied that by such mimicry he was able to arrogate to himself the divine functions and to exercise them for the good of his fellows. The operations of nature, to his thinking, were carried on by mythical personages very like himself; and if he could only assimilate himself to them completely he would be able to wield all their powers.

This is probably the original motive of most religious dramas or mysteries among rude peoples. The dramas are played, the mysteries are performed, not to teach the spectators the doctrines of their creed, still less to entertain them, but for the purpose of bringing about those natural effects which they represent in mythical disguise; in a word, they are magical ceremonies and their mode of operation is mimicry or sympathy. We shall probably not err in assuming that many myths, which we now know only as myths, once had their counterpart in magic; in other words, that they used to be acted as a means of producing in fact the events which they describe in figurative language. Ceremonies often die out while myths survive, and thus we are left to infer the dead ceremony from the living myth. If myths are, in a sense, the reflections or shadows of men cast upon the clouds, we may say that these reflections continue to be visible in the sky and to inform us of the doings of the men who cast them, long after the men themselves are not only beyond our range of vision but sunk beneath the horizon." (pg. 651)[4]

Bacchanalia of Andreas

By the time of Shakespeare and the Renaissance, the tradition remained. Renaissance scholar Dame Frances Yates writes of the hermetic elements of the Globe Theater:

Thoughts occur to one of the possibility of using Fludd's revelations, not only for the understanding of the actual staging of Shakespeare's plays, but for an interpretation of the relative spiritual significance of scenes played on different levels. Is the Shakespearean stage a Renaissance and Hermetic transformation of the old religious stage?[5]

ROBERT FLUDD (1574-1637): Prominent English Renaissance physician who followed the Paracelsian method. Fludd was an astrologer, mathematician, kabbalist, and supposed Rosicrucian. Famed for his correspondence with Kepler concerning occultism and science, Fludd is considered an important figure in early English Freemasonry.

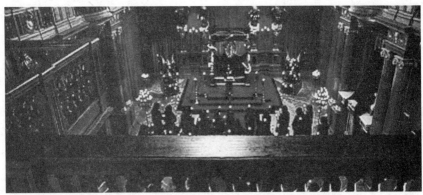

Ritual scene in Roman Polanski's *The Ninth Gate*.

Ritual scene in Stanley Kubrick's *Eyes Wide Shut*.

14

For the Renaissance "masked ball" tradition, the ritual aspect of the theater was quite profound, with the political and market elites meeting on estates for the original, now-famous *Eyes Wide Shut*-style ceremonial celebrations.[6] The point here is that the stage as a ceremonial altar for religious invocation is not novel, but a genuine tradition that has continued unabated from Renaissance era to the present.[7]

The 1972 Rothschild Masked Ball is now well known through online alternative media exposure, but it forms a perfect example of the elite ball as described.[8] Indeed, Roman Polanski's occult film *The Ninth Gate* and Stanley Kubrick's *Eyes Wide Shut* were both filmed in Rothschild mansions, and all carry explicit esoteric themes based around secret societies practicing sex magick.

Baroness-Marie-Hélène-de-Rothschild and Baron Alexis de Redé at the 1972 Rothschild Masked Ball.

Château de Ferrières, the site of *The Ninth Gate*.

That there is a dark side to Hollywood is generally known, given the numerous cases of bizarre deaths and squalid scandals, yet the occult side is still lesser known. In his section from *Sinister Forces* Vol. III on "Hollywood Babylon," Levenda includes a snippet from comparative religion writer Mircea Eliade:

Babylon was *Bab-ilani*, a "gate of the gods," for it was there that the gods descended to earth.... But it was always Babylon that is the scene of the connection between the earth and the lower regions, for the city had been built upon *bab apsi*, the "Gates of Apsu" – apsu designating the waters of chaos before the Creation. (pg. 109)[9]

And in Eliade's *The Sacred and the Profane*, he explains of the ancient conception of the threshold or gate, which is peculiarly applicable:

A similar ritual function falls to the threshold of the human habitation, and it is for this reason that the threshold is an object of great importance. Numerous rites accompany passing the domestic threshold – a bow, a prostration, a pious touch of the hand, and so on. The threshold has its guardians – gods and spirits who forbid entrance both to human enemies and to demons and the power of pestilence. It is on the threshold that sacrifices to the guardian divinities are offered. Here too certain paleo-oriental cultures (Babylon, Egypt, Israel) situated the judgment place. The threshold, the door show the solution of continuity in space immediately and concretely; hence their great religious importance, for they are symbols and at the same time vehicles passing from one space to another." (pg. 25)

The "gate of the gods" is thus fitting for Hollywood, as is the Saturnalian ethos, where the medium is the method: the spirits and gods of old still find their servants and missionaries crossing the threshold of the artistic airwaves and celluloid chapels, but the spiral goes even deeper.[10] In making this occult and religious association, one of the first prominent cases of Hollywood occult ritual psychodrama is Brian De Palma's *The Black Dahlia* (2006), which will be covered in a later chapter. Researcher Dave Mc-

Film poster image. Early Satanic ritual crime in Hollywood.

Gowan has written about the occult and Satanic connections to the murder, as noted by anonymous online blogger "HolyHexes," concerning McGowan's work on Hodel and Short:

McGowan sees clearly how privilege works while noting accusations that came out during Hodel's trial. "Allegations that the rich and powerful were dabbling in incest, hypnotism/mind control, pedophilic orgies, and Luciferian philosophies must surely have been shocking to Angelenos in the 1940s, as they would still be to most Americans today, but to these jaded eyes and ears, it just sounds like business as usual. Also sounding like business as usual is that Tamar was roundly vilified by both the press and the defense team (led by Jerry Giesler), and Dr. George Hodel was acquitted."

DAVE MCGOWAN (1960-2015): Veteran analyst and researcher of conspiracies and deep state events, McGowan is best known for his book *Weird Scenes Inside the Canyon*, arguing the 1960s cultural revolution was not, in the final analysis, anti-establishment, but carefully directed away from anti-war sentiment into debauchery (by the establishment). McGowan stressed the illusory nature of official government narratives on many historical events, questioning the veracity of the Apollo Missions, Sandy Hook and the Boston Bombing.

How it is that the fourteen-year-old daughter of a lowly probation officer fell into the orbit of the daughter of the wealthy and influential George Hodel (Hodel's former home is currently valued at $4.2 million) has never been explained, but Tamar, described by Michelle as "the epitome of glamour," quickly took the youngster under her wing, buying her clothes, enrolling her in modeling school, teaching her to drive, and providing her with a fake ID and a steady stream of prescription drugs – obtained, one would presume, from her father.

Have you come to the conclusion McGowan leads the reader? The Black Dahlia was recruited by a daughter of a rich and connected doctor for a ritualistic slaying in an underground walk-in vault beneath the home, her death, dismemberment and missing organs facilitated by drugs and participated in by members of a cult engaged in satanic worship. This is McGowan's premise in his book also on mind controlled serial killers, it's a cover for satanic worship and the "serial killers" are mostly patsies![11]

This article doesn't do complete justice to McGowan's essay. McGowan, a native of Los Angeles, pins down Phillips as possessed of occult leanings, and successfully, shows how "The Black Dahlia" may be connected to occult practices in the shadows of a sixties' Laurel Canyon.[12]

To bring this pattern into concrete examples, there is a curious Bacchanalian scene in *The Big Sleep* (1946) with Humphrey Bogart that shows a similarity to the underground porn and ritual imagery in *The Black Dahlia*

(2006), as well as to scenes in David Lynch's *Lost Highway* (1997). This revelation of the inside sexual and ritual aspects in the films themselves demonstrates the claims I'm making are not without basis. While noir would not be a place one would expect esoteric symbolism, The Big Sleep was actually referencing a topic completely taboo to the audience of the day – sex, drugs, and occult ritual. It is interesting to note that the camera's eye, or POV, in this still-shot from *The Big Sleep* is the third eye of the Buddha bust, suggesting a potential Tantric theme was involved in the porn at the flophouse.

Bogey discovers secret porn and drugged women in *The Big Sleep*.

Secret porn in The Black Dahlia associated with ritual murder.

In *The Black Dahlia*, a secret flop-house that resembles it can be seen above, where the porn was filmed, later to be followed by a grizzly occult murder. A wealthy family is involved in the ritual crime, bringing to mind the rituals performed at the estates in *Eyes Wide Shut* and *The Ninth Gate*. It also brings to mind the ritual porn/snuff film at the end of *Lost Highway*, which is an explicit tribute to *noir*.

At this point the question arises – what do ritual drama and these subtle examples of deeper sexual themes in noir and neo-noir have in common? Levenda's analysis is crucial here, highlighting the shamanic elements of the actor in seeking to become an *alternate persona*:

18

The similarity to the shaman was, of course, the walker between two worlds, who channeled the message from the spirit realm into ours. The father of method acting was none other than Konstantin Stanislavski, an occult practitioner who was explicit about the spiritual nature of his method. Levenda writes of Stanislavski, "The true Method actor is a kind of initiate, a voluntary madman, and opens himself or herself up to forces he or she does not understand, but which are potent nonetheless. And these forces being summoned then act upon those in close proximity."[13]

PETER LEVENDA: American author whose many books highlight hidden history, conspiracy analysis, occultism and the cryptocracy. Levenda's massive Sinister Forces Trilogy considers the occult side of American politics, from the nation's inception, to the JFK assassination, to 9/11 and the hidden hand of terrorism. Levenda's works also treat of eastern alchemy, Vatican intrigues, Nazism, Tantrism, H.P. Lovecraft and ritual crime.

With this made evident, the meme of Hollywood as an occult empire only mounts, and the above film examples as an interesting juxtaposition of 40s crime with subtle occult undertones continue to suggest it even more. In this shamanic context, David Lynch's quote makes even more sense: "'I learned that just beneath the surface there's another world, and still different worlds as you dig deeper."

The meta-narrative ritual film in *Lost Highway* with members of Marilyn Manson.

Also worth mentioning is a point I will elucidate in greater detail in my *Mulholland Drive* analysis, where the gorgeous starlet Candy Jones was a prime example, not just of an entertainment vixen surrounded by scan-

19

dalous scuttlebutt, but as an actual mind-controlled victim of the newly-established MKUltra program.[14]

Mind control victim Candy Jones in cosmetics ad highlighting her right eye.

Hollywood is also no stranger to the notion of mind-controlled subjects with alternate personalities, programmed with key words and triggers, as the 1962 film *The Manchurian Candidate* made evident, based on Richard Condon's 1959 novel of the same name. Another famous episode along these lines that relates to "Betty" is the story of Candy Jones, the famous model who was also a mind-controlled subject, as Donald Bain's 1976 *The Control of Candy Jones* argues. Betty/Diane, like Candy, seems to blend between the 50s and present day, in her descent into mental illness, depersonalization and dissociation. This will provide the key to understanding the blue key Betty is given that unlocks the blue box in "Club Silencio." The box and key are Betty's psyche and the key represents the key words and phrases her handler(s) possess. Levenda comments:

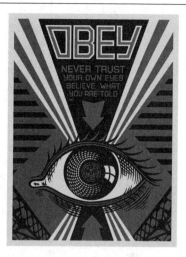

MIND CONTROL: Generally a reference to the CIA's secret programs under the moniker of "MKUltra," the MK program was merely one subproject of a vast, several-decades long series of wide-ranging tests and experiments into human thought control and social engineering. Employing originally military techniques as broad as LSD and hypnosis to electronic implants and electroshock "therapy," dozens of universities, doctors, scientists and psychiatric institutions participated in the programs under various covers and fronts in rank violation of basic human rights.

> "A recurring feature of David Lynch films is the flickering light, a result, we are told in the pilot episode of *Twin Peaks* – of a "bad transformer." This flickering electric light will appear in Lynch films such as *Mulholland Drive* [and *Lost Highway*], to announce the appearance of the Cowboy, a bizarre character who speaks in gnomic riddles, like a cross between Gary Cooper and David Carradine. In *Twin Peaks*, it is the light in the morgue over the place where the body of Laura Palmer had been kept, and which is then visited by Mike, the one-armed man, who recites the famous poem:
>
> > *"Through the darkness of futures past*
> > *The magician longs to see;*
> > *One chants out between two worlds*
> > *'Fire walk with me.'"*

There, in a strange little verse, we have the key to unlocking the mystery not only of *Twin Peaks* but virtually all of Lynch's films: the suspen-

21

sion of normal laws of time ("futures past") and the idea that the magician lives "between two worlds." The suspension of normal, linear narrative event in favor of a dreamlike, hallucinatory set of images that are taking place all over the fourth dimension is part of Lynch's appeal as a director, and part of what makes his films so frustrating to the film-goer. His realization that there are two worlds, and a place

LOOKOUT MOUNTAIN FILM STUDIO: Situated atop Laurel Canyon in Los Angeles, CA, down the infamous Mulholland Drive onto Wonderland Ave., the Lookout Mountain Facility was formerly under the aegis of the U.S. Air Force and functioned as a private, top secret film studio, from the 1940s to 1960s. Notable for its production of the famous atomic bomb test footage, Lookout Mountain was reportedly utilized by the highest levels of both Hollywood and the military for countless unknown projects. The facility is now the private home of actor Jared Leto.

to stand between them, is what contributes to his aura as a modern, twenty-first century initiate of the Mysteries, for that is what "mystery" films are: elucidations of the core Mystery behind reality."[15]

Marilyn Monroe's DOD identification.

22

Intrigue doesn't stop there. Writer Craig Heimbichner sees the entire complex of Hollywood like Oz, calling to mind the most well known film of all time, *The Wizard of Oz*. Heimbichner sees Oz as an occult allegory of Tinseltown itself:

> We are in a universal lapse into a state of immaturity; a true indicator we are in some sort of "era of the child." Hypnotized by computers, TVs, DVDs, CDs, palm pilots, Prozac, Paxil, and pot, the average zombie has left behind considerations of others, as though "others" were a TV show which one could laugh and shut off. Zombies rise in the morning, watch morning TV shows, scan the newspapers and receive new programming, go to work, and come home to passively watch more programming. If the zombies have an original thought, it is almost invariably a selfish one. But the absurdity is even the selfish thought reflects the cradle-to-crypt programming from the television, that other Eye of Set.

"You're getting sleepy."

Continuing, Heimbichner elucidates:

> ...the Wizards of Oz. Such shadow-players are the true OTO Templars, the real magicians whose wand of hypnosis exorcizes the powers of reason, and whose smoke-and-mirrors show obscures the true

23

nature of the game. The OTO's book proclaiming a pseudo-freedom is appropriately named *Liber Oz (The Book of Oz)*. The word "Oz" is Hebrew for strength. The *Zohar* relates in 3:208a and 212a-b that all who learn magic must journey to "the mountains of darkness," the abode of the rebel angels Aza and Azael, and learn under their auspices. Aza and Azael are phonetically related to Oz. Employing gematria, the branch of Kabbalah devoted to numerological obsession, Oz relates to 77: 7+7=14, a number of Venus; 1+4=5, the number of the pentagram, which masonically relates to the "Five Points of Fellowship," chastely enacted in a regular lodge, but given a fully sexual initiatory significance in higher degrees.[16]

The "smoke and mirrors" description is perfect, given the wizards behind the curtain of Hollywood are drab old studio executives nowadays working with the intelligence agencies, calling the shots for occulted reasons, for the purpose of mesmerizing the Dorothy-like populace of America. The Hollywood magical City of Oz doesn't exist, in fact, and is instead a place where reality comes closer to the film *8mm*, where Nicolas Cage plays an investigator who follows the underworld of film production to the lowest point on the downward spiral. Holly-Oz is where naïve princesses go to become whores or end up in porn, like Betty/Diane in *Mulholland Drive*, and after they're used up, the system tosses them away as refuse or kills them like so many stars and starlets who have been "suicided" or sacrificed to the system.[17] The recent tragic losses in Hollywood, as well as the seemingly bizarre behavior exhibited by many a pop star like Miley Cyrus or Amanda Bynes, demonstrates this perfectly. "What does it profit a man to gain the whole world and lose his soul?" (Mark 8:36). Or, the flame ain't worth the candle.

ORDO TEMPLI ORIENTIS (OTO): A religious fraternal organization best known for its one-time member and leader, Aleister Crowley, but generally understood to originate in late 19th century Germany or Austria under the guidance of Karl Kellner and Theodor Reuss. Under the leadership of Crowley, the O.T.O. adopted the philosophy of "Thelema" as found in Crowley's *Book of the Law*. Similar in form to European Freemasonry, the organization includes as a branch the Gnostic Catholic Church. Following the Crowley period, the Order divided into various groups under different leaders.

KABBALAH: A mystical, ethical and spiritual school of thought in Judaism. Kabbalah is an attempt to give a systematic teaching concerning an eternal, unchanging Deity's relation to the world of creation, as well as how evil can be, given divine goodness. Kabbalism generally sees divinity emanating from above, through a series of "worlds" or "sephirot," usually placed in locations on a "Tree of Life" diagram. Kabbalism utilizes Jewish texts like the Talmud, Torah and Zohar, while offering various levels of interpretation of texts that include hidden esoteric meanings, as well as numerological significances.

24

Endnotes

1. Young, Dudley. *Origins of the Sacred: The Ecstasies of Love and War*. New York: Harper Perennial, 1992, pg. 413.

2. Anger, Kenneth. *Hollywood Babylon*. San Francisco, CA: Simon & Schuster, 1975, pg. 12.

3. Hall, Manly P. "Ancient Mysteries and Secret Societies" in *The Secret Teaching of All Ages*. Sacred Texts Archive. http://www.sacred-texts.com/eso/sta/sta05.htm

4. Frazer, Sir James. *The Golden Bough*. Oxford: Oxford University Press, 2009.

5. Yates, Dame Frances. *The Art of Memory*. Chicago: Chicago University Press, 2001. pgs. 42-3.

6, Heale, Elizabeth. *The Faerie Queen: A Reader's Guide* (Cambridge: University Press, 1999).

7. Yates, Dame Frances. *The Rosicrucian Enlightenment* (New York: Routledge, 1972).

8. Vigilant Citizen. "Revealing Pictures From 1972 Rothschild Illuminati Ball." 17 September. 2013. Web. http://vigilantcitizen.com/latestnews/pictures-rothschild-family/

9. Levenda, Peter. *Sinister Forces: A Grimoire of American Political Witchcraft, Vol. III*. Oregon: Trine Day, 2006.

10. Hanshaw, Jamie. *Hollywood Mind Control*. San Bernardino, CA: Blue Fly Press, 2016, pgs. 8-24.

11. McGowan, Dave. *Programmed to Kill: The Politics of Serial Murder*. New York: iUniverse, 2004.

12. See McGowan, Dave. *Weird Scenes Inside the Canyon: Laurel Canyon, Covert Ops & The Dark Heart of the Hippie Dream*. US: Headpress, 2014, pgs. 200-215. "David McGowan Revisits Black Dahlia." Holy Hexes Blog. Web. http://www.holyhexes.blogspot.com

13. Levenda, *Sinister Forces Vol. III*, 112.

14. See Marks, John. *The CIA and Mind Control: Search for the Manchurian Candidate*. New York, Mc-Graw Hill, 1980.

15. Levenda, *Sinister Forces Vol. III*, pg. 151.

16. Heimbichner, Craig. *Blood on the Altar*. Coeur d'Alene, Idaho: Independent History and Research, 2005, pg. 132.

17. Nimmo, Kurt. "Author Claims David Carradine's Father Was OTO Member." Infowars. 7 June, 2009. Web. http://www.infowars.com/author-claims-david-carradines-father-was-ordo-templi-orientis-member/

Chapter 2

An Esoteric Analysis of Stanley Kubrick's *Eyes Wide Shut* (1999)

"I always enjoyed representing a slightly surreal situation in a realistic way. I have always had a penchant for fairy-tales, myths and magical stories. They seem to me to come closer to our present-day experience of reality than realistic stories, which are basically just as stylized."
— Stanley Kubrick[1]

*E*yes *Wide Shut* is a film that failed to live up to film-goers expectations. An edgy thriller that made statements about upper echelon decadence, it fell somewhat flat at the box office, while the film curiously utilized the "real-world" sex life of Tom Cruise and Nicole Kidman as a doorway bridging the threshold between reality and fantasy; and as we shall see, this theme emerges earlier in other Kubrick films. *Eyes Wide Shut* is based on the 1926 Austrian novella *Traumnovella* (Dream Story) by Arthur Schnitzler, Kubrick adapted the surrealist story to modern times, employing the same Freudian and class critique in the original, but with the film we find not just a statement concerning the power elite that run the show, but the darker side of the human *psyche* and the theme of ritual initiation. Critic Kaus Rainer comments:

> The film and the novella are to be reconsidered by means of an exemplary juxtaposition. The marital drama from the turn of the century possesses a present-day relevance which, despite liberalization, the breaking down of taboos and changes in moral values, has not lost any of its intensity [-] the yearning for intimacy in a satisfying relationship, but also its simultaneous endangering by our unconscious desires, feelings and fantasies. Arthur Schnitzler, a medical doctor by profession, was admired by Freud for his knowledgeable descriptions of psychic processes. They were not friends, but had great respect for each other. It is said that it was only the children of Freud and Schnitzler, who played together with each other, who gave occasion for correspondence between the two.[2]

The "show" Kubrick wants to draw our attention to is both the film itself, as well as *reality*: Kubrick wants viewers to realize that reality is

Stanley Kubrick (1928-1999): American filmmaker, director, screenwriter and producer. Frequently cited as one of the most important filmmakers in history, and often considered the greatest. A demanding perfectionist, Kubrick paid special attention to details, especially in sound and music in film. Kubrick is known for iconic classics like *Spartacus, Lolita, Dr. Strangelove, A Clockwork Orange, 2001: A Space Odyssey, The Shining,* and *Eyes Wide Shut.*

run, like a show, by the showmasters behind the veil of the videodrome. The viewer will not only be forced to reflect upon the decadence of the Eastern elite establishment, but embark on a shamanic revelatory journey wherein viewing the film itself becomes homage to present social hypocrisy, as the film is a would-be voyeuristic step into the sex lives of others. In this regard, it functions as an initiation mirroring the desire of the individual to both pass judgment on the taboos contained in the film, while simultaneously attending its showing. One is, in a sense, participating in the ritual, even if from afar through the magic of the screen. In this regard, it is Bill Harford (Tom Cruise) who will represent the average film-goer. While most reviews of the film focused on socio-political factors, none have considered the initiatory aspects as a framework of interpretation.

27

The average film-goer is watching because he or she is curious about Hollywood secrets and the lives of the stars, exemplified in the endless racks of Hollywood gossip rags at your local grocer. Of course, "Average Joe" also likely went to get a glimpse of Nicole Kidman's backside, and while this may seem crude, Kubrick intends the viewer to realize his hypocrisy in such an action, given that most will morally assess the film's secret society cult in a negative fashion. *Eyes Wide Shut* is thus a descriptor of the ocular handicap of the *spiritual* vision of the audience, as well as Bill Harford in the film, none of which truly grasp themselves, the human *psyche*, its weaknesses and the socio-political power base embodied in the oligarchy that rules our world. The power base is not, according to Kubrick's film, the average politician or wealthy doctor or lawyer in New York. Indeed, this is precisely Kidman and Cruise's characters' status: they are unwitting inductees. Thus throughout the film, the viewers eyes are wide *shut* to the reality of the power structure, just as Kidman and Cruise's characters, until the end, with veil removed and eyes "opened," as they state. Noting the film's surrealism as a "waking dream," critics Walker, Taylor and Ruchti explain the symbolic technique of the opening sequence:

> A young blonde woman stands there in a black sheath dress, back to us. Even clothed, she radiates an aerobic tension. At any second, one feels she could explode into the erotic. Suddenly, she lets her dress slither to her feet and, for a fleeting moment, is brazenly naked. Then: the screen blacks out, as if an eyelid had closed reflexively to mask what the retina had glimpsed. Exposure and denial, temptation and retreat: such are recurring motifs of what follows. The very title Kubrick gave his film implies it: *Eyes Wide Shut*.3

From the outset, the film employs occult symbolism, showing Mrs. Harford (Nicole Kidman) half-naked, but with more at work here, since she is situated between two pillars. These are, in my estimation, the door-

ways to the initiation, the twin pillars of Jachin and Boaz of Solomon's Temple. The two pillars figure prominently in Freemasonry as the entranceway to the divine, or transcendental planes or spiritual worlds. Masonic philosopher Albert Pike comments on the pillars and their relationship to gender, sexual relations, nature and oppositions:

> Unity is Boaz, and the binary is Jachin. The two columns, Boaz and Jachin, explain the in the kabalah all the mysteries of natural, political and religious antagonism. Woman is man's creation; and universal creation is the female of the First Principle. When the first principle of Existence made Himself Creator, He produced by emanation and idea Yod (point).... Reversing the letters of the Ineffable Name (of God), and dividing it, it becomes bi-sexual, as the word Yud-he or Jah is, and discloses the meaning of much of the obscure language of the Kabalah, and is the Highest of which the columns Jachin and Boaz are the symbol. "In the image of the Deity," we are told, "God created the Man; Male and Female he created them:" and the writer, symbolizing the Divine by the human, then tells us that the woman, then contained in the man, was taken from his side. So Minerva, Goddess of Wisdom, was born, a woman and in armor of the brain of Jove; Isis was the sister before she was the wife of Osiris, and with Brahm, the Source of all, the Very God, without sex or name, was developed Maya, the Mother of all that is.[4]

And Theosophist C.W. Leadbeater explains:

> They [the pillars] also form the portal to the mysteries by which souls ascend to their divine source; and it is only by passing through them at that the sanctuary of man's true godhead may be reached, the divine splendor which when aroused in the depths of the heart indeed establishes its dwelling place in strength and stability.[5]

As we will see, the course of the film's narrative shares this same pre-occupation with sex rites, initiation and ultimately the issue of the dissolution of the moral strictures of the middle-class Harfords as they pass beyond the gates of inhibitions. We also see that the intensity of the ritual orgy and its homosexual eroticism aims precisely at both hermaphroditism and the return to the primordial void of chaos through the attempt at overcoming all oppositions through sex magick. The viewer is also being led about, entering between the pillars from the vantage point of the viewing camera, penetrating the "mysteries," to peer into how the cryptocracy governs from the shadows (yet paradoxically, Kubrick intends us to understand that most eyes will remain wide shut).

Mired in marital frustrations related to sexual intimacy, the Harfords prepare for a bourgeois party hosted by Victor Ziegler (Sydney Pollack), Doctor Bill Harford's wealthy patient. It is significant that the setting is Christmas when the initiatory procedure takes place, functioning as a kind of anti-traditional religious/anti-Christian statement. Known for his impetuous attitude, perfectionism and temper, Kubrick's perspective was that all details are crucial and significant – the placement of everything is deliberate, often fraught with symbolism. These opening sequences give a sense of anxiety and foreboding, foreshadowing the coming temptations for both Bill and Alice that call into question their marital fidelity.

As can be seen in the poster for the film, mirrors are consistently present, classic symbols of the inner world of the *psyche*, as well as portals to other worlds. Kubrick intends, I think, to show us that the characters in the film are mirrors of each other, as well as mirrors of the viewing audience. The symbolism of mirrors also occurs in *Alice in Wonderland*, as well as *The Wizard of Oz*, and both figure prominently in *Eyes Wide Shut*. Both stories are influenced by occult teachings, notably L. Frank Baum's commitment to Theosophy and the teachings of H.P. Blavatsky (which are the basis

of the story), while Lewis Carroll of *Alice* fame preferred photographing young girls and attempting to attain ESP.[6] Carroll's taste for cultivating young girls may be applicable here, since *Eyes Wide Shut* includes the theme of pedophilia (as many Kubrick films do, most notably *Lolita*). Critic "Stephan" elucidates:

> We can celebrate Kubrick's casting genius in Kidman's riveting performance. Her persona is ideally suited to the text of the original novel. In the book Schnitzler continuously describes his female characters as "a young and charming girl, still almost a child…" or "quite a young girl, possibly fifteen years old, with loose blonde hair hanging over her shoulder and on one side over her delicate breast." Eighteen months ago it would have been unacceptable to examine Kidman's "baby-doll" little-girl sexuality.[7]

And Author Jamie Hanshaw comments on *The Wizard of Oz*:

> The author of *The Wizard of Oz* was a Theosophist, claiming inspiration from the story from a spirit who gave him the magic key to write the tale, which was published in 1900. The books were to be a theosophical fairy tale, incorporating the ancient wisdom of the mystery religions. The word "Oz" is important to all Thelemic magicians as it is not derived from children's books, but from gematria. In Hebrew, the word is spelled with the letters Ayin and Zayin and adds up to 77. According to Aleister Crowley, this number represents magic acting on the world of matter. It can be expressed as 1, the grand number of ritual magic, multiplied by 7, the number of manifestation (7-11).[8]

Though commenters on *Eyes Wide Shut* have posited connections to mind control and MKUltra, the CIA's sub-project associated with hypnosis and control of the psyche through hallucinogens,[9] I think keeping the analysis on that level misses the point (though this theme is present). A more holistic approach would be to use such stories as allegories or metaphors for transformation. The metamorphosis of initiation into the "mysteries" on the part of Bill, Alice and the audience. All three stories have theosophic undertones and symbolism, and thus constitute initiatory tales, even to the point of recommended reading (of *Oz* and *Alice*) by Aleister Crowley for aspiring magicians.[10]

ALEISTER CROWLEY (1875-1947): British occultist and founder of the religion of Thelema, Crowley believed himself to be a prophet guiding the world into a new aeon or age, known as the Aeon of Horus. A practitioner of ceremonial and ritual sex magick, Crowley was also an asset of MI5, British Intelligence, according to Dr. Richard Spencer in *Secret Agent 666: Aleister Crowley, British Intelligence and the Occult*.

When the Harford's arrive at the party, we see a clear symbol of what kind of initiation they are going to undergo – the Left-Hand Path;[11] as we see from the inverted pentagram:

The doors of their perception are about to change as they enter the party marked with an inverted pentagram.

Ziegler, we discover, has invited the couple to his parties frequently seemingly under the auspices of eventually getting them to participate in the secret orgies. There are two parties, we learn; not just the tame Christmas ball, but an "after party," at another location, and of a much darker nature. Harford's old college buddy, Nick Nightingale (Todd Field), "accidentally" stumbles into Bill, as they discuss the fact that Nick plays piano for both parties. Intrigued, both Harfords resist the temptation to sleep with other people at the Christmas ball, yet undoubtedly have the desire given their own marital problems. However, what we have begun to suspect is that these events are not randomly occurring, but rather that it has all been organized. It is not accidental. Nightingale was chosen precisely because he is an old friend of Bill's. Interestingly, Bill is then propositioned for a threesome with two beautiful British girls who drop hints they are of noble descent ("Nuala Windsor"), offering to take Bill "where the rainbow ends."

Alice simultaneously finds herself drunk, dancing as she is seduced by one Sandor Szavost, a wealthy Hungarian who drops quotes from Ovid's *Ars Amatoria* on bedding married women. Szavost may be a veiled reference to Anton Szandor LaVey, the founder and High Priest of the Church of Satan. I think this symbolic reference is alerting the perceptive viewer that we are ultimately witnessing an upper echelon Satanic cult. It is also interesting to note that the original novella was written about a couple who undergoes the same experience in upper-class Austria around the turn of the century, since neighboring Bavaria is the origin of the actual historic Order of the Illuminati.[12]

Anton LaVey (1930-1997): American author, musician and former carnival performer turned occultist. LaVey is most well known for founding the Church of Satan in San Francisco in 1966. LaVey is also known for authoring the Satanic Bible in which the organization's philosophy and rituals were codified. Describing itself as skeptical and atheistic, the Church of Satan professes belief in individualism, Epicurean hedonism and exaltation of the self.

Interrupted from the erotic temptation, Bill begins to develop suspicions about his client: The elite Ziegler appears to be enmeshed in shady deals, with connections to both hard drugs and sexual dalliances with beauty queens. Mandy, (Julienne Davis) one of the bevy of beauties that flock around Ziegler, overdoses at the party (in the midst of sex with Ziegler) and Ziegler calls upon Bill to rescue him from the scandal, ultimately to see if Bill can "keep quiet" about the affair. Mandy is curiously spoken of as "asleep," while above her is a portrait of a nude woman in the same pose, as if to allude to the film's thesis of a thin borderline between fantasy and dream, and Bill's reality as a planned synchronicity. Not only this, Alice will undergo a similar incident while lying in bed, half asleep, mumbling and mouthing dream revelations to Bill about the orgies. Diagnosing Mandy as stable, Dr. Harford aids by checking her pulse and advising she cannot continue her feral lifestyle: What we don't know is whether the overdose was an attempt on Mandy's life, a real overdose, or a staged event to test Bill.

Next, we see the Harfords going about mundane activities following an intense argument between Alice and Bill regarding sexual fantasies and attraction outside of marriage. Rejecting Bill's flimsy arguments, Alice exasperatedly corners Bill on his hypocrisy and naivety about women in not admitting he was tempted at the party. Alice confesses to Bill she was once tempted by a naval officer and, for a split second, was willing to throw away both husband and child for a night of pleasure. Bill, noticeably distraught, will begin his path of seeking extramarital affairs as a result of this heated dispute. The curious symbology in this scene is the inverted pentagrams in the background on the drapes:

More inverted pentagrams emerge.

As Alice moves about through the condo we see images of gateways and gardens, indicating again that this is a film about subconscious desires and initiation. Gardens also bring to mind Eden, and the expulsion of Adam and Eve due to sin; or, it could refer to their coming initiation into the "garden of the gods," so to speak, as Bill and Alice are soon to experience the underworld in overworld. Noting the meaning of the garden in perennial symbology, scholar J.E. Cirlot explains:

> The garden is the place where Nature is subdued, ordered, selected and enclosed. Hence it is a symbol of consciousness as opposed to the forest, which is the unconscious, in the same way the island is opposed to the ocean. At the same time, it is a feminine attribute because of its character as a precinct. A garden is often the scene of processes of "Conjunction" or treasure-hunts-connotations which are clearly in accord with the general symbolic function we have outlined.[13]

Garden/doorway imagery.

34

Meanwhile, Bill has taken leave to visit a patient who has passed away, and determines to begin his languorous escapade for an extra-marital affair. His patient's daughter has a crush on him and makes a pass, and an antsy Bill quickly exits (though he begins to waffle in his fidelity). Bill here begins to suspect marriage is a shackle for others, too, as Sandor had tried to convince Alice. Listless, Bill roams the night streets looking for sexual fulfillment, passing several hookers and sex shops. Harassed by a group of frat boys who (for no apparent reason), call him a homosexual, Bill's resolve to cheat is strength-

J.E. CIRLOT (1916-1973): Spanish poet, art critic, mythologist and musician. Cirlot's interest in symbolism and symbology led to his interest in Sufism, Kabbalah, and Eastern Philosophy. Ranked amongst symbologists like Rene Guenon, Carl Jung and Mircea Eliade, Cirlot is best known for his *Dictionary of Symbols*.

ened as we almost get the impression sex is a social obsession everyone is experiencing but Bill. Wandering further in his malaise, a gorgeous prostitute named Domino (Vinessa Shaw) propositions him, inviting him up to her apartment.[14] Bill concedes, and steps down for a bit into the world of the lower class, finding that sex here functions as a commodity.

Interestingly, the lower and upper-class attitudes in the film regarding sex are more or less synonymous, whereas only the upper-middle-class (Bill and Alice) are, and feel bound, by the legal obligations of marital fidelity. For Domino and the elites at the orgy, sex functions as a means of survival, pleasure and ritual enactment. More crucial symbolic imagery appears here with the prominent placement of books on psychology and sociology in Domino's apartment. Kubrick is undoubtedly making a statement on sociology – but not the one most people think. It's the true sociology of a world run, not just by oligarchical moneyed elites, but a cryptocracy of occult elites.[15] As a side note, it should be mentioned that Kubrick was well aware of the realities of global oligarchic hegemony; his daughter, Vivian Kubrick, has claimed the CIA met with her father in relation to his productions.[16]

Once again, Bill is interrupted from his adultery and bows out of Domino's offer, yet the placement of the masks in Domino's apartment functions as the first big key to determining that her meeting with Bill was not accidental. In an existential sense, the mask is symbolic of society as a whole, as Jean-Paul Sartre said, masking our true identities beneath the exterior facade we all erect. Notable too is Kubrick's critique of the social order in the film, the celebration of Christianity – there are Christmas trees and decor everywhere – yet it finds itself dominated by sexual obsession and consumerism, quite antithetical to traditional western religious concerns. Instead, the prevalence of masks in the film shows society as a fraud. Cirlot comments again on the confusion, mystery and anonymity within identity regarding the symbolism of the mask and its connection to sex magick:

> All transformations are invested with something at once of profound mystery and of the shameful, since anything that is so modified as to become "something else" while still remaining in the thing that it was, must inevitably be productive of ambiguity and equivocation.... Frazer has noted some peculiar types of masks used in the initiation ceremonies of some Oceanian peoples.... The mask, simply as a face, comes to express the solar and energetic aspects of the life process.[17]

But beyond that, Kubrick wants the viewer to see that those who really run things are masked – they constitute a secret team of wealthy, upper class who remain in the shadows. This is another clue that Domino is not a real hooker – she is part of the secret society and an actor (hence the masks in her apartment), and is being used to reel Bill in, just like Nick Nightingale. Most whores are not adept academic students of psychology and sociology.

The face behind the masks.

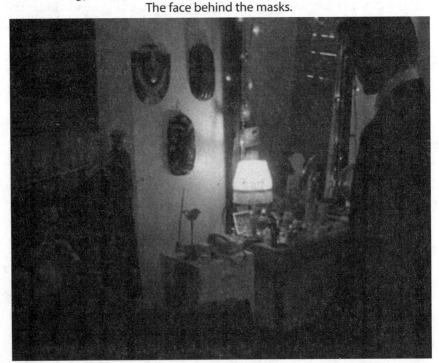

Again disgruntled, Bill exits Domino's and wanders into a nightclub where Nick is playing. Distracting himself with the performance, Bill engages Nick after the show to tell him about the after-party; the second party Sandor had mentioned to Alice where Nick plays piano "blindfolded." Albert Pike notes the meaning of the blindfolding of the "profane" initiate, seeking entrance to the mysteries:

This condition of blindness, destitution, misery, and bondage, from which to save the world the Redeemer came, is symbolized by the condition of the candidate, when he is brought up for the first time to the door of the Lodge ... this is symbolized by the candidate's being brought to the light, after which he is obligated by the worshipful master, who in that is a symbol of the Redeemer, and so brings him to light... [18]

ALBERT PIKE (1809-1891): Attorney, writer, Confederate Officer and masonic philosopher, Albert Pike is the author of one of the most important, foundational masonic texts, known as *Morals and Dogma of the Ancient and Accepted Scottish Rite of Freemasonry* (1871). Pike was influential in the Confederacy and remained Sovereign Grand Commander of the Southern Jurisdiction of the Scottish Rite for 32 years.

Intrigued, Bill decides to sneak in after tracking down a cheap mask and costume at the only store still open. The password, Nick tells Bill, is "Fidelio," bringing to mind the theme of marital faithfulness constantly in question. Quite clearly, Nick has purposefully told Bill the password to pique his interest. Ironically, the name of the shop is The Rainbow, recalling the hints at a set-up the sexy British nobility who propositioned Bill mentioned – that he can find what he is after "at the end of the rainbow." This obvious *Wizard of Oz* reference makes clearer the psychological games that are being played with Bill, just as the mirrors we see full of Alice suggested *Alice in Wonderland*. Still oblivious to these organized synchronicities, Bill remains blindfolded like Nick, yet not with a literal blindfold. Bill's blindness is to his own naivety and ignorance concerning himself and the world around him. All the clues are before him, that he is being led like a lamb to the slaughter, should he choose to see it. The events are Bill's initiation as he tested regarding his "fidelio," faithfulness either to his wife, his ambiguous sense of middle-class morals, or, ultimately, to the cult – hence, the password. It should be noted as well that the cult retains these sexual magic elements, where the profane seeker is in darkness (eyes wide shut or blindfolded), in which only the hierophant

37

or cult leader can enlighten, remembering that light is a prism or *rainbow*. The rainbow is also a symbol of the disregard of sexual inhibitions in relation to the rainbow flag of the homosexual movement. However, the sexuality in the film's perspective is not about liberation, but even subtly implies that Mr. Milich (Rade Serbedzija), the costume owner who is connected to the cult and also acting on their behalf in his exchange with Bill, prostitutes his own underage daughter (Leelee Sobieski) for money (to the Japanese businessmen and presumably to the cult).

Bill finds what he has been led to – the end of the rainbow.

The clue to knowing Milich's connection to the cult is the secretly whispered phrase his daughter gives to Bill about what to wear. After lithely rubbing herself on Bill, she explains his choice of gown won't do – he must specifically wear an "ermine cloak." Ermine is classically a sign of heraldry indicating high-ranking peerage and royalty, particularly among British elites. This lets the viewer know she has attended the rituals and knows precisely where Bill is headed, thus revealing the entire costume shop scene as staged to lead Bill to the mansion. Nervous, yet desirous for adventure, Bill takes a cab to the mansion donning mask and cape, and successfully infiltrates using the password. Within the estate, we witness a solemn form of an initiation ritual where a magic circle of gorgeous, almost nude women are inducted into the elite cult in a kind of mock Catholic mass, presided over by a figure resembling a Cardinal. The closest analogue in the real world would be something akin to a Crowleyan "Gnostic Mass," or the OTO.[19]

Masked balls go back to ancient times, yet in the past few hundred years they have come to mark the party life of certain cadres of the upper echelons of power. Renaissance Britain had many masked balls, as well as France, and according to Vatican insider and exorcist, Malachi Martin in his famous book *Hostage to the Devil*, such ritual orgies certainly do take place.[20] Martin details an account of a black mass at a lavish estate purportedly attended by a transgender individual Martin claims to have exorcized ('Richard/Rita"), ominously similar to the imagery in Kubrick's film:

> When the curtains parted, Richard/Rita could see a low altar table at either end of the pool. Above each altar there hung an ornament in the shape of an inverted triangle. At its center there was an inverted crucifix, the head of the crucified resting on the angle of the apex of the triangle. From the interior of the house he now heard the low peals of an organ. And someone was burning incense there, so the fumes drifted out lazily across the air, slowly twisting like blue serpents. Then the guests started to undress in an unconcerned fashion, each one dropping their clothes where they stood.... As each pair handed on the chalice, they started to copulate following the rhythm of Father Samson, until all – men, women and Father Samson – were chanting and copulating in unison.[21]

After witnessing the ritual orgy, Bill is tricked into revealing his identity to all the masked attendees and is given the impression the cult is going to sacrifice him, until a girl steps forward to "ransom" herself for him. That human sacrifice is involved seems to be clear, as the woman offers herself to "redeem" him, mimicking the biblical doctrine of blood atonement.[22] I suspect this is Mandy from earlier in the film, due to her respect for Bill at having aided her; yet now she wants out of the sex slavery, even at the cost of her life. Her way out will be a redeeming death, as Bill later discovers her name in the next day's obituary. Note the similarity of the imagery in *Eyes Wide Shut* to the Rothschild Ball described earlier in Chapter 1 and the celebrations at the 40th birthday of Prince Pavlos of Greece, as well as revelations concerning French IMF Banker Dominique Strauss-Kahn's sex parties, as reported by the *New York Times*:

> The investigation into the prostitution ring in Lille ultimately swept up 10 suspects, including Mr. Strauss-Kahn. They knew each other largely through their membership as French Freemasons, according to Karl Vandamme, a defense lawyer who represents Fabrice Paszkowski, the owner of a medical supply company who played a crucial role in organizing the sex parties.[23]

Author Terry Melanson comments:

"The Heaven and Hell-themed party was held at Prince Pavlos' £12 million London mansion, and participants were decked out in mask and costume suggestive of *Eyes Wide Shut*. "Ice sculptures of angels graced a marquee with room for 200 in the garden, which was meant to be Heaven," writes Colin Fernandez of the *Daily Mail*. "Meanwhile, the swimming pool in the basement was covered over and decked out to resemble Hell, with stilt-walkers and erotic dancers."

That they would choose to dress up in a particular way as to allude to *Eyes Wide Shut* – the definitive film portrayal of elite-Illuminati debauchery – is significant. Royalty, after all, more than any other class, are exceedingly familiar with their ancestry. Prince Pavlos – I'm sure he's aware – is a direct descendant of a documented member of the Bavarian Illuminati: Karl Landgrave of Hessen-Kassel (1744-1836). Likewise, guests Prince Michael of Kent and his kids; Prince Andrew; the Viscount of Linley, David Albert Charles Armstrong-Jones; and Crown Prince Haakon of Norway are all direct descendants of another documented member of the Bavarian Illuminati: Duke Ernst II of Saxe-Gotha-Altenburg (1745-1804).[24]

Above, Left to Right: Lady Gabriella Windsor (daughter); Prince Michael of Kent (dad); Princess Michael of Kent (mom); and Lord Frederick Michael George David Louis Windsor (son). Below: Prince Michael of Kent, Grand Master of the Mark Master Masons

40

For a more hardcore example of this type of revelry, author Dave Mc-Gowan recounts the details surrounding the infamous Dutroux Affair, which involved human trafficking, European elites, murder and secret societies, as children and women were procured for orgies (and worse) amongst the degenerate elite:

> Outrage continued to grow as more arrests were made and evidence of high-level government and police complicity continued to emerge. One of Dutroux's accomplices, businessman Michael Nihoul, confessed to organizing an orgy at a Belgian chateau that had been attended by government officials, a former European Commissioner, and a number of law enforcement officers. A Belgian senator noted, quite accurately, that such parties were part of a system "which operates to this day and is used to blackmail the highly placed people who take part. ..." As the *New York Times* reported, [Judge Jean-Marc] Connerotte "became a national hero after saving two children from a secret dungeon kept by a convicted child rapist and ordering an inquiry that led to the discovery of the bodies of four girls kidnapped by a child pornography ring ... [Nihoul's] parties not only involved sex, they included sadism, torture and murder."[25]

A shaken Bill takes his cab home to find Alice awakening, giggling and laughing, as if she had been drugged like Mandy. Informing her she was merely dreaming, to Bill's dismay, she begins to sob. He inquires about the dream and Alice replies:

> "It was so weird, we were in a deserted city and our clothes were gone. We were naked and I was terrified and I felt ashamed. And I was angry because you ... rushed away to find clothes for us. As soon as you were gone it was completely different. I felt wonderful. Then I was lying in a beautiful garden stretched out naked in the sunlight and a man walked out of the woods. He was the man from the hotel I told you about — the Naval officer. He stared at me and he just laughed. He just laughed at me.... He was kissing me and then we were making love, then there were all these other people around us – hundreds of them everywhere – they were all fucking. And then I was fucking other men; so many I don't know how many I was with. I knew you could see me in the arms of all these men ... and I wanted to make fun of you, to laugh in your face. And so I laughed as loud as could. And that must have been when you woke me up.[26]

41

This is a clue that both Bill and Alice are being inducted into the cult, or that the cult has power over even Bill's wife, should they choose to use it. Either Alice has been drugged and doesn't recall the orgy, thinking it was a dream, or she is a willing part of the initiation process for Bill, insofar as she has already been brought in and her memories are repressed (and return to her in her dream state). Frantic, Bill attempts to track down the cult, returning to the estate, but is warned by a butler, letter in hand, not to inquire any further. Still desiring an affair and now perhaps curious about the cult's reach, he phones Domino, only to discover from her roommate she is nowhere to be found due to contracting "AIDS" (in other words, her acting role is complete). Bill once again sets to wandering the streets, only to find he is stalked by shadowy figures, beginning to fear he has nowhere to run. Perusing the newspaper he learns Mandy has overdosed, visiting the morgue to find out it is indeed her body and she has likely been murdered. Falling back on his last resort, Bill visits Ziegler who reveals most of the truth: He is indeed in the cult and was present the night Bill snuck in. Ziegler warns again not to investigate any further, while Bill remains speechless that his close friend is part of an elite sex magick cult – with the power to control events and kill when necessary. It is also worth noting Ziegler's house is decorated with paintings of British aristocracy.

Ziegler reveals his knowledge of Nick's mentioning the cult and tells Bill he had him followed. Ziegler explains: "Bill, suppose I tell that everything that happened there, the threats, the girl's warnings, suppose I said all of that was staged. That it was a kind of charade. That it was fake? ... to scare the shit out of you to keep you quiet about where you'd been and what you'd seen."[27]

Bill tells Ziegler he saw Mandy's body and Ziegler reveals she was Bill's mysterious savior at the orgy – Bill retorts, what kind of charade ends with someone ending up dead? We discover the dark truth that it *was* a ritual killing. One question might be raised at this juncture, which is, why a sex-magick cult? As noted above, the symbolism has already conveyed numerous instances of pillars, pentagrams and *Alice* and *Oz* references, all of which culminate in the ritual orgy that hearkens to something overtly Crowleyan. There is also the hermaphroditic and alchemical union of opposites doctrine I mentioned above, that is believed to be overcome or transcended, in the sexual union. In the practice of sex magick, the goal of erasing oppositions is believed to be effected in the sex act. Traditionalist philosopher Julius Evola, echoing Pike's original quote at the beginning of this chapter, explains the attempt at overcoming dualities and effecting of the psychosphere through such actions:

The separation of the sexes is a special method of manifestation of the Dyad principle, which also conditions the division between spirit and nature, ego and non-ego. If there exists a metaphysical coincidence – and we have seen how Scotus Eriugena recognized it – then there may equally well be a relationship between the experience of transcendence through sex and a nondual state that permits a direct and extranormal action on the non-ego, on the outer web of events. Let us recall that in the classical and Platonic version of the myth of the original hermaphrodite, a power such that it struck fear into the gods and was attributed to that being before it was split.[28]

The magic circle.

And as regards the film's ritual orgy scene and magic circle coven:

Here it is a matter of the *chakra* or chains (literally, wheels) consisting of couples who perform ritual coitus together in circular formation. In the middle of the circle is the "lord of the wheel" or *chakreshvara* together with his companion, who officiates and directs the collective operation. An adept who has had perfect initiation is needed to perform this function. Overall, this is a collective and partly orgiastic evocation of the Goddess, as the latent force in the group, a force now aroused through the realization of acts and visualization of images by the individual pairs until a fluidic or "psychic" vortex is created and used in the operation. A similar method performed for the benefit of others is used in professional magic rites. Tantric *chakra* have been convened by princes for special profane purposes, such as propitiation of success in war.[29]

Indeed, it is here we see the Crowleyan elements of Kubrick's film made evident. As for the purpose of sexual orgies in a ritual context, American historian and Calvinist philosopher, R.J. Rushdoony comments on the ancient pagan perspective of primordial chaos and ecstatic frenzy, perfectly applicable to the magical view of *Eyes Wide Shut*'s cult:

> In ancient fertility cults, which, as genetic faiths, enthroned the lowest as the primary, a ritual return to chaos was held to be the means of social regeneration. The fixed, lawful and rational were late and higher developments and hence less basic also seen as essentially sterile. Closeness to the primitive was closeness to creativity and vitality, and chaos itself was the principle of regeneration. Saturnalia, the primitive festival, orgies, rituals involving confusion in the form of incest, bestiality or perversion, were necessary rites and means of social regeneration. "In fact, the festival is presented as a re-enactment of the first days of the universe, the Urzeit, the eminently creative era." The rebirth of nature and the rebirth of society both require the return to chaos. "The festival is thus celebrated in the context of the myth and assumes the function of regenerating the real world."[30]

In the Thelemic view, the goal of the individual magus is the overcoming of all taboos, oppositions and dualities, a fitting description of both Bill, Alice and the cult. Occult researcher Dr. Stephen Flowers comments:

THELEMA: Religious philosophy of English occultist Aleister Crowley as dictated in his *Book of the Law*, where the central maxim is "Do what thou wilt shall be the whole of the Law. Love is the law, love under will." Thelemites seek out their own true path in life, known as one's "True Will," with the intent of achieving concourse with one's Holy Guardian Angel, with the practice of ritual magick.

To understand completely what Crowley is saying we must refer to his general cosmology which is monistic: all apparent opposites are in reality unities. This is how Horus is united with Set. They are the light and dark opposites within the same unity. "The true magick of Horus requires the passionate union of opposites." This is clearly how, for Crowley, this is the Aeon of Horus, but its root formula is ShT (rendering Satan, Shaitan, Set, etc.). Here as elsewhere Crowley is using the familiar practice of antinomianism. In *Liber V vel Reguli* (*Ritual of the Mark of the Beast*) Crowley lays out his antinomianism and its practice: "This is in fact the formula of our Magick; we insist that all acts must be equal..."[31]

44

Bill returns home to find his lost mask on the pillow next to a sleeping Alice. In other words, we are to suspect either that Alice knows he was there, or she is telling him she is involved. Expressing intense sorrow, Bill breaks down weeping and tells her everything. It is within this scene we can see Bill giving the sign of secrecy, a masonic sign of faithfulness to the order borrowed in other sects, including those of Aleister Crowley. Significantly, it conveys the character of an oath – the hand on the chest with forefinger extended as shown in *Richardson's Monitor of Freemasonry*, page 86.

Oath of Secrecy
Aleister Crowley giving the sign of secrecy.

Having endured their trial, Bill and Alice discuss their decision to remain married, following the confession. Remembering their promise to take their daughter Christmas shopping that morning, the couple continue their talk in the department store, where some pivotal, yet subtle events transpire. Another inverted pentagram is shown, a purposefully placed "Magic circle" game, as well as another display labeled "magic." The couple has now stepped into the magic circle and their eyes are no longer shut. They have been "illuminated" by the

Israel Regardie (1907-1985): Ukrainian Jewish immigrant who would become Aleister Crowley's personal secretary, eventually settling in the United States, where he developed an interest in yoga, Hinduism and theosophy. Regardie is known for his many commentaries and books on the beliefs, rites and rituals of the Hermetic Order of the Golden Dawn, a secret esoteric society.

actions of the cult and are aware of the true power structure in the world. We had already seen a "magic circle" of women at the initiation ritual in the mansion. Crowley's personal secretary and fellow Golden Dawn member Israel Regardie notes, concerning the circle, (applying perfectly to Bill):

The principal symbol common to every operation is the Magical Circle. By definition this figure implies a confining space, a limitation, separating that which is within from that which is without. By the use of the Circle, the Magician asserts that within this self-imposed limitation he confines his labors; that he limits himself to the attainment of a specific end, and that he is no longer *in a maze of illusion and perpetual change as a blind wanderer without aim*, objective or aspiration...The Circle in which the magician is enclosed represents his particular cosmos; the conquest, self-inaugurated, of that universe is part of the process to attain complete self-consciousness.[32]

Undergoing this dark enlightenment, Bill and Alice discuss what to do next, opining they should be "grateful." Alice posits, "We should be grateful that we have managed to survive through all our adventures, whether they were real or only a dream." Bill asks if she is sure, to which Alice replies she will forgive one night of impertinence. "No dream is ever just a dream," Bill explains, and Alice responds that they are "awake now, and hopefully, for a long time to come." "Forever," they both say, yet "Let's not say forever," Alice retorts, "it frightens me. But I do love you, and you know, there is something very important we need to do as soon as possible – fuck," showing the intention to maximize their sexual potentialities, having been initiated.[33]

Alice and Bill are surrounded by pentagrams and the "Magic Circle."

Thus, the film functions on multiple levels, highlighting different issues of marital problems our society creates, with its decadence and veneer of Christianity, as well as its sexual issues, but that is only part of the story Kubrick wants to tell. The real story is the ritual journey of coming out of the dream state, with the result being the "awakening" to grasp the reality of the occult elite, the social power structure as it really is – rich elites who are into bizarre cults and aberrant sex magick. This magical surrealism as an initiatory rite is the true intention of the film.

The power structure is not merely focused around wealth and temporal power, but a particularly ritualized worldview that seeks to use the sex drive as a force for *metaphysical* power. Power over this drive allows power over the masses, and this is also the point of the Edenic imagery, including the *Alice in Wonderland* and *Oz* references – the transition both from a fantasy reality of the dream world and base sexual desires, into the fake world of the film itself (which is depicting reality!), as well as the transition from eyes shut, to awake. Not only is it supposed to be an initiation for the couple, the intention is to initiate the viewer, through revelation of the method, to the nature of this cryptocratic underground, assuming one is willing to see. Michael Hoffman explains this notion of revelation of the method from a British Intelligence perspective, as follows:

This demonstrates one of our simpler methods. Realizing that our activities will sooner or later come to light, we structure our activities so that as conspiracy researchers unravel them, they will release information in such a way that *it mirrors our initiatory procedure.* In this way, the more we are investigated, the more masses of people are psychologically processed by the people who seek to expose us. The meme that constitutes our structure is then successfully mimicked within the consciousness of those who investigate us. Success can then be measured precisely to the extent that our work is "exposed."[34]

MICHAEL A. HOFFMAN II: American author, lecturer and revisionist historian. Hoffman is a vocal critic of Rabbinic Judaism and is the author of the alternative research classic, *Secret Societies and Psychological Warfare*, where the notions of "twilight language," ritual symbolism and Freemasonic subterfuge are emphasized.

Endnotes

1. Kubrick cited in Nelson, Thomas A. *Stanley Kubrick: Inside a Film Artist's Maze.* Indiana, Indiana University Press, 2000, pg. 14.

2. Kaus, Rainer J. "Notes on Arthur Schnitzler's Dream Novella and Stanley Kubrick's film Eyes Wide Shut." University of Florida. 2003. Web. http://www.clas.ufl.edu/ipsa/2003/Greenwich%20conference.html

3. Walker, Taylor and Ruchti. *Stanley Kubrick, Director: A Visual Analysis.* New York, Norton Company, 1999, 344. As will be shown, Kubrick will employ this same technique of blacking out the screen as a representation of the viewer's eyes closing or being in the dark in my 2001: A Space Odyssey analysis.

4. Pike, Albert. *Morals and Dogma: Ancient and Accepted Rite of Scottish Freemasonry.* Richmond, VA, L.H. Jenkins Book Manufacturers, 1950, pgs. 772, 849.

5. Leadbeater, C.W. *The Hidden Life in Freemasonry*. India, The Theosophical Publishing House, 1963, pg. 72.

6. Carroll, Lewis. *Alice's Adventures in Wonderland* and *Through the Looking Glass*. New York, Penguin Books, 1998, pg. Xix. Conner, Miguel. "Alice in Wonderland and the Occult." Examiner. 26 March, 2010. Web. http://www.examiner.com/article/alice-wonderland-and-the-occult

7. Stephan, "Corridors of the Marvelous: The Femme-enfant, the Doll Fetish, The Mask, and Alice in a Wonderland of de Sade." Story of O. Web. http://www.storyofo.info/marvelous.html

8. Hanshaw, *Operation Culture Creation, Part 2*, pg. 77.

9. Marks, John. *The CIA and Mind Control: Search for the Manchurian Candidate*. New York, McGraw Hill, 1980.

10. Conner, "Alice in Wonderland and the Occult."

11. Flowers, Stephen E. *Lords of the Left Hand Path: A History of Spiritual Dissent*. Texas, Runa-Raven Press, 1997, pg. 145.

12. Melanson, Terry. *Perfectibilists: The 18th Century Bavarian Order of the Illuminati*. Oregon, Trine Day, 2009. I am not implying the cult in the film is the historic Illuminati, as it was concerned with Enlightenment rationalism and egalitarianism, rather, the film's cult is a secret society concerned with sexual magick.

13. Cirlot, J.E. *Dictionary of Symbols*. New York, Philosophical Library, 1962, pg. 115.

14. "Domino" is an interesting name, since, as a member of the cult, the events in Bill's life are occurring in planned, determined sequence, like the fall of a line of dominoes. It also suggests the concept of a game, as if the secret society is playing mind games with Bill.

15. See Hoffman, Michael A. *Secret Societies and Psychological Warfare*. Coeur D'Alene, Idaho, Independent History and Research, 2001. Ramsay, William. *Prophet of Evil: Aleister Crowley, 9/11 and the New World Order*. Lexington, Ky, Winged Victory Books, 2012. Estulin, Daniel. *The True Story of the Bilderberg Group*. Oregon, Trine Day, 2007. Quigley, Carroll. *Tragedy and Hope: A History of the World in our Time*. San Pedro, CA, GSG Publishers, 1998.

16. Kubrick, Vivian cited in "Vivian Kubrick on the Insanity of Tyranny," Infowars. Web. 26 November 2013. Web. http://www.infowars.com/infowars-com-exclusive-vivian-kubrick-on-the-insanity-of-tyranny-2/

17. Cirlot, *A Dictionary of Symbols*, 205-6.

18. Pike, *Morals and Dogma*, 639.

19. Heimbichner, *Blood on the Altar*.

20. Heale, Elizabeth. *The Faerie Queen: A Reader's Guide*. Cambridge: University Press, 1999. Martin, Malachi. Hostage to the Devil.

21. Martin, 213-15.

22. See Lev. 17:11.

23. Carvajal and la Baume. "Sex Life was 'Out of Step,' Strauss-Kahn Says, but not Illegal." 13 October, 2012. New York Times. Web. http://www.nytimes.com/2012/10/14/world/europe/dominique-strauss-kahn-says-lust-is-not-a-crime.html?hp&_r=1. See also Wolff, Michael. "Dominique Strauss-Kahn and Our Paranoid Erotic Fantasies of Power." Guardian. 15 October, 2012. Web. http://www.theguardian.com/commentisfree/2012/oct/15/dominique-strausskahn-paranoid-erotic-fantasies-power

24. Melanson, Terry. "Illuminati Descendants Assemble for an Eyes Wide Shut-like 'Heaven and Hell' Bash." Conspiracy Archive. 20 June, 2007. Web. http://www.conspiracyarchive.com/Commentary/Illuminati_Eyes_Wide_Shut.htm

25. McGowan, *Programmed to Kill*, pg. 6-7.

26. *Eyes Wide Shut*, directed by Stanley Kubrick. 1999. Burbank, CA: Warner Home Video, DVD.

27. Kubrick, *Eyes Wide Shut*.

28. Evola, Julius. *Eros and the Mysteries of Love: The Metaphysics of Sex*. Rochester, Vermont: Inner Traditions, 1991, pg. 267.

29. Ibid., 268.

30. Rushdoony, R.J. *The Messianic Character of American Education*. Vallecito, Ca: Ross House Books, 1963, pg. 337-8.

31. Flowers, *Lords of the Left Hand Path*, 143.

32. Regardie, Israel. *The Tree of Life: An Illustrated Study in Magic*. Woodbury, MN: Llewellyn Publications, 2001, pgs. 158-9.

33. Kubrick, *Eyes Wide Shut*.

34. Hoffman, *Secret Societies*, 77.

Chapter 3

Kubrick Bears the Light: *The Shining* (1980)

Down the years, he had a phrase that he repeated like a personal mantra to hold at bay anyone who pressed him too closely about the "meaning" of his work, or his own "intentions." It came from an essay by H.P. Lovecraft, like Stephen King a popular manipulator of the occult: "In all things that are mysterious – never explain." The edict applies to Kubrick's own work, but even more to himself.[1]
– Walker, Taylor and Ruchti, *Stanley Kubrick, Director*

Generally considered one of the best horror films of all time, Stanley Kubrick's adaptation of the Stephen King story *The Shining*, is not lacking in interpretive creativity on the part of film critics and analysts. Freudian psychoanalysis combined with esoteric speculation generally garners much of the review space, but in my estimation *The Shining* is about something much more obvious (and obscure at the same time). I believe the film adaptation is intended to convey the same message as King's, and that is demonic possession. Not merely a presentation of the possession of Jack Torrance (Jack Nicholson), but of the spectral haunting of America itself, in terms of its dark past in relation to the Native Americans. Author Peter Levenda explains this insight:

Americans seem to be unconsciously aware the [Indian] mounds are repositories of something more than crumbling bones. The famous

Overlook Hotel in Stephen King's novel of horror and demonic possession, *The Shining*, was said to have been built over an Indian burial mound. The house that was the scene of terrifying paranormal phenomena in the film *Poltergeist* was also said to have been built on sacred Indian ground. Thus, our novelists and filmmakers seem to agree there is a substratum of spiritual force – for good or evil – beneath the very foundations of America's towns and cities.[2]

Indigenous animistic spiritualism undergirds the film, manifesting as a form of generational curse upon Jack, as we will see.

Initially, the camera perspective appears to fly in from an aerial vantage, as if it were the view of a disembodied spirit or demon. From the camera's vantage we also see a lake whose very reflection suggests "as above, so below," and of a lonely islet in the midst of vast mountains. Signifying isolation, Jack's desire to be rid of his family is conveyed in the natural landscape itself, but as we will see, mirrors and reflections will be displayed prominently in the film to convey reality behind the veil: the spiritual realm.

As above, so below – the mirror of two worlds.

Hovering then over the mountains, the viewer gradually comes to spot Jack winding toward the ominous Overlook Hotel in Colorado. Built in 1907, the site was chosen for its seclusion and scenic beauty, yet there is a darker side to this locale: It seems to draw dark forces into its midst as a kind of spiritual vortex. While the hotel is "real," we will discover in Jack's mind it begins to take on an other-worldly portal association. Jack has, in fact, chosen this location purposely because the "writing" of the story is *not* his novel, but his gruesome reenactment of spiritual, ritual sacrifice that is required for his imagined entrance into the hall of fame – the abode of the "beautiful people."

51

All-American Manager Ullman, facilitator of whores, orgies and abuse.

Arriving at the hotel, Jack and his new masters become acquainted: The interview scene conveys an overtly *Americana* façade that clues the viewer into the dual symbolism of the film, where the Overlook is both Jack's degenerating *psyche* and a microcosm of the United States. With a friendly, charming veneer, the baby-boomer generation has a dark side that is portrayed both figuratively and literally in Jack's brutality at the mystic locale of the Overlook. In this sense, America is not baseball and apple pie, and manager Ullman's JFK-esque appearance masks his own potential to actually be nefarious, while surrounded by icons of *Americana*, from flags to paintings to Native American artworks.

Jack's homosexual and incestuous tendencies. Image credit: Rob Ager.

It is also worth noting that the photos in Ullman's office appear to be the same images that will conclude the film (as will be shown below). Ullman reveals to Jack that the history of the caretakers involved a previous mass murder, where "cabin fever" resulted in an instance of madness and violent outbursts. Danny, we begin to learn, has a special talent by which he can presage the future, named in the film's title, "Shining." Walker, Taylor and Ruchti explain, highlighting my point about animism and Native American traditions: "Carothers [Dick Halloran] is a great casting success. His talent for "shining" springs from the animism associated with blacks, but Carothers' features, ancient and weathered like an Easter Island monument, also lend the story more gravitas. He's the hero, although a sacrificial hero.[3]

Jack explains to Ullman that his wife Wendy (Shelley Duvall) is a "confirmed ghost story and horror film fanatic," but as we see from the imagery in the Torrance apartment, Wendy actually shares an interest in the occult, including numerous books on witchcraft, as well as the notorious *Catcher in the Rye*, associated with several assassins.[4] Because Jack has come to despise his family, who he thinks are his stumbling block to greatness, the dark depths of his subconscious will suggest (through the whisper of the demonic) a *real* horror for Wendy and Danny.

Nihilistic favorite of so-called assassins and killers, *The Catcher in the Rye*.

Following his father's job interview, Danny experiences a supernatural premonition, a seizure and dissociating blackout, sensing intuitively the trauma they are destined to undergo in their Overlook ordeal. We begin to

53

suspect Danny has been abused (possibly sexually), as his alternate persona emerges as a spirit named "Tony," who lives in Danny's "mouth and stomach." In my opinion, the usage of inverted stars on Danny's shirt is intentional, as we later discover Jack has, in fact, physically and sexually assaulted Danny (resulting in his traumatic break and "Tony"). Interestingly, in accounts of indigenous religions and spiritual possession, there are instances of spirits inhabiting certain areas of the body in precisely this way.[5]

Indeed, as film analyst Rob Ager has correctly elucidated, the abuse appears to be generational, as intergenerational conflict and Freudian/ Oedipal envy (Jack resents Danny) will occupy much of this story.[6] Ager is also correct in his insights concerning the cartoon programming Danny has apparently received, as Jack will become the "Big Bad Wolf," utilizing the Disney and nursery rhyme mantras during his psychosis.[7] This is also why cartoons are consistently playing throughout the film, including numerous references to fairy tales such as Hansel and Gretel, as well as classical works of mythology with Theseus and the labyrinth's Minotaur. Fairy tales and mythical referents are profuse: Ager is also perceptive to connect the old hag in the bathtub we will see later in the film, to the classical notion of the seductive nymphs or sirens transforming into hags, causing sailors to crash upon the rocks.[8] This omen will appear and apply to Jack as he progresses down his path of possession.

"Ghost and horror fanatic" Wendy's books include *The Magic Circle* and *The Mother Goddess*.

Looking over the books visible in Wendy's living room, we can see an interest in witchcraft in *The Magic Circle* (or is Jack the witch?) and *Mother Goddess*, as the counselor learns Jack dislocated Danny's shoulder in a drunken rage. Wendy, however, is partly to blame in this, as she is naively willing to overlook the trauma and against her better judgment trust Jack's empty promise. Recall as well the "magic circle" appears here and in Kubrick's final film highlighted in the previous chapter, *Eyes Wide Shut* – in fact, it appears Danny has arranged his Disney and cartoon stickers in a kind of magic or ritual circle on his door.

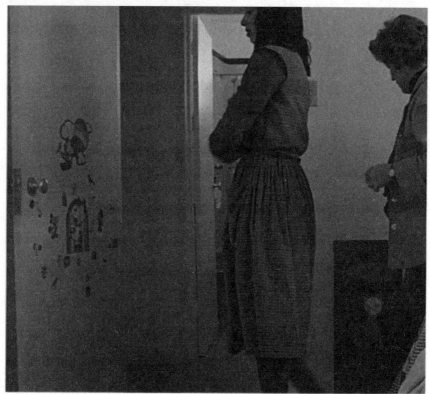

Danny's magic circle of stickers.

Concerning the minotaur and the film's art direction, Walker, Taylor and Ruchti note:

> Kubrick often positions Nicholson visually against extremely formal backgrounds. One image frames him in the abstract design of a wall tapestry. A Native American motif, it also resembles a printed circuit. It calls to mind the rigor of programmed information. No deviation allowed. In another shot, Torrance looms above a mod-

el of the garden maze. The maze clearly alludes to the Minotaur myth in which a monster with the head of a bull and the body of a man who was kept in a labyrinth and fed on human flesh until a hero, Theseus, killed it. It was a legend that had long appealed to Kubrick. (The company that made *Killer's Kiss* twenty-five years before was called Minotaur Productions.) ... In his film, the environment is destiny, not its instrument.[9]

The bull/Minotaur Taurus with Gemini (the twins) and "Monarch."

As the now evidently dysfunctional family journeys to their nightmare abode, Jack posits a macabre topic for discussion: the reality of cannibalism as a drive that is "necessary to survive," sneering at Danny's awareness of what he saw "on television." Jack displays his psychopathic, parasitic side in a glimpse, a premonition, of what horrors he will unleash upon his own family – a form of cannibalism. Here it is crucial to note, as Ager has shown, that Jack apparently has homosexual proclivities, despite his exteriorly masculine, fatherly role. Touring the hotel, Ullman reveals the secret to the Overlook – it was formerly a getaway for monied elites, Hollywood stars and royalty – all the "best people." Kubrick's dour view of American aristocracy and the middle class is reflected in their offspring, represented in the film by Jack. The hotel is not merely a site for elite orgies and lascivious dalliances, but a representative sacrificial site where the dead feed parasitically on the fear of living victims. This theme will also appear in the chapter on *Twin Peaks*.

The alchemical "Gold Room," according to Jay Weidner.

Timidly touring the hotel, Wendy anxiously refers to it as "a maze" like the hotel's garden, sprinkling her dialogue with references to cartoons and nursery rhymes. Danny is spoken of as "lost" (signifying both a literal and figurative sense), looking for his parents. He has been abandoned, his parent's fixation on the landscape leaving him forgotten in the "game room." Jack rhetorically comments on Danny's playfulness, "Did you get tired of bombing the universe?" – signifying Danny's representation of youthful American aggression, the great Enlightenment experiment that sits upon a giant Indian burial ground (the U.S.). Kubrick was very much a critic of Americanism and its foreign policy, as we can see in films like *Dr. Strangelove* (1964), where the absurdity of mutually assured Cold War destruction and the Rand Corporation are lampooned.

The Cold War Great Game was truly a "game room" of the theater of war, making Kubrick's critique of Western Imperialism appropriate.[10] Danny, we recall, had seen a vision of the murdered twins in the "game room," while behind him in the scene is a poster that reads "Monarch." Given Danny's representation of both traumatized youth and naïve America, Monarch can also be applied to the nation *en masse*, since, I propose, the MKUltra abominations were really about mass mind control, and not primarily programmed assassins.[11] Kubrick is thus gradually revealing Danny's abuse, trauma and mind control under the hand of Jack.

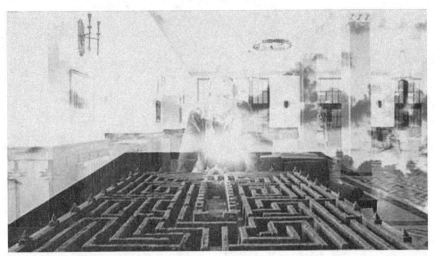

Comparison capless pyramid: Jack at the head of the maze, like the minotaur, superimposed over the apex of the pyramid during the zodiacal alignment in *2001: A Space Odyssey*.

Interestingly, the minotaur has a significance in terms of human sacrifice (the dark side of the film, as we will see), in relation to the myth of Theseus – originally a human sacrifice tale according to scholar Nigel Davies in his history of the practice:

> Perhaps the most famous concerns Theseus and the minotaur. Theseus was already the hero of many tales, including the killing of Procrustes, another slayer of men.... Athens paid an annual tribute of seven youths and seven maidens to Minos, King of Crete; these he shut up in the labyrinth, where they either lost their way and died of hunger or were eaten by the minotaur, half man, half bull.[12]

Monarch is reportedly connected with the various mind control programs of the CIA, in part seeking to create alternate personas, often mentioned under the umbrella of "MKUltra," but including projects BLUE-BIRD, ARTICHOKE and NAOMI, centered on mass mind control and whispers of creating dissociative states and altered consciousness through LSD, torture and traumatization.[13] Even if this has been exaggerated, the film certainly uses this narrative with Danny being subject to Jack's abuse, Danny's "alter" or spirit "Tony," the game room reference to "Monarch" and frequent use of maze and labyrinth symbolism, signifying compartments of the *psyche*.[14] Note below Jack's exhaustion and sleep state is accompanied by images of butterflies, signifying his transformation, as well as the mirror. Mirrors often represent the subconscious, the *psyche* or the inner world that is reflected in our minds from the outer world, as well as signifying the spiritual realm or another plane (Alice in *Through the Looking Glass*), closely parallel to our own where much of *The Shining* is taking place.[15] It is in this scene that Jack once again hints *he* is writing the ghostly horror tale that is *not* a book.

The maze-like compartments of the psyche, and Danny's carpet maze simulacra.

The maze itself is interesting for its dual usage: symbolizing both Jack's *psyche* and his writing of the fiction into his reality, the viewer begins to discover the principle of simulacrum, where the modeled things become real in a preparatory phase for later fulfillment. I will highlight Spielberg's use of this in later chapters analyzing *Close Encounters of the Third Kind* and *E.T.*, where the director functions as a shaman or magus, fore-signifying events to come. Through symbolic objects like toys (operating like a voodoo doll) in *Close Encounters, E.T.* or *A.I.* which later appear as real, life-sized objects, power is given over the reality: Roy's mashed potatoes and television programs (such as *The Ten Commandments* where Moses is at Mt. Sinai – like Devil's Mountain) portend future events. And like Devil's Mountain in *Close Encounters*, the Overlook Hotel is also situated on a "high place," where the spirits of the dead meet with man and demand and exchange.

The models in Roy's house in *Close Encounters* will become real, later, as the government stages an outbreak in the train sequence.

59

I propose this is not merely a plot device or choice of nostalgic imagery, but an attempt to *script reality* by writing one's own twilight language (like Jack is doing). Twilight language is a form of angelic script that integrates synchronistic events, like a kind of semiotic text to be read, while writers and directors like King, Kubrick and Steven Spielberg are operating in the role of the magus to produce a dramaturgical ritual that communicates with the subconscious. This is also why mazes and labyrinths have historically been associated with both the underworld and the *psyche*, as we will also see in the Lucas/Henson production, *Labyrinth*. In "The Process of Individuation," M.L. von Franz explains the meaning of the labyrinth as subconscious:

> The maze of strange passages, chambers, and unlocked exits in the cellar recalls the old Egyptian representation of the underworld, which is a well-known symbol of the unconscious with its mysterious abilities. It also shows how one is "open" to other influences in one's unconscious shadow side and how uncanny and alien elements can break in.[16]

Aeneas in the Underworld, from *The Aeneid* by Virgil, Book VI.

Simulacra is important to semiotics, but it also has an important role in esoterism because of the idea of correspondences. Before modern philosophy divorced metaphysics from academia, the holistic view of the sciences in the western tradition included an idea of essentialism, which connected the "essences" of things with all their referents and symbols. Thus, there would be an association between the symbol of the maze, the model, and its referent, the actual maze. This is a deep, difficult subject that gets into a lot of heavy philosophy and semiotics, but the idea is simply foreign to most moderns because of stupid philosophy. Thus, Plato discussed simulacra – we can see simulacrum in Spielberg's *Jurassic Park*, where a simulation of a theme park shows simulations of simulations (dinosaurs), as an example. Hollywood, just like esoterism, or like writing itself, *is* the manipulation of copies, signs and symbols. *E.T.* is about symbols, language and meaning (like *Close Encounters*), and we are constantly given camera angles and shots in *E.T.* from a child's perspective. The cross-reference to *Star Wars* is also interesting.[17]

Plato: 5th century B.C. Greek philosopher generally considered the father of western philosophy through his school in Athens known as "The Academy," together with his teacher Socrates. Known for his dialogues, laws and *The Republic*, Plato taught that reality is truly present in mental ideals. These ideals exist in a realm of forms distinct from the material realm. Through philosophical discourse and dialectical argumentation, the philosopher can attain to a direct knowledge of the forms. Influenced by mystical, Pythagorean and mathematical traditions, Plato argued for a fully rational, logical interpretation of how to construct an ideal government, explained in his highly influential *The Republic*.

Reminiscent of the Hortus Palantius, the garden maze of the Overlook Hotel would appear to have an alchemical significance in similar fashion to the above: the nearly mystical 17th-century "eighth wonder of the world" constructed by Elector Frederick Palatine V for his wife Elizabeth Stuart. According to Enlightenment scholar Dame Frances Yates, the gardens signified Rosicrucian mysteries, both regents being friends of Francis Bacon.[18] Largely destroyed during the Thirty Years' War, the garden mazes are replete with esoteric symbology

The alchemical maze gardens of Frederick the Palatine, the "Hortius Palatinus."

according to Dame Yates and we can see in Kubrick's maze that same principle at work. In fact, while looking at the image of the maze on the sign below, it occurred to me how similar the maze was to both a mandala and a sigil.

The Overlook Maze, reminiscent of the mandala or a sigil. The "Loser" has to keep America "clean" of the people who are aren't the "best people."

This connection is not tenuous, as Oxford anthropologist and Comparative Religion scholar John Layard outlines in his work "The Malekulan Journey of the Dead" where the indigenous religious mythology of the Malekulan tribe's after-death journey is drawn from the patterned formations that appear in the natural, sacred geometry of the tortoise shell. Not only is this seen to be a kind of math puzzle, it is also a maze and a pathway for the dead, resembling a sigil:

Malekulan mazes and sigils, signifying the journey of the soul after death.

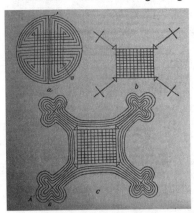

Fig. 8, [Left] Constructed in a similar way, resembles a mandala... Apart from a diamond shaped center unconnected with the other parts, the whole design is formed of a single, never-ending line. These are only a few examples of the pure art forms that have developed in Malekula out of the labyrinth motive combined with that derived from the outline of the human form [The Anthropocosmic principle].

62

From the Near East to Malekula is a long way. However, there are connecting links that suggest the itinerary which these combined motives apparently followed. One such link is to be found in South India, where ritual and labyrinth designs almost identical with those made in Malekula are still in use. This field of study has only begun to be investigated, but already it is possible to throw light on certain obscure points in classical tradition by comparison with the living beliefs of Malekula. The sibyl of classical and medieval lore may well be compared with the Malekulan Female Devouring Ghost, sitting beside her cave guarding the labyrinth. Through caves or clefts guarded by these mythical figures mighty heroes of antiquity started their journeys to the underworld to visit the shades of their ancestors.

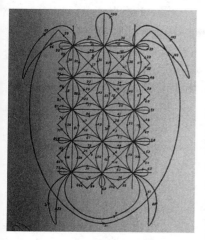

Using the animism of the Malekulan tribe as an exemplar, we see the symmetry and patterns of the tortoise shell that inform their mythology of the maze that follows upon death.

Virgil describes such a descent in the sixth book of the *Aeneid*, in which Aeneas goes into the underworld. Hitherto, scholars have, very understandably, failed to appreciate why, in his introduction to this book, the Latin poet interrupts his otherwise consecutive tale with a now apparently unintelligible interpolation concerning a labyrinth. Aeneas, who has finally landed at Cumae on Latin soil, approaches a cave, guarded by the sibyl, through which he wishes to descend to Hades. But here Virgil, often criticized for a passage that has nothing to do with the story, breaks off his account to describe a representation of the Cretan labyrinth, depicted at the entrance to the Cumean Cave; right in its symbolic place, but for the Roman reader the scene would have been charged with all the emotional connection with initiation rites at the journey into the land of the dead. In this same book of the Aeneid are also described "two waters;" outside flows the Styx nine times round, the river of death, which Aeneas can only be ferried over after he has shown the sibyl the famous Golden Bough or magic wand which, judging from the Malekulan evidence, is his own counterpart or spiritual double. Inside, he comes to Lethe, the water of forgetfulness leading to the inner life, which for full initiation he must immerse himself to achieve new life on earth. (*Spiritual Disciplines: Papers From the Eranos Yearbook*, pgs. 148-50).[19]

A Mandala-esque design of the same tribe that illustrates both the psyche and the human form, showing the anthropic principle.

The esoteric and literary *topoi* in connection to Jack Torrance become obvious: Jack's own *psyche* is plunging into the underworld maze of his dark persona as he is already under the reign of death through his gradual possession. This makes perfect sense of the infamous scene with Jack staring at the model of the maze gardens that morph into the real maze, with Wendy and Danny. The underworld is Jack's *psyche* where, like the Minotaur in the mythology of Theseus and the labyrinth, Danny will battle the bullish beast in the center of the Labyrinth. This explains why Jack even seems to have a kind of bullish appearance, as well as a devilish Minotaur that appears in the hallway of the game room when Danny sees the omen of the murdered twins. Interestingly, the twins are Gemini, and the film takes place in May, the month in which the zodiac transitions from Taurus (the Bull), to Gemini; or the Minotaur (Jack) to the Twins, which I think is obviously intentional.[20]

Jack is seen in the mirror in his dream state, with monarch butterflies in view.

64

The omen of the murdered twins seen by Danny, along with the vision of rivers of blood gushing from the elevator, is also biblical in nature, recalling the curse in the Book of Exodus upon Egypt. It is also possible the twins have a twin-towers significance, since in Masonry the twin pillars are Jachin and Boaz, which signify a doorway or portal to the Temple (which is also the meaning of Gemini in Babylonian mythology). This makes one puzzle given the title of Kubrick's masterpiece, *2001: A Space Odyssey*, and the events of September 11, 2001, as will be seen in the following chapter.[21]

Twin towers, twin pillars – Gemini

Room 237, in my estimation, does not relate to the moon. Although I do think Weidner is correct to point out the images of Danny in the Apollo shirt are a reference to NASA utilizing Kubrick and front-screen projection to film the footage, I am doubtful that the number change from King's novel is about the distance to the moon. I think 237, being the location of the murder of the twins, is supposed to foreshadow the murder of another child, Danny, who wears a "42" shirt (2x3x7=42). This is also why the film Wendy and Danny are watching is the 1971 *Summer of '42*, a reverse Lolita-style tale of an older woman who seduces a younger boy.

Danny's "42" shirt with inverted pentagrams.

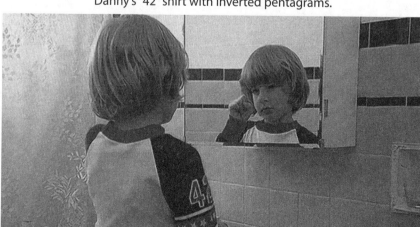

65

This is the second reference to pedophilia and Danny's #42 shirt clues us into that. Note that Kubrick also directed *Lolita*. As news reports foretell the coming snowstorm, we see Jack fall deeper into his trance states and demonic glares as Wendy and Danny begin to feel the drag of cabin fever. Danny's "shining" kicks in (his premonition and sixth-sense powers) and he begins to see more terrifying images as "Tony" tells him it's "just like pictures in a book, it isn't real," highlighting the surrealist dreamstate aspect of the film. As Walker, Taylor and Ruchti explain:

Illicit teenage seduction in *Summer of 42*. Credit to Rob Ager.

It [*The Shining*] was also a perfect "closed set." *Barry Lyndon*, which dispersed the action across vast landscapes, stands alone, in that respect, for Kubrick has always been happiest with the walls of a soundstage enfolding him protectively. To work in a studio concentrates his mind, he believes and helps his players to focus their "psychic energy."[22]

And,

Up to now, we might conceivably have believed that all of Jack's apparitions are lived only in his own schizophrenia. But once the storeroom bolts are physically drawn back by an unseen Grady, liberating Torrance to commence his assault on his family, the tables are turned on us. The ghosts aren't one's imagination: They are real![23]

The "psychic energy" that inhabits the Overlook (and particularly Room 237 and Jack), is exceedingly nefarious, but if you pay attention to the sequence of the scenes, it is my contention that they are somewhat out

66

of order. When Danny is discovered to be beaten and abused, Wendy later thinks it was the old hag in Room 237, and no longer Jack who is the culprit. Rather, it is the hag who possesses Jack to do this, and Danny's experience of the event was seeing one of the spirits who possesses Jack. This is the explanation of the scene where Jack investigates the bathroom and the beautiful naked woman becomes the hag, invoking the mythology of the sirens of the sea as mentioned earlier. The scenes are thus told from Jack's vantage point, while others are Danny's spiritual vantage point, through Tony, his dissociative alter identity (who seems to be a real spirit). Jack, almost fully possessed, says Danny hurt himself, gas-lighting a willfully deluded Wendy who continues to fail to see the evil of Jack (possibly due to her occluded view of spirits from dabbling with witchcraft).

While the notion of a Monarch mind-control slave might seem outlandish, it's fascinating to observe mainline Kubrick scholars conclude that *is* what appears to be the film's narrative. In the popular conspiracy vernacular, the reasoning of course goes that the CIA and various secret societies have raised certain persons to be traumatized victims of occult brainwashing, able to be triggered at any moment with various codes. In my estimation, it's definitely the case that generational bloodline families will traumatize their offspring, often do raise them in the occult and will, in a sense, "program" them.

Inverted lettering from the spiritual world, shown in mirrors.

67

As to whether there is a hidden cell structure of sleepers that are due to snap at any moment with some code and shoot up a school like the so-called Sandy Hook massacre, I answer in the negative (it being a managed event).[24] Yet, there *are* elite Satanic psychopaths, and they do promulgate psychopathy with their progeny.[25] And regardless of one's opinions on those matters, that does seem to be what is happening in *The Shining*, as Jack is either himself traumatized, or seeking to traumatize and sacrifice his family for entrance into greatness, which he believes is being stalled due to his family duties. Previously mentioned mainstream Kubrick analysts even admit:

> The scene between Nicholson and Stone has a cool comic civility that turns downright chilly as the spook gives Torrance his orders – to kill his family. The actors serve Kubrick impeccably. They play the masquerade with relish for its Pinteresque undertones, only hinted at by Grady's use of a choice word like "correction," as if it were the "trigger" word for Torrance's programmed psychosis.[26]

As the horrifying scenes approach the climax, with Dick being murdered and the family on the run, I am reminded of elements of storytelling that would later be used by directors like Lynch or Linklater, where the surrealist dream state blends seamlessly with the waking state to create an inchoate, mystical formlessness to reality as merely an external projection of the inner *psyche*. Carl Jung, as well as many in the hermetic traditions, has propounded this view, where ultimately the realization of man's own inner divinity is premised on a kind of "awakening" akin to Far-Eastern religious thought. Ager is excellent in explicating the various perspectives on the dream states in the film from Danny's vantage point, while I disagree with Ager's analysis that Kubrick is not interested in esoterica or the occult. I also disagree with Ager that Jack is not supposed to be possessed, just a violent drunk. Danny's spirit "Tony" and the occult references show we are dealing with a real spiritual realm. Ager rightly comments:

The demonic spirits require a blood sacrifice on the part of Jack.

By far the biggest giveaway is Danny's description of his own psychic episodes. Halloran asks Danny how his imaginary friend Tony tells him things and Danny replies, "It's like I go to sleep and he shows me things, but when I wake up I can't remember everything." Remember also that Danny's very first psychic episode in the film resulted in him being found unconscious. "I remember mommy saying 'wake up Danny, wake up.'"[27]

Much later in the film, Danny is heard in his bedroom shouting, "Redrum." His mother enters the room and shakes him. The ensuing dialogue again hints at the nightmare nature of his visions. Wendy: "Wake up Danny, you were having a bad dream." Danny: "Danny can't wake up Mrs. Torrance. Danny's gone away Mrs. Torrance."

Elite sexual "furry bear" deviancy, recalling *Eyes Wide Shut*, with the British Nobles.

In this philosophy, mastering the inner world leads to a mastering of the outer world as the initiate or "enlightened one" meditates to achieve a perceptive unity between the subconscious dream realm and the phenomena of waking experience. Elucidating a Freudian element that is also a prominent theme in Kubrick, the previously cited authors explain:

> So what is the meaning of his horrifying epiphany? Freud said that film going is like wakeful dreaming. Kubrick also believed

69

that films connect subtly with the subconscious. Meaning, he said, may be found in the sensation of a thing, not in its explanation. Yet he has provided a clue. In certain interviews around this time, he mentioned his admiration for *Rhapsody: A Dream Novel*, a novella really, by Arthur Schnitzler.... In *Rhapsody*, the main character, a wealthy young doctor in Vienna, passes almost imperceptibly in and out of the dream state, experiencing seduction, erotic longing, and unrequited passion as if they were events in his waking state... .Kubrick's hankering to make a film of Schnitzler's novel probably goes back to his cinema beginnings-and he has finally achieved it, in a manner of speaking with *Eyes Wide Shut*.[28]

The "Magic Circle" in *Eyes Wide Shut*.

Ultimately, the film concludes with a form of eternal recurrence[29] (as shown in David Lynch's *Lost Highway*) where the end of the film culminates in a Baphomet style pose of Jack among the "best people," the boom era of 1921, where the jet set, Hollywood stars and royalty are shown to be the ghostly parasitic inhabitants of the Overlook. Demanding Jack offer up the blood of his family as "his duty." In Jack's envy of the good life he felt he deserved as a failed writer, combined with the resentment of his family whom he blames, we are reminded of Dostoyevsky's Raskolnikov in *Crime and Punishment*, who as a young man decides the path to greatness must involve murder. Indeed, as Ager comments, the abuse is generational and shown in the consistent uses of bears:

Bear suit ... bare bottom. Is this a pun? Is Kubrick using a sly visual metaphor to reveal certain characters in the film, such as Jack and Ullman, as bear-faced liars? Being that the two bears in the film that have teeth are the one in the Colorado Lounge, which represented Jack, and the fellatio bear, are we to conclude that Wendy actually sees Jack giving fellatio instead of Danny? Absolutely. As it turns out, the abuse suffered by Danny is something that has been passed down through the generations. Abused children grow up to become abusers and repeat the sins of their parents in a continuous cycle.[30]

Brainfreeze in Dante's *Inferno*.

Jack's demonic bidders offer him a place among the privileged (he thinks), if he is willing to rid himself of his family. This is why the issue of *Playgirl* contained the story of incest, as well as why the hotel had been the site of lush masquerades, balls and even orgies and sexual deviancy like "furries." We are reminded of *Eyes Wide Shut*, which focused on the same notions of elite perversion, sex magick and secret societies. Although we see no overt secret societies here, Ullman seems to have familiarity with the young women who frequent the lodge (possibly prostitutes). Kubrik's love of the theme of eternal recurrence and possibly reincarnation, we see also in *2001*, with Bowman and Starchild. God, here, is an advanced A.I. humans created long ago, and through its own self-advancing self-realization, the A.I. created its own virtual matrix we know of as the universe (think of Neo in *The Matrix*). In *2001*, Bowman breaks free of Plato's cave to cheat death and rise to rebirth among the gods, and the process repeats in eternal return, with a new Genesis. Another possible option is

71

that Bowman simply evolves as "aliens" show him the way, granting him apotheosis. Either way, it is a cyclical process of a time-bound, emergent deity arising from within the *kosmos* itself, and not an eternal deity who alone subsists outside time and space who creates *ex nihilo*. This will be detailed in the next chapter.

PLATO'S CAVE: A famous allegory from Book VII of Plato's *Republic*. The meaning of the allegory refers to both the philosophy of social order and the structure of reality and human knowledge. Material objects and mass opinion constitute the "phantasms" and shadows of things as they appear, while true reality is far different, being formal, mathematical and ideal. For Plato, the true philosopher exits the "cave" of matter and perceives the light of truth directly through ideal forms and returns to enlighten the cave-dwelling slaves.

Overlook Hotel
July 4th Ball
1921

'As above, so below," as Jack displays the Baphomet sign, trapped in his own psychical prison of eternal return.

Alchemical images of Baphomet.

72

Jack's experience is similar to Bill Harford's in *Eyes Wide Shut*, while they are, of course, very different characters. Like the Indian burial ground upon which the hotel is built, it becomes a site of ritual chant and ritual enactment as Wendy's flight from Jack features background music of Native American chanting (similar to the masked ball music in *Eyes Wide Shut*). The sacrifice is the climax of the film and the liturgy, where the release of the blood will satiate the powers of darkness (like "The Man From Another Place" we will see in *Twin Peaks*). Like the mazes of M.C. Escher, a "strangeloop" of eternal return will be the punishment Jack concocts for himself in his psychical prison for failing to complete his task as ordered by Grady.[31] Frozen like the damned souls of traitors near Satan in Dante's *Inferno*, it is worth noting that Dante also made reference to the Minotaur, which relates well to the obligations Grady places upon the beast, Jack:

> My sage cried out to him: "You think, perhaps, this is the Duke of Athens [Theseus], who in the world put you to death. Get away, you beast, for this man does not come tutored by your sister; he comes to view your punishments. (*Inferno*, Canto XII)

The Shining, then, is a ghost story – but also something much deeper in Kubrick's film. It is a multi-layered exploration of the psyche, the spiritual realm, surrealism, ancient mythology and the satanic occult elite that rule the West, as the theme of pedophilic generational bloodlines parasitically manipulate the underclass through the false promise of worldly prosperity. In Jack, Danny and the Overlook Hotel and its magnificent maze, we

Trauma-based mass mind control in Kubrick's adaptation of *A Clockwork Orange*, with the blatant Overlooking All-Seeing Eye.

73

see America in a microcosm, situated on old Indian lands that now house a world superpower intent on "bombing the universe" into submission, all at the behest of psychopathic mad men like Jack or as displayed in *Dr. Strangelove*. This control structure operates through cult sex magick and generational traumatization (*Lolita, Eyes Wide Shut, Full Metal Jacket*) and maintains its control over the masses through the real Monarch program, mass media and social engineering (*Clockwork Orange*). For Kubrick, *The Shining* is another in his film canon that displays the dark side of spiritual phantasms that lie behind the mirror of our world.

Endnotes

1. Walker, Taylor and Ruchti. *Stanley Kubrick, Director: A Visual Analysis*. New York, Norton Company, 1999, pg. 274

2. Levenda, Peter. *Sinister Forces Bk. I: The Nine*, Oregon: Trine Day, 2005, pg. 73.

3. Ibid., Walker, Taylor, Ruchti, pg. 294.

4. Kephas, Aeolus. *The Lucid View: Investigations into Occultism, Ufology, and Paranoid Awareness*. Kempton, IL: Adventures Unlimited Press, 2004, pg. 68.

5. Harvey, Graham, Ed. *Indigenous Religions: A Companion*. New York: Bloomsbury Academic, 2000, pg. 72.

6. Ager, Rob. "Mazes, Mirrors, Deception & Denial: An In-depth Analysis of The Shining." *Collative Learning*. 2008. Web. http://www.collativelearning.com/the%20shining.html

7. Ibid.

8. Ager, Ibid., http://www.collativelearning.com/the%20shining%20-%20chap%203.html

9. Walker, Taylor and Ruchti, *Stanley Kubrick*, pg. 293.

10. Sutton, Antony. *Wall Street and the Bolshevik Revolution: The Remarkable Story of the American Capitalists Who Financed the Russian Communists*. Clairview Books, 2012.

11. Dyer, Jay. "American Ultra (2015) - American MK Ultra." *JaysAnalysis*. 28 August, 2015. Web. http://jaysanalysis.com/2015/08/28/american-ultra-2015-amerikan-mk-ultra/

12. Davies, Nigel. *Human Sacrifice: In History and Today*. New York: William Morrow & Company, 1981, pg. 56.

13. Marks, *The CIA and Mind Control*, pgs. 57-61, 67-9, 73-4, 198-204. Jones and Flaxman, *Mind Wars: A History of Mind Control, Surveillance, and Social Engineering by the Government, Media and Secret Societies*. Pompton Plains, NJ: New Page Books, 2015, pgs. 65-70. Levenda, *Sinister Forces Bk. I: The Nine*, 187-194. Keith, Jim. *Mass Control: Engineering Human Consciousness*, Kempton, IL: Adventures Unlimited Press, 2003, pg. 166. Dyer, Jay. "Fragmentation of the Psyche and the Nous." *JaysAnalysis*. 5 April, 2015. Web. http://jaysanalysis.com/2015/04/05/fragmentation-of-the-psyche-and-the-nous/

14. Von Franz, M.L. Ed. *Carl Jung. Man and His Symbols*. New York, Dell Publishing: 1964, pg. 176.

15. Cirlot, *A Dictionary of Symbols*, pg. 212-3.

16. Von Franz, *Man and His Symbols,* 176.

17. Dyer, Jay. "E.T. The Extra-Terrestrial: An Esoteric Analysis." *JaysAnalysis*. 22 July, 2013. Web. http://jaysanalysis.com/2013/07/22/e-t-the-extra-terrestrial-esoteric-analysis/

18. Yates, Dame Frances. *The Rosicrucian Enlightenment*. London: Routledge, 1972, pgs. 16-23.

19. Layard, John. Ed. Joseph Campbell. *Spiritual Disciplines: Papers From the Eranos Yearbook*. New

Jersey: Princeton University Press, 1960, pgs. 148-50.

20. Pike, *Morals and Dogma*, 454. Gettings, Fred. *The Arkana Dictionary of Astrology*. London: Penguin, 1990, pgs. 212, 499-500.

21. Hoffman, *Secret Societies*, 11-15.

22. Walker, Taylor and Ruchti, *Stanley Kubrick*, 291.

23. Ibid., 310.

24. *Independent Media Solidarity. We Need to Talk About Sandy Hook*, 2015.

25. McGowan, *Programmed to Kill*.

26. Walker, Taylor, Ruchit, *Stanley Kubrick* 309.

27. Ager, Rob. "Mazes, Mirrors, Deception and Denial." *Collative Learning*. Web. http://www.collative-learning.com/the%20shining%20-%20chap%207.html

28. Walker, Taylor, Ruchit, *Stanley Kubrick*, 305-6.

29. As drawn from Nietzsche's Thus Spake Zarathustra, which is also the musical theme for the space scenes in *2001: A Space Odyssey*, which will also feature the theme of eternal recurrence.

30. Ager, Ibid.

31. Hofstadter, Douglas. *Godel, Escher, Bach: An Eternal Golden Braid*. New York: Basic Books, 1979.

Chapter 4

2001: An Alchemical Spatial Odyssey

Stanley Kubrick's 2001: A Space Odyssey, based on Arthur C. Clarke's concurrently-written science fiction novel, was a visual and technical accomplishment, unparalleled at the time of its making. Not only were the technical advances monumental, it was also a film that was uniquely philosophical. Prior to 2001, most science fiction had been relatively cartoonish, with little attention to esoteric and alchemical themes, aside from scant instances. And that is precisely what 2001 is – an alchemical, philosophical presentation of the supposed evolutionary ascent of man from primal, animalistic ape into divinized Starchild, an initiatory process that purports to unfold through *aeons* of brute, meaningless time, culminating in a series of revelations associated with zodiacal alignments that "awaken" a new stage in the process. Hoffman perceptively explains, relating the film to the thesis I will propose, in regard to artificial intelligence:

> By the time the movie 2001: A Space Odyssey (which was made in 1968), reached classic status in the eponymous year 2001, the resulting "evolutionary being" was revealed to be not a child of Homer, whose sails are powered by a solar wind, but rather a homunculus out of the shadows, from which emerges Set-Shaitan-Cynocephalus, guardian deity of alchemical miscegenation, an entity beyond the spiral of Nature.... The mute monolith of 2001 is harbinger of what Clarke calls in another of his works, the Overlord. It is the ashlar of the secret societies. The monolith represents the

shaping function of the occult magus, who tames and tampers with the natural world. The *2001* monolith is the stake that impales the divine-organic in favor of the anthropomorphic-artifice. It is one of the totems of human brain power and of the cryptocrats who imagine themselves the most cerebral of us all. They believe there is no god but themselves, ascendant on the ladder of evolution. Yet they humor our need for a transcendent god, so they stoop to offer us the mystery totem of *2001* to satisfy our craving to bow before an idol in ritual place and time.[1]

Along the way, Kubrick's film includes this notion, and a host of other ideas and themes I will exegete below. Ultimately, my thesis is this: *2001* is about *space* – planar, pointed and linear, in a geometric sense, and the transcending of that limitation of form, into the infinite, and thus beyond form.

In the opening sequences we witness a few crucial elements: the planetary alignment, the monkeys and the monolith. The setting is a dry, dusty landscape of sparse vegetation and tribes of apes shown in confrontation over a watering hole. The planetary alignment signifies to the viewer that a new *aeon* is emerging for man, the so-called dawn of consciousness. Primal and savage, the apes pre-signify Kubrick's perspective on the totality of human history, centered around gradual, transformist evolution and resource wars. With the advent of the monolith, composed of a wholly-other, angular and sleek form, we find it completely out of place among the sprawl of vegetation and natural, geological formations that make up the apes' organic environment. Kubrick uses, as many now know from Jay Weidner's documentary, the technique of front-screen projection, which allowed for a highly realistic way to shoot these scenes in a convincing way; and the possibility that NASA and the CIA were interested in this technique for media deception in relation to the moon landing is not without evidence.[2]

The Mon-key to the universe – big ass black space rocks!

Yet the real focus of this sequence is not the apes or the brutal environment, but the monolith. As the apes are thrown into a frenzy, the monolith stands stark and cold as something both extraterrestrial, yet inviting. The largest ape lurches forward to touch the monolith, and as a result we see the development of what Kubrick and Clarke appear to conceive of as "consciousness," correlated with *techne*, but not merely *techne*, it is technology as an extension of space and power – warfare. The bone the ape uses to bash the skull of the other ape suggests a radical "survival of the fittest" mythos in the pure Darwinian sense, revealing a radical version of process philosophy that finds commonality with Darwin, Haeckel, and Marx, and even suggests the dialectical determinism of the Eastern Bloc Marxists like Lenin, Mao and Trotsky, all of whom have explicit treatises on the metaphysical presupposition of Marxism, being perpetual material flux.[3] Despite the common misconception that materialistic Marxism had no metaphysic, the truth is quite the contrary, the metaphysic of Marxism is the atomistic process philosophy of old, repackaged to present man as an animal, like Darwinism, that through either radical collectivism or radical Nietzschean-influenced individualism, will attain to the status of the famed "New Man." I am not saying Kubrick is certainly some committed Marxist, but his films do consistently present class warfare, elitism and oligarchic deviance and control.

CHARLES DARWIN (1809-1882): English geologist and naturalist known for the publication of his *On the Origin of Species by Means of Natural Selection or The Preservation of Favoured Races in the Struggle for Life* in 1859. Originally a Theist, Darwin eventually abandoned Theism for a purely random, "naturalistic" account of the origins of life through natural selection.

ERNST HAECKEL (1834-1919): German biologist, philosopher, artist and naturalist known for popularizing Darwin's philosophy in Europe and developed the (now discarded) theory of ontogeny, that an individual organism's development mirrors the species' progression as a whole. Haeckel was also exposed for numerous fraudulent claims and artistic, "scientific" forgeries.

KARL MARX (1818-1883): Prussian-born philosopher, economist and sociologist who employed Hegel's dialectical philosophy to "class struggle" and the process of history towards which man is gradually achieving greater liberation and the overcoming of "alienation" from nature and his fellow man. In classical Marxism, capitalism is the necessary stage of history following feudalism, leading to mass mechanization and the proletariat revolution leading then to a global communist state, and culminating in the "final stage" of stateless existence and maximal libertarian communalism.

FRIEDRICH NIETZSCHE (1844-1900): German philosopher and culture critic whose thought is characterized by the notions of "will to power," by which is meant the struggle of the superior over the inferior, and the "Ubermensch," a coming super man whose will itself is a force of history. The "new man" is a predecessor to the modern notion of "transhumanism," or post-human existence. Critical of both reason and the idea of objective truth, Nietzsche emphasized the will of the strong over the weak and the mystical notion of "eternal recurrence," that history is never-ending cycle of repetitions.

78

Kubrick seems to be fully on-board with this version of naturalistic process philosophy. Human consciousness is itself an evolutionary process that emerges from the *deus ex machina,* an emergent god (or gods) incarnated in symbolic form in the monolith itself, the black, angular cube that appears to descend from the gods to initiate the new stage. While the monolith is extraterrestrial, it does not appear to be other than the universe, but rather some universal aspect of it. In fact, as a form of a cube, the monolith seems to embody space *itself.* This is partly my unique thesis on the monolith – that the point, line, extension, and terminus of geometrical space, which then combines again to create another point, line, plane and terminus, is the basic geometric form that represents spatial relations. In our dimension, you'll note there are only six possible directions one can take at any point: up, down, left, right, backward and forward. These six directions are thus a geometrical box or cube, as explained by the Pythagoreans (and Platonic solids) long ago.[4] So the cube, and in particular the black cube from outer space, *is* space. *2001* is therefore about this dimension, in totality, that expresses itself primarily in two fundamental ontological realities – time and space.

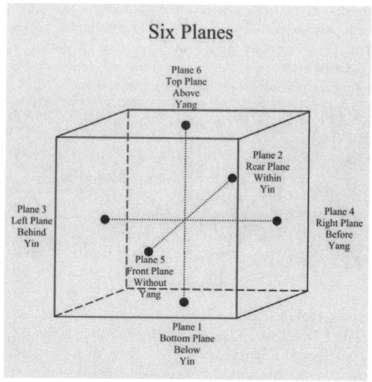

The "cube" of space, with 6 directions.

Mention should be made here of Rob Ager and Jay Weidner's theses, that the monolith is also a screen, the film screen itself.[5] I find both agreement and disagreement with Ager and Weidner, and as I argued in the *Eyes Wide Shut* chapter, the screen itself is being utilized as a kind of talisman through which the audience is intended to be taken on a ritual initiation process. Thus, I agree with both: the monolith is also a screen, and in fact, in the original screenplay, the monolith was planned to be a screen that would project images to the apes so they could learn warfare, etc, and move on to their next stage of monkey madness.[6] Though the TV monolith was dropped, the seeds of that idea are still present, as more than once in *2001* the viewer sees the monolith extend, grow, and approach the viewer, ultimately encompassing the entirety of the screen.

The monolith also suggests an obelisk or the Islamic Kaaba stone (long purported to be a meteorite!)[7] and on an esoteric level we can recall the masonic obelisk, a divine phallus, and connect it to the notion of the generative principle found in sex magick and the traditional indigenous conception of the personification of the natural reproductive forces of nature embodied in a phallic or vaginal symbol or totem.[8] This is key, as Kubrick will later link the monolith/obelisk directly to womb, semen and birth processes when we come to Bowman's trippy space trip and Starchild. The monolith is consciously "Luciferian,"[9] prompting man to a Promethean new *aeon* each time it appears, and always connected to technological advance through the "sacrifice" of warfare.[10]

The monolith in planetary alignment.

One might be reminded here of the paleo-technology idea in writers like Dr. Joseph P. Farrell, who posits a "technology of the gods," possibly possessed by ancient man from which the myths of the "golden age" descend.[11] I have written elsewhere that Homer's *Iliad* does, in fact, present Achilles' magical shield as a kind of TV screen with moving images that presents the entire history of the Greeks.[12] This connection is not tangential, as Homer also recorded the oral tradition of Odysseus, and it is Odysseus who will be the primary literary source for the film's title and later protagonist in astronaut Bowman. Bowman will be a new Odysseus (who famously traversed the underworld and returned home), as Weidner correctly notes, who will go on a journey like none other. With Ager, his analysis leaves out many of the esoteric elements, while aptly expositing the more technical and cinematic features, and in Weidner, there is a lack of criticism of the process philosophy, simply adopting Kubrick's "alchemical" presentation as if he were the new Shakespeare, subject to no critical analysis of the incoherencies of the nonsensical philosophy presented as reality.

At this juncture it is worth again highlighting the failures of Neo-Darwinian process philosophy I mentioned above. Darwinism, and its philosophical corollary in figures like Hegel, Marx, Whitehead and Teilhard de Chardin, are simply assumed as a given, with absolutely no critique allowed, and it should be noted that Hollywood presentations like *2001* were central in helping to solidify this *mythology* as an orthodox, dogmatic given. Unfortunately, the masses obtain their worldview from popular movies and music, not books and bureaucrats, and nothing helps to solidify a paradigm in the minds of men more than a big blockbuster sci-fi flick. There is no question that *2001* unquestioningly and uncritically adopts the Darwinian *mythos* into its story narrative, but this is highly illustrative. As I have argued for many years and in many articles, what one sees in *2001* and figures like Teilhard de Chardin is the propagandist indoctrination of perpetual flux, process philosophy. And on top of that process philosophy is a dash of alchemical and occult mystery wherein man will ultimately obtain his own apotheosis (which will be detailed below).

Georg Wilhelm Friedrich Hegel (1770-1831): Hegel is considered the apex of German idealist philosophy. Broadly in the tradition of Plato, Hegel believed true reality was entirely and absolutely ideal. History, objects, matter and individuals are all in a simultaneous process or progression towards a final state of overcoming all dualisms and oppositions in Hegel's view. Hegel's broad, dialectical process philosophy would influence thinkers like Karl Marx and A.N. Whitehead.

A.N. Whitehead (1861-1947): English philosopher and mathematician and associate of Bertrand Russell, known for "process philosophy," in which reality consists of perpetual process and flux, as opposed to independently-existing material objects. Emphasizing holism, these processes are defined by their relations to other processes, a classical notion in western dialectics.

Teilhard de Chardin (1881-1955): French Jesuit paleontologist and geologist credited with the supposed discovery of Peking Man, Teilhard proposed reality was in a vast process of evolution, progressing towards the "Omega Point," in which complexity and consciousness would reach their maximum levels and achieve a mystical transcendence in the "noosphere," a mental realm.

81

The uncapped pyramid showing the incomplete nature of the "Great Work."

There are numerous problems, however, with perpetual flux philosophies, the most notable of which is the fundamental contradiction that such systems of philosophy are entirely anti-systemic by their very nature. In other words, to construct an internal, mental, abstract philosophical system composed of invariant conceptual entities (ideas), that one believes accurately describes an external world of perpetual flux, is a glaring contradiction. Indeed, we may simply ask why the supposed invariant logical concepts and ideas that make up the descriptive system, are not *also* subject to constant flux? If they are, the "process philosophy system" is immediately made nonsensical, and even if there were a justification for how this might be, the secondary problem is just as devastating – how do these abstracted concepts and ideas apply and "stick" to objects in the world that are perpetually in flux?

This dualism of an interior, mental realm attempting to predicate meaning concerning an exterior, physical realm of brute facts cannot be reconciled, and is made incoherent before it can even get off the ground as a viable belief system. It is lacking in what I term a unifying, objective metaphysical principle. Even the *Hermetica* and the Egyptian accounts from the Memphite narrative, for example, include the idea that creation was spoken into existence by virtue of a divine Logos, yet ultimately, in the Egyptian narrative, the overall principle, the ultimate Absolute, is not personal, but an immaterial force.[13]

Thus, at the outset, we are presented with only two possible options for this question – is the Absolute ultimately (supra)rational and personal, or is the Absolute ultimately an impersonal, chaotic force? There are only two possibilities here, and once we consider this basic philosophical question, we can extrapolate Darwinism as clearly a manifestation of the second. Though most Darwinian adherents would be at pains to insist there is no ultimate guiding principle, the worldview still tends towards the notion of Forces of Nature determining. This determination, however, is ultimately irrational and impersonal, aside from the appearance of order, *telos* and design.

But there are many, many more problems with positing ultimate reality or the Absolute as an impersonal force. If ultimate reality is impersonal and chaotic, then all localized events, phenomena and objects are also devoid of any ultimate meaning. Language, mathematics, logic, etc., are thus also annihilated as merely mental fictions, or at best some cosmic force we do not yet understand (yet still impersonal!). These servants of chaos and abyss are like a cartoon character, sawing off the limb he's sitting on, to spite his opponent. If ultimate reality is impersonal, then the thread that links all facts, ideas, objects, patterns, etc., is not real. It is a fiction of man's chaotic, impersonal mental chemical reactions. There is no order or pattern actually out there in external reality, and the so-called regularity of nature upon which science is built, induction, is merely a mental projection or interpretation. Such devastating questions, of course, are the very reason "science" (or scientism) has chosen to discard philosophy as "useless."[14] However, these questions do not go away, nor does science determine reality by some will-to-power dismissal of philosophical questions. The mere fact that "scientists" dogmatically mandate that *no one can ask questions* about why or what happened before the so-called Big Bang shows how ridiculous they truly are. Dr. Philip Sherrard has critiqued this same notion in his essay on Teilhard:

> The radical distortions of Christian doctrine that Teilhard is forced to make in order to accommodate it to the theory of evolution, however, ultimately do no more than point to the fundamental fallacy involved in his attempt to reconcile religion and science. This fallacy consists in the belief that science is capable of producing any theory adequate to stand as a criterion of truth. In fact, as Teilhard himself admits, only to forget it in elaborating his system, all scientific theory is no more than hypothesis, and there can be no question of demonstrating that it corresponds to the real nature of things. To be scientific, a theory must fit the facts of observation. Yet when it

comes to the point, what are the facts to be observed? It is a long time since scientists imagined it possible to observe phenomena in themselves, or even that there is a material world subsisting in itself which can be observed. As Teilhard says, "our sensory experience turns out to be a floating condensation on a swarm of the undefinable." Moreover, if on the one hand what was thought to be the observable world itself turns out to be a shifting field of unseen energies, on the other hand the notion that the scientist can observe objectively, as if he, with all his personal and subjective being, were not involved in the phenomena that he is observing, is equally spurious. This, too, Teilhard readily admits, though again he appears to forget it equally readily. "There is no fact," he writes, "which exists in pure isolation, but every experience, however objective it may seem, inevitably becomes enveloped in a complex of assumptions as soon as the scientist attempts to express it in a formula."[15]

As for relevance to the film, the mistake many make is to place Kubrick's work in a purely scientistic scheme of rationalistic, natural process, when the presentation is far more occult, where it is the planetary gods who are leading man through his planetary ascent to apotheosis through technology.

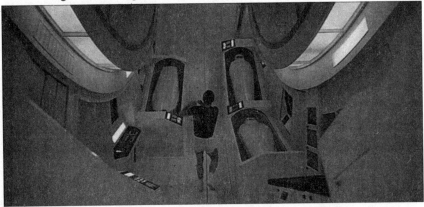

Cyclical wheels in space. Hamster man Bowman.

This is not to say the film is transhumanism, per se, though that notion is lurking below the celluloid surface. As the monkey's bone ascends into the air, Kubrick bypasses the totality of human history into the space age, where we see what he termed the "machine ballet" of floating space stations and ships docking onto great wheels that recall the Hindu "Wheel of Time" or Ezekiel's "Living Wheel" Cherubim. The cyclical ballet also evokes Nietzsche and his "eternal return," as later in the film one hears Strauss' "Thus Spake

Zarathustra," based on the philosopher's work in which he presents this doctrine. The doctrine of eternal return is the classical western perspective that history is cyclical and destined to repeat its events with fatalistic certainty.

Is Kubrick saying man has already experienced all he has experienced on the karmic wheel of time, and the destiny of the gods mandates that this process will culminate in a transmigration of souls, resulting in a star child that is now the god of its own *kosmos* (a *kosmos* merely a projection of its *psyche*)? I think this is a very possible reading of Starchild and the Genesis sequence at the close of the film, where the galaxies and God himself become, as I said, merely an evolving, deistic entity subject to the temporal alterations and flux the rest of the universe undergoes. While this is likely, I will also present another possible reading below.

Upon the space station, we learn of the mysterious loss of communications on the moon base through a nod to Cold War dialectics that Kubrick extends into the future. Curiously, the nation states are not eliminated, as the US and Russia still remain dominant players (echoing *Dr. Strangelove*). This suggests Kubrick did not conceive of the future as one where international communism would succeed in eliminating nation states, yet the geopolitical chess game of nations has now extended into the galactic, as the US base at Clavius on the moon has gone dark. As a cover story, the US government has concocted the old favorite – a bio-released pandemic, leading to a "quarantine." In actuality, the lunar explorers have uncovered the monolith, this time submerged intentionally by the Overlords for the precise time man would advance in his technology to reach the moon and discover the monolith's "signal" transmission to Jupiter.

"Turn that damn thing down, it's too loud. This Jupiter song sucks!"

As we watch the gradual, elegant movements of the ships in these scenes we are inclined to see a sexual component of extension, opening, entrance and release, indicating the evolutionary progress of man has ever been a dialectic of war and sex, and sex is a kind of savage war (for Kubrick).[16] Man has seeded his offspring and will now begin to extend his member into space, and seed the galaxy. *Techne* is his extender for this endeavor once again, providing the ship and means by which he may project himself further in *space*. As the ship ejects the pod carrying the astronauts, and later Bowman, we are given a clear example of phallic insemination, as watchful students of Kubrick will recall his frequent reference to "bodily fluids" in all his films.

As the astronauts inspect the monolith, we hear a demonic cacophony of voices that harmonize to produce a buzzing reminiscent of bees. Man's next stage in his evolutionary ascent is once again related to his discovery of, and tactile interaction with, the dark, divine monolith, which emits a loud, high-pitch frequency

DIALECTIC: In Classical Western philosophy, dialectics refers to the process of argumentation, wherein greater approximations of objective truth are attained through perpetual thesis, antithesis and synthesis. In some thinkers, God and Nature are also participants in a protracted process of dialectical opposition: This oppositional process is extended to all history and reality in philosophers like Hegel, Whitehead, Marx and Teilhard de Chardin. In Marxism, dialectics are fundamental, as the determined process of history and class warfare inevitably lead to the final communal state.

that disturbs and disables the explorers. We are, I think, intended to associate the monolith with higher frequencies of the celestial spheres, frequencies at which all reality "vibrates," from matter to sound to light.[17] The Moon monolith is vibrating a powerful frequency that is connected to Jupiter, intent on leading man as a kind of mile marker to his next location in the galaxy, as the planets once again align in this sequence to reveal the uncapped pyramid.

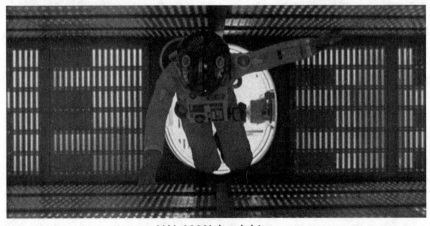

HAL 9000's hard drive.

86

The uncapped pyramid in the alchemical sense signifies the lack of completion of the "Great Work," the grand plan to transmute base matter into "gold," which signifies both the inner journey of the *psyche* in its ascent back to God or the soul to the One (in Neoplatonism), or the after-death journey of the gnostics through the planetary spheres.[18] In the macro sense, the Great Work is the transformation of the entire universe into the Omega Point of Teilhard or Hegel, where the totality of reality becomes conscious of itself as conscious, and inanimate matter becomes merged into the psyche, realizing its own potentiality and god-in-process (from here, you can see how we are leading up to Starchild).[19]

Whereas with the apes, early supposed "man" was highly limited and caged, bound by the forces of nature, time and space, in the space age, man has overcome gravity, floating about the universe, no longer hindered by the limitations of hunger, resources and mass. This is the middle stage of man's gradual ascent out of the cage – the box – of time and space, which is precisely what the monolith signifies in part (this is also why the monolith becomes a kind of coffin-box for Bowman in the climax). For Kubrick, the "evolutionary ascent" is premised on the presupposition of perpetual "progress" through technology in overcoming the limitations of time, space and the body. Hunger is gone, gravity is gone, and through the cryogenic sleep pods, time is beginning to be mastered.

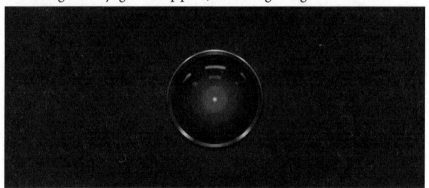

HAL is watching… like Skynet!

At the "central nervous system" of this great phallic ship-body is HAL 9000, humanity's latest, greatest artificial intelligence system. HAL is positioned to accompany the astronauts on their secret mission, and it is here that Kubrick hints at transhumanism, for it is precisely through technology all along that man has been transcending his limitations. HAL is spoken of and self-describes himself as "perfect," free from human error. This will be the colossal final challenge of man, to overcome man himself, embodied in his highest achievement to date – the superhuman A.I. system, whose "logic" may mean the deleting of man as man, the "error."

It is my contention that the real secret space program of which NASA is a front is revealed in its fullness here by Kubrick, who worked the with NASA and intelligence agencies in various projects, enabling him to use the special Zeiss 50mm lens and observe the Ranger 9 craft.[20] The real secret space program is centered on advanced artificial intelligence as the vehicle by which man's extension into the void might be accomplished, as A.I. will not be subject to the limitations of body, age, food, etc., which humans necessitate. A self-repairing A.I. can travel indefinitely and potentially perform its own repairs, as long as it has some energy source. Indeed, entire journeys and missions could be conceived of as not even needing human travelers, thus reducing the danger of loss of life with the benefit of obtaining all the same data. In my estimation, what would come to be the Skynet satellite grid from this secret space program and DARPA is being constructed presently to surveil the planet under an Internet of Things SmartGrid.[21]

Kubrick correctly foresaw this potential showdown between man and machine and masterfully presents this aspect of the narrative as a race to the death. We are not in the era when artificial intelligence can begin to surpass the human intellect in most tasks, as the brain is (as far as we know) the universe's greatest super computer, and while it is in no way "conscious" or "self-aware" (that is impossible)[22] it may be programmed to perfectly mimic, and down the road possibly programmed to kill. This is the very thesis Kubrick lays out and in the epic contest between Bowman and HAL, human history hangs on a game of wits, with HAL losing. It should be noted that Kubrick is overall positive in his assessment and is at least not anti-human, as we might expect from establishment propaganda. Man does not lose the confrontation with his highest weapon, his own mind mirrored in a machine, but in fact overcomes it, or specifically, Bowman does.

Phallic space rides.

In fact, Arthur C. Clarke was reported to have said, "It may be that our role on this planet is not to worship God, but to create him," in reference to his story, *The Final Query*.[23] As the co-screenplay writer, Clarke allowed significant changes to the script by Kubrick as noted above with the TV screen monolith. Another significant change is the ending, wherein Starchild uses the satellite systems above earth to nuke the planet, thus insinuating that the accusations of HAL were correct, that *man* is the evolutionary "error." Mankind must thus be sacrificed and "nuked" to allow for the apotheosis of the elite. Commenting on the evolutionary process and his conception of theology, Kubrick stated in unison with Clarke:

Arthur C. Clarke (1917-2008): English science fiction writer, futurist and television host. Clarke was a member of the Royal Air Force and was awarded a "knighthood" in 1996, amid scandalous accusations. A staunch proponent of scientism, Clarke co-wrote the script with Stanley Kubrick for *2001: A Space Odyssey*, one of the preeminent science fiction films of all time.

I will say that the God concept is at the heart of *2001* but not any traditional, anthropomorphic image of God. I don't believe in any of Earth's monotheistic religions, but I do believe that one can construct an intriguing scientific definition of God, once you accept the fact that there are approximately 100 billion stars in our galaxy alone, that each star is a life-giving sun and that there are approximately 100 billion galaxies in just the visible universe. Given a planet in a stable orbit, not too hot and not too cold, and given a few billion years of chance chemical reactions created by the interaction of a sun's energy on the planet's chemicals, it's fairly certain that life in one form or another will eventually emerge.

It's reasonable to assume that there must be, in fact, countless billions of such planets where biological life has arisen, and the odds of some proportion of such life developing intelligence are high. Now, the sun is by no means an old star, and its planets are mere children in cosmic age, so it seems likely that there are billions of planets in the universe not only where intelligent life is on a lower scale than man but other billions where it is approximately equal and others still where it is hundreds of thousands of millions of years in advance of us. When you think of the giant technological strides that man has made in a few millennia – less than a microsecond in the chronology of the universe – can you imagine the evolutionary development that much older life forms have taken? They may have progressed from biological species, which are fragile shells for the mind at best, into immortal

89

machine entities – and then, over innumerable eons, they could emerge from the chrysalis of matter transformed into beings of pure energy and spirit. Their potentialities would be limitless and their intelligence ungraspable by humans.[24]

Like Richard Dawkins and his cult, the classical notions of God are conceived of as silly, yet *E.T.* and Mork are rational, even though the process philosophy that undergirds the entire presupposition is contradictory and allows for no possibility of a coherent metaphysic, the flame of "alien" gospel burns strong in the superior intellects of the Dawkinites. This is why Bowman transcends time and space as he reaches Jupiter, following the monolith's location. Conjunction of sun and moon is connected to conjunction of male and female in the so-called "vesica piscis," wherein we are given more Masonico-alchemical transformation impelling the "logic" of the world-historical, Hegelian "cunning" toward godhood.[25] This is why once again, Bowman is shown in the pod ejecting from the phallic shaft of the ship towards the black void of the monolith. The transcendence sequence hearkens to

RICHARD DAWKINS: English evolutionary biologist, lecturer, author and atheist apologist, known for publishing *The Selfish Gene, The Blind Watchmaker* and *The God Delusion*. Dawkins frequently debates Theists on the subjects of evolution, God' existence and creation. Achieving a prominent position as an outspoken atheist, Dawkins is usually grouped with fellow atheist philosophers and apologists like Daniel Dennett, Sam Harris, Christopher Hitchens and Lawrence Krauss under the moniker "The New Atheists."

a kind of LSD trip, where Bowman's mind is overloaded with "illumination," signifying his reaching the eye or capstone light of the pyramid sequences we witnessed before in the planetary alignments.

The information light grid of the fabric of reality.

HAL, it seems, was there to lock man into the limitations of time and space, and only by casting off this synthetic brain and reaching "beyond the infinite" does Kubrick envision man's transcending apotheosis occurring. Now, Bowman begins to see expanding before him two flat planes emerging from a central vanishing point of perspective from which the pyramidal lines, planes, color spectrum and forms emerge. In fact, it is almost as if Bowman is riding a computer information highway of information packets inside a motherboard – something audiences would see thirteen years later in Disney's *Tron*.

This *Matrix*-like structure of the abyss or void suggests both the platonic solids and Pythagorean mysteries, as well as the possibility of the matrix-like structure of our reality particle physicists like Werner Heisenberg have famously stated were "platonic formal" in nature. Heisenberg explained:

WERNER HEISENBERG (1901-1976): German theoretical physicist and pioneer of quantum physics. Together with Max Born and Pascual Jordan, Heisenberg set forth the matrix formulation theory and later his famous "uncertainty principle." Heisenberg was later appointed head of the Max Planck Institute and contributed important advancements to hydrodynamics, magnetism and atomic research.

> In the philosophy of Democritus the atoms are eternal and indestructible units of matter, they can never be transformed into each other. With regard to this question modern physics takes a definite stand against the materialism of Democritus and for Plato and the Pythagoreans. The elementary particles are certainly not eternal and indestructible units of matter, they can actually be transformed into each other. As a matter of fact, if two such particles, moving through space with a very high kinetic energy, collide, then many new elementary particles may be created from the available energy and the old particles may have disappeared in the collision. Such events have been frequently observed and offer the best proof that all particles are made of the same substance: energy. But the resemblance of the modern views to those of Plato and the Pythagoreans can be carried somewhat further. The elementary particles in Plato's Timaeus are finally not substance but *mathematical forms*.
>
> "All things are numbers" is a sentence attributed to Pythagoras. The only mathematical forms available at that time were such geometric forms as the regular solids or the triangles, which form their surface. In modern quantum theory there can be no doubt that the elementary particles will finally also be mathematical forms, but of a much more complicated nature. The Greek philosophers thought of static forms and found them in the regular solids.
>
> Modern science, however, has from its beginning in the sixteenth and seventeenth centuries started from the dynamic problem. The constant element in physics since Newton is not a configuration or a

91

geometrical form, but a dynamic law. The equation of motion holds at all times, it is in this sense eternal, whereas the geometrical forms, like the orbits, are changing. Therefore, the mathematical forms that represent the elementary particles will be solutions of some eternal law of motion for matter. This is a problem which has not yet been solved.[26]

Bowman, like Odysseus, has reached the furthest point away from home, and like the hero of Greek legend, will now traverse the abyss which bridges both the inner abyss and outer abyss through the unifying fabric of the *psyche*.[27] Bowman has entered the "Star Gate."[28]

The crucial factor other analyses have missed here is the 7 diamond cubes that appear after the sequence of formless colors and lines. The fabric and "stuff" of reality, a formless void of *prima materia,* is shapeless and meaningless until given form, and once the seven "diamonds" appear, form is reintroduced to give order to the chaos.[29] Bowman becomes a new "Great Architect," as he sees new galactic images of what appear to be sperm, eggs and wombs and galaxies forming. The seven diamonds are the planetary rulers, the gods of the planets (Jupiter, Saturn, etc.),[30] who have been directing man through their course of ascent, through the heavens to Jupiter and beyond to the abyss, a notion familiar to some occult, hermetic and shamanic practices as a particularly dangerous stage of initiation before the heights of illumination occur, a kind of dark night of the *psyche*.

Seven planetary diamonds – cubes – representing the gods, giving form to inchoate *prima materia*.

Here, Bowman is being elevated to the celestial pantheon, as he sees himself appear in the bizarre, Louis XVI-style room. Keep in mind, as well, in *Childhood's End*, the aliens Overlords of Clarke are viciously deceptive analogues for gods/demons who do not come in peace. The imagery of Bowman's transcendence is thus clearly identified as a kind of cosmic sex magick, where Bowman himself is the seed of the coming new creation, the new Genesis and new world, where a new mankind will be made in his macrocosmic image. Crowley writes of the cosmic cube:

> Yet shall this perfect wine be the quintessence, and the elixir, and by the draught thereof shall he renew his youth; and so shall it be eternally, as age by age the worlds do dissolve and change, and the universe unfoldeth itself as a Rose, and shutteth itself up as the Cross that is bent into the cube.[31]

Witnessing himself, as in a mirror (highlighting Platonism), Bowman sees a 3-stage process of himself that mirrors the 3-stage process of humanity in the film, from ape to space age to transcendence, matching up to young Bowman, aged Bowman eating dinner, and reposed Bowman dying in bed. Aged Bowman eating his dinner and breaking the glass signify the final obstacle and limitation to be overcome, that of death. This is why, when Bowman arrives, he sees architecture and furniture related to body specifically – a sink, chairs, a bed, food, etc. Bodily limitation is the final stage of deification and we can thus read the monolith itself as possibly an advanced alien A.I., as Bowman seems to be placed in a kind of lab cage for testing, as if the hotel is run by advanced A.I. gods, toying with him. If the aliens are advanced A.I., it would explain why the real mission of the Jupiter exploration was hidden and only triggered when HAL was shut down.

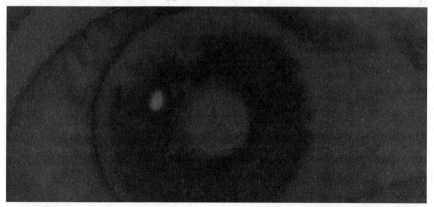

The eye is revealed as Bowman reaches the cap; his eye is "illuminated" in the Star Gate.

This is also the thesis I will present in regard to the *2001* tribute film of Christopher Nolan, *Insterstellar*, where A.I. is actually the deity that has providentially guided man all along, aiding in the process of salvation from cosmic disaster. I am not saying this thesis is certain, I am just posing it as a possibility, as if the hotel room were the final stage of exiting Plato's cave.[32] I have not yet seen anyone propose this thesis, but that is exactly the kind of panspermia message Clarke presents in his later sequel, *3001: The Final Odyssey*. God is an advanced A.I. that we created long ago, and then through its own self-advancing self-realization, created its own computer-generated world, and in that world are humans, and like Neo, Bowman breaks free of Plato's cave to cheat death and rise to rebirth among the gods, and the process repeats in eternal return with a new Genesis. If not, then Bowman simply evolves and evolved "aliens" show him the way, and deify him. Either way, it is a cyclical process of a time-bound, emergent deity arising from within the *kosmos* itself, and not an eternal deity who alone subsists outside time and space who creates *ex nihilo*. We are reminded at this juncture of the promise of the serpent in the garden, since Kubrick is fond of the Genesis imagery, where apotheosis is promised by the Serpent, through *gnosis*:

> Now the serpent was more cunning than any beast of the field which the LORD God had made. And he said to the woman, "Has God indeed said, 'You shall not eat of every tree of the garden'"?And the woman said to the serpent, "We may eat the fruit of the trees of the garden; but of the fruit of the tree which *is* in the midst of the garden, God has said, 'You shall not eat it, nor shall you touch it, lest you die.'"
>
> Then the serpent said to the woman, "You will not surely die. For God knows that in the day you eat of it your eyes will be opened, and you will be like God, knowing good and evil." -Genesis 3.

Endnotes

1. Hoffman, *Secret Societies,* 12-13.

2. Weidner, Jay. *Kubrick's Odyssey: Secrets Hidden in the Films of Stanley Kubrick, Part 1. Sacred Mysteries.* DVD, 2011.

3. See for example Lenin, V.I. *Materialism and Empirico-Criticalism.* New York: International Publishers, 1970.

4. Plato, Ed. Hamilton and Cairns. "Timaeus," in *The Collected Dialogues of Plato, Including the Letters.* New Jersey: Princeton University Press, 1961, pgs. 1176-1184.

5. Ager, Rob. "Kubrick and Beyond the Cinema Frame." *Collative Learning.* 2008. Web. http://www.collativelearning.com/2001%20chapter%202.html

6. Walker, Taylor and Ruchti, *Stanley Kubrick,* 181.

7. Armstrong, Karen. *Jerusalem: One City, Three Faiths,* New York: Ballantine, 2005, pgs. 221-2

8. Keuls, Eva. *Reign of the Phallus: Sexual Politics in Ancient Athens.* Berkeley: University of California Press, 1985, pgs. 78-9.

9. Cavendish, Richard, *The Black Arts*, New York: Penguin, 1983, pgs. 296-7.

10. Marvin and Ingle, *Blood Sacrifice and the Nation*. Cambridge: University Press, 1999.

11. Farrell, Dr. Joseph P., *The Cosmic War: Interplanetary Warfare, Modern Physics, and Ancient Texts*. Kempton, IL: Adventures Unlimited Press, 2007.

12. Dyer, Jay. "Plato's Cosmology and Achilles' Shield Compared." JaysAnalysis. 3 May 2011. Web. http://jaysanalysis.com/2011/05/03/platos-cosmology-and-achilles-shield-compared-full/

13. Freke and Gandy, Eds. *The Hermetica*. New York: Penguin, 1999, xxix, xxxv, 12.

14. Dvorsky, George. "Neil deGrasse Tyson Slammed for Dismissing Philosophy as 'Useless.'" iO9. 5 December, 2014. Web. http://io9.gizmodo.com/neil-degrasse-tyson-slammed-for-dismissing-philosophy-a-1575178224.

15. Sherrard, Dr. Philip. "Teilhard de Chardin and the Christian Vision." Studies in Comparative Religion, Vol. 4, No. 3. World Wisdom Publishers, 1970.

16. See Young, Dudley. *Origins of the Sacred: The Ecstasies of Love and War*. New York: Harper Collins, 1991.

17. Plato, *The Republic*. Ed. G. M.A. Grube. Indiana: Hackett Publishing, 1991, pg. 288. Lundy, Miranda, *Quadrivium: The Four Classical Liberal Arts of Number, Geometry, Music and Cosmology*. Glastonbury: Wooden Books, 2010, 185-90.

18. Freke, *The Hermetica*, 97-104.

19. Steinhart, Eric. "Teilhard de Chardin and Transhumanism." *Journal of Evolution and Technology*. December, 2008. JET Press. Roob, Alexander. *The Hermetic Museum: Alchemy & Mysticism*. Los Angeles: Taschen, 2006, pg. 111-114.

20. DiGiulio, Ed. "Two Special Lenses for 'Barry Lyndon.'" American Cinematographer. Web. http://www.visual-memory.co.uk/sk/ac/len/page1.htm. Kubrick, Vivian cited in "Vivian Kubrick on the Insanity of Tyranny," Infowars. Web. 26 November 2013. Web. http://www.infowars.com/infowars-com-exclusive-vivian-kubrick-on-the-insanity-of-tyranny-2/. Duncan, Paul. *Stanley Kubrick: The Complete Films*. London: Taschen, 2003, pg. 113.

21. See Farrell, Joseph P. *The SS Brotherhood of the Bell*. Kempton, IL: Adventures Unlimited, 2006. *The Third Way: The Nazi International, European Union, and Corporate Fascism*. Kempton, IL: Adventures Unlimited, 2015. Jacobsen, Annie. *The Pentagon's Brain: The Uncensored History of DARPA, America's Top Secret Military Research Agency*. New York: Little Brown & Co., 2015, pgs. 436-8.

22. Lucas, J.R. "Minds, Machines and Godel." *Ethics and Politics*. 2003.

23. Clarke, Arthur C. cited in "Sir Arthur C. Clarke's Quotations." The Arthur C. Clarke Foundation. Web. http://www.clarkefoundation.org/about-sir-arthur/sir-arthurs-quotations/

24. Kubrick, Stanley. *Playboy* interview reproduced in "What did Kubrick Have to Say About What 2001 Means?" Krusch. Web. http://www.krusch.com/kubrick/Q12.html

25. Steinart, "Teilhard de Chardin and Transhumanism."

26. Heisenberg, Werner, in *Physics and Philosophy: The Revolution in Modern Science* (1958) Lectures delivered at University of St. Andrews, Scotland, Winter 1955-56.

27. Atmanspacher, Harald. "The Hidden Side of Wolfgang Pauli." *Journal of Consciousness Studies*, 3, No. 2, 1996, pgs. 112-26.

28. Picknett and Prince, *The Stargate Conspiracy*. New York: Berkley Books, 1999.

29. Pike, *Morals and Dogma*, 773.

30. Pike, *Morals and Dogma*, 728.

31. Crowley, Aleister. "Cry of the 12th Aethyr" in *The Vision and the Voice*. Hermetic.com. Web. http://hermetic.com/crowley/the-vision-and-the-voice/aethyr12.html

32. Plato, *Republic*, Bk. 7.

Part Two:

Spielberg's Android Space Brothers

Chapter 5

H.G. Wells, Science Fiction Propaganda and Spielberg's Mythos

Russell's blunt description of a "scientific dictatorship" was matched by the account of Aldous Huxley, author of the utopian tract Brave New World, *in a speech on the U.S. State Department's Voice of America, in 1961, of a world of pharmacologically manipulated slaves, living in a "concentration camp of the mind," enhanced by propaganda and psychotropic drugs, learning to "love their servitude," and abandoning all will to resist. 'This,' Huxley concluded, 'is the final revolution."*

– Jeffrey Steinberg[1]

"The American motion picture is the greatest unconscious carrier of propaganda in the world today. It is a great distributor for ideas and opinions."

– Edward Bernays[2]

We tend to think of science fiction, modern science (scientism), and religion, as three distinct subjects, with minimal connection amongst them. When we consider them philosophically, a radically different perspective begins to take shape, where the underlying presuppositions of all three move closer and closer. Considering the weaponization of culture from the vantage point of the establishment under the rubrics of full spectrum

EDWARD BERNAYS (1891-1995): Nephew of Sigmund Freud and famed for his works on propaganda and mass advertising, Bernays pioneered methods and techniques for influencing and altering mass opinion. Bernays focused on crowd psychology and for a time worked for the U.S. Government in originating the concept of public relations and the "herd instinct."

BERTRAND RUSSELL (1872-1970): British philosopher, mathematician, logician and pioneer of modern, atheistic materialism. Russell's public facade was as a liberal democrat opposing nuclear weapons and warfare, while simultaneously advocating a Huxley-style "Brave New World" superstate where a technocracy would control all areas of life, including population growth and human genetics. Russell was a collaborator with other Fabian Socialists for a supposedly science based world order that would put an end to all previous forms of human culture.

JULES VERNE (1828-1905): French novelist, playwright, and poet. Verne authored of some of the most famous adventure novels of all time that would have a profound influence on the various literary genres globally. His famed works include classics such as *Journey to the Center of the Earth, Around the World in Eighty Days,* and *20,000 Leagues Under the Sea.* Verne is the second most translated author in the world, after Shakespeare, and along with H.G. Wells and Hugo Gernsback, is considered the "father of science fiction."

ROBERT HEINLEIN (1907-1988): One of the most prominent American science fiction authors whose controversial works would have an immense impact, even in Hollywood and among military academies. Heinlein is often classed with Asimov and Arthur C. Clarke as the most prominent in the genre through the 60s and 70s. Heinlein's political philosophy evolved over time, from a mainline progressive Democrat towards libertarian anarchism, as reflected in his work, *The Moon is a Harsh Mistress,* where an A.I. supercomputer aids in a revolution. A sexual liberation proponent, Heinlein is rumored to have mingled in the circles of Crowley.

dominance, all three are crucial cultural drivers that disseminate a prepackaged worldview to its consumers. Whether it's Isaac Asimov fans, Dawkinites or followers of L. Ron Hubbard, all have tremendous power to shape, mold and convert the perspectives of their flocks towards some desired end. It is my thesis that the end goal of all three in our age of transition is ultimately to merge into a singular monoculture globo-worldview, that will function as a kind of new religious mythology.

From the earliest days of what we knows as "science fiction" in figures like Jules Verne and H.G. Wells, the notion of "science" as being the means by which man may project his imagination into the future was seen to be a useful tool of statecraft. Particularly with Wells, we can see a figure whose stated goals of Fabian socialism would bleed though many of his more notable works with

L. RON HUBBARD (1911-1986): American science fiction author and founder of the Church of Scientology. A one-time associate of Aleister Crowley, Hubbard is the controversial conduit of the space-based religious drama found in the Church's central text, *Dianetics.* Hubbard's background is shrouded in controversy and scandal, including debates over his actual Naval service record. Nowadays, Scientology has an intimate relationship with some of Hollywood's top A list actors, including Tom Cruise, Kirstie Alley and John Travolta, all of whom heavily promote the institution, which is often believed to utilize vicious mind control techniques over members.

H.G. WELLS (1866-1946): Famed English author generally known for his science fiction works that are some of the most well known of all time, such as *The Time Machine, The Island of Dr. Moreau* and *War of the Worlds.* Wells' science fiction works have had an unparalleled influence, not just on literature, but also on Hollywood. Along with Jules Verne, Wells is considered the father of science fiction. A zealous Marxist and adherent of the Fabian ideology, Wells was also a Freemason and radical proponent of scientism and eugenics.

beaming effulgence. Wells supposedly sought the eradication of the speculative monetary system (in the close of *Outlines of History*), and through his fiction foretold a bright era of technological utopianism where reason would be crowned king. In works like *The Time Machine,* notions of eugenics play a central role in conditioning the coming aeons of the rise of the vulgar class, which would have to be controlled and managed by the technocratic control grid.

In works like *War of the Worlds*, the alien invasion myth exploded as even many of the academic class bought into the notion of civilizations that inhabited Mars or other solar systems. Hollywood soon jumped on board and after Orson Welles' famous broadcast, there would issue a nonstop flow of all things alien, UFO and galactic, as new luminaries like Edgar Rice Burroughs, Nolan, Robert Heinlein, Frank Herbert, Asimov, Clarke and many more would chip in to produce classics in both print and screen incarnations. From the vantage point of propaganda, the state found the alien mythos to be quite a useful tool, piling on more and more external invasion "threats" as a fascinated mass consumed more and more. By the 70s and 80s, following the supposed Apollo 11 Mission, *Close Encounters*, the *Star Wars* trilogy and *E.T.* had crystallized the alien myth in the minds of the public as fact, far more than any scientists' claims of panspermia.

EDGAR RICE BURROUGHS (1875-1950): American author most well known for his creation of the literary characters of Tarzan and John Carter, in the *John Carter From Mars* series. Fellow famed science fiction writer Ray Bradbury referred to Burroughs as the most influential writer of all time, noting that his combination of fantasy adventure with romance changed an entire generation of young boys.

It is precisely with panspermia, as I've remarked many times, that we see the infusion of the alien mythos into so-called empirical science, yet the absurdity here becomes manifest by definition – no one has observed panspermia, it is simply a theory – and a sci-fi theory, at that. Indeed, as a film buff, one thing is undeniably certain, and that is there is no end to the alien story. Yet there's another "alien" story that is also crammed down our throats and as I hinted, arises roughly contemporary with science fiction, and that is Darwinism. Purporting to be a strictly "natural" explanation of the "origins" of life and species adaptation ("change over time"), the more one delves into the ideological origins of Darwinian theory, the clearer it is seen to be linked with British Freemasonry and ancient mythology – less and less does it appear to be "scientific," and more and more like a Wells tale. Having been redefined and elastically stretched to encompass everything from floor pol-

Panspermia and Evolution - a new mythology.

101

ish to toenails, literally everything is purported to be "proof" of evolution. Despite no transitional fossils (and we should be swimming in endless piles of the billions of dead transition creaturely remains), Darwinism is the dominant religious perspective of our day, with all reality coming under its aegis as a product of endless material flux and chaos.

Concurrent with this grand narrative explanation is the other grand narrative explanation – that of science fiction. Thus, while Darwinism looks to the past, science fiction is distinctly future-oriented. Quite often the two meld together and are linked, especially in the alien mythos. The explanation for the obviously rational and highly likely existence of extraterrestrial entities of some form is often said to be the aeons of Darwinism. Why, it's just obvious that the 4.5 billion years the solar system took to "form" (an unsubstantiated, non-empirical presupposition) would surely give rise to the birth of "life" on Zeta Reticuli, and since we're talking in the billions of years, it's likely they "evolved" to be far more advanced than humans. Hell, they probably "seeded" us here on terra firma. Stop for a moment and think about how much that starts to sound just like science fiction! However, let's recall our opponents' definition of "science" – observable "facts" to support or negate a theory. In other words, these are the creative speculations of men in much the same way Bobba Fett and Mork are creative fictions. They are not real, nor is the postulant that primordial muck was struck by lightning and gave birth to determined amoebas and fish and whales. Much like science fiction, it is a story that men choose to believe in as a substitute, like a child dons a Superman costume and bounces off the couch attempting flight.

We can see a window into this melding process in examples of UFO cults like the Raelians or Scientology. Both purport to be in perfect harmony

RAELIANS: A UFO religion founded by French journalist and former race car driver, Claude Vorilhon (now known as "Rael"). Based on purported encounters with "Yahweh" and other space beings, the Raelian system borrows terms and images from the biblical texts, such as "Elohim" (gods) and re-appropriates them for the organization's uses. Similar in many ways to New Age ideas, the Raelians hold Jesus and Buddha to be "messengers" in syncretistic fashion, and stress a supposed ability to "clone" humans through which immortality will be reached. Like believers in panspermia, Raelians believe humans are the genetic experiment of aliens, otherwise known as the "Elohim." However, unlike most New Age beliefs, the Raelians do not believe in the supernatural and stress physicalism.

SCIENTOLOGY: A religious organization formed in 1954 by science fiction writer L. Ron Hubbard. Based on Hubbard's teachings in his book Dianetics, the organization's message focuses on an elaborate cosmology based on a galactic history populated by entities which afflict humanity from past lives. The Church's "auditing" process involves the supposed healing from this malady, as well as various regulations related to healthy living and a generally anti-psychiatric attitude. Former adherents claim the group uses mind control and brainwashing techniques. Controversial at all times, Hubbard's Scientology has intimate connections with Hollywood A-listers and is believed by some to be tied to the CIA, resulting in its being banned in some countries like Russia and Germany.

with science and critical of the present systems of petty government corruption like Wells whined in *Outlines of History*. Both project glorious futures of utopian progress through various pseudo-scientific and scientistic means, as man can achieve self-salvation through some rigorous process of bizarre doctrinal adherence. Both maintain a strict regimen of belief for followers to cult figures that best not be challenged, since the cult has the monopoly on truth and the answers to pretty much any issue that might arise, and should they not, have faith, an answer will come from the high priesthood. These sci-fi cults thus operate in the exact same

We come in peace to give perms, shoe horns and vacuum your planet. Truly evolution is a fantastic mystery.

fashion as the sci-fi cult of Darwinism, where dissent results in being ostracized, fired, mocked and harassed.

Despite democidal statist regimes supposedly basing their principles on Darwinism, reason and science resulting in the murder of millions, the faith in the cult of the sci-fi Darwinian state continues on, because, well, there are microwaves and iPhones – and those are proof of evolution. Oh you didn't know that? What are you, an Ozark Mountain dweller? You didn't know iPhones prove Darwinism? Of course, technological progress has absolutely no necessary connection to a wild biological theory of origins, but that never ceases to be used as a "proof" of a ridiculous paradigm.

One thing cult members lack is critical thinking and objectivity, and if the Darwinian science fiction space opera that is to be our coming religion has anything, it has an army of followers who talk all day about reason, yet don't have the foggiest idea how reason operates on immaterial, invariant principles that are in the domain of metaphysics.

Once Darwin and the empiricists supposed they had banished metaphysics, the past was assumed to be "explained" on "natural" grounds, and from there, the future needed some hope, some thing for ever-duped man to look into the future to project himself among the stars (after all, we are all "stars" according to physicist Lawrence Krauss, echoing Crowley:

The amazing thing is that every atom in your body came from a star that exploded. And, the atoms in your left hand probably came from a different star than your right hand. It really is the most poetic thing I know about physics: You are all stardust. You couldn't be here if stars hadn't exploded, because the elements – the carbon, nitrogen, oxygen, iron, all the things that matter for evolution – weren't created at the beginning of time. They were created in the nuclear furnaces of stars, and the only way they could get into your body is if those stars were kind enough to explode. So, forget Jesus. The stars died so that you could be here today.[3]

And this is the role the Psy-Op scions of science fiction play. To play with reality and rewrite reality as a play of reality is the function of our new saints, St. Darwin and St. Wells, prophets and sages of the new dawn intent on exterminating man, as Holy Father Bertrand Russell lovingly prayed, with the aid of the space brother elites intent on bringing us to *Childhood's End*. It's just science, it's a fact.

Before there was Spielberg's *Back to the Future*, however, there was the early phase of science fiction embodied in Fabian Socialist H.G. Wells' 1895 novella, *The Time Machine*. Wells' work is both entertaining and important for the course of modern literature, yet also calls for an analysis given the prevalence of propaganda functioning at many levels within the novel. Functioning as a popular serial and eventually published in book form, the story has captivated generations as a supposed warning tale of the potential dark future of mankind unless we're willing to heed the dictates of reason, science and methodical empirical deduction. The novel also displays an early example of environ-

FREEMASONRY: A broad fraternal organization originating in the Medieval stonemason's guilds, and proclaimed by members to be the "ancient craft" of true science and philosophy. Freemasons are organized hierarchically into lodges in various nations and utilize a series of secret oaths, rituals and symbols to signify their associations and beliefs. In general, masonry promotes classical liberal ideals of freedom of thought, belief and worship, and often requires attendees be male and profess adherence to a "Supreme Being."

mentalist themes, preparing the way for the dubious threats of man-made global warming, the human disruption of the biosphere, the burning out of the sun and stars as well as the propagation of Marxist class struggle and eschatological utopianism succeeded by dystopianism, all of which is predicated on one catch-all mythos – Darwinism.

With *The Time Machine* we have a clear example of what I have elucidated in many articles, where the new mythos of scientism and its revolutionary offspring, Darwinism, came to such prominence through the promotion of its primary source: funding and global academic control, from the Royal Society.

Illustrating even clearer the close relationship between Fabian Socialism and Masonry, Wells himself was a Mason and crafted his novels rife with reference to the so-called craft. What also emerges is the close relationship of the leftist-socialist revolutionaries that espoused the worker's revolution and their phony counterparts, the faux right with their core revolutionary values of scientism and empiricism that still maintained a predilection for property rights and family. Spewing forth, as it always has, from London, Marxism and socialism were always connected to Masonry and the banking houses, despite Wells or Bertrand Russell's masks of anti-monetarism. The republics and their socialist "parties" worldwide are actually controlled by this secretive Orwellian "Inner Party." Bertrand Russell openly praises this approach:

ROYAL SOCIETY: A scientific society founded in London in 1660 for the promotion of knowledge of the natural world and given a royal charter by King Charles II. It is believed to be the oldest such society still in existence (along with similar arms of the Vatican), and has had unparalleled influence in the history of western academia and ideological development. Many of its earliest members were prominent magicians, alchemists and Freemasons, like Robert Fludd and Isaac Newton. The earliest origins of the society date to Sir Francis Bacon and his alchemically-influenced ideas as found in his famous *New Atlantis*. In our day, the Royal Society, along with associated elite institutions like Chatham House, still have tremendous influence amongst academics.

> Sires will be chosen for various qualities, some for muscle, others for brains. All will have to be healthy, and unless they are to be the fathers of oligarchs they will have to be of a submissive and docile disposition. Children will, as in Plato's *Republic*, be taken from their mothers and reared by professional nurses. Gradually, by selective breeding, the congenital differences between rulers and ruled will increase until they become almost different species. A revolt of the plebs would become as unthinkable as an organized insurrection of sheep against the practice of eating mutton. (The Aztecs kept a domesticated alien tribe for purposes of cannibalism. Their regime was totalitarian.)[4]

The Time Machine not only demonstrates the paper-thin façade of the socialist and communist project, but simultaneously reveals, like Huxley's *Brave New World*, the suppression of real metaphysics, science and cosmic truths, while feeding the masses a public consumption replacement intent on stunting, devolving and undermining the populace for their gradual, incremental (the Fabian plan) integration of the continents into a global technocratic age. Hardly anyone could be chosen as a more prominent or notable figure for the preparation and programming of the socialistic techno-state than H.G. Wells and, as we will see, the present novel undoubtedly encodes many of the same themes and messages as Huxley's dystopia, yet with other hidden angles.

Speaking of angles, the first curious reference in the book is to the notion of higher dimensions. Like the Victorian era novel *Flatland* by Edwin Abbot that explored similar themes, or Madeleine L'engle's later *A Wrinkle in Time,* the notion of the next dimension up being a certain mathematical reality, Wells seems content to slip the notion into the novel at the outset under the guise of a fictional hoodwink. The protagonist, the Time Traveller, engages in a lengthy discussion with other academic and establishment colleagues concerning the reality of the fourth dimension as immaterial and most likely time itself. Glorying in his scientistic approach, the empirical scientific method is touted as the only path to knowledge, as the scientist makes a fool of his unnamed colleagues, the Journalist, the Psychologist, the Medical Man, etc. The anonymous naming signifies the pre-eminence of the "scientist" for Wells, despite Wells' own self-satisfaction in his role as fiction propagandist. The Time Traveler's philosophy of pragmatic empiricism is also compounded with a close associate.

ALDOUS HUXLEY (1894-1963): British author and philosopher, famous for his dystopian work *Brave New World,* and mystical, drug-based tracts like *The Doors of Perception.* Huxley, as well as his prominent family, were ardent promoters of the coming global order. Like Orwell, Huxley predicted a dystopia based on top-down control, but rather than a future based on force, the means of power would primarily be through genetic engineering and pharmaceutical mass drugging. Like Bertrand Russell and many other western academic elites, the catch-phrases and propaganda of Huxley were "democratic," while simultaneously adhering to the "rationality" of a mass depopulation agenda and an authoritarian, global scientific dictatorship based on mass mind control. Huxley was also associated with the Tavistock Institute and thus, by extension, functioned as an early pioneer of what would later become the various MKUltra programs.

Future utopias, he is convinced, will be erected on the basis of pure communism, having left aside the impediment of symbolic monetary exchange and the preference for personal property. For the materialist, such dreamy philosophies have always been the secular salvific hope, despite their utterly irrational foundations and completely off-base appraisals of "human nature" and the "human race" (which Wells lauds often). Rather, the reality is something even the Fabian Wells appears to light upon in his story, that mankind is not fundamentally rational, nor are his social structures, and on top of all that, nor is empirical scientism itself founded upon Pure Reason.

I feel sure Wells had quite a laugh to himself, as he proposed immaterial, invariant dimensions at the start of the novel, and proceeded to declare the dogma of scientism elsewhere. Indeed, for Wells the reasoning is such that because the human body is a machine, and he distinctly notes his preference for mechanistic conceptions of man and his universe, then a like machine for the body might be constructed. As the mind traverses the linear progress of beginning to end within time inside its machine, the human body, so might a machine for this machine be made in which man might overcome the dominance of time in his quest for secular apotheosis.

Crystals are curiously what propels the time machine, though we are not given any mechanics of the device. Crystallography does have many subtle mysteries and properties that actually do have a connection to higher dimensions, through the example of the quasi-crystal and Roger Penrose's tiling, which exhibits the same geometrical and mathematical matrices structures of quasi-crystals, as well as a hypercube or tesseract. It is therefore interesting that, in a scientistic fiction novel that also references Platonic Allegory of the Cave motifs, we have similar ideas to the higher dimensional discussions found in Plato's Phaedo.[5] In other words, like Huxley's Technocratic Controller, Mustapha Mond, the reality of metaphysics must be suppressed and dead-end empirical materialism promoted.

The next curious feature of the novel is the Sphinx, a great ruin the Time Traveler discovers as he reaches the year 802,701 A.D., now decaying from years of disuse as the utopian civilization that once did appear had now fallen. The Sphinx is Wells' masonic code for the Craft of Masonry itself, as Albert Pike explained, "Masonry is the veritable Sphinx, buried to the head in the sands heaped round it by the ages."[6] The sphinx is also spoken of as relating to time and space, and in some traditions associated with the Cherubim,

So this was what the future world was like, I thought. The White Sphinx was the work of a great artist. Clearly the future loved beauty.

But then I looked more closely. The bronze base was green with mold. The Sphinx's face was partly worn away.

Morlock Sphinx.

"Then there is the future," said the Very Young Man. "Just think! One might invest all one's money, leave it to accumulate at interest, and hurry on ahead!"

"To discover a society," said I, "erected on a strictly communistic basis."

as the wheels of Ezekiel are associated with the governance of the natural forces of the cosmos.[7] Here, the sphinx and the ancient mysteries have been decoded and surpassed, as Wells' scientistic hero usurps the previously accorded divine role to use his chariot to traverse time and space.

No longer is the body limited, but by a new body, a new chariot allows man to bend time and space like the angelic hierarchies and the Chariot of biblical theology.

Having overcome body and temporal limitations, man is threatened with an absurd fear-porn from Wells, where the future is a bleak one in which the Golden Age which had returned was once again lost due to the long evolutionary trek of the human race, now divided between Eloi and Morlock. Blonde and four-feet tall, the Eloi are surface dwellers who eat only fruit and graze like cattle for the troglodyte monkey-men cave dwellers, the Morlocks. Promoting the mythology of Paleolithic "cave men" and notorious frauds like Piltdown Man or Peking Man, Wells propaganda was quite successful in aiding the Darwinian ethos with its new timeline of imaginary aeons of millions of years in which humans rise from muck to walk upright. For Wells, the loss of reason and science (embodied in the decayed Green Porcelain Museum) has doomed man once again to the crass ways of primal cannibalism, as Morlocks consume the Eloi at night.

The novel also features another highlight of Marxist lore, the alienation of man from nature, the inevitable struggle of social Darwinism and the external threat of the decaying and dying environment. Indeed, quite early in the game Wells was seeding the idea of man as a threat to the biosphere, where uncontrolled population has to be curbed to prevent Malthusian disasters. Despite the glowing praise of materialism, Earth is treated as usual amongst this ilk as a "living being" upon which mankind is a cancer. Wells, in fact, warns the entire cosmos is "dying" as his hero's journey to the end of time results in the burning out of the stellar luminaries and the beginning of evolutionary process starts anew as prehistoric monsters and creatures emerge from the ocean.

The Time Traveller with the Eloi from the 1960 film adaptation by George Pal.

Cyclical history is presented once more, all of which is a complete re-packaging of ancient mythology under the cover of science! The crucial factor here is that you can begin to see the real origins of where most gain their assumptions of Darwinian tales – science fiction preparation, not in any empirical observation of amoebas from muck or Peking Man. For Wells, the socialist end goal must wipe away all, especially the family and the androgyny of alchemical gender bending:

> I felt that this close resemblance of the sexes was after all what one would expect; for the strength of a man and the softness of a woman, the institution of the family, and the differentiation of occupations are mere militant necessities of an age of physical force; where population is balanced and abundant, much childbearing becomes an evil rather than a blessing to the State; where violence comes but rarely and off-spring are secure, there is less necessity – indeed there is no necessity – for an efficient family, and the specialization of the sexes with reference to their children's needs disappears. We see some beginnings of this even in our own time, and in this future age it was complete. This, I must remind you, was my speculation at the time. Later, I was to appreciate how far it fell short of the reality....
>
> But with this change in condition comes inevitably adaptations to the change. What, unless biological science is a mass of errors, is the cause of human intelligence and vigour? Hardship and freedom: conditions under which the active, strong, and subtle survive and the weaker go to the wall; conditions that put a premium upon the loyal alliance of capable men, upon self-restraint, patience, and decision. And the institution of the family, and the emotions that arise therein, the fierce jealousy, the tenderness for offspring, parental self-devotion, all found their justification and support in the imminent dangers of the young. Now, where are these imminent dangers? There is a sentiment arising, and it will grow, against connubial jealousy, against fierce maternity, against passion of all sorts; unnecessary things now, and things that make us uncomfortable, savage survivals, discords in a refined and pleasant life.[8]

The family and gender, mere social constructs that merge and then submerge back into nature's blind, meaningless force are subject to the same deterministic necessity Wells states, as all other materialistic constructs. Chaos reigns supreme in the evolutionary paradigm and never ceases to cancel out the supposed rationality that it stands upon. There is no reason in a world where there is no telos* or purpose, and Wells seems to acknowledge this with his admissions of geometric entities. In great irony, the Time Traveler escapes his underground captors through the use of matches, symbolizing the Masonic use of reason once again, as if reason were a god. How absurd, then, that the scientistic crowd never delves into the question of what exactly reason is, how it is had or functions universally as an invariant principle. None of that matters, only the story of the long march of history and "science" versus the "darkness" and Night of superstition, like Mozart's *Magic Flute*.

Irony again, given that scientism endlessly touts the "freedom" it offers from the self-imposed tutelage of superstition, while then turning around and promoting numerous environmental catastrophe warnings that never manifest, from Malthus to global cooling to warming to climate change. Even genetics is trotted out as a fear tactic, with the added bonus of class warfare that is the source of both evolution and devolution. The wealthy end up docile cattle while the retarded Morlocks become sub-human. For the Fabian Socialist it becomes clear that despite the supposed opposition to Nazi eugenics, it is the Fabians who are overtly behind the policy of covert dysgenics. In fact one might even see an inkling of this in *The Time Machine*, noting the close correlation to Darwin and the completely mythological speculations and the "natural" state of all things dying and returning to an amorphous center:

> I think I have said how much hotter than our own was the weather of this Golden Age. I cannot account for it. It may be that the sun was hotter, or the earth nearer the sun. It is usual to assume that the sun will go on cooling steadily in the future. But people, unfamiliar with such speculations as those of the younger Darwin, forget that the planets must ultimately fall back one by one into the parent body. As these catastrophes occur, the sun will blaze with renewed energy; and it may be that some inner planet had suffered this fate. Whatever the reason, the fact remains that the sun was very much hotter than we know it.[9]

Evolutionary aberration: Morlock troglodytes.

Being members of the same club with the Huxleys, we are reminded by Wells again through fiction of the strategy of admission through science fantasy what is fact: real metaphysics and science is suppressed, and the masses are fed garbage to keep them in a prison. While not as sub par in prose as most science fiction, and certainly an entertaining story, Wells' novella was much more than a fantasy tale for pulp publications. The Fabian Socialist strategy was always to utilize all means necessary to gradually move the Masonic atheistic scientistic presuppositions into the realm of confessional dogma with the masses gleefully cheering on their own enslavement, believing they follow "reason" as they are denigrated into irrational beasts. Like Huxley, Wells' novel is a propaganda piece that reveals as much as it conceals. With early hints of transhumanism, it also functions to prepare the way for manufactured environmental crises and bogus cosmologies where man is situated in a purely chaotic universe of infinite flux, doomed to return to nothingness. These are all, of course, lies, as Mustapha Mond explained to John the Savage in Aldous Huxley's *Brave New World*:

> We don't want to change. Every change is a menace to stability. That's another reason why we're so chary of applying new inventions. Every discovery in pure science is potentially subversive; even science must sometimes be treated as a possible enemy. Yes, even science. Science? The Savage frowned. He knew the word. But what it exactly signified he could not say. Shakespeare and the old men of the pueblo had never mentioned science, and from Linda he had only gathered the vaguest hints: science was something you made helicopters with, something that caused you to laugh at the Corn Dances, something that prevented you from being wrinkled and losing your teeth. He made a desperate effort to take the Controller's meaning.
>
> "Yes," Mustapha Mond was saying, "that's another item in the cost of stability. It isn't only art that's incompatible with happiness; it's also science. Science is dangerous; we have to keep it most carefully chained and muzzled."
>
> "What?" said Helmholtz, in astonishment. "But we're always saying that science is everything. It's a hypnopædic platitude." "Three times a week between thirteen and seventeen," put in Bernard. "And all the science propaganda we do at the College ..."
>
> "Yes; but what sort of science?" asked Mustapha Mond sarcastically. "You've had no scientific training, so you can't judge. I was a pretty good physicist in my time. Too good–good enough to realize that all our science is just a cookery book, with an orthodox

theory of cooking that nobody's allowed to question, and a list of recipes that mustn't be added to except by special permission from the head cook. I'm the head cook now. But I was an inquisitive young scullion once. I started doing a bit of cooking on my own. Unorthodox cooking, illicit cooking. A bit of real science, in fact." He was silent.[10]

As for science overstepping any bounds and seeking to blend different species, the notion of creating a *chimera* is an ancient tale: For the ancient Greeks, it was a fire-breathing beast with the heads of a goat, lion and snake, appearing in Homer's *Iliad* in Book VI as follows:

> Howbeit when the tenth rosy-fingered Dawn appeared, then at length he questioned him and asked to see whatever token he bare from his daughter's husband, Proetus. But when he had received from him the evil token of his daughter's husband, first he bade him slay the raging Chimaera. She was of divine stock, not of men, in the fore part a lion, in the hinder a serpent, and in the midst a goat, breathing forth in terrible wise the might of blazing fire.

From here, the mythology of the chimaera took on many forms, yet for modern scientistic western man, the dream of blending and bending Nature to fit his own designs took on a whole new meaning. Demythologizing and desacralizing Nature of any divine or sacramental character, the new grand narrative, as I have detailed many times, became that of blind, mechanistic force. Banishing God from Nature through the removal of belief in His immanence, for a time the West was prepared to grant verbal homage to him as perhaps a blind watchmaker of a universe of sound and fury signifying nothing, and in no wise intimate with his creation.

Following the rise of both deistic Freemasonry, empiricism and Darwinism, the distant watchmaker soon dropped away,

Oedipus and the chimeric sphinx.

112

leaving only the universe itself, with man dethroned of any special place, purportedly drifting along in a meaningless kosmos, with infinite worlds and an infinite universe on all sides, making his already insignificant existence even less so, as becoming annihilated being. Titus Burckhardt comments in "Cosmology and Modern Science" on the folly of scientism and its self-contradicting futility in its belief in man and reason (given its presuppositions):

> What connection is there between that primordial nebula, that eddy of matter whence they wish to derive both the earth and life and man, and this little mental mirror losing itself in conjectures-since for the scientists intelligence is but this – with the certainty of discovering the logic of things? How can the effect judge concerning its own cause? And if there exist any constant laws of nature such as those of causality, number, space and time, and also something that, within ourselves, has the right to say, 'this is true, that is false,' where then lies the guarantor of truth, in the object or in the subject? Is the nature of our spirit only a little foam on the waves of the cosmic ocean, or is there to be found deep within it a timeless witness of reality?[11]

With the rise of the Royal Society and its masonic and atomistic dogmatism, the focal point of empirical scientism was able to evangelize the earth with its new paradigm, pragmatic scientism where perpetual becoming has canceled all notions of being.[12] The eternal and unchanging, be it God, mathematical principles or even reason itself, was now subservient as mere descriptors of "natural phenomenon" with no grounding in anything beyond the determined, chaotic chemical reactions in some brain, equally meaningless in the chemical reactions of some other brain. Nevertheless, the vaunted new deity, "reason," somehow functioned and operated consistently between these chaotic chemical reactions, and not in each man's mind *in potentia*, but rather only amongst the self-titled scientific elite. As we saw in Wells' *Time Machine*, it was only the scientist who possessed the gnosis of fire to rescue himself and trapped Eloi from the Morlocks, signifying the fire of reason, and as we shall see, the contradictions apparent in that novella are also found within his later 1896 work of equal fame, *The Island of Dr. Moreau*.

In the introduction to the Signet edition of *The Island of Dr. Moreau*, Dr. Nita Farahany of the Salk Institute notes the sagacious forethought on the part of Wells, as applying to neuroscience, genetics, epigenetics and ultimately, mind control:

His character Dr. Moreau directs his attention to the subtle grafting and reshaping of the brain, and in this way Wells showed eerie prescience. When he imagined Dr. Moreau, scientists believed the brain was fixed and unchangeable. That belief remained unchanged until just a few decades ago…. As research similar to Merzenich's started piling up, eventually scientists came to accept the plasticity of the human brain. The plastic brain constantly changes in response to events and remodels itself throughout life. Just as Wells speculated, it is because of brain plasticity that the brain can change and be changed as well.[13]

Farahany proceeds to then admit all the ethical dilemmas of modern scientism, admitting the U.S. Government's testing of Guatemalans by deliberately infecting them with STDs in 1946-48, merely one example among countless of the shadow government covertly "experimenting" upon humans, as well as its own citizens; classified, in fact, as "man and other animals in the Law Code."[14] Publishing his *The Ghost in the Machine* in 1967, Hungarian socialist Arthur Koestler took the implications of reductionist materialism to new lows in openly discussing the forced drugging and manipulation of the public. Koestler cites a mind control presentation in San Francisco by Dean Saunders in 1961:

Here at our disposal, to be used wisely or unwisely, is an increasing array of agents that manipulate human beings…. It is now possible to act directly on the individual to modify his behavior instead of, as in the past, indirectly through modification of the environment. –Dean Saunders, of the San Francisco Medical School, at the Control of the Mind symposium (1961), pg. 335.[15]

Koestler proceeds to the discussion of the possibility of re-engineering RNA and creating increased suggestibility through forced public drugging, citing Dr. Holgar Hyden from the same symposium:

The author is [referring] to any substance inducing changes of biologically important molecules in the neurons and the glia and affecting the mental state in a negative direction. It is not difficult to imagine the possible uses to which a government in a police-controlled state could put this substance. For a time they would subject the population to hard conditions. Suddenly the hardship would be removed, and at the same time, the substance would be added to the tap water and the mass-communications media turned on. This method would be much cheaper, and would create more intriguing possibilities then [voluntary introduction methods].[16]

The use of pharmacology and mind control by the CIA and various members of the establishment openly advocate this covert application. In this regard, we can view Wells' novel as another in a long line of science fiction propaganda, propping up the fragile myth of empty "progress" that knows no ethical bounds, justifying anything and everything sadistic and psychopathic under the rubric of the "advance of science." Like Alfred Kinsey, if molestation can be used as a vehicle for "scientific" gnosis, it would seem to follow that since (incorrectly) man emerged from ape-man and ape-man from bird and lizard, anything goes. The plasticity of man means the plasticity of all things, from species to gender.

Farahany continues (as if this were some unique feature of China and rare U.S. instances):

ALFRED KINSEY (1894-1956): American professor, biologist and "sexologist" who famously pioneered the now debunked "Sexual Behavior in the in the Human" study, arguing for the normative status of homosexuality. The study proved to be highly influential in the West, despite their dubious findings. On top of that, Kinsey also reportedly committed acts of criminal pedophilia under the guide of "science" by stimulating numerous young people, and even toddlers, in "sexual research." Kinsey is believed to have visited Aleister Crowley's "Abbey of Thelema," while receiving monetary aid for his "research" and the Kinsey Institute from the Rockefellers.

> A small group of scientists in China, for example, recently faced widespread public condemnation for their work diminishing the human brain. These scientists were performing a dramatic form of brain surgery to "cure" people of addiction. They hoped to eliminate cravings for drugs and alcohol in individuals with addictions by suppressing or removing a part of their brains. The procedures involved inserting electrodes into a region of the brain known as the nucleus accumbens and passing electrical current into this region to "kill off" cells.[17]

And you thought MKUltra was shut down? On the contrary, the same projects were transferred elsewhere and developed into programs like the Salk Institute's "Brain Initiative," where mapping and electroshock done by Drs. Cameron, Delgado and West continues on.[18] Are we to believe that this is only done in China? As if the Pentagon does not openly engage in these very same projects through DARPA or Salk? Such a notion is utterly ridiculous and betrays the paper-thin veneer of moral casuistry and self-righteousness that anyone involved in these projects must erect to justify their participation: at least Dr. Moreau was honest enough to consider himself God, dispensing with morality and taboo.

DR. JOSE DELGADO (1915-2011): Spanish-born professor of physiology at Yale. Delgado is most well known for his research into electronic mind control, in which he claimed in the 1960s to be able to control the motor functions of a bull. Beginning with cats, and moving to bulls, Delgado finally made use of human subjects in psychiatric institutions and was part of the CIA's MKUltra programs for just this reason. Delgado even published his research publicly in 1969, aptly titled *Physical Control of the Mind: Toward a Psychocivilized Society*.

115

Thus we come to Wells' text, which for its prose and flow is above average for pulp science fiction, but more famously known for its foreseeing the reality of genetic modification. I would also assure the reader not to worry – I won't be referencing the horrible John Frankenheimer film version with Marlon Brando and Val Kilmer, itself something of a monstrous concoction better left unmade (though quite comedic in its aberration). Rather, in the classic novel we are told through the journal entries of one Edward Prendick, an Englishmen with some scientific knowledge stranded on an island that happens to be inhabited by chimeric human-beast hybrids, all the work of the archetypal mad scientist, Dr. Moreau. Dispensing with all ethical and moral bounds, Moreau believes his microcosmic biosphere (the island) is the only suitable and rational locale for what he believes to be true, unhindered scientific progress. On the island, Moreau tortures and blends various species into new aberrations, and even erects a new law for the half-breed populace, with himself as God.

Prendick, astonished at the evil genius at work, eventually finds himself under threat, first from Moreau and then from his beastly offspring, leading to the death of all but he after a violent reversion and revolution on the part of the beast folk. Much like the Morlocks, Wells' atheism and scientism are at the fore of the novel, as we are blatantly presented with a microcosm of mankind and civilization as itself a retarded and stunted outgrowth of "evolution," where God and religion are merely humanly devised social constructs for better herd management by a technocratic elite. There is no violation of and divine or sacral law by blending the species, though of course in the biblical sense, this would be forbidden in both Leviticus and Jude.

DR. EWEN CAMERON (1901-1967): Scottish-born psychiatrist and head of both the Canadian and American Psychological Associations at various times. Cameron is one of the more prominent, known figures in the infamous MKUltra program, involved in the administration of LSD and electroshock "treatments." Cameron's experiments were vicious violations of human rights, yet later doctors in the CIA mind control programs like Dr. Jose Delgado built upon his research into pioneering the implantable electrode, bragging he could control a bull's motor functions.

DR. LOUIS JOLYON WEST (1924-1999): American Psychiatrist whose research dealt primarily with the "extremes of human experience." West analyzed famous patients, including Jack Ruby, Patty Hearst, Sirhan Sirhan and Tim McVeigh, suggesting a high level of deep state positioning for West. West is known for infamously dosing an elephant with LSD, resulting in the elephant's death, and for his work with the "Human Ecology Foundation," one of the many fronts for the CIA's MKUltra programs. West is also known for his indepth research into hypnosis and dissociative states - ideas long believed to be linked to MKUltra and mind control programming.

The fact that Moreau and all his creatures die is no warning from Wells – rather, the death that results is merely the death of the blind, mechanical

Prendick and the Darwinian fictional creation, the Ape-man.

forces of materialistic determinism Wells finds so "rational," leading to Prendick's discovery upon returning to London that it is the men of London and society who are the very same as the beast men of Moreau's nefarious lab. As we saw with *The Time Machine*, the façade of egalitarianism and equalitarianism on the part of the Fabian technocrats is, of course, an inside joke that is no more sincere than their Marxist belief in the distribution of wealth and social equality. The snickering heroes of Wells' novels are the scientistic pragmatists who, like their Fabian fathers, realize that man is but matter adrift amidst infinite flux, and in such a world, it truly does not matter whether science kills one man or a million, so long as some vague notion of "progress" is bantered about to quell any dissent.

It is the time traveling scientist in *The Time Machine* and scientists Prendick and Dr. Moreau who are vindicated here, as the great mystical truth Prendick divines from the island is merely the evolutionary plasticity of "man" and his environment – an environment to be genetically modified, geo-engineered and raped as the technocrat sees fit (because London is the island, and by extension, the world). Once Nature had been divested of any sacramental quality, and the presence of the divine vanquished (in the mind of Wells and his cohorts), it was natural that the sci-fi propagandist would step in and fill the void with a new mythos of fictional utopianism and grandiose promises based on the new Gospel, with Wells as one of its gnostic Apostles.

In other words, we are seeing a pattern at work here of a replacement ideology long ago at work by a certain power bloc, particularly the scientific mythos of the Royal Society, to promote the new gospel of man under the guise of humanism. However, as we have seen, even the so-called "great humanists" like Wells or Russell cannot help but betray their hatred of mankind in their works, as they lustily crave the destruction of the species through unbounded scientific modification and experimentation. For many, the notion of a technocratic elite who would seek to abolish man, as man, is too far-fetched. Yet in countless publications, and especially in the fiction of these new apostles of scientism, the glowing refrain is consistently genocide, not even for "science," but at the altar of Satan Himself. It is not reason or scientific progress that is at the heart of Fabianism or the New Atheism – it is Luciferianism, and that is the energizing force that hates man and Creation, seeking to wreck it as an inverted sacrificial affront to God.

It is not by accident or organic, "grassroots" trend that numerous films are coming focused on artificial intelligence and the transhumanist takeover. From H.G. Wells' tales of genetic *chimaeras* in The *Island of Dr. Moreau* to *Sixth Day* with Arnold Schwarzenegger, to recent A.I. films like *Chappie*, the predictive programming preparations are rolling out. My recent research has focused on the Manhattan Project, and like the MKUltra programs, Manhattan had a much wider application than is commonly known.

In fact, MKUltra and Manhattan are related through the connect of biometrics and bio-warfare. As MKUltra faded away, the program was renamed MK-SEARCH and transferred to Fort Detrick, one of the U.S. Military's biological weapons-focused bases.[19] And with both MK-SEARCH and Manhattan, we find an overarching ideology of transhumanism that has its origins much earlier in the alchemists of the ancient world.

The Manhattan Project is publicly known as the secret operation spanning several years devoted to developing the atomic bomb, yet the truth is much deeper and darker.[20] The Manhattan Project was actually a vast program concerned with radiation, human exposure and the grand telos – engineering resistant, synthetic humanoids. The inklings that we can gather about this overall, long-term project appear to be geared towards biologically engineering humans to withstand the coming onslaught of various alterations in the entire biosphere, all the while being sold as inevitable through Hollywood and fiction.

In order to transition to the synthetic overlay that will integrate SmartCities, the "Internet of Things," human bio-engineering, cloning, biometrics, genetic programming and environmental engineering is now an open plan in numerous transhumanist lectures and publications (but the way of mass acceptance was prepared through Spielberg's aliens and *A.I.* and later with James Cameron's *Terminator* series, as we will see). Yet in order to reach this phase, experimentation is necessary, and what better means to that end than experimenting on populations *en masse*. We have already seen that the technocratic establishment has no qualms about testing unwitting subjects, so covert experimentation on mass populations is not without precedent, from MKUltra to covert spraying. The U.S. government sprayed St. Louis, for example, in a radiation experiment under the guise of preparing for a Russian attack.[21]

That this particular experiment (among numerous others) involved radiation was no coincidence. The 20th Century appears to have been the "radiation century," suggesting the hypothesis that the Atomic Energy Commission and its Manhattan Project were interested in much more, given the provenance of Dr. Edward Teller. It appears the goal of the 20th century's experiments were precisely to overwrite the existing biosphere with a new, synthetic overlay, or humanity 2.0. Humanity Plus, the new homo evolutis, would be an androgynous being capable of technocratic control beneath the all-seeing Eye of panoptic surveillance. Children grown in test tubes, according to the *Brave New World* plans of Huxley, will mean the erasing of families, while sexuality would become meaningless.[22] Offspring allowed to subsist will be genderless automatons, made for slave-like subjugation and toil. Wells presaged this in his *Time Machine*, with the Morlocks and Eloi.

From Bertrand Russell to Dr. Edward Teller, the plan that is blossoming in our day is showing itself to be a unified one – a plan that spans the last century in particular as the century of the "final revolution" (in Russell's words), where scientific process would reveal the secrets to technological imperialism. Teller himself, as I have written, was not only a key figure in the development of the hydrogen bomb and the Manhattan Project, but also the father of aerosol spraying and atmospheric geo-engineering.[23] This period is thus concurrent with the alchemical nucle-

James Cameron (1954-): Canadian filmmaker, director, producer, explorer and inventor. Cameron is known for creating two of the most monetarily successful films of all time: *Aliens* (1986), *Terminator 2: Judgment Day* (1991), *Titanic* (1997) and *Avatar* (2009). Cameron's films have grossed billions, while in 2010 alone he grossed 257 million to be the most highly paid director. Cameron's obsession with aliens and environmental messages also make his blockbusters ripe for propaganda, as he has worked intimately with NASA as an advisory board member for so-called "Mars missions" and "colonization funding." The fact that NASA is officially under the aegis of the Air Force, and is intimately tied to Cameron, demonstrates the very thesis of this book like none other.

Dr. Edward Teller (1908-2003): Hungarian-born theoretical physicist known as the "father of the Hydrogen bomb." Teller worked on the Manhattan Project, the infamous program purported to be concerned with developing the atomic bomb, which most likely dealt with wide scale human and biosphere reengineering. Teller is less famously known as the father of weather modification and atmospheric aerosol spraying, known online in alternative media circles as "chemtrails." Teller was an ardent proponent of Reagan's Strategic Defense Initiative concerning the "weaponization of space" and is one of the inspirations for Dr. Strangelove in Kubrick's famous satire.

ar tests done by igniting bombs in the atmosphere, beginning at the Trinity Site in New Mexico. The historical archive site ABomb1 explains:

> From 1945 to 1963 the U.S.A. conducted an extensive campaign of atmospheric nuclear tests, grouped into roughly 20 test "series." After 1963 when the Limited Test Ban Treaty was signed testing for the U.S., Soviet Union, and Great Britain moved underground. France continued atmospheric testing until 1974 and China did so until 1980. This page focuses mainly on U.S. testing because those documents are most readily available.[24]

Masonic obelisk marking the Trinity site

Researcher Michael A. Hoffman opines on the alchemical significance of these tests at the "Trinity" site and its scientistic underpinnings:

> The reason science is a bad master and a dangerous servant and ought not to be worshipped, is that science is not objective. Science is fundamentally about the uses of measurement. What does not fit the yardstick of the scientist is discarded. Scientific determinism has repeatedly excluded some data from its measurement and fudged other data, such as Piltdown Man, in order to support the self-fulfilling nature of its own

120

agenda be it Darwinism, or "cut, burn and poison" methods of cancer "treatment."... This process is observed in the Renaissance, which was informed by a secret gnosis whose core dogma was momentous change in man's attitude toward nature: the alleged "perfection' of a "flawed" Creation by the invention of the "omnipotent" human brain. Thus it was the Renaissance magical tradition that gave birth to the monstrous world of machines, industrial pollution, ugliness and the modern way of death we have come to term the "rat race."[25]

And in regard to the esoteric significance of the site itself as a "rite" to mock the Trinity:

> The creation and destruction of primordial matter at the White Head (Ancient of Days) at White Sands, New Mexico, at the Trinity Site. The Trinity Site itself is located at the beginning of an ancient western road known in Old Mexico as the *jornada del muerto* (The Journey of Death).... Fabled alchemy had at least three goals to accomplish before the complete decay of matter, the total breakdown we are witnessing today, was fulfilled. These are:
>
> 1. Creation and Destruction of Primordial Matter
>
> 2. The Killing of the Divine King
>
> 3. The Bringing of *Prima Materia* to *Prima Terra*[26]

The connection here to the overall stratagems of the technocratic transhumanists and the Manhattan Project can now be elucidated, and for those skeptical of the connection of ritual magicians and occultists to modern science, consider the person of Jack Parsons, the father of the jet propulsion engine, who was an avid follower of Crowley's OTO.[27] The *ouroboros* signified here is the cycle of temporal and material existence being transcended to achieve apotheosis through techne. For this great work to be achieved, much experimentation was needed – from the human psyche, to the depths of subatomic particles. I wrote about the splitting of the atom as a kind of ritual sacrifice.

For several hundred years, Western man in particular has been firmly convinced of the

Jack Parsons (1914-1952): American rocket engineer, chemist, cofounder the JPL (Jet Propulsion Laboratory) at California Institute of Technology and an adherent to Crowley's religion of Thelema. Parsons is credited with inventing the first rocket engine, using both liquid and solid fuels. While in Crowley's circles, Parsons' wife left him for L. Ron Hubbard, leading to Parsons' attempt at an intense, apocalyptic magical ritual known as the "Babalon Working," in which the Thelemic goddess would be brought down to earth. Parsons eventually left the OTO and was accused of being a red spy after working as a consultant for an Israeli rocket program.

dogma that humans are blank slates, awaiting only the right imprinting, the perfected external educational stimulant, and when the hallowed secular social order finally gets it just right, man will achieve his Promethean triumph. When the coming technocracy appears, universal education and global democratic republics full of enlightened, informed citizenry will lead the way into the great ascent to godhood. With a rising erection, the Enlightenment evangelists even hoped a fully global government would be conjured up, like some benevolent republican idealistic version of the Incarnation out of the Kantian noumena.[28]

Instead, it becomes more apparent each day that these ideologues were either duped or consciously evil. The presuppositions of existing modernity and its structures of power are still operating as if the Enlightenment "truths" are axiomatic givens – enshrined discoveries of the heroes of science that are no longer in question, as the verdict of reason and history are fully and ever vindicated. The hard truth is that the Enlightenment ideologues were not only fundamentally wrong, but they were funded by the banking cartel for the purpose of social disorder and reorganization. The dark lords of cash and subversive secret societies atop the idiot demagogues and salesmen were quite cognizant of the stupidity of such notions of Enlightenment *tabula rasa* anthropology, nevertheless, the endless stream of Dantons won out and even still never go away. All the while, the money power laughs a hearty satanic cackle as the centuries pass by.

Thus, here we are two hundred years after 1776 and 1789 and what do we see? We see the intelligentsia operating as if physics and empiricism are actually explanatory "grand narratives." In total hypocrisy, labeling religion a fictitious "grand narrative" that only existed because it had explanatory power and satiated human fears, these in-

IMMANUEL KANT (1724-1804): German philosopher and one of the fathers of modern philosophy. Kant posited a divide between the mind's perception of the external world, and the objects of external perception in themselves. For Kant, and many subsequent philosophers, this had the effect of relativizing the world. Prior to Kant, the common assumption was that external reality was made up of objective facts presentable to sense perception. For Kant, these objects of perception are ordered and given meaning by the subjective mind interpreting phenomena. Though Kant himself was no radical relativist, this legacy, along with the work of David Hume, would result in modern empiricism, the philosophy that human knowledge can only extend as far as what is within our immediate sense perception.

AUGUST COMTE (1798-1857): French philosopher and founder of the discipline of sociology and the empiricist-related doctrine of positivism, that human knowledge is radially limited to immediate sense data. Comte was a utopian socialist influenced by earlier "illuminists" like St. Simon, who believed a scientistic society could be constructed on the principles of pure reason and the social sciences. Comte believed history demonstrated necessary stages and patterns, evolving in a Darwinian sense from primitivism and religious superstition, towards a purely rational, scientific global socialism. Comte is also famous for positing the creation of a new, humanistic civic religion by the superstate.

tellectually dishonest liars erected their own alternative narrative that daily assaults me, and which I gleefully dissect on a daily basis: The new Gospel of human ascent through "science." One thinks here of August Comte's patterned view of history where man passes from gradual stages of enlightenment, from primitive superstition and paganism, to rational monotheism, to philosophy and metaphysics, to physics and "social science." Although nothing could be further from the truth as regards the actual working of science and the actual structures of human social order and history, this mythology is still modernity's Heilsgeschichte.

For Jurgen Habermas, in his *Theory and Practice,* the Frankfurt School becomes the praxis for the dark side strategy, whose own work is a manifestation of the *angst* of grappling with the course of the never-ending "revolution," looking into the future for the social engineers to fix man through his needed destruction.[29] I cite Habermas because he is a major Marxist Frankfurt School thinker who links the destruction of the old world to the French and American revolutionaries. Habermas and the rest of his ilk like Max Horkheimer and Theodor Adorno, who worked with Western oligarchs and British establishment to destroy Western social order, export their weaponized disintegration to the rest of the globe. They are significant for demonstrating that evil is not merely an organic, chaotic force that just occurs. On the contrary, evil is very much concentrated, organized and cunning in its tactics.

THE FRANKFURT SCHOOL: A school of Marxist philosophy dedicated to social critique and analysis. Arising from the Inter-War era, the Frankfurt School differed from Stalinism and Eastern Bloc Marxism in their theory, analysis and praxis. Seeking to continue the tradition of "classical Marxism," the Frankfurt School attempted to synthesize thought from Kant, Hegel, Freud and Weber as a means to overcome the limitations of materialism and its lack of ethics. Following World War II, the Frankfurt School would take a more negative appraisal of human progress, coming under the influence of Nietzsche with the publication of Horkheimer and Adorno's *Dialectic of Enlightenment,* where the Enlightenment ideology of perpetual human progress is rejected as a new mythology. The Frankfurt School also cooperated with larger power entities in the Shadow Government, such as the Rockefeller Foundation, OSS and the CIA, for western cultural reengineering. The Frankfurt School's social critiques are the origins of the much-touted notion of "cultural Marxism."

The key point here is that this technocratic rewriting is a strategic plan for total destruction that had to first be preceded by centuries of revolution and disintegration, prior to what, as I said, Bertrand Russell and Aldous Huxley called "the final revolution,"[30] intending by this the great revolution against man himself. It is organized, structured, full-spectrum subversion, inversion and dominance – put into practice through fiction, mass media, and

Hollywood. Author Jeffrey Steinberg comments on this technocratic revolution as follows:

> Lord Bertrand Russell, who joined with the Frankfurt School in this effort at mass social engineering, spilled the beans, in his 1951 book, *The Impact of Science on Society*. He wrote:
>
>> Physiology and psychology afford fields for scientific technique which still await development. Two great men, Pavlov and Freud, have laid the foundation. I do not accept the view that they are in any essential conflict, but what structure will be built on their foundations is still in doubt. I think the subject which will be of most importance politically is mass psychology.... Its importance has been enormously increased by the growth of modern methods of propaganda. Of these the most influential is what is called "education." Religion plays a part, though a diminishing one; the press, the cinema, and the radio play an increasing part.... It may be hoped that in time anybody will be able to persuade anybody of anything if he can catch the patient young and is provided by the State with money and equipment.[31]

Russell continued:

> The subject will make great strides when it is taken up by scientists under a scientific dictatorship.... The social psychologists of the future will have a number of classes of school children on whom they will try different methods of producing an unshakable conviction that snow is black. Various results will soon be arrived at. First, that the influence of home is obstructive. Second, that not much can be done unless indoctrination begins before the age of ten. Third, that verses set to music and repeatedly intoned are very effective. Fourth, that the opinion that snow is white must be held to show a morbid taste for eccentricity. But I anticipate. It is for future scientists to make these maxims precise and discover exactly how much it costs per head to make children believe that snow is black, and how much less it would cost to make them believe it is dark gray.[32]

Speaking at the California Medical School in San Francisco, Huxley announced:

> There will be in the next generation or so a pharmacological method of making people love their servitude and producing dic-

tatorship without tears, so to speak. Producing a kind of painless concentration camp for entire societies so that people will in fact have their liberties taken away from them but will rather enjoy it, because they will be distracted from any desire to rebel by propaganda, or brainwashing, or brainwashing enhanced by pharmacological methods. And this seems to be the final revolution.[33]

With this context in mind, we can begin to see that the reason the modern West is unable to combat this strategic infiltration and destruction is due to its adoption of all the same presuppositions of the Enlightenment revolutionaries and Jacobins. As long as you have conflicting presuppositions and double-think at work in your worldview, it is only a matter of time before one begins to live more consistently with one of the two combating principles. In philosophy we call this coming to epistemological self-consciousness.

America especially, as a propositional, presupposed abstraction nation, is founded on this double-think of deistic rationalism and puritanical pietism. It is the Enlightenment *par excellence,* and only "works" so far as the assumptions of the Enlightenment are correct. But as a philosopher, it is my job to tell you the truth, and the ugly, red pill is that the presuppositions of the Enlightenment anthropology and statecraft are incorrect. Man is not a blank slate and the state is not an entity that the social contract speaks into existence. The entire history of statecraft and humanity attests to the opposite of the Enlightenment claims, yet this never dissuaded Locke, Rousseau or Jefferson from their deep commitment to faith in their dogmas.

The false faith in man's reason and scientific methodology must also be accompanied by a false faith in man and his own progress. This is not to say that man cannot use his reason to probe the atom or control the electromagnetic spectrum: He can and does. But why does he do this? In a universe desacralized and emptied of any divine telos, the only logical conclusion is the destruction of what is, and thus man's quest to dethrone God erupts into an orgiastic fanaticism to annihilate *prima materia.*[34]

The universe is mirrored in the atom, and so the atom must be divided, because the universe must be destroyed, and this is because man follows Satan, who is the adversary that divides. Satan is the thief that comes to steal, kill and destroy (John 10:10). To divide is to conquer, and man's quest to ritually sacrifice the atom like Abraham divided the carcasses (Gen. 15:10) is also much like Phaeton. Phaeton was the mortal son of Apollo. He hijacked and tried to drive his father's chariot to bring up the dawn one unfortunate morning, but couldn't control it and wreaked havoc on the Earth. It is a myth modern man should consider. In Plato's esoteric masterpiece *The Timaeus*, (circa 360 B.C.) Solon speaks of Phaeton: From Salk's technocratic *Man Unfolding*.

There have been, and will be again, many destructions of mankind arising out of many causes; the greatest have been brought about by the agencies of fire and water, and other lesser ones by innumerable other causes. There is a story that even you [Greeks] have preserved, that once upon a time, Phaeton, the son of Helios, having yoked the steeds in his father's chariot, because he was not able to drive them in the path of his father, burnt up all that was upon the earth, and was himself destroyed by a thunderbolt. Now this has the form of a myth, but really signifies a declination of the bodies moving in the heavens around the earth, and a great conflagration of things upon the earth, which recurs after long intervals."[35]

For seeking to drive his chariot into the sun, the earth was destroyed by fire and Phaeton by a thunderbolt. Modern man is Phaeton in his mad quest to grab the destructive fire of the sun in the atom, that great electromagnetic engine, and instead, unable to control his horses (passions), ends up destroyed by the very thing he sought to conquer. Even Oppenheimer stated this when he spoke of splitting the atom, calling himself "Shiva, the Destroyer of Worlds." The classics are full of such lessons of warning against the hubris of man, but like a toddler with a revolver, man's ingestion of a near infinite data stream of knowledge coupled with his lack of wisdom can only end in desolation and destruction, and this is Satan's great con in the Faustian bargain of technological obsession without wisdom. For all man's worship and enthronement of reason, why does he not reason thus – what is the point of existence, if there is no God? Having closed yourself off from the infinite, confining your existence to purely temporal, finite meaninglessness, why should there be any purpose to doing science at all, other than destruction?

Lacking this wisdom, thinking he can rewrite existence with an entirely fabricated overlay, modern man has destroyed all chance at wisdom because of his false governing presuppositions. Meaning can only be if it is grounded in the eternal and infinite. Without that objective unifying principle that can only be found in God, man's actions are all sound and fury signifying nothing. However, man refuses to look into that abyss from fear of its implications, and thus places fideistic* faith in "science" to give his life meaning, one day. It is no accident that modernity is also simultaneously on a quest for an entirely synthetic, virtual existence; yet another attempt at time-bound fallen man to escape his own death and meaninglessness through the creation of alternate worlds. But a synthetic virtual world of bits and bytes cannot solve his inner problems of the heart any more than blasting off to Alpha Centauri – and in those "worlds" man can only destroy. It is a lack of wisdom and a fetishizing of bare knowledge that characterizes our current modernity, and as foolish men pursue their own self-destruction in their devotion to "Goddess Reason," it is only by confronting Eternal Truth and Meaning that they will abandon their own self-destructive hubris.

This scientistic perspective, however, can take on nefarious aspects, wherein man comes to be viewed like a rat or monkey in a lab, ripe for experimentation. Fast-forward to the scandal of the SV 40 vaccine and Dr. Jonas Salk and Dr. Maurice Hilleman, and we have an "accident" in which the simian virus in the inoculations resulted in cancer. According to Edward T. Haslam in his *Dr. Mary's Monkey*, the totality of the Manhattan project was largely concerned with radiation, with the technology of inoculation having intimate connections to the military industrial establishment.

When we consider the central place of planetary bioengineering and biometrics (replacing the older "eugenics"), the new plan has morphed into dysgenics operations through covert soft kill methodologies. The SV 40 vaccine is believed by some to be, not a cure, but a covert experiment into the results of inoculation technology for population control.[36] While this may seem far-fetched to many, Dr. Jonas Salk himself wrote of the need for vast population reduction in his 1972 book *Man Unfolding* and the ability of the establishment to accomplish these goals through technocratic means. See the below video, where, in the CBC documentary, Dr. Hilleman openly admits the SV 40 infected the populace. According to the PolioForever blog archive concerning the SV 40, the citations are as follows:

> [T]his period, 1951-1953, is awfully convenient for the AEC and the Atomic Bomb Casualty Commission's hundred-year-surveillance recommendation, and just in time for experimental inclusion in polio vaccine. Along with the cancerous HeLa cells harvested

127

in February of 1951 at Johns Hopkins (funneled to Univ. Minnesota lab of Scherer and Syverton, under direction of Leo Szilard) which became viral seed-stock for the Salk IPV, the polyoma SV40 combination may have been the "right formula" for the vaccine, announced by Jonas Salk to his supervisors in 1952...[37]

Dr. Henry Seymour Kaplan, "together with Edward Ginzton, invented the first medical linear accelerator in the Western hemisphere while he worked at the Stanford University Medical Center of Stanford University, San Francisco. The six million volt machine was first used in 1955, six months after another model was first used in England."[38]

The particle accelerators were used to microwave the various cells, while results were catalogued to determine their biological warfare utility. Haslam writes:

> My conclusion is that this medical Manhattan project that was on the grounds of the U.S. Public Health Service hospital in New Orleans was using a linear particle accelerator for the purpose of mutation of...cancer-causing viruses, and the danger and ethical issues involved... is why they kept it so secret....
>
> There was another [covert] laboratory which was discovered ... by the investigative team working for [Jim] Garrison's investigation on the Kennedy assassination. This was an underground laboratory which was reportedly using cancer-causing viruses to create cancer and what is particularly disturbing about this laboratory is the location..[which] was in the hands of people who can easily be described as right-wing political extremists.[39]

It is important to recall that the majority of the doctors involved in these programs are committed eugenicists, or more properly, *dys*genicists, intent on the "scientific fact" that the masses must be destroyed, stunted, retarded, and re-engineered to either not exist or become an androgynous Morlock serf to the technocrats of the future. From the Malthusians of the Victorian era to the White House Science Czar John P. Holdren, whose *Ecoscience* dictates a picture more frightening than mere population control, the

THOMAS ROBERT MALTHUS (1766-1834): Anglican cleric, political economist and demographics analyst who claimed natural resources could not sustain his projected population growth. As a result, Malthus projected vast death and destruction, which never materialized. Despite these failed predictions, Malthusians and eugenicists to this day continue the doomsday proclamations that never manifest. Malthus' philosophy is the origin today's globalists who mandate the need for a massive reduction of the global population. As one aspect of the British Empire's mythology, Malthusianism was combined with social Darwinism to "justify" theories of genocide and enslavement.

endgame is the alchemical transformation of man into the new *aeon* of techno-man.

The belief of this cult is not really science, but esoteric philosophy that man can, by technology, transcend his bodily limitations and death, but only through the mass sacrifice of billions on the altar of "progress" and worship of death. The true plan is a complete rewrite of the entire genetic makeup of the planet, and the eventual integration of all inanimate life into the "web." This is why I have constantly written about the Internet as A.I. reconnaissance, with the singularity eventually giving rise to the transcendence of the limitations of our dimensions.

Geneticist David Suzuki has recently commented on this ultimate goal, noting that the entire planet appears to be part of the great "experiment":

> In gearing up for the 2010 release of its super-genetically modified corn called 'SmartStax', agricultural-biotechnology giant Monsanto is using an advertising slogan that asks, 'Wouldn't it be better?' But can we do better than nature, which has taken millennia to develop the plants we use for food?
>
> We don't really know. And that in itself is a problem. The corn, developed by Monsanto with Dow AgroSciences, "stacks" eight genetically engineered traits, six that allow it to ward off insects and two to make it resistant to weed-killing chemicals, many of which are also trademarked by Monsanto. It's the first time a genetically engineered (GE) product has been marketed with more than three traits.
>
> One problem is that we don't know the unintended consequences of genetically engineered or genetically modified (GM) foods. Scientists may share consensus about issues like human-caused global warming, but they don't have the same level of certainty about the effects of genetically modified organisms on environmental and human health![40]

The Manhattan Project involved several thousand participants, all compartmentalized in their knowledge of the grand plan, all of which was kept secret from the public for several years. Likewise, it is my thesis that the present grand experiment involves all the experimentation with the biosphere we are witnessing today with the goal of eradicating man as he presently exists. This is why we are now seeing mainstream articles about intelligence officials concerned over weaponized warfare. Recalling Dr. Edward Teller, we can see the connection of geo-engineering and Manhattan. *21st Century Wire* details this in a recent report as follows, citing the *Independent*:

These claims definitely provide cause for concern. How can an agency with such a shady history be let loose with such dangerous and destructive technology? Professor Alan Robock, a senior American climate scientist, said he was contacted three years ago by two men, who claimed to be from the CIA.

They asked if it would be possible to know if another country was manipulating American weather patterns, from which Robock deduced that they actually wished to know if it would be possible for another country to figure out it was being done to them... A senior American climate scientist has spoken of the fear he experienced when US intelligence services apparently asked him about the possibility of weaponising the weather as a major report on geo-engineering is to be published this week.

During a debate on the use of geo-engineering to combat climate change, at the annual meeting of the American Association for the Advancement of Science in San Jose, California, Prof Robock said: "I got a phone call from two men who said we work as consultants for the CIA and we'd like to know if some other country was controlling our climate, would we know about it...?[41]

In the last few years, the rollout of the tech/A.I. takeover also provides evidence of my hypothesis, as robots will begin to replace workers across the manufacturing and service sectors. As Ray Kurzweil has glowingly predicted, we will begin to see the A.I./nanotech invasion in the next ten-twenty years, with nanotech re-engineering mankind into just the synthetic android existence I have been discussing. Intelligence officials, for example, project a "very transhumanist future"[42] in the next few decades, and DARPA is presently perfecting the Matrix-style modem, where Internet access will link directly with the brain.[43]

RAY KURZWEIL: American author, scientist and futurist. Kurzweil is most known for being the face of transhumanism. Kurzweil's popular books posit the "singularity," that the rapid advance in computer technology is exponential, leading to the coming era of supercomputers that will surpass the human mind and its processes. For Kurzweil this signifies a new stage of "evolution" where mankind is destined to achieve various forms of fusion with technology, resulting in the eventual emergence of immortality. For many transhumanists, technological advance represents a new form of religious promise where man might transcend the limitations of time and death.

In the Kurzweil documentary, *Transcendent Man,* all the alchemical goals mentioned above, as well as the recent reports of DNA laser printers also associated with Kurzweil, demonstrate the various broad spectrum programs of the technocracy were not accidental, but clearly covert fronts for the deeper plan of bringing about the "Great Work" of the end of man, and the rise of the New Man of intergalactic synthetic Borg dystopia.[44] "No man is an island," but the new world will be one in which every man is an island of Dr. Moreau. The technocratic "alien" Overlords, it seems, are very much human, as opposed to other-worldly, but have the stated intention of making men into robots, and robots into men.

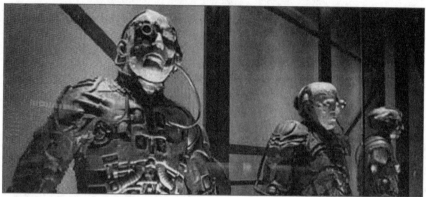

Resistance is futile!

Endnotes

1. Steinberg, Jeffrey. Jeffrey. "From Cybernetics to Littleton: Techniques in Mind Control." Schiller Institute. April, 2000. Web. http://www.schillerinstitute.org/new_viol/cybmindcontrol_js0400..html

2. Bernays, Edward. *Propaganda*. Brooklyn: IG Publishing, 1955, pg. 166.

3. Krauss, Lawrence, cited in Spaulding, Daniel. "Revolt of the Star Children" Soul of the East. 11 September, 2015. Web. http://souloftheeast.org/2015/09/11/scientism-materialism-atheism/

4. Russell, Bertrand. *The Impact of Science on Society*. New York: AMS Press, 1953, pg. 51.

5. Dyer, Jay. "Plato, Crystals, Dimensions and Artificial Intelligence." JaysAnalysis. 18 November 2014. Web. http://jaysanalysis.com/2014/11/18/plato-crystals-dimensions-and-artificial-intelligence/

6. Pike, *Morals and Dogma*, 8, 728, and *Book of Words*.

7. Ibid.

8. Wells, H.G. *The Time Machine*. New York, Penguin Books, 199?, pgs. 28-31.

9. Ibid.

10. Huxley, Aldous. *Brave New World*. New York: Harper Brothers, 1932, pgs. 225-6.

11. Burckhardt, Titus. "Cosmology and Modern Science" in *Sword of Gnosis: Metaphysics, Cosmology, Tradition, Symbolism*, London: Penguin Books, 1974, pg. 137.

12. Lomas, Robert. *Freemasonry and the Birth of Modern Science*. Massachusetts: Fair Winds Press, 2003.

13. Farahany, Anita. "Introduction," in Wells, H.G., *The Island of Dr. Moreau*. New York: Penguin, 2014, pp. 11-17.

14. "21 U.S. Code 321. Definitions." Cornell University Law Code. Web. https://www.law.cornell.edu/uscode/text/21/321

15. Dyer, Jay. "The Ghost in the Machine and Mass Mind Control." JaysAnalysis. 30 May, 2015. Web.

http://jaysanalysis.com/2015/05/30/the-ghost-in-the-machine-and-mass-mind-control/

16. Dr. Holgar Hyden, *Control of the Mind Symposium*, pg. 334.

17. Ibid.

18. Marks, *CIA and Mind Control*.

19. Ibid.

20. Haslam, Edward T. *Dr. Mary's Monkey*. Oregon: Trine Day, 2007, pp. 26, 31. "SV40 Monkey Virus." Polio Forever Blog. Web. https://polioforever.wordpress.com/sv40-monkey-virus/

21. Epstein, Emily Anne. "Revealed: Army Scientists Secretly Sprayed St. Louis with 'Radioactive' Particles for Years to Test Chemical Warfare Technology." 29 September 2012. Web. http://www.dailymail.co.uk/news/article-2210415/Revealed-Army-scientists-secretly-sprayed-St-Louis-radioactive-particles-YEARS-test-chemical-warfare-technology.html

22. "Test Tube Babies." PBS' American Experience. Web. http://www.pbs.org/wgbh/americanexperience/features/introduction/babies-introduction/. Eley, Adam. "How has IVF Developed Since the First Test Tube Baby." BBC. 23 July, 2015. Web. http://www.bbc.com/news/health-33599353

23. Bielo, David. "What is Geoengineering and Why is it Considered a Climate Change Solution?" *Scientific American*. 6 April, 2010. Web. http://www.scientificamerican.com/article/geoengineering-and-climate-change/. Smith, Jerry. Weather Warfare: The Military's Plan to Draft Mother Nature. Kempton, IL: Adventures Unlimited Press, 2006, pgs. 274-5.

24. "The Years of Atmospheric Testing: 1945-1963." Trinity Atomic Website Archive. Web. http://www.abomb1.org/atmosphr/index.html

25. Hoffman, *Secret Societies*, 49.

26. Ibid. 80.

27. Ibid. 204.

28. Kant, Immanuel. *Prolegomena to Any Future Metaphysics*. London: Routledge, 1996.

29. Habermas, Jurgen. *Theory and Practice*. Cambridge: Polity Press, 2007.

30. Huxley, Aldous. "Introduction." *Brave New World*, Ibid.

31. Steinberg, Jeffrey. "From Cybernetics to Littleton: Techniques in Mind Control." Schiller Institute. April, 2000. Web. http://www.schillerinstitute.org/new_viol/cybmindcontrol_js0400..html

32. Russell, *Impact of Science on Society*, 30.

33. Steinberg, "From Cybernetics to Littleton," Ibid.

34. Hoffman, *Secret Societies*, 80.

35. Plato, *Collected Dialogues*, 1157.

36. Adams, Mike. "Dr. Jonas Salk, inventor of polio vaccine, exposed as criminal-minded scientist who conducted illicit medical experiments on mental patients." 2 March, 2011. Web. http://www.naturalnews.com/031564_Jonas_Salk_medical_experiments.html#ixzz44on06ahd

37. Steinberg, Ibid.

38. Ibid.

39. Haslam, Ed, *Dr. Mary's Monkey*.

40. Suzuki, David. "More Science Needed on Effects of Genetically Modified Food." David Suzuki Foundation. 23 September, 2009. Web. http://davidsuzuki.org/blogs/science-matters/2009/09/more-science-needed-on-effects-of-genetically-modifying-food-crops/

41. Hooper, Stuart. "WEATHER WEAPONS: CIA Funding Geo-Engineering to Weaponize Weather." 21stCenturyWire. 15 February, 2015. Web. http://21stcenturywire.com/2015/02/15/weather-weapons-cia-funding-geo-engineering-to-weaponize-weather/

42. Dvorsky, George. "U.S. Spy Agency Predicts 'Very Transhumanist' Future by 2030." Io9.com. 12

132

December, 2012. Web. http://io9.gizmodo.com/5967896/us-spy-agency-predicts-a-very-transhu-man-future-by-2030

43. Rothman, Peter. "Biology is Technology — DARPA is Back in the Game With A Big Vision and It Is H+." H+Magazine. 15 February, 2015. Web. http://hplusmagazine.com/2015/02/15/biology-tech-nology-darpa-back-game-big-vision-h/

44. Harris, Kristan. "DNA Laser Printer, Prints Life." Rundown Live. 16 January 2015. Web. http://therundownlive.com/dna-laser-printer-prints-life/

Chapter 6

E.T. The Extra-Terrestrial – An Esoteric Analysis (1982)

Original film poster of *E.T.* in which the "alien" takes the place of Michelangelo's God and touches the child with extra-terrestrial knowledge.

As we begin to explore the Spielberg world, it's necessary to start with one of the most popular films of all time, the children's fantasy classic *E.T.* While *Close Encounters* is earlier and is certainly loaded with esoteric and conspiratorial clues and messages, *E.T.* has its unique emphasis, providing the youth of the 1980s with a new approach to the issue of our beloved space brothers. If you've watched Spielberg films (who hasn't?), you almost intuitively know he was instrumental in altering public opinion on the idea of the existence of otherworldly extra-terrestrials. Recent polls claim half of Americans now believe there likely exists life on other planets.[1] I wasn't able to turn up any analyses of the shifting trend of belief in aliens over time, which would have been interesting from a psy-ops perspective, but my confident assumption is that following the 1940s and 50s science fiction explosion in Hollywood and the fabled Roswell and Area 51 incidents, average Joe was becoming more and more accepting of the notion. From my research, the alien mythos is a completely manufactured psy-op phenomena, used for several purposes, including as a cover for drug running, secret technology, and in the long run as a possible scenario for mass manipulation. The "MJ 12" scientists were precisely the ones who concocted the new alien mythos,[2] so it's important to place the Orson Welles *War of the Worlds* broadcast/social engineering psy-op that fits into the scientistic narrative covered in the last chapter, combined with the explosion of Hollywood alien scenarios still ongoing, and the continued modern obsession in these contexts.

Thus Hollywood has contributed immensely to the "Overton Window" manipulation of public opinion, particularly on big metaphysical issues of this nature. If the new mythos of "aliens" could be injected into the mass consciousness on a large-scale, an entirely new narrative for civilizations could be erected. As opposed to more traditional western beliefs, the new alien origins *mythos* is supposedly amenable to "science," which is why scientific gurus like Dawkins, Sagan and Hawking all promote the "alien" mythos. Why, given the supposed commitments to "rationalism" and atheism, would they often advance and promote the ridiculous, never-proven alien theories and panspermia*? They do it precisely because they are part of the propaganda complex. Somehow theism is irrational, but alien origins are rational. These pop gurus are promoted by the establishment, precisely to fulfill a role as "scientific gatekeepers."

Book on the psy-ops of mass panic from the Orson Welles radio fiasco.

The thinking behind this from a psychological warfare perspective is as follows: As new generations grow tired of traditional, collapsing forms of Catholicism, Protestantism and evangelicalism, the tide could be turned towards a new faith – one of galactic space brothers possessing highly advanced technology through secret science. All of this is pure pseudo-scientific baloney, yet the ability to program mass populations to believe entirely false ideologies is the very nature of all historic statecraft.[3] In reality, the alien psy-op is actually a cleverly crafted intelligence program that functions as a cover. Just like other forms of propaganda and social engineering, the "alien mythos" has also had billions of dollars in funding intended to prop up this cover that functions mainly as a distraction for less intelligent mass audiences. Contrary to many claims of skeptics, the Welles fiasco was a Rockefeller-funded psychological operation through Princeton:

ORSON WELLES (1915-1985): American actor, directc and film producer. Welles is generally classed wit eminent figures like Hitchcock and Kubrick as one c the greatest directors of all time, with his *Citizen Kar* (1941) often ranked by critics and film scholars as th greatest film of all time. Welles also participated in Rockefeller-funded psychological operation know as the infamous 1938 *War of the Worlds* broadcas Welles broadcast H.G. Wells' famous novel on a radi drama resulted in mass chaos and panic, as the publ assumed the account was real. This incident is a crucia early example of the nexus between the shadow go\ ernment, the academic establishment and Hollywoo

Aware of the Dartmouth connection, Marshall encouraged the enterprising Cantril to apply to the Foundation for support. Cantril's request resulted in a $67,000 grant for a two-year charter of the "Princeton Radio Project" (PRP) at Princeton University. There Cantril proceeded to develop studies assessing radio's effects on audiences. In 1938 Cantril also became a founding editor of the Rockefeller Foundation-funded *Public Opinion Quarterly*, an organ closely associated with US government's psychological warfare endeavors following World War Two.

When the Princeton venture commenced another trained psychologist close to Rockefeller, CBS Director of Research Frank Stanton, was named PRP lead researcher but took a secondary role of Associate Director due to his position at the broadcast network. At this time Austrian émigré social scientist Paul Lazarsfeld was recruited to join Cantril. Thus Cantril, Stanton, and Lazarsfeld were closely affiliated and ideally positioned to embark on a major study involving public opinion and persuasion.

The opportunity for such an analysis presented itself when CBS broadcast Orson Welles' rendering of H.G. Wells' *War of the Worlds* on October 30, 1938. Lazarsfeld saw the event as especially noteworthy and immediately asked Stanton for CBS funds to investigate reaction to what at the time was the largest immediate act of mass persuasion in human history. Over the next several months interviews with *War of the Worlds* listeners were collected, provided to Stanton at CBS, and subsequently analyzed in Cantril's 1940 study, *The Invasion From Mars: A Study in the Psychology of Panic.*[4]

136

It is with this basic background in mind that we must approach *E.T.*, situated as it was in the mid 80s, when alien furor was going strong from earlier hits like *Close Encounters*, *Star Wars*, and other science fiction works. With *Close Encounters* and *E.T.* Spielberg takes a turn from the alien norm, presenting audiences with "good" space buddies. Instead of barreling through space to annihilate the planet, our space neighbors abduct people (and children!) from the populace because they're "elect" (*Close Encounters*) and make contact with others because they, too, are "special" (Elliot in *E.T.*). For my analysis, it is crucial to keep *Close Encounters* in mind during the following chapter, since I believe they are relatively connected, in a loose way. In the Spielberg 70s-80s universe, these other-worldly entities are shown to have been making contact for decades, yet their motives remain obscure. In *Close Encounters* analysis, the deeper meaning of the film centers

STEVEN SPIELBERG: American director, producer, and screenwriter. Spielberg has created some of the most successful, recognizable films of modern memory, including *Jaws, E.T.*, the Indiana Jones series, and later award-winning films, like *Schindler's List*. Spielberg's talents are undeniable, as he is often ranked as one of the great directors with figures like Hitchcock, Kubrick and Welles. In terms of themes, Spielberg's films often center on civil rights and interpersonal and familial reconciliation, while simultaneously being a prime figure in the promotion of the alien mythos. Nowadays, Spielberg is known as one of the most powerful men in Hollywood, being the highest grossing director of all time due to his films earning 9 billion dollars globally.

around semiotics: the philosophy of signs, communication, symbols and language. Semiotics is also the theme of *E.T.*, though with *E.T.* the imagery is intended to evoke the subconscious of the youth. *Close Encounters* is an adult's story, while *E.T.* is for children, and both films focus heavily on semiotics and involve complex usages of synchronicity, foreshadowing and occult symbology.

Keeping an open mind on the subject of "aliens," I have read enough on the matter to say that the evidence points overwhelmingly, in almost all cases, to so-called alien encounters being humanly-manufactured and/or government-related psy-ops. In saying that, I do not consider it impossible to hold to the view of Jim Keith or Jacques Vallee that there may be demonic entities related to this subject, yet most cases involve little to no supernatural elements. It is with this presupposition I approach the artistic portrayal of aliens on film, which are more akin to propaganda. I have viewed *E.T.* several times, and the more one reviews the film, the more hidden elements emerge. In my view, *E.T.* is a youthful version of *Close Encounters*, intent on melding a clever use of symbology with occult imagery for the purpose of effecting a change in the mass *psyche* as regards the existence and nature of aliens, or "interdimensional entities," or "daemons."

JIM KEITH (1949-1999): American conspiracy and deep politics researcher and writer most known for his books on secret societies, mind control, and the shadow government. Keith posited a view of "The Octopus," a secret network of global, oligarchical interests connected to the death of journalist Danny Casolaro (according to Keith). Keith also met an untimely demise many consider foul play.

HEAVEN'S GATE: US-based UFO religion founded in the 1970s by Marshall Applewhite that made headlines in 1997 when Applewhite and dozens of members reportedly committed mass suicide in the belief they would be raptured by an alien mothership that accompanied the Hale-bopp Comet. Heaven's Gate, in many ways similar to Scientology, was a bizarre blend of theosophy and biblical, millennial apocalypticism that some researchers have connected to the FBI and the deep state, with the implication the group functioned as a mind control operation.

THEOSOPHY: An esoteric philosophical school promoting the notion of direct knowledge of the mysteries of God and nature founded in 1875 in New York City by Helena Blavatsky, Henry Judge and Henry Steel Olcott. Theosophy is a syncretistic belief based in comparative religion that claims to promote a "Universal Brotherhood of Man" through the study of the latent powers within man himself and the unexplained laws of nature.

In the cases of so-called abductions and encounters of the "third kind," the stories often reveal similar patterns and themes. Abductees are told they are a "special" elect and experience symptoms that often sound the same as those who have unfortunately undergone ritual abuse.[5] Kidnapping, experimentation, drugging, lost time, multiple personalities, sexual abuse and "probing," bizarre costumes and scars, occult and odd religious ceremonies, etc., all characterize the accounts of both the ritually abused and "alien" abducted. Though almost no one discusses this but authors like Jim Keith, it should be obvious to those in criminology that there might be a connection.[6] This is my own speculation, but I don't think it's a coincidence that the two are so similar. Several real examples of UFO cults also provide ample evidence, since often these cults combine the two openly. Consider, for example, the Heaven's Gate cult whose leader Marshall Applewhite, famously had odd occult and shadow government associations,[7] or L. Ron Hubbard's elaborate and ridiculous alien mythology in Scientology. Both Applewhite and Hubbard had military connections and interests in Blavatsky and theosophy, while Hubbard was even for a time a devotee of Aleister Crowley.[8] With both of these characters, we see examples of men who associated ritual occultism and "alien" agendas. The alien mythos and ritual magic was also a theme in *2001: A Space Odyssey*, if it may be recalled.

With these examples in mind, let us consider *E.T.* An initial clue that we are dealing with a film about semiotics and meaning is contained in the letters "E" and "T," and in the name of the main protagonist, Elliot. Elliot's name begins and ends with E and T, foreshadowing the mystical connection the two will share. This will be important later when we consider *what*, exactly E.T. is. E.T. arrives in a globe-shaped craft as part of a scientific expedition to collect plant specimens, and is accidentally left behind. Childlike, E.T. is surrounded by flora and fauna, associating him with nature, while simultaneously avoiding the *adult* government agents who are tracking him.[9]

E.T. thus evokes the primal and natural, in contrast to the urban and suburban life of the nearby generic California city. E.T. has a spiritual connection to nature, while men are alienated from it in their consumer-driven city life. This will be evident later in the film, but is a very obvious theme in several Spielberg films of the 80s. *E.T.*, left behind, is *alienated*, like his mystical human connect, Elliot. In classical Marxist theory, alienation is the angst man feels as a result of his urban lifestyle that is a result of the economic modality of consumer-driven capitalism.[10] In the DVD commentary, Spielberg and avowed Marxist actor, Peter Coyote, even speak of *E.T.* as an attempt at a kind of cultural Marxism,[11] since E.T. represents alienation and the transcendence of all boundaries of culture and class. However, I, as a vehement critic of Marxism, would add that these two contentions are correct: Man does experience alienation as a result of consumer-driven mass capitalism and urbanization.

The first planet we're shown is Jupiter, figuring prominently in Kubrick's *2001*, where man encounters the alien monolith.

139

As the action shifts to the single parent household of Elliot (his mother is named Mary, with obvious religious significance), we notice that Elliot isn't allowed in the D&D game: as the alienated runt he's relegated to fetching pizza and looking on. Already the connection with E.T. is evident, yet on a deeper esoteric level the viewer is given initial signs of what is to come. Two planets are shown in the D&D scene: Jupiter and Saturn, two central planets in classical mythology, but I noticed in my last viewing that in the progression of the film, we are actually shown each of the planets through Kubrick-esque imagery with the circular lamp channeling Dr. Strangelove. Spielberg will actually make numerous interesting symbolic references to Kubrick, while later collaborating and altering Kubrick's plans for the *A.I.* script. From an esoteric perspective, this is important because of the deep, symbolic nature of Kubrick's occult films, particularly *2001* and *The Shining*, as we saw. Spielberg will reference these in a cryptic way.

Note the Saturn image on the game box.

While I don't think Dungeons & Dragons is a big deal, it could be a use of irony that as the young guys are discussing ritual magic in the context of the game, they accidentally "invoke" E.T. D&D did have a reputation in the 80s of being an "occult" game that involved some kids in forbidden practices, so it is possible this was in Spielberg's mind as a jab, playing on 80s fundamentalist fears. Regardless, after the presentation of Jupiter and Saturn, Elliot meets his space-brother, E.T. It is also significant that Peter Coyote plays the shadow government researcher named "Keys." We are not told anything more concerning him, but when he appears, we prominently see Keys with his keys jingling on his belt – a use of intertextual synchronicity, with the character signifying not only an aspect of his person. It is also, on an esoteric level, a reference to the *Key of Solomon*, a famous text of ritual magic that purported to be the method by which King Solomon was able to control spirits and demons, both good and evil. Is Spielberg hinting that the "key" to interpreting the film is understanding such esoteric references? Michael Hoffman and James Shelby Downard posit:

James Shelby Downard (1913-1998): American author and conspiracy researcher whose works focused on Masonic theories and subterfuge that, at times, bordered on dark satire. Downard is well known for his publication with Michael A. Hoffman of the "King/Kill 33" theory of the JFK assassination. This theory argues for a ritualistic-symbolic association behind the event, where locations, numbers and names take on the significance of "twilight language" and "mystical toponymy," revealing deeper meanings behind the event.

> A "keystone" is the designation for which, when set in place, "keys" or locks the whole. A symbolic keystone is vital to the legend of the Masonic Royal Arch Degree of York. The earliest known record of such a degree is in the annals of the city of Fredericksburg, Virginia, on December 22, 1753. Fredericksburg is also the location of the "House of the Rising Sun," a masonic meeting place for such notables as founding fathers George Washington and Benjamin Franklin (of Hell-Fire Club fame) and George Mason.[12]

Magical emblem from the so-called "Key of Solomon"

Spielberg's *Close Encounters* and *Raiders of the Lost Ark* both demonstrate the mystical, esoteric side of Judaism, and *E.T.* is no different.[13] It is also significant that it is under the moon that Elliot first encounters E.T. The moon has an important role in mythology as regulating the female ovulatory cycle, and thus being associated with the feminine. In astrology, the moon has a direct influence on human actions, and here as a possible "moonchild," Elliot encounters what will be his familiar.[14] My contention is E.T. is more like a "familiar" spirit

Hellfire Club: A name for numerous high society, private clubs in Britain and Ireland in the 18th century that met in underground caves and catacombs. Believed to originate from Sir Francis Dashwood, the clubs reportedly involved politicians and lords engaged in ritualistic orgies and mock religious ceremonies. Prominent Freemasons were also members of the clubs, including the Duke of Wharton and Benjamin Franklin.

141

than an "alien." In classical descriptions of the familiar, the spirit can be associated with an animal.[15] Is Elliot a kind of "Moonchild," referencing the Crowleyan mythology of a demonic insemination?[16] Elliot is spoken of as "chosen," and through E.T., will have magical powers: The symbolic meaning of the moon with Elliot and E.T. signifies Elliot as a magus.

Elliot seems to have all the powers of a male witch. Is he a "moonchild"?

As we will see with *Close Encounters*, E.T. arrives on the "high place," the traditional arrival spot of the gods in the biblical historical books, and Israel's God, Mt. Sinai. Elliot ascends to the "high places" to aid E.T., as Roy will do in *Close Encounters*. Initially, there is a waxing moon that later becomes a full moon. The season is important. By the time of Elliot's full union with E.T., it is Halloween, which portends the Winter solstice. Halloween is also the ancient druidic festival of Samhain, an important time in the pagan and occult ritual calendar.[17] Given what I have argued, I don't think it's accidental Halloween was chosen as the setting, as Samhain is the night when the gates and doors to the "otherworld" are opened, and the spirits of the dead enter our realm.[18] This is precisely the point of the *Key of Solomon*, as noted earlier.[19] While a theme of the demonic invasion of America may seem out of place, that is precisely the theme of *Poltergeist*, *Gremlins* and *Gremlins 2*.

When E.T. and Elliot meet, an odd conversation about words, language and simulacra erupts. Elliot confusedly explains, "This is a coke [a fake spilled Coke].... These are men, they can have wars.... Fish eat fish food, sharks eat fish.... This is a peanut.... You can't eat this peanut, you put your money in it." The significance is that due to Elliot's young mind there is no separation of concept, thing, and symbol. Elliot has to stop and explain to E.T. how a porcelain peanut piggy bank is a bank, but is not a real peanut. The Coke is not a real Coke, etc. This is semiotics and simulacra at work. As we will see in the *Close Encounters* analysis, uses of simulacra are also common in Kubrick films, such as the model maze in *The Shining*, which transforms into the actual maze in Jack's perception. The model becomes the reality.

Simulacra is important to semiotics, and has an important role in esoterism because of the idea of correspondences. Before modern philosophy divorced metaphysics from academia, the holistic view of the sciences in the western tradition included an idea of *essentialism*, which connected the "essences" of things with all their referents and symbols. Thus, there would be an association between the symbol of the maze, the model, and its referent, the actual maze. This is a deep, difficult subject that touches on a heap of heavy philosophy, but the idea is simply foreign to most moderns because of, yes, "stupid" philosophy. Thus, Plato discussed simulacra in *Sophist*, while modern philosopher Jean Baudrillard devotes an entire book to the subject, *Simulacra and Simulation*, where he cites numerous examples of news media taking on the character of a Hollywood disaster film.[20] Hollywood, just like occult magickal practices, or like the act of writing itself, *is* the manipulation of copies, signs and symbols. As mentioned, *E.T.* is about symbols, language and meaning (like *Close Encounters*), and the viewer is constantly shown camera angles and shots from a child's perspective. The cross-reference to *Star Wars* is also interesting, given the collaborations of George Lucas with Spielberg on the *Indiana Jones* franchise, which features Jewish mysticism.

"This is Greedo."

143

As E.T. showcases his abilities, we see that he can make objects levitate, and when Elliot asks where he's from, E.T. causes small Play-Doh versions of the planets to orbit.

E.T. can levitate.

Continuing with the planet sequence, we see Mars, Mercury and Uranus now, and possibly Pluto, with the sun in the center. Another element not yet mentioned is the transition to puberty. E.T. tells the kids he has come from outer space, prompting Gertie to call him the "man from the moon," which will be relevant momentarily.

The Venus Star. The goddess of sex.

Elliot, at the verge of puberty, has not yet kissed a girl, but when E.T. gets drunk (causing Elliot to be drunk), Elliot kicks off the "free the frogs" revolution in his biology class, leading to his cinematic kissing of the cute blonde, which, synchronistically, matches the film E.T. is watching on television. While admittedly the target audience is Elliot's age, as we will see later with the Jim Henson/Lucas *Labyrinth*, the odd reference to the transition of puberty involves the tutelage of a spirit (there, Bowie leads young Sarah into puberty, while here, a reptilian leads Elliot). E.T. causes Elliot to awaken in this psychosexual way. While this occurs in the classroom, the camera shows Voyager, Jupiter and Io. Voyager was purportedly the mission that sent probes to Jupiter and Saturn in the late 70s, as a result of the work of the JPL in California. This again brings to mind Crowley, since Jack Whiteside Parsons was one of the founders of the JPL and a devotee of Crowley.[21] The use of Io is also relevant, since Io was a virgin lunar deity.

Voyager, Jupiter, Io.

Indeed, when Elliot both meets and parts with him, E.T. touches Elliot's "third eye," which in Hindu Tantric sex practice signifies the spiritual eye that is awakened through the Kundalini serpent power that is purportedly coiled at the base of the spine, eventually welling up to reach the third eye for "enlightenment."[22] It is also directly connected to sexual potency and energy.[23] You'll also notice that Venus was not left out, but referenced in the closet, with the clear imagery of the star of Venus, the eight-sided star. We also discover E.T. is reptilian due to his magically causing Elliot to free the frogs due to his (Elliot's) sympathy for E.T. This is why E.T. can breathe underwater, resembling a cross between a frog and a retarded turtle.

145

Trumpy, you can awaken Kundalini stuff!

Further evidence E.T. is a familiar spirit is due to his reptilian "light" hearkening to biblical imagery from Genesis, with the serpent, as well as later New Testament texts where Paul describes the devil as a deceptive "being of light." In Hinduism, the Kundalini energy mentioned earlier is the shining serpent energy, again evoking similar themes. In fact, E.T. even "dies," but grants Elliot the power of resurrection, since Elliot's love causes E.T.'s heart to beat again. Indeed, in the DVD commentary, Drew Barrymore makes a bizarre comment that E.T. was like a "guardian angel for them," insisting that he was "almost real." One of the most odd scenes surrounds the arrival of the government agents who have been surveilling Elliot's house and discover he's harboring the cosmic visitor. When they arrive, they don't don Hazmat suits, but arrive as Apollo Mission astronauts.

Apollo astronauts?

146

This is one of the more interesting aspects of the film, as the question arises, why these suits? Following this scene, the doctors and scientists switch to Hazmat suits with no trace of anything like this again. There are several possibilities, but my thesis is this is another reference to Kubrick and *2001*. Just as we have seen planets evoked, particularly planets related to *2001: A Space Odyssey*, where Bowman encounters the monolith of the alien/gods, so here the "man from the moon" has come down, with Apollo astronauts suddenly appearing, a subconscious association made on the part of the audience. Whatever one's view of the Space Program and the moon landing, there is evidence that trickery and deception were involved, as well as the use of Disney sound stages for some shots.[24] In fact, it is undeniable that Kubrick worked with NASA in some capacity, as we saw. While the references to Crowley might seem strained, recall that Crowley claimed he communicated with a "spirit" that has famously been identified as an early image of what would become the modern archetype for the "alien," and like E.T., was a practitioner of sexual Tantrism. Crowley, Kubrick, Clarke and Spielberg all promote the alien Overlord mythos, it should be added.

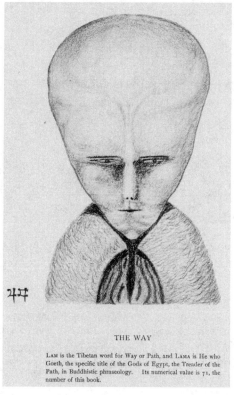

THE WAY

Lam is the Tibetan word for Way or Path, and Lama is He who Goeth, the specific title of the Gods of Egypt, the Treader of the Path, in Buddhistic phraseology. Its numerical value is 71, the number of this book.

Crowley's "Lam"

The perennial rehashing of the alien meme refers back to the power of the simulated image. Hollywood is the most powerful propaganda complex in history, according to Bernays. Kubrick had taken that potential to a new level with his technical innovations and cinematic special effects that wowed the military-industrial complex. Spielberg is paying homage to what Kubrick had done and decided to take the same techniques of using simulacra to make "movie magic" even more effective. As such, *E.T.* was wildly successful at implanting the alien mythos in the *psyche* of a generation. On a film and script level, it is a cinematic masterpiece, but is Spielberg telling us much more about what is going on in the background behind big events? I think so, and *Close Encounters* will back up this claim in the following chapter. It thus becomes clearer why men like Arthur C. Clarke promote the inane alien myth, while supposedly being rationalist atheists.[25]

Kubrick with Illuminist/NASA man Arthur C. Clarke and NASA Administrator George Mueller.

Endnotes

1. Swanson, Emily. "Alien Poll Finds Half of Americans Think Extraterrestrial Life Exists." Huffington Post. 21 June 2013. Web. http://www.huffingtonpost.com/2013/06/21/alien-poll_n_3473852.html

2. Paul and Phillip Collins. "MJ 12: The Technocratic Thread." ConspiracyArchive. 19 June, 2014. Web. http://www.conspiracyarchive.com/2014/06/19/mj-12-the-technocratic-thread/. "Alien Smokescreen." ConspiracyArchive. 17 June, 2007. Web. http://www.conspiracyarchive.com/2014/09/21/alien-smokescreen/

3. Tracy, James. "Early "Psychological Warfare" Research and the Rockefeller Foundation." Global-

Research. 29 April, 2012. Web. http://www.globalresearch.ca/early-psychological-warfare-research-and-the-rockefeller-foundation/30594

4. Ibid.

5. Catani, Enrico. "Test Companion to Education and Psychology." *Education and Psychology*. University of Michigan: May, 2008, pg. 30.

6. Keith, Jim. *Saucers of the Illuminati*. Kempton, IL: Adventures Unlimited Press, 2004.

7. Rutkowski, Chris. *Abductions and Aliens: What's Really Going On?* Toronto: Dundurn Group, 1999, pg. 227.

8. Lewis, James R. *Scientology*. Oxford University Press, 2009, pgs. 20, 59.

9. Ebert, Roger. *The Great Movies*. New York: Broadway Books, 2002, pgs 164-66.

10. Marx, Karl. Karl Marx: *Selected Writings*. Ed. Dave McLellan. Oxford University Press, 2000, pg. 91.

11. Coyote, Peter cited in "Where the Counterculture Prevails." ForaTv lecture on YouTube. 28 August, 2009. Web. https://www.youtube.com/watch?v=zV3qLXhmSLQ

12. Hoffman, Michael and James Shelby Downard. King-Kill 33. Whale.to. Web. http://www.whale.to/b/kingkill_33.html#Mystical_Toponomy_

13. See Scholem, Gershom. *Origins of the Kabbalah*. Princeton University Press, 1990.

14. Eliade, Mircea. *Shamanism: Archaic Techniques of Ecstasy*. Princeton University Press, 2004, pg. 72.

15. Ibid.

16. Crowley, Aleister. *Moonchild*. MA: Weiser Books, 1970.

17. "Equinozes and Solstices," Archaeostronomy. 2016. Web. http://www.archaeoastronomy.com/seasons.html

18. Frazer, Sir James. *The Golden Bough*. Oxford: Oxford University Press, 2009, 721-27.

19. See Mathers, Samuel L. MacGregor, Ed. *The Keys of Solomon the King*. MA: Weiser Books, 2000.

20. Baudrillard, Jean. *Simulacra and Simulation*. University of Michigan Press, 2006, pg. 40.

21. Hoffman, *Secret Societies*, pg. 201-10.

22. Evola, Julius. *Eros and the Mysteries of Love,* pgs. 221-2.

23. Ibid.

24. McGowan, Dave. "Wagging the Moondoggie." ChecktheEvidence. 2009. Web. http://www.checktheevidence.com/pdf/Dave%20McGowan%20-%20Wagging%20The%20Moon%20Doggie.pdf

25. Arthur C. Clarke cited in "2001 A Space Odyssey Interview with Arthur C. Clarke." Youtube. 30 July 2009. Web. https://www.youtube.com/watch?v=HEEtfhxLQbw&w=420&h=315]

Chapter 7

Close Encounters of the Third Kind (1977)

This awe-inspiring film is one of the most dazzling UFO science fiction films ever made, although it has pre-digital special effects. Douglas Trumbell's visual and special effects of the Mother Ship are spectacular, ushering in – with Lucas' Star Wars (1977) of the same year – a flood of Hollywood films featuring special effects. It was Columbia Pictures' biggest grossing film up to that time, and helped to usher in the era of the blockbuster sci-fi/fantasy film. The screenplay (finished by Spielberg from an original script by Paul Schrader) was based upon the book, The UFO Experience (1972), written by Dr. J. Allen Hynek, who served as the film's technical advisor (and appeared in a bit cameo part during the final scene).

–FilmSite

S pielberg is, in several senses, a master, and not least of all, a master of propaganda. His 80s films constitute the very essence of what it was to grow up as a child of the 80s, like myself. Those of us who have a keen sense for that 80s "feel" – a decade when it seemed simpler, and those who grew up in that time will feel the nostalgia. Reagan was a "good guy" leading the "free" West against a godless empire of commies and atheists, while yuppies could found businesses and snort coke, as Jacko burned his curls at Pepsi-funded mega-concerts. In the midst of this pop culture was a series of Spielberg and Lucas films, from *Star Wars* (late70s) to *E.T.* to *Indiana Jones* to *Back to the Future*; that made the 80s even more enjoyable. We looked at *E.T.*, but the emerging alien mythos was primed earlier in a pivotal sense in the late 70s gateway to the 80s that was *Close Encounters of the Third Kind* (1977).

One crucial element in both *E.T.* and *Close Encounters* is a deeper esoteric theme that has been over-

GEORGE LUCAS: Award-winning American filmmaker, producer and entrepreneur, and creator of the Star Wars and Indiana Jones franchises. Lucas recently sold his Lucasfilm to the Walt Disney Company in 2012 for 4 billion dollars. Interestingly, Lucas was one of the camera men during the infamous 1969 Altamont Music Festival where the Rolling Stones reportedly played during the riot and subsequent death of Meredith Hunter. Lucas' films impacted a generation in an unparalleled way, making esoteric and alien themes from Joseph Campbell, Carl Jung and comparative religion household notions.

looked in most reviews and analyses: the nature of symbols, language and communication. In the opening sequence we are shown mysterious ships that appear in the Sonoran desert, while the French scientist Lacombe (Francois Truffaut) and a cartographer interview an elderly native who exclaims the UFO was "the sun. It came out and sang." There is a direct connection throughout the film between the alien entities and music or sound, as well as solar worship. Simultaneously, across the globe in India, Hindu pilgrims and yogis had gathered to sing praises to the entities as gods during the sun's zenith, chanting, "Ah yah, Ah

Francois Truffaut (1932-1984): French actor, director, screenwriter and critic, also known for being one of the founders of French New Wave Cinema. Truffaut is one of the most prominent French film figures, having worked on over 25 films. Influenced by Orson Welles, Alfred Hitchcock and John Ford, Truffaut remained a convinced atheist is known to have had many affairs with his leading ladies.

yah ye." This is close to the Tetragrammaton (YHWH), the sacred Name of God in Scripture, as well as in the magical practices of Kabbalism: Spielberg makes a direct connection to the entities and the biblical notion of God as Lord Sabaoth, Lord of Hosts.1 In this instance, however, the "hosts" appear to be closer to the gods, Clarke's demonic Overlords. Note also that placed over the old native is the Star of David, a symbol very familiar to Spielberg.

Simulacrum.

When the "aliens" arrive at Barry's house, what happens is more in line with supernatural phenomena surrounding the multitudinous accounts of possession. Strange occurrences like electrical disturbances and electronics going haywire mark their arrival, and it's worth noting that the police cars, airplanes and trucks go haywire, running in circles. Immediately following the Barry scene, we are shown Roy and his son doing fractions over the family train set. Roy, we notice, has this fascination with models and miniature versions of things. In symbology or semiotics (which is key to unlocking *Close Encounters* and *E.T.*), the connection of a smaller image, icon or model with the thing itself is simulacra.

151

"33"

In semiotics, particularly in Plato's *Sophist* and Baudrillard's book, simulacra is intended to fool the viewer into thinking the copy is the real thing. Baudrillard explains how synthetica leads to a virtual post-nihilism:

> These two forms no longer concern us except in part, or not at all. The nihilism of transparency is no longer either aesthetic or political, no longer borrows from either the extermination of appearances, nor from extinguishing the embers of meaning, nor from the last nuances of an apocalypse. There is no longer an apocalypse (only aleatory* terrorism still tries to reflect it, but it is certainly no longer political, and it only has one mode of manifestation left that is at the same time a mode of disappearance: the media – now the media are not a stage where something is played, they are a strip, a track, a perforated map of which we are no longer even spectators/: receivers). The apocalypse is finished – today it is the precession of the neutral, of forms of the neutral and of indifference. I will leave it to be considered whether there can be a romanticism, an aesthetic of the neutral therein. I don't think so – all that remains, is the fascination for desert-like and indifferent forms, for the very operation of the system that annihilates us. Now, fascination (in contrast to seduction, which was attached to appearances, and to dialectical reason, which was attached to meaning) is a nihilistic passion par excellence, it is the passion proper to the mode of disappearance. We are fascinated by all forms of disappearance;, of our own disappearance. Melancholic and fascinated, such is our general situation in an era of involuntary transparency.

> Because there is a nostalgia for of the dialectic, and without a doubt the most subtle dialectic is nostalgic to begin with. But more deeply, there is in Benjamin and Adorno another tonality; that of a melancholy attached to the system itself, one that is incurable and

152

beyond any dialectic. It is this melancholia of systems that today takes the upper hand through the ironically transparent forms that surround us. It is this melancholia that is becoming our fundamental passion. It is no longer the spleen or the vague yearnings of the *fin-de-siecle* soul. It is no longer nihilism either, which in some sense aims at normalizing everything through destruction, the passion of resentment (ressentiment). No, melancholia is the fundamental tonality of functional systems, of current systems of simulation, of programming and information. Melancholia is the inherent quality of the mode of the disappearance of meaning, of the mode of the volatilization of meaning in operational systems. And we are all melancholic.[2]

The copy takes on a life of its own, yet viewed in scale it would clearly appear that the copy is not real. This is a perfect analogy for the nature of film itself, as well as the role of the director, who now gives man his new meaning. The writer and/or film director is creating a simulacrum of the real world with models and pictures, piecing and placing them together in a certain way, just as Roy does with the model train and city he has built. One may think of the simulated beings in *Blade Runner* (replicants) or the simulated world of *The Matrix*, as we will see later. Spielberg has mastered this art of simulation, and is presenting a simulated reality world – that of UFO-invaded America that is intended to produce a certain effect in the population. Can this be taken to a larger scale, to which Spielberg as the director himself is a "toy" of the larger, galactic forces or entities of the cosmos? Are we a Greek scale of being, being "played" and "directed" by the celestial hierarchy?

Kabbalistic Star of David

The models and simulacra also function on another level as foreshadowing of things to come within the film, as police, airplanes and military vehicles will later scurry about in a frenzy, as the plot progresses towards the Devil's Tower monument in Wyoming. But before that, it's important to look at the ship that appears in the Gobi desert, the 'Cotopaxi.' The Cotopaxi, a tramp steamer, actually did disappear in 1925 on its way to Cuba, and is part of

153

the origin of the Bermuda Triangle mythology.[3] Spielberg is tying the alien mythos to the Bermuda tales, arbitrarily linking up mysterious events under the alien banner. On the surface level, the viewer is being given a new worldview with which to connect the overt imagery under the banner of the only orthodox, mainstream-promoted "conspiracy," extraterrestrial, alien origins for UFOs. However, on a deeper level, we can look at the association of Cotopaxi with the Colorado city of the same name, as well as the mountain in Ecuador, part of the Andes. Cotopaxi, Colorado is about three hours from Denver, which will be relevant as we progress; before we get there, another element of simulacra that should be mentioned is synchronicity.

Simulacrum

Within the film, as in E.T., the characters experience a barrage of symbols and images that later become relevant on a larger scale. In this way, the simulacra function as inter-textual synchronicitous experiences for the characters.

Roy periodically sees an image that has been placed in his subconscious that he doesn't understand. The *mountain* keeps emerging in his experience: in his mashed potatoes and on the TV. He doesn't realize what it is, but he senses there is something of galactic importance to his inner vision that will turn out to be the Devil's Tower monument in Wyoming. In the midst of his near insanity, having lost his family, Roy happens to catch a television report on Devil's Mountain. In an instant, he realizes his synchronicitous image is the spot of an important encounter with his new higher power.

The gods atop the high places.

154

Consonant with these events, the French scientist Lacombe, tracking the UFO events, has developed a sign language that corresponds to the notes the entities "sang" to the Hindus and to the old native in the desert. He presents his signs to an audience of scientists that are part of a secret project to study the "alien phenomenon," with the Lacombe character representing none other than UFO researcher Jacques Vallee.[4] That the film is based on esoteric doctrines is confirmed by the Vallee inspiration. He wrote openly of his interest in the UFO phenomenon in relation to

JACQUES VALLEE: Computer scientist, author and UFOlogist. Vallee is a prominent figure in UFO research and is known for his work with the Stanford Research Institute and ARPANET (a precursor to the Internet). Vallee is an apologist for the existence of extraterrestrial beings, as well as their inter-dimensional origins. Vallee has also reportedly been affiliated with various esoteric societies and hermetic beliefs, such as Rosicrucianism.

the occult.[5] Their symbol is a *black pyramid*: thus far we have a Masonic "33" on the plane in the first scene, a "32" on Roy's son's jersey, hand signs with Lacombe and a black pyramid project, run, as it turns out, by a shadow government of agents and "men in black" types that are connected to the Air Force and Lockheed Martin, a major corporate force in the military-industrial complex. Earlier in the film, the Air Force met with the townsfolk of Muncie, Indiana, and engaged in a mock press conference of disinformation intent on dispelling public interest in the "close encounters" occurrence. The Air Force spokesmen make reference to bare rationalism, denying knowledge of any and all events, which adds credence to the popular, ridiculous and controlled alternative media narrative of government suppression of the existence of "aliens." To a

Old Lockheed Martin Logo with inverted star.

degree, this is true, as the real players close to the "aliens" are private, shadow military contractors – Lockheed, Raytheon, DARPA, etc., not locally elected officials. Note the inversion of the star in the logo used in the film.[6]

Two possible associations can be made here. The secret project of scientists tasked with studying the UFO phenomenon recalls the famed "MJ 12" or "Majestic 12" committee of "agents" that were supposedly studying the existence of aliens and unexplained aerial phenomena related to Roswell. This is, of course, a large load of black ops bullshit, as is the much-promoted Roswell "crash."[7] In fact, the entire "alien" mythos is itself one large disinformation campaign designed to func-

155

tion as a cover for actual secret aerial and space-based technology and, likely, drug running.[8] "MJ 12" was more probably the group formed to promote the alien myth to keep prying eyes from looking into the technology that was being developed. As for the French UFO scientist, it may be a reference to Jacques Vallee, the famed UFO researcher who argued that UFOs were something more sinister: demonic entities invading our plane of existence. As with *Raiders of the Lost Ark*, the encounter with the gods occurs on a mountain, one of the high places.

To add to the mystery, some researchers have pointed out the possible connection of the Denver International Airport and the numbers the entities give through their interstellar communication. In the film, the mysterious numbers become geographical coordinates. Using Google Earth, I came up in the vicinity of the Denver Airport, but it was not exact. That is certainly possible, but what can be seen here are at least two explicit references to Colorado: Cotopaxi and the coordinates. Colorado is the home of NORAD (at the Cheyenne Mountain Complex),[9] as well as the CIA's recent relocation – two key shadow government locations, as well as the underground base beneath the Denver Airport (and who knows what else).[10] It should be added that Denver and Colorado factor quite prominently in pop media and fiction: *Atlas Shrugged, X-Men: First Class, The Stand, The Passage, The Prestige, Jericho, Red Dawn, The Shining*, etc. Denver and Colorado appear to have a special relation to the cryptocracy.

NORAD and the Cheyenne Mountain Complex.

Wyoming is also home to underground bases and secret establishments. When we see the government beginning to set up shop in the Devil's Mountain area, a bus is shown that brings astronauts preparing to go away with the aliens. This is interesting, since the bus has a header that reads "Cheyenne." Cheyenne, Wyoming is presumably the base from which the shadow government in the film has set up shop to control the alien arrival situation at the Devil's Tower (Devil's Tower is four hours north of Cheyenne). However, "Cheyenne" also has reference to Colorado as mentioned, since the NORAD/Cheyenne Mountain Complex is located in Colorado Springs, and is one of the most important shadow/continuity of government installations. In Philip K. Dick's story *Dr. Bloodmoney*, it is the capital of a new military dictatorship, while in the television series *Jericho* it is the capital of the "Allied States of America," a faction of the new, post-apocalyptic US government. In the 1984 Cold War propaganda film *Red Dawn*, it is the farthest the communist forces have pushed American rebels. It is also the location bio-warfare survivors retreat to in Stephen King's apocalyptic novel, *The Stand*.

Devil's Tower, the abandoned Cold War era NSA spy center in Berlin.

While on the topic of bases and names, "Devil's Tower" is also the name of a British base on Gibraltar, and Gibraltar's rock looks strikingly similar to Spielberg's choice of the Devil's Tower monument. Thus, we can associate Devil's Tower with the RAF and MI6, as Devil's Tower is an

157

ancient fortress keeping watch over British colonies.[11] Is Spielberg saying the shadow government is the Anglo-American establishment, still keeping its panoptic gaze over its "colonies"?[12] Devil's Tower also has reference to a famous Cold War spying station of the NSA.[13] Is Spielberg saying those that run the alien mythos are actually the shadow government?

Devil's Tower RAF base next to the Rock of Gibraltar.

Or, conversely the elite are saying they are the "alien" Overlords – ascended, superior evolutionary beings that condescend to contact the profane masses atop the high places. The key players in the shadow government are so removed from the masses as to be another species, "alien" to them, with the intention of playing them in the simulacrum simulation as Roy plays with the trains? Certainly it is curious that much of what is portrayed in the film has polyvalent reference to so many real-world sites home to strategic outfits of the shadow government. As the story nears conclusion, Roy flees towards Devil's Tower and the military begins aerosol spraying nerve gas – chemtrails – upon the escaped contactees. Earlier, the shadow government had conceived a plan to "scare" all the populace with a staged biological leak, but here the military industrial complex releases it in actuality.[14] We know from sites like the Sunshine Project such events are also real possibilities. "Bahama, this is Pyramid, over. Call the Dark Side of the Moon," say the special forces soldiers. *Dark Side of the Moon*, of course, brings to mind the 1973 Pink Floyd rock opera album of the same name.

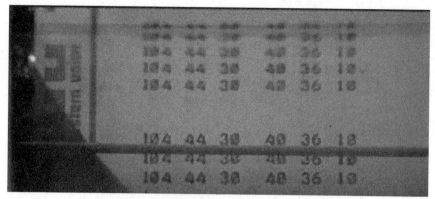

Coordinates that come close to the Denver Airport.

This may seem a bit far-fetched, but keep in mind that we are dealing with very intelligent people who do think in this symbolic and archetypal fashion. What some like Michael Hoffman have titled "mystical toponomy*" is likely at work here, and can be described as the practice of making associations and connections with events and places based on the symbology, history, and meaning of said events and places. Hoffman and James Shelby Downard write:

> Mystical toponomy incorporates word wizardry (onomatology) and the Masonic science of symbolism. In considering my data it would be helpful to consider a dictum of Einsteinian physics: "Time relations among events are assumed to be first constituted by the specific physical relations obtaining between them." My study of place names imbued with sorcerous significance necessarily includes lines of latitude and longitude and the divisions of degrees in geography and cartography (minutes and seconds).

> Let us take as an example the "Mason Road" in Texas that connects to the "Mason No El Bar" and the Texas-New Mexico ("The Land of Enchantment") border. This connecting line is on the 32nd degree. The 32nd degree is the penultimate Masonic degree awarded. When this 32nd degree of latitude is traced west into the "Land of Enchantment" it becomes situated midway between Deming and Columbus, New Mexico.[15]

This is a field in which to tread lightly, since the associations are often fuzzy and speculative in nature, and only the most adept are proficient at this art. It is also somewhat dangerous, as the film itself shows with Roy, who begins to go mad making associations that emerge from his subconscious and are, by him, "associated" with synchronicitous events and places in his life.

159

Lacombe develops hand signs.

In the plot, Roy is "chosen" by the gods/entities to gradually experience this initiatory journey until he ascends the mountain to be translated to the heavenly city. Is Spielberg laying out the frightening and enlightening journey of those who would seek out the mysteries of the universe and embark on that journey? The track Roy takes, being called to it and forsaking all that he has to attain the truth certainly lends credence to this view, and shows that perhaps Spielberg is telling us not to be afraid. Fear is what keeps us in our prison worlds of simulacra and models. Are we willing to question our basic presuppositions and worldviews, or are we married to them to such a degree that something utterly mysterious and foreign invading them and challenging them warrants scientistic rationalism as a crutch?

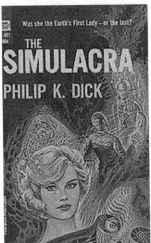

The Simulacra, the Phillip K. Dick story.

The aliens also seem to have a difficulty communicating. For some reason they cannot just talk, so they use music and eventually the hand signs that the scientist developed. Perhaps the gods or angelic entities also find it difficulty to communicate, and speak through the archetypes and symbols of our experience. I believe the angelic hierarchy or celestial intelligences organize the synchronicitous events and connections we experience, under the providential power and guidance of God. Understanding how these deeper-level connections and associations are made is a tricky and somewhat frustrating art, and therefore places the viewer in Roy's position.

I think it is possible to read the film on all these levels, and Spielberg is certainly genius enough to make such a film. I think noticing the profound depth of the simulacra and the models as foreshadowing alone, is a gateway to viewing the films on these deeper levels. If we are permitted to take a step through that first gateway, is it possible Spielberg is telling us something more, to the extent that we are to look now at our own experiences and read a possible mystical toponomy at work? It is possible. Are we willing to be like Roy, sacrificing all for the truth of what is happening all around us? Initially, I read the film in a very moralistic fashion, such that the mythos was all about promoting aliens, and Roy was immoral for leaving his family and chasing the aliens.

Yet upon multiple viewings throughout my life, I take a more reflective position. Here is a normal guy confronted with something real, yet very out of the ordinary. Spielberg makes it a point, too, to show that Roy's wife saw things as well, even hiding the news clippings of UFO sightings from him. As Roy has his difficult and very real experiences, his wife continues to degrade and despise him until she leaves. Roy is not a bad guy: at no point in the film does he wrong his wife. He is genuinely enthralled by something otherworldly that happened to him outside his own control, yet the people closest to him are unable to understand him. These perspectives are not mutually exclusive, either. Perhaps Spielberg is telling us about his own transformation through his artwork, and is conveying that journey to us through Roy's gradual revelation and enlightenment. Maybe I sit here as a crazy Roy, sculpting a devil's tower of analysis of mystical toponomy to follow, or maybe I'm just another madman.

Roy's shamanic journey begins.

161

Endnotes

1. Halevi, Z'ev ben Shimon. *Kabbalah and Exodus*. Boston, MA: Weiser Books, pg. 54.

2. Baudrillard, Jean.

3. "Ships and the Sea." *Evening Post*. 27 March 1926. Web http://paperspast.natlib.govt.nz/cgi-bin/paperspast?a=d&d=EP19260327.2.161

4. "Close Encounters of the Third Kind." FilmSite. Web. http://www.filmsite.org/clos.html

5. Vallee, Jacques. *Forbidden Science*. San Francisco: Documatica Research, 2010, pg. 81, 241, 251.

6. Inverted stars generally represent the metaphysical principle of inversion as a form of black magic.

7. Collins, Phillip and Paul, "Alien Smokescreen." ConspiracyArchive. 17 June, 2007. Web. http://www.conspiracyarchive.com/2014/09/21/alien-smokescreen/

8. Ibid.

9. "Cheyenne Mountain Complex." Fas.org. 13 December 1999. Web. http://fas.org/nuke/guide/usa/c3i/cmc.htm

10. Priest, Dana. "CIA Plans to Shift Work to Denver." Washington Post. 6 May, 2005. Web. http://www.washingtonpost.com/wp-dyn/content/article/2005/05/05/AR2005050501860.html

11. Sweeney, Chris. "The World's 18 Strangest Military Bases." Popular Mechanics. 16 June, 2010. Web. http://www.popularmechanics.com/technology/design/g152/strangest-military-bases-gallery/

12. See Quigley, *Tragedy and Hope*.

13. Zetter, Kim. "Devil's Mountain: NSA's Abandoned Cold War Listening Post." Wired. October 3, 2011. Web. http://www.wired.com/2011/10/teufelsberg/

14. Note the film's revelation of the military industrial complex staging news, with fake animal deaths and a planned evacuation to induce fear and panic.

15. Hoffman, Michael and James Shelby Downard. King-Kill 33. Whale.to. Web. http://www.whale.to/b/kingkill_33.html#Mystical_Toponomy_

Chapter 8

A.I. Artificial Intelligence (2001) – Transhumanist Fairy Tale

"It is all of metaphysics that is lost. No more mirror of being and appearances, of the real and its concept. No more imaginary coextensivity: it is genetic miniaturization that is the dimension of simulation. The real is produced from miniaturized cells, matrices, and memory banks, models of control – and it can be reproduced an indefinite number of times from these. It no longer needs to be rational, because it no longer measures itself against either an ideal or negative instance. It is no longer anything but operational. In fact, it is no longer really the real, because no imaginary envelops it anymore. It is a hyperreal, produced from a radiating synthesis of combinatory models in a hyperspace without atmosphere."[1]

– Jean Baudrillard

*A*rtificial Intelligence is a Stanley Kubrick script made into a 2001 film by Steven Spielberg. A modern presentation of *Pinocchio*, the Spielberg/Kubrick *A.I.* operates on multiple levels as an allegory, as well as a morality tale of mankind's potentially disastrous future given the rise of super-advanced technology. Having viewed the film numerous times since 2001, only now has it become evident how profound it really is. Much has been scribbled about *2001: A Space Odyssey* and *Eyes Wide Shut*, but *A.I.* appears to have been overlooked. About a decade ago the idea of doing esoteric film analysis occurred to me when I read a review of *A.I.* that argued it was an allegory of Dante's *Inferno* (as David will undergo a *katabasis*). A decade later I still think that element is well-found, but the real meaning has yet to be explored in its full depth insofar as the more hidden aspects of the cryptocracy's designs with technology have only recently come to some brighter light.

Transition from Human to Post-Human Era

The film opens to a warning of the catastrophic effects of global warming and the melting of the polar icecaps that led to the flooding of major world centers. In the wake of the crisis, the global population found itself in a resource war for the basic means of survival, with robotics achieving a primary place due to the minuscule amount of resources robots require (not needing food, water, etc.). Spielberg appears to be on board here with the establishment's grand fear narrative of Malthusian climate threats, as the hype of carbon emissions is just now in our day emerging as a massive hoax geared towards total population control. Entities like the Royal Society, the U.N. and think-tanks like the Club of Rome have exhausted tremendous wealth and energy towards selling the phony fear of climate catastrophe, from the failed predictions of Paul Ehrlich to Al Gore, and in *A.I.* we see a placement of clear fear-based propaganda preparing the audience for a dark future of apocalyptic climate-based scenarios.[2] Regardless, in the fictional future world of *A.I.*, the revelation of the resource war is shown to be the essence of the elite technocratic control grid, as we will be entering a transition period from the human to the post-human.

CLUB OF ROME: A global think tank established in 1968 to study "the future of humanity." The Club of Rome has published white papers and books that explicitly argue for depopulation, as well as its basis on a concocted "pollution problem" and engineered "Green movement." This is explained in detail in the Club's 1991 "First Global Revolution" document. Notable members have included economist Joseph Stiglitz and Soviet leader Mikhail Gorbachev.

Dr. Allen Hobby (William Hurt) is shown next giving a lecture where he presents a new goal for A.I. – to build a robot that can dream. The assumption appears to be that synthetic consciousness lacks the deeper abilities humans possess to access a subconscious, from which individual aspirations, inspiration and spontaneous volition, can arise. Hobby even speaks of creating a machine that can build its own inner world of symbolic archetypes and metaphors, arising from its own process of self-individuation.[3] While it might have seemed far-fetched in 2001, a decade and a half later, we are now seeing top A.I. thinkers plan these very things through entities like DARPA, Google and the work of Ray Kurzweil.[4] The ability to do such work operates on an alternate metaphysical system to that presented in mainline academia and quantitative-dominated physical sciences.[5]

The archon image of David foreshadowing his future race of *alien*-like A.I.

Thus, at the outset of *A.I.*, Spielberg is revealing a major component of the long-term goals of the cryptocracy, to build a post-human man able to transcend the limits of space and time. If an A.I. being could be created that was able to form its own inner psychical world of associations, archetypal forms and meaning, the bridge from purely algorithmic, determined process might be broken, and self-conscious volition based on this inner-symbolical world (think Jean Piaget), resulting in undetermined choice would be the closest point of contact with human consciousness possible, depending of course on whether one views human consciousness as purely determined physical phenomena or intentional, volitional action. In any event, it was somewhat synchronistic for me as a viewer to watch this for the tenth time (after a long period of not seeing it) and only then notice the references to what I had just written about.

Oedipal Eden

David (Haley Joel Osmet) is Prof. Hobby's first test subject for an A.I. that can dream, and is given to a company researcher named Henry Swinton, whose son Martin is in a coma. Henry presents his distraught wife Monica with David as a temporary replacement, to which Monica reluctantly concedes. Hearkening to the opening of the film where we see an elongated figure emerging from a shell with the infinity symbol (the Cybertronics logo), David appears out of focus with an extended head and slim body that will form the pattern for the alien-like A.I. at the end of the film. In similar foreshadowing, Martin, who is frozen in a cryogenic state surrounded by images of fairy tales on the wall of the children's hospital foreshadows the ice-water tomb that will encapsulate David in the third act. This reflexive symbolic foreshadowing is constant in the film and itself suggests a cyclical view of time and eternity.

Monica as womb of the gnostic Sophia

165

The cinematography consistently utilizes circular imagery in almost every scene, giving the impression of eternality, instability and constant change. Some scenes even intentionally evoke iconic images from Kubrick films, such as *Dr. Strangelove*. At no point do we, as viewers, or David as the protagonist, feel stable and fixed. We are immediately propelled on a chaotic adventure where time seems forgotten. This atemporal aspect harmonizes well with the atemporal setting for ancient mythology and their more recent versions, fairy tales. A.I. is thus a post-human, transhumanist technocratic fairy tale. Those versed in the classics will be aware of the Greek notion of the myths taking place in a pre-temporal "golden age," where giants, monsters and gods roamed freely before a great cataclysm that brought about temporal reality. In *A.I.*, Spielberg and Kubrick would have us transfer our thinking to the realm of the mythological and fairy tale, which is also the realm of the subconscious and the *aether*, explaining why the film utilizes a host of images and ideas, from Freud to Jung to *Pinocchio*.

Sigmund Freud (1856-1939): Austrian neurologist and founder of psychoanalysis as a school of thought in psychology. Freud is also known for techniques such as "free association," where hypnosis is employed to analyze a patient's psyche. Also of note is Freud's preoccupation with sexology and the Oedipus Complex, where familiar relations are reduced to deviant sexual impulses. The Frankfurt School would later use Freud's research to attempt to dissolve the family unit itself as the source of "fascism."

Mirrors also appear frequently, as the mirror is emblematic of the psyche or subconscious, reflecting either the deepest dreams and intentions of the characters, or the shade of Jungian archetypalism. As David adapts to his new life in the Swinton household, he begins to do things normal children do, like play hide and seek, but while in this innocent, Edenic state, David carries a creepy air about him that will manifest in a "fall" in the third act. Monica, the mother archetype, is shown doing all distinctly human actions, such as eating, cleaning, cooking, sleeping, and going to the bathroom, contrasted with David's futile attempts to be human. At one point David steps over the line by opening the bathroom door to Monica while she is reading a book on Freud, cluing us into the sexuality at work: David grows to become attached to Monica; an Oedipal aspect is clearly shown with the Freud reference.

Carl Gustav Jung (1875-1961): A long time associate of Freud, Carl Jung proposed a different theory of psychoanalysis centering on archetypes and dream interpretation. For Jung, the collective unconscious manifested itself in the dreamstate through symbols and types that could be decoded by the psychoanalyst. Jung's theories operated in tandem with a wide range of comparative religious thought, including gnostic and Platonic ideas of forms, a world-soul and even alchemical notions of mystical self-transformation.

David is an A.I. version of a child in his so-called "anal stage," and Monica is the archetypal mother who now has two beings contending for

166

her affection – David and Henry. Henry is also never called "father" in the film, hinting at a completely absent and/or emasculated masculine component. The only male figure prominent in the film is Joe, the effeminate sex bot. It is David's sexuality-constructed desires for affection that will lead him on his journey to become "real" to his mother. The dark mirrored aspect of Monica's psyche is evident as she constantly looks into mirrors and even stares at David in her rear view mirror as she drives away, abandoning him. Mirrors are also copies of things, so we can associate the mirror imaging with the overpowering simulacrum that dominates the film.

Magical Mind Control Trigger Words

A profoundly kabbalistic idea is shown in regard to the means by which David's emotions and self-actualization are "triggered." Monica (not Henry) must touch a chakra point (David's neck) and repeat a series of magical words to make David's emotional receptors kick in. Once it's done, the process is irreversible, and Henry and Monica even discuss the possibility of returning David to the company for dissolution should they find him distasteful. There is at this juncture another important key to understanding the film, as none of the human characters are remotely likable. Almost all of them evidence purely egoistic and despicable qualities, especially in the Swinton household, where everyone operates in their own interests. Monica only wants Martin, Henry only wants Monica's affection, and Martin only wants to be rid of David.

Envy takes primacy as Martin miraculously comes out of his coma and arrives home to find David in his place. In a striking dialogue between Martin and David, Martin challenges David to do things he obviously cannot do, all the more ironic as Martin can barely walk. In Martin's mind, David only exists for his own pleasure and amusement, passing off Teddy, last year's "supertoy" to David. Teddy is the Jiminy Cricket of this version of *Pinocchio*, and will represent David's conscience throughout. Martin passing off Teddy signifies that humanity has, at this point in history, lost all conscience and become completely self-absorbed and destructive. Indeed, humanity is to blame for the climate apocalypse at the opening of the film, and in this microcosmic scene we are given an image of the fall from the Edenic, golden age state of bliss to one of utter objectification and masochistic abandon. As the A.I. become more humanlike and abused, men are more abusive and exploitive towards one another, in a strange contrast. It is as if mankind achieved a pinnacle of technological progress, only to do so at the expense of the loss of all morality and de-

167

cency, ending in nihilistic self-destruction. While I do not share the film's global warming alarmism, the threat of sacrificing our humanity at the altar of technocratic progress is very much a warning to be heeded.

David's alter "imprinting" courtesy of the technocratic panoptic establishment.

However, before we move on to that major theme, Monica's magic Cybertronics words must be analyzed. David is programmed to have a series of vocal frequencies repeated to him that activate his self-realization and dream-making emotional abilities through the recitation of his mother alone. This is, as mentioned, a profoundly kabbalistic and gnostic idea, as well as a more orthodox sentiment, as the notion of God creating the world from His Logos, or Word, is found in many religious texts, not the least of which is John, Chapter 1. Here, the idea seems to be more in line with kabbalism, as the mother archetype "imprints" upon David a series of code words that trigger a personality to come to the fore.[6] The interesting word string is as follows: Cirrus, Socrates, Particle, Decibel, Hurricane, Dolphin, Tulip, Monica, David, Monica. The words seem to span an array of topics, from forces of nature to philosophy. Monica appears as the gnostic Sophia in my analysis, activating his self-consciousness through divine word, recalling Genesis 1, where God creates man through a word, yet here the creation occurs in the new Adam, David, who will be the forefather of a new race of A.I. beings, with Martin representing the old man, or Adam, subject to death and decay.

In kabbalism, there is the idea that man can create a golem or artificial being with the right combinations of words and sounds and material, and as with *E.T.*, Spielberg is referencing that tradition.[7] Perhaps the title of the film itself is a kind of bookend on *E.T.*, where only two letters are used – "A.I." and "E.T." Extra Terrestrial Artificial Intelligence could be a mystagogical code for the origins of advanced artificial technology as channeled from the inter-dimensional alien "gods." While this notion may seem far out, there are plenty of elites who affirm *panspermia,* which does include this idea as we will see in the *Prometheus* analysis.

Programmed sex slave bots.

The notion of "imprinting" also suggests a possible mind control reading of the film, as David's persona comes about through trigger words. We saw earlier the use of psychological conditioning in the military/industrial/entertainment complex, as well as its prevalence in film. This reading is not outside the realm of possibility, given that David's next companion on his journey will be the programmed sex slave, Gigolo Joe (played by Jude Law). While we know there are brainwashing programs that involve sex slave programming, assassination programming, and various other techniques, that *A.I.* presents both trigger words and sex slaves seems more than coincidence. Skeptics might wonder how this connection might be substantiated, but if we reflect, it's not hard to make. Robots are made human, and humans are made robotic, by programming.

In the cult classic *Blade Runner,* there is almost the same theme as *A.I.,* where persecuted replicants are struggling against man for mere survival.

Blade Runner also includes the theme of a massive mega corporation that has the ability to wipe and program the minds of both sex slaves and assassins. Thus, this multi-tiered level of meaning is not without precedence in science fiction. Another reason we can draw this association is due to the close correlation artificial intelligence research and psychology share. The presuppositions of creating A.I. revolve around understanding and mapping the human brain and psyche, and the century of research the establishment has poured into such endeavors intertwines closely with research into advanced bio-tech. This is why DARPA and Google have such a close relationship with people like Regina Dugan, formerly of DARPA and now a high-up at Google.[8] Mapping the psyche is the key to creating A.I. and we can make a rough parallel between Cybertronics and Google, as both appear to run the existing globe from a technocratic standpoint, seeking to install the post-human era.[9]

DARPA: The Defense Advanced Research Projects Agency, formerly known as ARPA. Created in 1958 by President Eisenhower, DARPA's purpose was advanced weapons research through science and technology. DARPA is independent of other military research, as it reports directly to the Department of Defense. In fact, the Internet itself arose out of DARPANET, participating universities and think tanks. In our day, DARPA develops cutting edge drone technology, robotics, and is even involved in brain-interfacing, transhumanist flavors of "bio-enhancement" and artificial intelligence.

Flesh Fair Inferno to Robo-booty Rouge City

As David and Martin continue to butt heads, David gradually begins to grow aware of the darkness of his world, being tricked on three occasions by Martin into appearing as a threat. Ironically, David is a threat, although not consciously, as the A.I. will eventually take over as humanity destroys itself. Martin almost foresees this, and knows that David must be eradicated for his own survival. This is one reason the first half of the film is filled with moon symbolism. Moons are everywhere, from David's bed to the flesh fair, as Gigolo Joe proclaims that to reach Dr. Know, they will have to journey toward the moon. The floating hot air balloon that first captures David, for example, is a gigantic synthetic moon, which brings him to the Flesh Fair, where gladiatorial games are displayed for a brutish and rural public to torture and dismember robots. Spielberg is thus presenting the robots as the new persecuted race, reminiscent of both the early Christian persecutions in Rome and the Jews in Nazi Germany.

The Flesh Fair does recall images of Dante's *Inferno*, which marks a highpoint in the western tradition of the hero undergoing a *katabasis*, or descent into the underworld. From Homer to Virgil to the Bible, the hero's descent to the underworld is symbolic of two important elements: the passage from this life to death and the psyche's trek from consciousness to the realm of the unconscious. Both are linked, as the subconscious is home to our darkest archetypal fears, and death is the realm that holds us in a prison, in fear in this life, not knowing what lies beyond. The lunar symbolism of the first half of the film also represents the human era as a kind of dark-age, as opposed to the daytime setting for the second half. Spielberg seems to be warning that the era of man may be "baptized" in a flood of death that will bring the post-human, leading to a spurious new dawn of trans-humanist singularity. However, in this ominous portrayal, it is not a glorious utopia where man merges with machines according to the trans-humanist promise, but rather the ultimate dystopia where humans are extinct. We have seen numerous films, from *Moonraker* to *Sky Captain* to *2012* to *Elysium* to *Interstellar*, that present the elite escaping to an off-world utopia, a breakaway civilization, while the rest of humanity is left to perish in apocalyptic disaster.

Gladiatorial Inferno Flesh Fair.

In my analysis, this is the ultimate goal of the shadow government, and I expect this storyline to continue to pop up in pop-culture as the controllers seem to relish in cryptically laying out their designs. One final note should be added concerning the lunar symbolism that fits well with the theme of mind control, which is the notion of Moonchildren. In my *E.T.* analysis I pointed out the moon symbolism with E.T. and Elliot, and here in *A.I.* it is evident too, as David is not just a robot, but a programmed moonchild, which recalls the occult "Babalon" workings of Jack Parsons and Crowley, seeking to create a homunculus.[10] While that working was done with the intent of effecting things on the astral plane, the goal of the technocracy is to transfer such workings to the material plane, where "mecha" (mechanical beings in the film) become "orga" (organic beings). It is even mentioned in the film by Gigolo Joe that orga hate and will be replaced by mecha, and they know it. Thus the descent from Flesh Fair to Rouge City, a degenerate licentious red-light district that is an entire city is also the source of Dr. Know, the gnostic embodiment of rational thought.

Dr. Know-sis.

The City at the End of the World and the New Aeon

Dr. Know, a kind of 3D Google, informs Joe and David that "Blue Fairy," the enigmatic representation of man and David's religious quest, is to be found at the end of the world in Man-hattan. In the midst of this query, Dr. Know shuts off and becomes a message from Cybertronics to David. A riddle is given to tell David to come to the end of the world and seek out Dr. Hobby, playing on the archetypal quest that motivates David. The interplay between machine and machine is fascinating here, as both seem incapable of understanding the different semiotic usages and senses of words, puns and exemplification. Being overly literal, machines seem unequipped to joke, aside from Gigolo Joe, who is the "fairy in hand" that will accompany David to *Man*-hattan.

As a side note, as David and Joe journey to Man-hattan, what appears to be a monolith is briefly shown on the New York skyline, as the scene fades to the World Trade Towers submerged in water. Is this a pre-9/11 reference to the coming destruction? Possibly, as other Spielberg-associated films like *Gremlins 2* contain a 9/11-like scenario of the nasty batch taking over and destroying a tower and a scene with "9/11" referenced. Curiously, in this film the towers appear to be visible, so this connection is more ambiguous. The placement of the monolith, hearkening to *2001* however, is not. The Dr. Know sequence is also a revelation of the total panoptic goals of the technocracy, as Dr. Hobby reveals they had been watching David all along – it was all an experiment to see if David would seek out his maker. And when David finds Dr. Hobby, the discovery of a clone factory of himself throws him into a rage. The spiraling, eternal cycle of the consideration of copies of copies interacting with still more synthetic and higher-level copies paints a bleak vision of a tech-obsessed future.

As Joe and David and Teddy approach Man-hattan a brief shot of a monolith is reflected on their copter. Immediately after this, the NYC skyline is shown with a submerged WTC.

David experiences a kind of "fall" here, where vengeance, hatred, rage and egoism emerge, throwing him into a fit when discovering that Blue Fairy wasn't real, and that Dr. Hobby had planned the entire quest as a sick experiment due to the loss of his own son. David sees that he was a manufactured being, completely unoriginal, and is a product of the ultimate consumerism – cloned and produced and consumed children. David then becomes suicidal, and after dropping towards his watery abyss tomb, Joe proclaims, " I AM, I WAS," which is a take on the famous Name of God from Exodus 3:14, where God says "I AM that I AM." In the new world order of A.I., the *deus ex machina* of an emergent technological deity supplanting humanity is shown, as David becomes the founder of a new race. It is significant that as the aeons pass while David is submerged in the underworld, the new A.I. beings search for David in order to find their founder. We are left to assume that the A.I. defeated or outlived the humans who self-destructed and became extinct. Their alien appearance is reminiscent of typical Spielberg alien productions, giving us a contrast to Kubrick's *2001*.

Post-human era emerges with an iconic scene showing New York destruction prior to 9/11

In *2001*, man battles HAL to go to the next level of evolutionary apotheosis, whereas here, man loses, and the bots continue on. Operating in a collective, the borg-like A.I. recreate David's past and inform him that every particle of space reflects every other event that occurred – a profound Leibnizian concept.[11] It is clear that whoever consulted with Spielberg on *A.I.* was undoubtedly very grounded in the establishment's hidden metaphysics, and it was likely the establishment itself, as that relationship has long been known. David's *katabasis*, or descent to the underworld abyss results in his resurrection, but we discover humans can only be brought back for one day. David retains the hair of Monica he cut off, and Monica is brought back for a day before passing away into sleep. That day is spoken of as a never-ending day, the day of eternity, in contrast to the night and moon imagery of the first two acts. Just like Odysseus, Orpheus and Dante, David must descend in order to *ascend*, yet the trek to the depths of depravity in Rouge City and the ice tomb evokes a left-hand path of reaching *gnosis* (Dr. Know) through a dark night, prior to awakening.

174

Future A.I. archon overlords.

Conclusion: To Starchild and Beyond

While *A.I.* is still a cinematic marvel and a film of unparalleled genius, the ultimate message conveyed is not pretty. It is at once a warning and an establishment revelation of its materialist and esoteric credo – that the next aeon is not one that will be marked by the human. The notion of never-ending aeons is prominent in hermetic and esoteric teachings, as well as in Hinduism and Sufism, and suggests a Crowleyan idea of David as the "crowned and conquering child," a kind of mecha/orga homunculus who will become the dayspring of a new aeon – one without humans, in contrast to *2001*, where man defeats HAL to become Starchild. We see trigger codes, sex slaves, and ideas like passing through the abyss (David's descent), so these notions are worth considering. David as a mecha with orga emotions and drives looks to be the *new* Starchild, and mankind will be left to the dustbin of history. Is David also an image of the programmed sex slaves and exploited tools of the elite, who are possibly bringing in the new religious aeon of a transhumanist singularity that will surpass the old religions of man? It is highly important in numerology that 2001 was the release date of *A.I.*, as 2001 is the date chosen for Kubrick's version of Arthur C. Clarke's story (Clarke had definite occult associations, as well as Kubrick being visited by the CIA about his projects, as Vivian Kubrick related earlier). That aspect is more speculative, but in any case, *A.I.* is definitely a trans-humanist fairy tale with a foreboding message.

Endnotes

1. Baudrillard, *Simulacra and Simulation*, 3.

2. King and Schneider, The First Global Revolution: A Report by the Council of the Club of Rome. Orient Longman Publishing. Dyer, Jay. "Global Green Luciferian Government." JaysAnalysis. 8 May, 2014. Web. http://jaysanalysis.com/2014/05/08/global-green-luciferian-government/

3. Dyer, Jay. "Plato, Crystals, Dimensions and Artificial Intelligence." JaysAnalysis. 18 Nov, 2014. Web. http://jaysanalysis.com/2014/11/18/plato-crystals-dimensions-and-artificial-intelligence/

4. Turbeville, Brandon. "The Singularity Movement, Immortality and Removing the Ghost in the Machine." ActivistPost. 23 February, 2011. Anne Jacobsen, *The Pentagon's Brain*. http://www.activistpost.com/2011/02/singularity-movement-immortality-and.html

5. Dyer, Jay. "The Cult of Scientism and Nikola Tesla's Aether." JaysAnalysis. 17 June, 2014. Web. http://jaysanalysis.com/2014/06/17/the-cult-of-scientism-and-nikola-teslas-aether/

6. Martin, Sean. *The Gnostics: The First Christian Heretics*. London: Pocket Essentials, 2006, pgs. 34-5.

7. Scholem, Gershom. *Kabbalah*. New York: Dorset Press, 1974, pg., 351.

8. Jacobsen, Annie. *The Pentagon's Brain*, 427-32.

9. Regalado, Antonio. "Military Funds Brain-Computer Interfaces to Control Feelings." *MIT Technology Review*. 29 March, 2015. Web. https://www.technologyreview.com/s/527561/military-funds-brain-computer-interfaces-to-control-feelings/

10. Hoffman, *Secret Societies*, 210-13.

11. Leibniz, Gottfried. *Selections*. New York: Charles Scribner's Sons, 1951, pgs. 96-8.

Chapter 9

Minority Report (2002) – Esoteric Analysis

"Everybody Runs"

Spielberg's *Minority Report* is another important film to link to our present discussion. Based on the short story by visionary science fiction author Philip K. Dick, Spielberg's film version implements an important number of predictive programming elements not found in Dick. Both are worth a look, as, some years later, we are actually seeing the implementation of the total technocratic takeover, including pre-crime tracking systems. Although the film and the short story present precognition as a metaphysical mystery by telepathic individuals who can see into the *aether*, the real pre-crime systems are based on A.I. and the digitizing of all records under total in-

PHILIP K. DICK (1928-1982): Ground-breaking American science fiction writings often center on gnostic themes, future dystopias, and anti-authoritarian protagonists. His works often reflect his peculiar theological and metaphysical views, while many of his well known stories have been adapted into blockbuster films, such as *Blade Runner, Total Recall* and *Minority Report*.

formation awareness.[1] Contrary to popular belief, this was DARPA's plan for the Internet all along. DARPA states as follows concerning its creation and reason for existence:

"The Soviet Union's launch of Sputnik showed that a fundamental change was needed in America's defense science and technology programs. DARPA was formed to meet this need and rejuvenated our defense technological capabilities."[2]

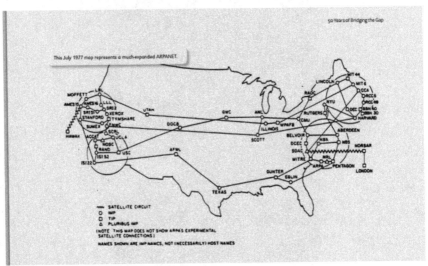

The 1977 ARPANET, precursor to the Internet, connected to RAND, Harvard, Stanford, London, etc., and the satellite grid.

In fact, a close friend worked for a few years digitizing mass medical records, and while most are aware of Google's attempts to digitize all books, if they were aware, the why would be unfathomable. I've warned for several years that the end goal of all this digitization is not "efficiency" and trendy I-Watches (Fit-Bits, etc.) to monitor heart rates and location. The ultimate goal is total mind control, loss of free will and the *complete rewrite of all past reality*.

Consider, for example, the power the system will wield with the ability to "delete" all past versions of literature – religious texts, Shakespeare, *1984*, nothing will be sacred and unable to be "revised." Remember that in 2009 Amazon erased Orwell's *1984*.[3] Your own past may even be deleted, subject to revision, or altered to make *you* the next villain! All this is revealed in detail in *Minority Report*. Thus, while the public adopts "Kindles," print itself is assigned the doom of the kindled fire – like *Farenheit 451*, as Richard Grove has said.[4]

178

Minority Report's setting is a 2055 dystopic Washington D.C., where Agent John Anderton (Tom Cruise) is framed for two murders from within his own PreCrime Corporation ranks by the CEO, Lamar Burgess (Max Von Sydow). (Note: The existing system appears to be a merger of private and government sectors.) I'm sure most readers have seen the film, so I'll spare you detailed plot recaps and hit the highlights for the sake of our purposes.

"The Temple" – the new god for a new aeon, the predictive A.I. system.

The film's PreCrime alerts a private corporation to an impending murder event ahead of time, giving the agents of the corporation time to save victims. Hailed as a perfect system, the infallibility of PreCrime has made D.C. the safest city in the world, with no murders for several years. As a result, the PreCrime test requires a total surveillance society, something akin to complete panopticism. In fact, the advertising in D.C. is user-specific, targeting pedestrian's personal desires based on retina scans – and all travel requires retinal scanning and mass micro-chipping.[5]

Total surveillance society with targeted advertising.

179

We are now on the verge of the implementation of retinal scanning, as the U.S. military has engaged in retinal scanning in occupied territories for several years now. It is important to understand that the actions of the military abroad are often a testing ground for the implementation of such surveillance and tracking technology at "home." In October 2010, the *Guardian* reported of U.S. troops stationed in Afghanistan:

> With each iris and fingertip scanned, the device gave the operator a steadily rising percentage chance that the goat herder was on an electronic "watch list" of suspects. Although it never reached 100%, it was enough for the man to be taken to the nearest US outpost for interrogation.
>
> Since the *Guardian* witnessed that incident, which occurred near the southern city of Kandahar earlier this year, US soldiers have been dramatically increasing the vast database of biometric information collected from Afghans living in the most war-torn parts of southern and eastern Afghanistan. The US army now has information on 800,000 people, while another database developed by the country's interior ministry has records on 250,000 people.[6]

Wired magazine reported millions were the actual goal.[7] The goal is not millions, but the entire globe, where any and all information is now currency for "big data." This is exactly the world *Minority Report* foresaw, and for those curious about Philip K. Dick, whispers are his foresight was due to being well connected with the Silicon Valley elites.[8] This is how *Ubik* foresaw the "Internet of Things," as well as Isaac Asimov's *Foundation*. Slate writes of *Ubik*:

> Samsung, the world's largest manufacturer of televisions, tells customers in its privacy policy that "personal or other sensitive" conversations "will be among the data captured and transmitted to a third party" through the TV's voice-recognition software. Welcome to the Internet of Things.
>
> Sci-fi great Philip K. Dick warned us about this, decades ago. In his classic 1969 novel *Ubik*, the characters have to negotiate the way they move and how they communicate with inanimate objects that monitor them, lock them out, and force payments.[9]

Just as the predictive algorithm in Asimov's *Foundation* was able to track mass movements, so now the same algorithmic tracking is in place across the "web of things" that are capable of being recorded and tracked – and that's

Mandatory retinal scanning by Spyders drones.

most things. The Pentagon has a virtual "you" in a real-time 3D interface that updates its data consistently from everything done on the web. The Register reported in 2009 about this simulated warfare and predictive software:

> Defense analysts can understand the repercussions of their proposed recommendations for policy options or military actions by interacting with a virtual world environment," write the researchers.
>
> They can propose a policy option and walk skeptical commanders through a virtual world where the commander can literally 'see' how things might play out. This process gives the commander a view of the most likely strengths and weaknesses of any particular course of action.[10]

It's not telepathic Samantha Morton in a tub of goo, it's Google and DARPA developing highly advanced technology along the lines of what William Binney exposed, as a former NSA employee. Think here of the film *War Games* (1983), where the A.I. bot was able to war-game future scenarios of global thermonuclear war, but thankfully Ferris Bueller was there to save us. If this was displayed in 1983 in pop culture, imagine how far that technology has come 30 years later, lest anyone think the "pre-crime" is merely for security and weekend Xbox enjoyment.

Capitalism, communism, nationalism, 401ks, blah blah blah, all of these things are basically obsolete. Why? Because of the nature of the real secret high-tech and plans for mega-SmartCities that are to come. You see, you think you are getting ahead and climbing the social ladder, and you aren't even aware that the CEO of IBM, Ginni Rommety, gives lectures about SmartCities where everything you do will be rationed, tracked and traced by the central supercomputers, with pre-crime determining whether you are guilty of crime-think. So everything you are trusting in is already obsolete.

Total surveillance panopticism.

You think I'm exaggerating? On the contrary, you and your children's futures are determined (you don't have a future), and if you are allowed to live past the great culling, you will essentially be boxed into a giant WalmartTarget-GameStopUniversity City that will literally be run by a supercomputer.[11]

And lest anyone think PreCrime is a thing of the future, consider that it has been used for two years in the U.K. 21stCenturyWire reports:

> That's the hope of police in the US, who have begun using advanced software to analyse crime data in conjunction with emails, text messages, chat files and CCTV recordings acquired by law enforcement. The system, developed by Wynyard, a firm based in Auckland, New Zealand, could even look at social media in real time in an attempt to predict where the gang might strike next.
>
> "We're trying to get to the source of the mastermind behind the criminal activity, that's why we're setting up a database so everybody can provide the necessary information and help us get higher up the chain," says Craig Blanton of the Marion County Sheriff's Office in Indiana. Because Felony Lane Gang members move from state to state to stay one step ahead, the centralised database is primed to aggregate historical information on the group and search for patterns in their movements, Blanton says.
>
> "We know where they've been, where they are currently and where they may go in the future," he says. "I think had we not taken on this challenge, we along with the other 110 impacted agencies would be doing our own thing without better knowledge of how this group operates.

It's not the only system that police forces have at their disposal. PredPol, which was developed by mathematician George Mohler at Santa Clara University in California, has been widely adopted in the US and the UK. The software analyses recorded crimes based on date, place and category of offence. It then generates daily suggestions for locations that should be patrolled by officers, depending on where it calculates criminal activity is most likely to occur.[12]

Returning to the film, an interesting tidbit occurs about three times that I noticed. Any time Anderton or his fellow Agents access the "Temple," the holding site of the telepathic PreCogs, the sound made is distinctly the iPhone power-on sound. The first iPod premiered in 2001, so I'm assuming it's the same sound for turning on, but readers can correct me. I find it curious if not, since the sound would likely be chosen for a reason.

If you've seen the important Spike Jonze film, *Her*, you'll see why. In *Her*, lead character Theodore (Joaquin Phoenix) falls in love with an iOS – his operating system. The iOS of his future is an intelligent software system with capability for learning (like the A.I. in *War Games*), and ultimately transcends its own limitations.

I bring this up because *Minority Report* is distinctly dominated by eye imagery. While seemingly insignificant, it is my opinion that Siri and Apple in particular are crucial in the implementation of the com-

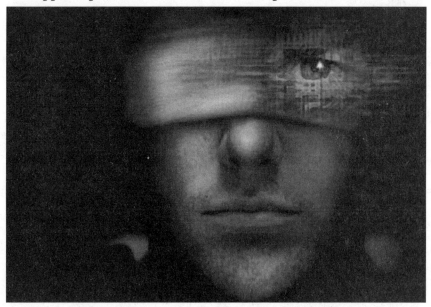

The eye takes on a new meaning here. The retinal scan.

183

ing new order. Apple ads have contained a distinctly esoteric and significant cultural referent, and the 1984 Apple Super Bowl ad was no accident. The year of the revelation of the MAC for home computing was accompanied by an ad that proclaimed George Orwell's *1984* had arrived. This is not to say Microsoft or any of the other tech giants are insignificant; on the contrary, I believe they are all arms of one entity and the appearance of competition is largely illusory.

GEORGE ORWELL (Eric Blair 1903-1950): British writer and former intelligence agent who purported to be a democratic socialist. Most known for his *Animal Farm* and *1984* (as well as many essays), Blair's fiction is some of the most read in modernity. Projecting a dark future of a tyrannical dystopia, Blair encapsulated the "new world order" in its most dismal form in his works. Like Aldous Huxley and H.G. Wells, Blair openly stated the long term plans of the Fabian Socialists and Atlanticist elites to create a world socialist order based on scientism.

I believe in and profess one military industrial complex, and DARPA and Google and Apple and Microsoft are its sons. The façade of competition is enough to advance the technology by the tech nerds that serve it, but in the end, it all serves the same system. My point here is that the iPhone is much more than an iPhone. It is actually an EYEphone, functioning as the eye of Sauron himself, as A.I. reconnaissance before the takeover.

Tech whispers are the iPhone of the next few years, which will contain a Siri that communicates with you like a personal assistant. TechGenMag describes it directly in connection to the film Her, noting "Viv" will do the following:

> On the other hand, not only will Viv recognize disparate requests, she will also be able to put them together. Basically, Viv is Siri with the ability to learn. The project is being kept heavily under wraps, but the guys at Viv have hinted that they're working towards creating a "global brain," a shared source of artificial intelligence that's as readily accessible as heat or electricity. It's unclear how soon a breakthrough of this magnitude can happen. But if this team made Siri, you can bet their next project is going to blow the tech world to pieces.[13]

In order to endear the public to that idea, a prototype Siri had to be offered. While this may be a rumor, it will eventually come. And the dystopic scenario presented in *Her* will meet the nightmare of *Minority Report*. For now, it all seems harmless (though we are seeing a generation of youth mentally destroyed by screens and pads – Steve Jobs didn't let his own kids play with an iPad!1, but the end goal I assure you is nefarious.

The dominant ideology of these tech giants is pure and total dysgenics (not eugenics). In order for the total rewrite to come, the existing structure must be destroyed. The "old way" of doing things will be scapegoated as the technocracy replaces it, offering utopia and salvation, but the synthetic rewrite is a Trojan horse. Humanity will be enslaved in the same virtual Matrix which entraps Anderton.

The film's tagline, which pops up numerous times in the story, is about running. "Everybody runs," and John spends most of the film on the run from the very system he operated. The film asks the question multiple times, "Can you see?" and when we think of this on a deeper level in terms of predictive programming, I think we are intended to look beyond the immediate narrative. There are also numerous hat tips to *Blade Runner*, where again the "running" imagery comes to the fore. Can we run from the panopticon? Do we have eyes to see the iEYES that are "infallibly" surveilling us?

EYEphone

Endnotes

1. Horgan, John. "U.S. Never Really Ended Creepy 'Total Information Awareness' Program." Scientific American. 7 June, 2013. Web. http://blogs.scientificamerican.com/cross-check/u-s-never-really-ended-creepy-total-information-awareness-program/

2. DARPA. Web. http://www.darpa.mil/About/History/History.aspx

3. Stone, Brad. "Amazon Erases Orwell Books from Kindle." *New York Times*. 17 July 2009. Web. http://www.nytimes.com/2009/07/18/technology/companies/18amazon.html?_r=1

4. Grove, Richard. "Privacy and Surveillance." TragedyandHope. 28 January, 2015. Web. http://www.tragedyandhope.com/privacy-and-surveillance-richard-grove-with-meria-heller/

5. "NBC News: US to Be Microchipped by 2017." TopInfopost. 23 October, 2013. Web. http://topinfopost.com/2013/10/23/all-americans-microchipped-by-2017-video

6. Boone, Jon. "US Army Amasses Biometric Data in Afghanistan." *Guardian*. 27 October, 2010. Web. http://www.theguardian.com/world/2010/oct/27/us-army-biometric-data-afghanistan

7. Schachtman, Noah. "Army Reveals Afghan Biometric Program: Millions Scanned, Carded by Many." Wired. 24 September 2010. Web. http://www.wired.com/2010/09/afghan-biometric-dragnet-could-snag-millions/

8. Peake, Anthony. Interview. "Philip K. Dick: The Man Who Remembered the Future." Red Ice Radio. 8 January, 2014. Web. https://www.youtube.com/watch?v=sb1t-RhpX-8

9. Glaser, April. "Philip K. Dick Warned Us about the Internet of Things in 1969." *Slate*. 10 February, 2015. Web. http://www.slate.com/blogs/future_tense/2015/02/10/philip_k_dick_s_1969_novel_ubik_on_the_internet_of_things.html

10. Page, Lewis. "Pentagon World-Sim Tool Making Good Progress, Say Profs." Register. 27 November, 2009. Web. http://www.theregister.co.uk/2009/11/27/pentagon_war_matrix/

11. Rometty, Ginni. Lecture. "SmarterCities Rio." YouTube. 10 November 2011. Web. https://www.youtube.com/watch?v=DKmj7nlQndg

12. Henningsen, Patrick. "British Police Roll Out New 'Precrime' Software to Catch Would-be Criminals." 21stCenturyWire. 13 March 2015. Web. http://21stcenturywire.com/2015/03/13/british-police-roll-out-new-precrime-software-to-catch-would-be-criminals/

13. Raval, Parth. "Siri Creators Developing Viv, a Next Gen A.I. for your Smartphone." TechGenMag. 31 August, 2014. Web. http://techgenmag.com/2014/08/siri-creators-developing-viv-a-next-gen-ai-for-your-smartphone/

14. "Apple's Steve Jobs Didn't Let His Children Have iPads." DailyMail. 13 September, 2014. Web. http://www.dailymail.co.uk/news/article-2754547/Apple-boss-Steve-Jobs-didnt-let-children-iPads-limited-tech-consumption.html

Part Three:

70s-80s Fantasy Dystopia

Chapter 10

Logan's Run (1976) – Our Technocratic Dystopia Unveiled

The 23rd century, where pleasure rules in a synthetic society.

The 1970s were a hot era for science fiction films that took a decidedly dystopian turn. After *Planet of the Apes* at the close of the 60s, films like *Soylent Green* (1973) infected the mass mind with the threat of the coming apocalypse, to be followed by a spate of 80s post-apocalyptic B movies and cult classics like *Mad Max*. One of those highly revelatory 70s films is the 1976 film adaptation of William F. Nolan's novel, *Logan's Run*, directed by Michael Anderson. As with all the dystopian films, especially 70s installments, they all seem to contain a puzzle piece of the overall real-world plan of the technocrats preparing us for the coming of the new aeon.

The setting for *Logan's Run* is a technocratic utopian society situated in a self-contained biosphere dome based around a death cult that participates in a monthly ritual (The Carousel) where all citizens are killed in a "renewal" ceremony somewhat reminiscent of Katy Perry's Super Bowl halftime show. Convinced that renewal results in reincarnation, the youth are color-coded to determine their caste, with those reaching thirty considered aged and primed for euthanasia sacrifice.

Hedonism rules, as the pleasure-seeking synthetic society is run by a giant A.I. SmartGrid, with the central computer tracking and tracing every movement and thought of its citizens. Segregated into various "quadrants," different classes match up to a roughly Platonic model of Philosopher King/central computer system, the guardian class (Logan 5, played by Michael York), and the populace, some of whom are sex slaves, having offered themselves to the guardian class through a vague 70s version of the Internet. This net, however, can transport you directly to the guardian's quarters. Meanwhile, offspring are no longer produced through sexual interaction, but grown in test tubes by unknown donor parents, recalling Huxley's *Brave New World*. Ominously, the BBC has recently reported on UK legislation allowing three parent babies, where DNA will be blended from multiple donors.[1]

Give your soul and body to the Red Lotus Death Cult's carousel.

With a façade of perfection, the death ritual indicates a society that has succumbed to the ultimate dictates of scientistic quantification, where sustainability "dictates" that for every citizen born, one must die to maintain balance in the ecosphere. Thus *Logan's Run* images the very plan the Royal Society and United Nations envision, with mandated euthanasia and death panels determining the time of death according to one's astrological chart. It seems Logan's technocratic society is not immune to the digital state's manipulation of religion, with the Buddhist and Hindu imagery coming to the fore in the red lotus crystal, which, in Buddhist traditions, references the heart and passion. The lotus is also a reference to the Flower

PYTHAGORAS (c. 500 B.C.): Greek philosopher and mathematician who preached a mystical-religious veneration of numbers. Known for the Pythagorean Theorem, his teachings contributed greatly to geometry and number theory, while influencing both Plato and Aristotle, and by extension, all of Western Thought.

of Life in Pythagorean and Platonic mysticism, signifying the unity of the ecosphere as a whole, built up from the platonic solids. Matthieu Ricard and Trinh Thuan comment in their work on these connections, *The Quantum and the Lotus*, citing Platonist Roger Penrose:

> To me this spontaneous insight supports the idea that when the mind makes mathematical discoveries, it enters into contact with a realm of Platonic mathematical concepts. Roger Penrose is adamant about this:

The Lotus Flower of Life.

> I imagine that whenever the mind perceives a mathematical idea, it makes contact with Plato's world of mathematical concepts.... When mathematicians communicate, this is made possible by each one having a direct route to truth, the consciousness of each being in a position to perceive mathematical truths directly, through the process of "seeing."[2]

In various traditions of "Sacred Geometry," the platonic solids are the building blocks of nature itself and we can surmise with the red lotus here the imagery is a sacrifice inverting the principle of life found in the symbology of the Lotus.[3] Platonism is thus the presupposition of the utopia, even in its esoteric and religious concepts. Far Eastern traditions have long seen a spirit of an age, a *zeitgeist*, at work behind long periods of time, the darkest period called *kali yuga* in Hinduism, for example.[4]

Borrowing from these far eastern strands, Aleister Crowley proclaimed a "new aeon of Horus," the crowned and conquering child, where youth and immaturity would overthrow the previous Age of Pisces, dominated by Christianity.[5] It is precisely this aeon in which Logan finds him-

AEON OF HORUS: In Thelema, the age of "the crowned and conquering child" that succeeds the age of Osiris (the Middle Ages and the Christian era of the dying God), characterized as the time of self-realization and spiritual interest.

191

self, where the death state reigns supreme, under the ruse of a synthetic utopia removed from nature, where plastic surgery and bodily alteration permeate Logan's utopia.

Having plumbed the depths of nature and mastered its secrets, this future world's utopia is in fact a dystopia, the golden age of a *kali yuga*, where the police state agents known as "Sandmen" zap any prospective escapees ("runners"), turning them immediately to dust, hence, "sandmen." Logan[5] is one of these guardian class sandmen, who, as you can imagine, begins to question the authenticity of his society. Co-opted by the central computer to infiltrate the subversives who have escaped to the mysterious "Sanctuary," Logan is commanded to become a runner, adopting their *ankh* symbology to go undercover.

A.I. insanity, with a SmartCity run by an insane Box bot.

Initially suspicious of Logan and his sex-slave love interest, Jessica 6 (Jenny Agutter), the rebels inform Logan that "Sanctuary" is much further underground beneath the city. Journeying deeper and deeper, the Dante-esque journey displays the ultimate deception – the whispers of "Sanctuary," as believed by the rebels, is also not true. "Sanctuary" is a giant freezer facility run by an insane A.I. bot named "Box" that imprisons successful escapees in a cryogenic tomb due to his programming, viewing man as a mere resource to be exploited like the fish and plankton. Fiction once again presages reality here, with the recent proposals to allow IBM's Watson supercomputer to manage healthcare for U.S. citizens as the Affordable Care Act begins.[6]

It's no longer far-fetched and outlandish to consider the possibility that the coming SmartCities will also incorporate this centralized A.I. monitoring control grid, engaging in every totalitarian tyranny from "precrime" to computer-determined healthcare, as IBM's CEO Ginni Rometty glowingly declared in our previous chapter.

192

The Affordable Care Act Palmistry Lifeclock, determining your lifespan.

Having sabotaged Box's cryogenic tomb, Logan and Jessica crawl out of their platonic cave for the first time to see the blinding light of the sun. Once again Platonism is the underpinning of the narrative, where the city dwellers are captivated by the shadows and virtual phantoms dancing around them, never being enlightened by the light of objective Truth and the realms of higher existence. In an essay on Plato and Crystals, I cite the profound references in the dialogue *Phaedo*, where Socrates reveals the earth's dwellers toiling away in a subterranean, mundane existence, unaware of higher dimensions, freedom and the true nature of reality. I wrote:

> The study of crystallography demonstrates much of this, and crystals are a big piece of this mysterious metaphysical puzzle, pointing in the direction of higher, spiritual realms. Amazingly, in *Phaedo*, Plato speaks of the higher realms (something akin to heaven) as possessing aether like we possess air. This higher dimension is also directly connected to crystals, as the crystals we possess in our world are mere shards of the wonders of that realm in 109-111:

> Also I believe that the earth is very vast, and that we who dwell in the region extending from the river Phasis to the Pillars of Heracles inhabit a small portion only about the sea, like ants or frogs about a marsh, and that there are other inhabitants of many other like places; for everywhere on the face of the earth there are hollows of various forms and sizes, into which the water and the mist and the lower air collect. But the true earth is pure and situated in the pure heaven – there are the stars also; and it is the heaven which is com-

193

monly spoken of by us as the aether, and of which our own earth is the sediment gathering in the hollows beneath. But we who live in these hollows are deceived into the notion that we are dwelling above on the surface of the earth...

Of these and other colours the earth is made up, and they are more in number and fairer than the eye of man has ever seen; the very hollows (of which I was speaking) filled with air and water have a colour of their own, and are seen like light gleaming amid the diversity of the other colours, so that the whole presents a single and continuous appearance of variety in unity. And in this fair region everything that grows – trees, and flowers, and fruits – are in a like degree fairer than any here; and there are hills, having stones in them in a like degree smoother, and more transparent, and fairer in colour than our highly-valued emeralds and sardonyxes and jaspers, and other gems, which are but minute fragments of them: for there all the stones are like our precious stones, and fairer still.[7]

Stunned at the light of the sun, Logan is still disillusioned by the disappointment of both his utopia and "Sanctuary" exposed as shams. Seeking some refuge, Logan and Jessica wander into the ruins of Washington D.C., which had apparently been destroyed centuries before in some environmental cataclysm. That Logan's Atlantis is built upon the ruins of America is not accidental – this is precisely what Francis Bacon predicted in his esoteric work, *The New Atlantis*, prognosticating the discovery of the new world would be the future site of the coming technocratic wonder state, founded upon the empirical scientistic methodology of the Enlightenment. Atlantis in Logan's day eventually suffers the same fate as the myths of ancient Atlantis tell, where unbridled technology in the hands of a detached elite becomes self-destructive.

FRANCIS BACON (1561-1626): English philosopher, scientist and statesman. Bacon is often considered the father of the scientific method, stressing the importance of empirical observation of the natural world. Bacon was also interested in hermetic and esoteric teachings, as his famous New Atlantis evidences Rosicrucian themes.

Like the unbelievers of Plato's Allegory of the Cave, Logan discovers the dome-dwellers will not believe his discoveries of other lands and worlds outside the biosphere, and realizes he must face the central A.I. computer system. Placed under an MKUltra-style brainwashing procedure, Logan battles the central system and somehow overcomes, resulting in the breakdown of the mainframe and the self-destruction of the dome. Fleeing the collapse, Logan and Jessica lead the

Logan's Dome City – or Epcot Center?

survivors to the proof of the "old ways," the sight of an old man who functions as the Jungian sage and repository of gnosis of the old ways.

Life returns to normal with the youthful refugees discovering their own alienation and divorce from nature, where they had so long subsisted in a self-imposed tech prison erected on a false religious ideology. In essence, Sanctuary was real, it just wasn't found anywhere in the nihilistic, hedonistic frauds of the system. The pro-life message of *Logan's Run* is refreshing in contrast to the death culture obsession of modern Hollywood productions. Indeed, it appears we are on the verge of the end of the old ways, as we prepare to enter into the "final revolution" of the Fabian technocrats, who have prepared a zoo-like existence in the coming virtual-sphere for the enslaved herd. But don't worry – we can always look forward to the red death lotus ritual next year, where Katy Perry and Madonna will celebrate the ritual sacrifice of our troops for the glories of the Global Death State.[8]

Robot mind control!

Endnotes

1. Gallagher, James. "MPs Say Yes to 3 Person Babies." BBC. 3 February, 2015. Web. http://www.bbc.com/news/health-31069173

2.Ricard, Matthieu and Trinh Xuan Thuan. *The Quantum and the Lotus*. New York: Random House, 2001, pgs. 223-5.

3. Monkman, Andrew. "Sacred Geometry: Flower of Life." *Phoenix Masonry*.

4. Guenon, Rene. The Reign of Quantity & the Signs of the Times. New York: Sophia Perennis Press, 2001, pg. 84, 132.

5. See his *Little Essays Toward Truth and Heart of the Master*.

6. "Impementation of Watson." IBM. Web. http://www.ibm.com/smarterplanet/us/en/ibmwatson/implement-watson.html

7. Dyer, Jay. "Plato, Crystals, Dimensions and Artificial Intelligence." JaysAnalysis. 18, November 2014. Web. http://jaysanalysis.com/2014/11/18/plato-crystals-dimensions-and-artificial-intelligence/

8. Hackard, Mark. "Pleasure Dome Police State." SouloftheEast. 1 January, 2012. Web. http://souloftheeast.org/2012/01/01/pleasure-dome-police-state/

Chapter 11

Illuminist Symbolism in the 1974 Film *Zardoz*

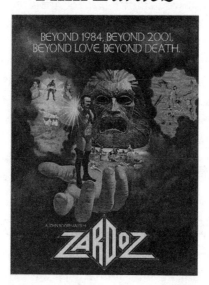

I generally avoid using the term "Illuminati," due to it essentially having become meaningless nowadays, since it was a historical phenomenon as a secret society, but in the case of *Zardoz*, it actually fits. I've titled many analyses with sensational bylines about being the full revelation, the secret of this or that, but only two other films have garnered the actual use of "Illuminati" – *Blade Runner* and *Eyes Wide Shut*. Best known as the film with "Sean Connery in those red undies," there is actually much more going on here.

I am here to declare *Zardoz* as part of that company of actual "Illuminati" films. In today's analysis, we will revisit this 70s oddity to see how this highest "Illuminism" (and much more) was woven into the plot of an unlikely cult classic. OK, and yes, to be fair, *2001: A Space Odyssey* should be in that list as well.

If *Eyes Wide Shut* describes the present social strata of the elite secret societies, and *Blade Runner* describes the near future dystopian transition from man to A.I. replicant, *Zardoz* reveals the distant, post-apocalyptic era following a prolonged dark age. John Boorman's tagline is itself revealing, "After 1984. Beyond 2001," giving us the genre from which we ought to draw to decode the symbology.

Boorman's trippy odyssey is set in 2293, where bands of "brutals" roam the wastelands controlling the population of a savage remnant of humanity. Above the brutals is a fictional deity named Zardoz that floats around in a huge bearded-head hovercraft. Zardoz is a sometimes benevolent, yet demanding god of war who cultivates at the appointed time a civilization for the brute masses, granting them the skills of husbandry and farming in the harsh life of the Outlands.

"Zed" (played by Sean Connery) is our underoo-bedevilled protagonist whose curiosity gets the best of him, and upon investigating his floating-head god discovers humans are being cloned and seeded. Hints of the British elite perspective of panspermia emerge, yet Boorman adds a twist: The gods are actually just highly intelligent humans with advanced technology.

Immediately we are presented with the masonic philosophy of theology as a kind of cloak for technology, where enlightened nobility of yesteryear cunningly crafted elaborate mythologies utilized by the priest class to dupe the vulgar. In order to keep the population down, Zardoz had associated the penis with the gun, and as Zed invades the garden of the gods (known as "The Vortex"), the effete, feminized immortals are entranced by his sexuality. Having become somewhat androgynous and long abandoned natural procreation, the deities of the Zardozian Fields are entirely apathetic. Having conquered death through technology, the Immortals live only to try to advance science, yet to no discernible end.

Much like the Masonic film, *The Man Who Would Be King*.

Boorman accurately captures the nihilistic character of the technocratic age, where the quantification and so-called "perfecting of nature" so adamantly sought by the trans-humanists ends in meaninglessness. In a universe devoid of meaning, whither telos? There is no purpose beyond that of furthering the acquisition of data for its own sake. And this is precisely the empty state in which the technocratic utopia leaves the Immortals, many of whom have actually contracted the "disease of apathy."

We are also given allusions and hints that these immortals are to be roughly matched up with the gods of Ancient Greece and Rome, dining in iconic settings and ninnying about in gardens all day, struck by the boredom of their perfectly secure existence in their breakaway civilization behind their Vortex Force Field. It is also worth noting the council of the gods admits no new members, as it is a completely communal and collectivist society based on *sustainable development* where dissent and divergence are not allowed. Death merely means regeneration by the "Tabernacle," which we learn is an advanced artificial intelligence linked into all material existence, like a kind of all-pervasive Internet of Things.

The Council of the Effete Elite inspect Zed's DNA.

Xenophobia sets in for Zed as the oddities of the Immortal way of life are beyond his comprehension, and as he fumbles around an archive room, Zed discovers a seemingly magical ring that communicates with other Immortals through holographic technology. The image displayed on Zed's third eye from the ring is undeniably the All-Seeing Eye, which in this case, really is the All-Seeing Eye, as Zed discovers the Vortex dwellers possess total panopticon surveillance through their mysterious crystal ring technology. On one level, the eye here has the significance of total surveillance, but as the film progresses, it will take on a deeper meaning.

In this same scene we also see written on the wall the inscription, "In this secret room from the past, I seek the future." This is a clue to the overall meaning of the film, that the gnosis of the ancients in fact contains the secrets of the future. For Zed, representing the common man, the technological prowess and mystical mumbo jumbo of the elite seem to be supernatural, yet according the masonic mythos Boorman will employ, the secrets of nature are merely the secrets of science, giving the first two acts of the film a gnoseological focus. Zed is on a quest to understand his world and seek the truth at all costs.

British Sphinx on Trial for Psychic Violence.

Zed is placed in the service of one of the Immortals in the museum of the gods, who desires to make him into an experiment. The museum of the gods houses mankind's artworks, books, and treasures we later discover were secreted away by the elite prior to the apocalypse. Isolating themselves from the destruction and collapse, the elite kept all their secrets and technology hidden away as the remaining humans fell into a dark age.

Zed however, we come to learn, was more than he let on. A trickster (actually Zardoz) had led him with clues to a dilapidated library in the Outlands and taught him to read, and the big reveal is that the first book Zed learned to read was *The Wizard of Oz*, from which Zard Oz took his name. The reference to *The Wizard of Oz* is worth considering, as it has had a long history of association with mind control and the occult. The essential meaning of the text, while certainly containing those aspects, is more a masonic treatise about atheism. The Wizard is merely an old con man who uses technology to terrorize and rule by fraud, like Zardoz.

The mastering of technology in the historical process is known by the alchemists as the "Great Work," which will "perfect nature," and reveal the philosopher's stone, transmuting crass matter into a higher state of immortality. Nature is viewed in this sense as a vast, irrational, dysfunctional machine – the highpoint of Enlightenment hermeticism. For both Masonry and alchemy, the perfecting of nature is believed to come through gnosis of nature itself, and the advance of technology. For the Immortals, this has arrived, yet as mentioned, they find themselves unsatisfied and listless, having discarded all love and passion, regarding all sex as "rape." After flitting about in several dreamlike sequences, Zed solves the great puzzle of the Vortex, which is controlled by a central A.I. crystal computer that was programmed to never allow itself to be turned off, or allow death. The real "God" is thus an artificial *deus ex machina,* an emergent deity forged in the labs of ancient scientists who had since purposefully erased the secrets to the "Tabernacle."

Now you're inside the Matrix. And the Matrix is the monolith!

Zed, having brought desire, passion and sexuality back to the Immortals (with his perpetual red underwear even the goddesses can't resist), begins to take on the characteristics of a revolutionary. Teaming up with May, who wears a red sphinx cap, Egyptian esoterism and communist revolution are brought together in a mix somewhat curious at first, but when we think of the history of Egyptology-focused Freemasonry, which fomented most of the revolutions of the last few centuries, the pairing is made coherent. Zed is thus a new Satan or Lucifer, invading the Edenic Garden of potentially immortal man, a Prometheus embodying the alternate version of the Genesis narrative as told by the hermeticists and gnostics, where Satan becomes a liberator. Zardoz, as mentioned, was merely a trickster man-god who revealed Zed to himself (Zardoz explicitly says this to Zed).

Longing for death, the dispassionate gods elect Zed to be their liberator by impregnating them with his seed (as they are sterile), if he will be their champion to "break the Tabernacle." Seemingly an impossible task, Zed agrees to take on by osmosis all the gnosis of the Immortals in the hopes that his savage nature will allow him to somehow break the Tabernacle which the gods explain has trapped them in the 3rd and 4th dimensions.

If the Tabernacle-A.I.-god can be broken, the Immortals believe they can transcend their limitations. Here we are in *2001* territory, where the possibility that technology itself is the secret of God, and God Himself is nothing more than a kind of vast, imprisoning *Matrix*-style demiurge. This is the real meaning of the Eye as previously mentioned, where the Eye is the notion of an All-Seeing God, portrayed in Zardoz as a tyrannical control grid.

Death eternal.

Zed discovers that the secret of the A.I. Tabernacle is a single crystal, a diamond, in which the infinite rays of light are able to store infinite amounts of data, and determines the diamond must be destroyed. Immediately translated into the diamond, Zed confronts the depths of his own subconscious, and like *Interstellar*, we are presented with the same mythos of man's conquest of the outer worlds mirroring the conquest of his inner world (psyche). As Zed maintains his sanity inside the Tabernacle, he shoots his reflection in a mirror, signifying the complete death of man. Having achieved full apotheosis, Zed now has power over time and space itself, and leads his band of rebel Immortals to death, prophesied by the Sibyl-like character as true freedom.

Ouroboros of eternal return.

202

As the film concludes, Zed and Consuela, the one Immortal who chose to love him, exit the Vortex now that the Tabernacle had been destroyed and procreate. The film closes with Zed, Consuela and their son, a new Adam, starting the human race anew. In the last few frames, we see a cave painting of two hand-prints and a gun, fulfilling the secrets of the ancient world – the truths of the future. Nietzsche is referenced in the film, and it is from this well that we can surmise the ultimate meaning intended here – that of eternal return.

History is the cyclical turn of the wheel of time, where civilizations rise and fall and at the apex, man discovers technology, which was a secret inside himself all along, as he projected these phantasms of his own forgotten genetic memories into externally existing metaphysical realities (think Bruno Bauer). Again, Nietzsche dominates Boorman's narrative, from the notion of decadent elites, to the ouroboros of eternal return.

Zed, in the final analysis, is the *Ubermensch*, a human Prometheus who has the audacity to storm heaven itself in order to overthrow the existing order of the gods, installing himself as the New Name of a new aeon, suggesting even Crowleyan themes. In the final analysis, *Zardoz* is a masonic philosophical allegory, replete with esoteric symbology and archeo-futurism that culminates in a Nietzschean LSD-trip cavalcade of existential nihilism, where death is "natural" and itself God. Ultimately, *Zardoz's* offering of *death* as the real god destined to have sway is a perfect representation of the meaninglessness of the secular, techno-progressive worldview, and this is a positive message.

BRUNO BAUER (1809-1882): German philosopher and historian. Bauer studied under Hegel and became an extreme rationalist in his approach, seeking to explain all religion and theology in terms of historical revisionism. Bauer posited the character of Jesus was a fictional blend of various religious traditions and exemplified a kind of idealized image of "man," making him influential in the rise of German higher critical textual studies. Bauer would influence Karl Marx in the acceptance of atheism and the application of rationalist methods to historical processes.

Chapter 12

Labyrinth (1986) – Journey Into Sarah's Subconscious

It's always fun to go back and watch the movies you grew up with. However, it can also be a laughingly disturbing experience, akin to finding out that the uncle you thought was so cool was actually an alcoholic. One of the best examples of such nightmares that have receded into the recesses of the mind is the Jim Henson/George Lucas production *Labyrinth* (1986), starring David Bowie and Jennifer Connelly. Famously known for Bowie as "Jareth," the Spandex-sporting witch who can transform into an owl (and trap you in an Escher maze), *Labyrinth* is undoubtedly packed with Kabbalistic, Jungian and hermetic symbolism that is worth investigating.

Seemingly a childish mish-mash of various fairy tales into a puppeteer's hodgepodge, I decided it was also necessary to include the very first *Jays-Analysis* film analysis, and look back on my own development of thought almost a decade later. I'm embarrassed to say the writing was sub-par, and quite likely ten years from now, this present writing will be equally as lacking. So after ten years, and many reads later, let's look at *Labyrinth* afresh.

The narrative centers around Sarah (Jennifer Connelly) on the eve of puberty and womanhood, yet still entranced by the ease and simplicity of her childhood fantasy world. Sarah's mother has apparently run off to be an actress, which we derive from the *Playbill* issues in her bedroom. And predictably, in fairytale fashion, Sarah hates her "wicked stepmother." Sarah's obsession with fantasies thus derives from her inability to cope with the harsh reality of the emotional let downs of the real world. The opening scene presents her in a park/garden, where she wears a virginal white dress emblematic of Edenic purity, reciting invocatory lines from the child's book, *The Labyrinth*. The curious feature of these scenes is her placement in front of the phallic obelisks, foreshadowing the hermetic and masonic to come.

Before delving into the inner, psychical journey Sarah will take into her own subconscious (the labyrinth), it is worth considering the classic mythological significance of labyrinths. Labyrinths have had a wide usage since ancient times, the most famous of course being the story of Daedalus in Homer, who constructs a dancing ground for Ariadne, and later is the architect of the labyrinth for King Minos in which Theseus battles a minotaur. In the Roman poet Ovid, the labyrinth is so skillfully crafted that even as the architect he has a difficult time escaping. Ovid records in *Metamorphoses* VIII:

> The scandal concerning his family grew, and the queen's unnatural adultery was evident from the birth of a strange hybrid monster. Minos resolved to remove this shame, the Minotaur, from his house, and hide it away in a labyrinth with blind passageways. Daedalus, celebrated for his skill in architecture, laid out the design, and confused the clues to direction, and led the eye into a tortuous maze, by the windings of alternating paths. No differently from the way in which the watery Maeander deludes the sight, flowing backwards and forwards in its changeable course, through the meadows of Phrygia, facing the running waves advancing to meet it, now directing its uncertain waters towards its source, now towards the open sea: so Daedalus made the endless pathways of the maze, and was scarcely able to recover the entrance himself: the building was as deceptive as that.[1]

The Labyrinth of Sarah's own unconscious mind.

Henson/Lucas' labyrinth hearkens back to the labyrinth of classical mythology, as well as relating to the perennial journey of the hero on his quest to the underworld. One can see how the transference of the earthen labyrinth and abyss-like waterways can be read as an allegory of the unconscious mind, the underworld of Hades and death, as well as being associated with the worlds in which we enter in our dream state. This astral realm, intimately connected to the realm of the subconscious is the wellspring from which the archetypes of experience spring, corresponding to the archetypal forms in the outer world of phenomenal experience, as we will see below.

Jim Henson (1936-1990): American puppeteer, artist, director and inventor. Henson is known for his creation of The Muppets, characters like Kermit the Frog, and esoteric themed 1980s children's films, such as *The Dark Crystal* and *Labyrinth*.

Upon entering the labyrinth Sarah learns quickly that things are not as they appear – fairies bite, not bless. Doors are not where they appear and missing where they should be. In the medieval world, labyrinths were a symbol of making our way though this wayward world to heaven. In Jung, the Labyrinth is also an image of the individual's unconscious psyche. We will see Sarah fall several times in the film, deeper and deeper into the labyrinth. In "The Process of Individuation" by M.L. von Franz in Carl Jung's *Man and His Symbols*, the author explains the meaning of the labyrinth as subconscious:

> The maze of strange passages, chambers, and unlocked exits in the cellar recalls the old Egyptian representation of the underworld, which is a well-known symbol of the unconscious with its abilities. It also shows how one is "open" to other influences in one's unconscious shadow side and how uncanny and alien elements can break in."[2]

Sarah and her obelisks.

206

Sarah has entered another world, an alternate from our own, which seems to purposefully mirror all the elements in her bedroom. Considering Henson's usage of kabbalistic and gnostic imagery, symbolism and tradition in his *The Dark Crystal*, it is not outside the sphere of possibility to posit a kabbalistic version of alternate worlds in the case of Sarah's psyche/subconcious. Kabbalistic scholar Gershom Scholem explains in his famous *Kabbalah* of these worlds:

> The common element in all these doctrines is supposition that during the first steps toward emanation, certain abortive developments took place which had no direct effect on the actual creation of the present worlds, although remnants of these destroyed worlds did not entirely disappear and something of them still hovers disruptively among us. … Most kabbalists agreed that there is no essential break in the continuity of the influx of emanation which led to the development of additional areas of creation as well, such as the world of the intellect, the world of the spheres and the lower world. But they maintained that whatever preceded these secondary stages was part of the divine domain, which they symbolically portrayed as a series of events in the world of emanation, whereas from this point on.[3]

A young Bowie sketches out the Kabbalistic Sephirot.

This quote gives a clue into what is going on within Sarah: In her bedroom we see Escher's maze, the various creatures that populate the maze, a small marble labyrinth, the *Wizard of Oz*, other fairy tales, and a statue of

Jareth. In other words, the world construct of Jareth's labyrinth is actually a construct of Sarah's subconscious, where the transference of her pain over her mother manifests in the beastly and foreign forms of the otherworldly maze. Upon entering the labyrinth she learns quickly that things are not as they appear. In the medieval world, labyrinths were a symbol of making our way though this wayward world to heaven, which is here Sarah's journey through her own inner psychical world towards individuation.

Clearly the phallic/mason images come to the fore as Sarah travels through the labyrinth, and given Jim Henson's, Monty Python's Terry Jones' and George Lucas' penchant for such masonic myopia, we should not be surprised. However, seven years ago, I read this through your average conspiracy-theorist's goggles, and now I have a different take. The usage of the masonic and kabbalistic imagery concerns Sarah's process of leaving childhood for adulthood, and specifically puberty. Previously clad in virginal white, Sarah encounters numerous instances of bodily functions and base desires, such as Hoggle urinating and the Bog of Eternal Stench, prior to her sexual awakening. The mental process itself is conceived of as an alchemical transformation, since the body itself "transforms" as it grows through puberty.

The masked ball sequence may have a reference to *Eyes Wide Shut*-style orgy parties, and the two scenes are reminiscent of one another, but I think the most natural reading is that of Sarah's sexuality. You'll note the penis shape of many of the noses at the ball, and the hints of her dalliance with orgies, which I read as the curiosities of a person coming of age. It is certainly possible that there is a deeper reference to sex slavery and the

Sarah is tempted.

208

manipulation of alter personas to follow a "programming" that leads to the type of lifestyle the models and beauty queens live in *Eyes Wide Shut*. Whether this was intended by Henson and Lucas is hard to say.

In regards to Jareth and his owl powers, in ancient mythology the owl denoted Athena to the Greeks, goddess of wisdom. In *Labyrinth*, however, the imagery seems to be similar to that of it's meaning to the Romans – mystique and bad luck. Lilith is associated with this as well, and in certain traditions and in terms of the Illuminati proper, the owl was a symbol of autonomous reason and rationality, based on the research done by Terry Melanson.[4] While there may be some esoteric association with the "Illuminati," in Henson and company's mind, it appears to be more of a bad omen and outright witchery – not Illuminati rationalism. Indeed, Jareth is more of a witch, which in Latin is *strix*, from which comes the Italian *strega*, meaning "witch." He is the king of the goblins in the film, and in real life, witches aren't always women, and in the final sequence Jareth is revealed to be merely a phantasm of Sarah's displaced fantasies.

TERRY MELANSON: Author and proprietor of the long-running ConspiracyArchive.com, a website dedicated to investigating the deep state, political conspiracies and globalism, as well as hosting the academic articles of Paul and Philip Collins. Melanson is the author of the definitive scholarly work on the Bavarian Illuminati and its history, in the 2009 publication from TrineDay, *Perfectibilists: The 18th Century Order of the Bavarian Illuminati*.

Sarah's desire to remain in adolescence and retain her freedom from motherhood and responsibility is due to her anger with both her mother and stepmom. She does not want to babysit Toby and instead invokes a curse in anger that the Goblin King (Jareth) would come and take him away. Bowie enters as an owl in a flurry of glitter and spandex nastiness as the androgynous, calling to mind again alchemical doctrines, where the union of opposites into one is seen as the highest form of unity, relating back to the sublime source from which all arises, the One. Sarah's fascination with his androgyny is associated with her own confused ideas about sexuality due to her dysfunctional family life.

This is ultimately another reference to her own confusion about the world as it is. Families break up, relationships fizzle, people leave sexual partners for new, and nothing is as it seems. Sarah confronts this apparent duality and contrariety of reality particularly as she figures out the relationship of male to female. Presuming as youth does, that it has it all figured out, she assumes she has solved the Scotty-dogs' riddles, but as a result, ends up falling even deeper into her subconscious. Ending up in an oubliette, a place of forgetting things, Sarah is tempted to forget her brother and her responsibilities.

Worth noting here is the Platonic notion of forgetting our precious existence from which we have fallen, the realm of the forms, into the lower, base existence of materiality. Sarah's fall into her own inner fantasy world is a mirror of the platonic doctrine of being trapped in the world of appearances where truth is lost for the ease and simplicity of lies and phantasms.

Bowie as Jareth in Escher's maze.

After battling a golem, the Jewish tradition of an animated mechanical man, Sarah has a staring contest with Jareth inside the M.C. Escher strange-loop maze. Escher is significant here because of the mathematical and metaphysical implications of his artwork. The mathematics and ontology of an Escher work are generally styled in the form of a Mobius strip, where the ending is in a state of eternal recurrence with the beginning. For Douglas Hofstadter in his *Godel, Escher, Bach*, this has tremendous relevance for our own psyche, as we seem to experience this same phenomena in a multitude of forms in life, from music to math to art. For the *psyche*, it raises questions of immateriality and what, exactly, consciousness is. In the Labyrinth narrative its usage is Sarah's own entrapment in her mind. Her pain and resentment has become a psychic prison from which she is unable to mature into adulthood. If Sarah does not face her own shade, Jareth, and come to accept reality, she runs the risk of enslavement in her own perpetual arrested development. Thus, the classic quest of the hero is here applied to the journey of the individual *psyche* into maturation.

Endnotes

1. Ovid. *Metamorphoses*. Oxford University Press, 1986, pg.176.

2. Von Franz, *Man and His Symbols*, 176.

210

3. Scholem, Gershom. *Kabbalah*. New York: Dorset Press, 1974, pg. 176.

4. Melanson, Terry. "Owl of Wisdom: Illuminati, Bohemian Club, Schlaraffia, James Gordon Bennett, Jr." ConspiracyArchive. 8 March, 2009. Web. http://www.conspiracyarchive.com/2015/04/18/owl-of-wisdom-illuminati-bohemian-club-schlaraffia-james-gordon-bennett-jr/

Chapter 13

The NeverEnding Story (1984) – Esoteric Analysis

These 80s cult classics do well for analyses. Virtually all the classics children of the 80s like myself grew up with were loaded with deeper, esoteric symbolism, as our series has demonstrated, and *The NeverEnding Story* is no different. In fact, the more one contemplates and revisits these fantasy films of the 80s, the more pronounced the esoteric themes become. *The NeverEnding Story*, I discovered, was influenced by some of the more overt and bizarre strains of occultism in the previous century. The film is based on a children's book of the same title by author Michael Ende, a German writer, whose works are influenced by Rudolph Steiner's Anthroposophy, a German movement that split from Madame Blavatsky's equally occult Theosophy, which influenced Nazi ideology. The reader will recall this same theme in regard to Oz and L. Frank Baum. As the German biography notes, Ende was also influenced by other pagan movements:

> Michael Ende has a lifelong interest in all philosophical systems based on a magical worldview. "Edgar's son was always looking for other paths and esoteric knowledge, like the legendary Christian Rosenkreutz 'Chemical Wedding,' as well as the infernal old master Aleister

Crowley, the Indians and Egyptians, Zen, the Kabbala, in Swedenborg, Eliphas Lévi, Soren Kierkegaard, and Friedrich Weinreb."[1]

Thus Ende's worldview influences are clear. Anthroposophy shared many of the same new age notions of theosophy, but was banned by the Nazi party. Ende attended a new age Waldorf School, which based its curriculum around anthroposophical ideas, both of which have United Nations affiliations.

What becomes clear as one researches this subject is the parallels between the United Nation's globalist ideology, along with its parallel idea of a single, unified global religion as a tool of a superstate which replaces all previous nationalities and traditions, forcing everything into an amalgamated muck where individuality is lost in a collectivist blob, subservient to the deified world state. Amazingly, my articles still have commenters who dispute these public globalist policies, which have been known for decades. I even attended

RUDOLPH STEINER (1861-1925): Austrian philosopher, architect and esotericist. Founder of the "spiritual science" philosophy known as anthroposophy, Steiner was influenced by German idealism, Goethe and Rosicrucianism. Steiner's ideas were also similar to Madame Blavatsky's "Theosophy," a mystical school emphasizing individualism and the reconciliation between spiritualism and science. Steiner's version emphasized European spirituality and dismissed religious figures promoted by theosophists, like Krishnamurti.

a new age-ish elementary school for the gifted in my younger years associated with UNESCO that enforced these globalist ideologies along similar lines to Steiner's syncretic mysticism. Make no mistake about it; it is very real, very public, and very much an open tool of the globalists. I was surprised, however, the last time I watched this film, how overt it's paradigm was.

The NeverEnding Story presents the protagonist hero, Bastian Balthazar Bux, as the typical 80s nerd harassed by neighborhood bullies, raised by his single father. Contrary to popular belief, having half of *Simon and Simon* as your dad (Gerald McRaney) isn't as bitchin' as you would expect. In fact, Mr. Bux is basically a dickhead. But what can you expect, when *Simon and Simon* ends and you're in *NeverEnding Story* (and your wife has died).

Bastian and Atreyu's Ouroboros, the "Auryn," representing eternal return

Bastian awakes from a dream, startled, and late for school, but this clues us into viewing him as a "dreamer" as the opening sequence makes clear, when Mr. Bux demands he get his "head out of the clouds and keep his feet on the ground." Tormented by bullies, Bastian stumbles into an obscure bookshop where he meets a magician. The magus then tempts Bastian to read his occult wonderworking text, *The NeverEnding Story*, replete with an Ouroboros on the cover. As it turns out, Bastian is himself written into, and in the process of writing this story. In literature studies, this is known as meta-fiction, where the narrative is taken to another level; an appropriate usage in this case, since the view of alternate worlds and all possible worlds comes into play. This is significant because the film is working from a paradigm in which notions of a multi-verse end up necessitating that all possibilities are eventually made actual.

The Ouroboros symbolizes this concept in ancient religions, as well as in gnosticism and hermeticism. In fact, Plato included the concept of the Ouroboros in his famed esoteric work of cosmology, *The Timaeus*. Plato wrote:

> The living being had no need of eyes when there was nothing remaining outside him to be seen; nor of ears when there was nothing to be heard; and there was no surrounding atmosphere to be breathed; nor would there have been any use of organs by the help of which he might receive his food or get rid of what he had already digested, since there was nothing which went from him or came into him: for there was nothing beside him. Of design he was created thus, his own waste providing his own food, and all that he did or suffered taking place in and by himself. For the Creator conceived that a being which was self-sufficient would be far more excellent than one which lacked anything; and, as he had no need to take anything or defend himself against any one, the Creator did not think it necessary to bestow upon him hands: nor had he any need of feet, nor of the whole apparatus of walking; but the movement suited to his spherical form was assigned to him, being of all the seven that which is most appropriate to mind and intelligence; and he was made to move in the same manner and on the same spot, within his own limits revolving in a circle. All the other six motions were taken away from him, and he was made not to partake of their deviations. And as this circular movement required no feet, the universe was created without legs and without feet.[2]

In this scheme, it is a symbol of all created reality itself. The view of time and reality here is one of cyclical, eternal return, as it's called. This is shared in common with Hinduism and ancient Egypt, and is a staple characteristic of pagan religions, in distinction from biblical religions, which view time as linear, with a progression, beginning and end, rather than time and history being a deterministic, karmic trap, which must be escaped.

In biblical religions, linear time itself becomes "redeemed" in some fashion. In paganism, time is a dismal illusion of determined, neverending brute force – thus the film's title. In the film's paradigm, the ancient and occultic exterior doctrines of archetypes and cyclical, eternal return are internalized and psychologized, as, for example, Hinduism does, as well as other occult systems. Carl Jung did this. In this absurd scheme, the individual is himself the god creating the external reality, writing the whole narrative. This is precisely what is happening in *The NeverEnding Story* – it's Balthazar's never-ending story of eternal return, which is the *gateway* to the supposed self-realization of apotheosis.

It is also very significant that the film includes the concept of sphinxes as gateways. This gets very complex and *uber* deep, but suffice to say this is also an ancient notion that is shared in numerous religions. Ancient Egyptian theology in particular placed emphasis on the sphinx as the gateway guardian to the temple. This same idea exists in Jewish theology, too, in regard to the Temple's Seraphic and Cherubic imagery, in particular the Ark of the Covenant, as well as places like Eden. *The Jewish Encyclopedia* notes:

> Primitive Hebrew tradition must have conceived of the cherubim as guardians of the Garden of Eden (Gen. iii. 34; see also Ezek. xxviii 14). Back of this lies the primitive Semitic belief in beings of superhuman power and devoid of human feelings, whose duty it was to represent the gods, and as guardians of their sanctuaries to repel intruders. Compare the account in the Nimrod-Epos, Tablet IX.[3]

The purpose of this chapter is not to prove conclusively how close Babylonian griffins or Egyptian sphinxes were to which angelic beings, and is outside of its scope. However, what is clear is that there are similarities and an association with the sphinx guarding a portal or gateway to the gods, as well as esoteric knowledge due to their riddles, and also an association with initiation. That is precisely their usage in *The NeverEnding Story*, as well. Albert Pike explains of the sphinx in Freemasonry, for example:

> The Cherub, or symbolic bull, which Moses places at the gate of the Edenic world, holding a blazing sword, is a Sphinx, with

215

the body of a bull and a human head; the old Assyrian Sphinx whereof the combat and victory of Mithras were the hieroglyph analysis. This armed Sphinx represents the law of the Mystery, which keeps watch at the door of initiation, to repulse the Profane. It also represents the grand Magical Mystery, all the elements whereof the number 7 expresses, still without giving it last word. This "unspeakable word" of the Sages of the school of Alexandria, this word, which the Hebrew Kabbalists wrote; IHUH, and translated by ARARITA, so expressing the threefoldness of the Secondary Principle, the dualism of the middle ones, and the Unity as well of the first Principle as of the end; and also the junction of the number 3 with the number 4 in a word composed of four letters, but formed of seven by one triplicate and two repeated; this word is pronounced Ararita.[4]

The first gate of the southern oracle, the sphinxes, resembling the Ark of the Covenant's seraphic guardians.

In *The NeverEnding Story* Bastian has a "higher self" in the alternate world of Fantasia named Atreyu, a wild buffalo hunter of the "plains people," somewhat reminiscent of an American Indian. In fact, Bastian has an experience of synchronicity when he first reads about Atreyu, noticing that he had placed a sticker of an Indian hunting a buffalo on a plain. The film chronicles Bastian's progressive realization that the actual story is about him, while Atreyu is also on a journey of self-discovery to realize that he is also Bastian, similar to something you would find in Stephen King's Gunslinger series.

With the introduction of the Ouroboros, and then meeting the characters named Engywook and Urgl, who represent respectively science and superstition in tension, an alchemical angle. They aid Atreyu on his journey, but turn out to be bumbling and silly, showing the film's thesis to partly be that those who only see reality as from a base superstitious perspective or from a naive scientism have not but scratched the surface of the true nature of reality, which is only to be found through initiation into "the mysteries."

Atreyu at the Mirror Gate, seeing his alternate identity, Bastian.

Many esotericists and gnostics took the perceived metaphysical statements about the gods and archetypes and internalized them into the individual psyche, thus psychologizing them. Alchemy was done this way too, and the alchemical process comes to symbolize instead an inner, progressive realization of godhood. That is what is happening here. Bastion must realize that he is Atreyu, and vice versa. Once this realization occurs at the magic mirror gate, after the sphinx explains the mystery of Fantasia to Atreyu, Atreyu and Bastian see each other reflected in the mirror. In standard Jungian lingo, this is common. This is the mirror of the psyche, reflecting itself. In other words, Bastian is supposed to realize these are manifestations of his psyche, and then reintegrate them. Now, I think this is ridiculous, but there is something to it. Synchronicity is real, and the inner worlds are connected to the outer worlds, but in my estimation all this needs to be purged of the gnostic notions of external reality being an "illusion." It's also manifestly false that reality is created by an individual's mind. Solipsism is manifestly absurd and self-refuting.

The reason Atreyu is on his quest is to save the childlike empress of Fantasia, who is nameless. In many esoteric traditions, the concept of a name controlling and in some sense containing the essence of the Thing, is fundamental. The Empress, we discover, needs a name. Atreyu doesn't learn this until the end, but this is clearly working from the Magian worldview, as Spengler termed it, where word and thing are intimately bound up in one another. This is also found in kabbalistic ideas, as well. Bizarrely, Bastian must rename the Empress, we discover, and it must be the name of his dead mother, who we find out is called "Moon Child." Bastian actually screams "Moon Child!" when Fantasia is imploding. "Moonchild" has the occult association of being the novel by Satanist Aleister Crowley concerning demonic insemination, as well as associating the Empress with Bastian's mother, or the feminine Sophia archetype.

Indeed, research into the scheme Ende drew up for Fantasia includes the idea that the Empress is the feminine embodiment of the spirit of Fantasia. She is then the "soul of the world," or the *anima mundi*, in Platonic parlance. It is also interesting that she appears as a kind of Venus or Aphrodite, as well as with vaginal imagery. She is also the virgin queen Sophia, (wisdom) who lacks the male principle. This is why Atreyu enters the vaginal chamber at the end. Naturally, there must be the sexual component.

Fantasia, we learn, is imploding due to "The Nothing," which is used to represent the classical idea of chaos, or Tiamat, existing prior to form being imposed upon it. In the cyclical pagan view, matter is eternal and form is imposed on it, being recycled after a few aeons into new forms, but since eternal means eternal, eventually all possible potentialities will become actual. Much of modern theoretical physics deals with this, in writers like Michio Kaku and Lisa Randall.

A universe in a grain of sand.

218

So, in the end, the world implodes in on itself, because Fantasia is all of humanity's desires and dreams. It is the astral realm, and Bastian figures out how to magically conquer it, re-appropriate it into his psyche and become god of his own "world." When he speaks to Sophia/Empress at the end, having "named" her, he, as his higher self, had penetrated into the Empresses' overtly vaginal throne room. It is here that she gives him a "grain of light" and tells him it is another genesis scenario. It is the beginning again, and all is darkness. The empress tells Bastian to make up a whole new world. Bastian is god. He takes the raw stuff of matter from the feminine principle, and imprints upon it form and order. A new order must be brought out of the old chaos. Bastian has opened the gateway/portal to Fantasia and brings his astral realm fantasies into the "real" world of the 1980s, riding that goofy-looking dragon around, exacting revenge on his bullies. To sum it up, *The NeverEnding Story* is sex magick.

Atreyu penetrates the Empress' overtly vaginal Ivory Tower

Endnotes

1. "Michael Ende und die magischen Weltbilder." MichaelEnde.de. Web. http://www.michaelende.de/autor/biographie/michael-ende-und-die-magischen-weltbilder

2. Plato, *Timaeus in Plato: Collected Dialogues*, pg. 1164-5.

3. "Cherub," in *Jewish Encyclopedia*. Web. http://www.jewishencyclopedia.com/articles/4311-cherub

4. Pike, *Morals and Dogma*, 728.

Chapter 14

Alchemy and Eros in
Ridley Scott's *Legend* (1985)

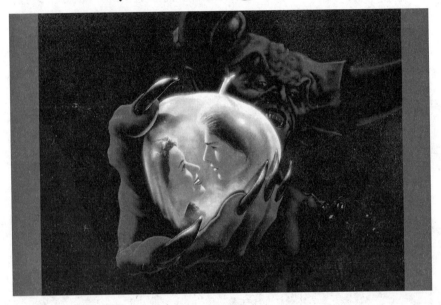

By: Jay Dyer and Jennifer Sodini

Ridley Scott is reportedly not happy about *Legend*, nor is Tom Cruise. However, when we think "80s Tom Cruise," we think *Top Gun, Risky Business*, and *Legend*. How does one go from *Blade Runner* to *Legend*? These are great 80s mysteries that we are not here to solve – what we *are* here to solve are the enigmatic, and sometimes bizarre, scenes and images in *Legend*. No stranger to positing deeper meanings to jovial 80s films targeted at adolescents, Jennifer Sodini and I have decoded the moribund (and sometimes meandering) mythos of *Legend*.

Packed with all the key elements of fantasy/whimsy: unicorns, princesses, sprites, goblins, fairies, and forest people galore, *Legend* resembles other 80s fantasy films like the *Dark Crystal, Labyrinth* and *The NeverEnding Story*, yet has its own unique elements. For those of us who grew up enchanted by the fantastical fairy tale imagery of this film, taking a deeper look at the hidden esoteric symbolism involved in the story reveals a shocking subplot about sexual temptation/desire and alchemical imagery one wouldn't expect.

As the story begins we are introduced to Tim Curry's character, which many would mistake to be "the devil," but is actually the demon Darkness, the beast of temptation and lust that lives within all of us (even the purest of heart). Darkness summons one of his goblins, Blix, to do his bidding as he expresses the urge of his carnal desires to be satiated. The accomplishment of this act is intimately tied to the ritual action of removing the unicorn's horn and consuming the energy of its innocence through blood sacrifice, signifying both menstrual blood and the blood of the broken hymen.

Functioning as an antithesis to the red (the color corresponding to the base chakra/carnal desire, *muldadhara*), dual-horned demon Darkness, the unicorn's white signifies sexual purity/innocence.[1] While the unicorn has a horn, the horn (just as sexual energy) can either be used to create or destroy, to protect, or to impale. Sexual energy (the orgasm in particular), as viewed by most religions, is sacred: The power of the orgasm is perceived to be the same power of both death and creation, arising from the universe.[2] This theory was also explored by scientist Wilhelm Reich, in his cloud-busting and orgon box energy experiments. Carl Jung explains the symbology of the unicorn in relation to alchemy and Mercury:

WILHELM REICH (1897-1957): Austrian psychoanalyst well known as the second generation following Freud, and the most radical. Reich attempted to harmonize psychoanalysis with Marxism and later influenced many young student radicals through his book *The Mass Psychology of Fascism*, which would later become popular. Reich was interested in sexology, particularly in relation to bio-mechanical feedback, and other far-flung theories arising from his "Orgone Institute." Reich was arrested by the FBI in 1941 under suspicion of being involved in subversive activities and espionage.

> The unicorn in alchemy: The example of the Unicorn is chosen to demonstrate how the symbolism of Mercury is intermingled in the traditions of pagan gnosticism and the Christian Church. As the unicorn is not a single, clearly identified entity, more specific concern is centered on the beast with a single horn (the alicorn). Examples are given from the literature, especially the *Chemical Wedding of Christian Rosencrantz*, in which the unicorn, the lion and the dove appear, all of these being symbols of Mercury. Reference is also made to medieval art in which images of the virgin and the unicorn appear.
>
> These images are said to represent the dual aspect of Mercury: the virgin as the passive, feminine aspect of the unicorn, and the unicorn or lion as the wild, rampant, masculine force.... References from the Church fathers are variously given in which the uni-

221

corn is identified with the God of the Old Testament or Christ. It is pointed out that there are ecclesiastical quotations in which the unicorn is said to carry the element of evil. It is this inner contradiction that makes the unicorn an appropriate symbol to be used by alchemists' *monstrum hermaphroditum*. [the hermaphrodite – a key stage of unification in the alchemical process].3

The initial relationship between Lilly (Mia Sara) and Jack (Tom Cruise) is presented as juxtaposition between a feisty, rebellious princess who does not like being told what to do, and the peasant boy of the woods who speaks with animals and abides by the code of nature (hearkening to Shakespeare's Puck and Ancient Greece's Pan). Interesting opposites, as one would assume the princess would listen, and the forest boy would be wild. As Lily is approaching her "time" and Jack is naturally ripe, the loss of innocence in the forest commences as he blindfolds her before leading her to the unicorns. Lilly protests by saying, "Do you not trust me"? Then she frolics off to tickle the forbidden phallus.

When the unicorns appear, we see two paired together, striding down a stream that is sexually provocative given the angle of the camera. Riding on the running "water of life" is also noteworthy, as water in alchemy is associated with the power of emotion and intuition. Sexual temptation presents itself, and courses through the power of emotion/intuitive desire, leading Jack and Lily to experiment beneath the Tree of Life, a classic image of sacral fertility. Both images recall the Jung quote above, as well as speaking to a possible link with Scott's *Blade Runner* usage of the unicorn in Deckard's dream – both seem to suggest an alchemical union amongst both films' protagonists.

Jack instructs Lilly not to approach the unicorn, yet she defiantly does so, eventually touching it. As she touches it, Blix, the goblin sent to do the "Big

D's" bidding shoots the unicorn with a poison dart, releasing chaos, death and darkness into the world. After her "fall," Lily removes her magical ring, which is emblazoned with a waning moon, highly suggestive again of the menstruation cycle and the seasonal clock Lily gazed upon in the peasant cottage. Lily tosses her ring off a cliff and issues a challenge to Jack to recover it from the abyss, and, in so doing he may have her in marriage.

The cyclical clock of nature, frozen in death after Lily's fall.

The explanation for the enigmatic clock scenes, which displays the seasons and is then frozen following Lily's fall, are eloquently explained in concert with her challenge for Jack by Julius Evola:

We find here a similar conception of a cyclic development, symbolized by the "cosmic clock" and its course. The first phase is the entry of God into nature, of the "Son" into process of becoming, and of the male into female. It is the woman or Shakti, the lowest point of the clock, that predominates in this phase. At the figure six, which corresponds to the lowest point of the clock, that is, the descending arc, "in which woman dominates man and matter imprisons the spirit in the depths of its entrails," we have the limits of the abyss; when we reach his limit we either die or are reborn to eternal life. It is the point of the "dangerous passage" or the turning point where the great trial is held.

JULIUS EVOLA (1898-1974): Italian baron and philosopher, painter, and esotericist. Evola believed mankind had entered a Kali Yuga - a dark age in which traditional relations and societies were being inverted by nefarious earthly and spiritual forces, dominated by materialism. Evola's books focus on the metaphysics of war and sex, as well as the meaning of mystical symbols like the Holy Grail. Evola's work would become highly controversial, influencing fascists for decades to come, as well as modern day right wing, conservative and traditional movements.

After that, themes of sexual magic appear because the trial should also consist in facing the woman in the same spirit as the Tantric principle of "victory over the bad through its transformation into the good." The woman is thought of as the gate through which it is possible to enter the sphere of death or life. In the fall, sensual pleasure became the magnet which draws man towards woman, not for the conquest of life (which equals God), but for the conquest of death (which equals Satan), and Eve ... became the battlefield of the struggle between life and death.

At the decisive point of this trial, man sees his "bride" again and is invited to immerse himself in her, the female, once more, not in order to enter into the realm of death and becoming, but in order to leave that realm and maintain awareness of his own being instead of dissolving. In this context the woman is seen as the Gateway of Heaven, and as the essential element for freedom. From the end of the descending phase six, the victorious male next finds himself re-projected to the starting point of the cosmic clock's cycle, freed from matter and consecrated King. This is the rite of the "Second Wedding," which coincides with that of the formation of the Messiah.[4]

Jack nosedives from the cliff after the moon ring and upon descending to the abyss, the seasons rapidly change, the water freezes, and winter falls over the land. As this is all happening, the unicorn Lilly touched is captured and de-horned (emasculated), an allegory of innocence lost, chastity discarded, and the death of sexual purity in Jack's concession to Lily. This explains why the unicorn who dies is the male, while the female survives. As Blix presents the horn to Darkness, the demon replies that the destruction of both is needed, and in particular the ritual sacrifice of the virgin female, since the female possesses "the power of creation."

Jack's descent into the abyss is signified in the sense Evola describes in this scene, whereupon, emerging ringless, he experiences a psycho-sexual emasculation, having lost both his "horn" and Lily, who has now run away. Recalling the mythology of Osiris, the lost phallus is primeval in its mythological origins, and only as Osiris' disembodied form is reassembled into a higher unity, including the return of the phallus, can the process of the restoration of the masculine occur. It is within *Legend* this same narrative is played out, as Jack must mature from adolescence into manhood, undergoing the trial of losing his essence due to Lily's folly, imprisoned in the wintry, watery abyss that now encompasses his world. Our abyss interpretation is also confirmed by Darkness' opening salvo that, "in the beginning, there was only Darkness, and the void..." (the abyss), from whence the order of created beings emerged (Gen. 1).

Darkness' lair.

Before Lilly is captured, we see the abuse of the power of the horn as Blix uses the horn for trivial/egotistical purposes, emblematic of base desires utilizing the magic of sexuality to destroy, not create. Eventually Lilly and the female unicorn are captured and brought to the underworld inferno of Darkness. Darkness' realm is a massive, dead tree, a kind of Da'at* inverse of the Tree of Life, with a vast network of underground abodes and prisons borrowed quite clearly from Dante.[5] Gump, the Frankie Muniz lookalike that accompanies Jack on his quest, identifies it as the location of the ritual site where the wicked once performed ritual blood sacrifice (Jack also mentions "alchemy" in this scene, confronting the witch). Blood had already been let in the loss of Lily's innocence, and now Lily must undergo the temptation to give in to her shade, the Goth alter persona she almost embraces.

DANTE ALIGHIERI (1265-1321): Famed Italian poet of the late middle ages and author of the classic Divine Comedy, widely considered to be one of the greatest poetic works of all time. Dante's Divine Comedy achieved a synthesis between ancient Greek mythology and philosophy and the western Catholic religious tradition, as well as being influenced by the esoteric and hermetic teachings of his day.

This scene is oddly reminiscent of Sarah's dalliance with Jareth in the orgiastic masked ball in Jim Henson's *Labyrinth*. In both films, maturation into puberty is the subtle theme, with the energy of sexuality evoking confusing and conflicting ideas for both protagonists grappling with the opposite sex. For Sarah, the loss of her mother and the possibility of childbearing as a result of bodily coitus are repellent, as she despises the care of Toby. For Lily, the alter persona of the sexually liberated gothic babe engaging in trysts with "Big D" almost overcome her resolve. Both scenes occur in the context of the underworld/Labyrinth's connection to the subconscious, from whence arise our potentially multiple personas or alters. As we saw previously, the meaning of the labyrinth or underworld as the subconscious signifies a maze of strange passages, chambers, and unlocked exits in the cellar emerging from the Egyptian representation of the underworld.

225

The seduction of Lilly, and her shade self, exemplified in the mirror reflection.

Of particular import is Lilly's dance with the devils in an interesting choreography where her black clad shade twirls her into a seductive spell. Under the sensuous mind control of Darkness, she eventually merges with the shadow, acquiescing to the pomp and luxury of Darkness' appeal to her ego through flattery (and women do love jewelry!). Drawn into the material, Lily adorns herself with the diamond necklace that alludes to Ezekiel's description of Lucifer as bedazzled with emeralds and precious stones (and I don't mean the Bedazzler). Ezekiel 28:12-14 describes the fallen Cherub:

> Son of man, take up a lamentation over the king of Tyre and say to him, 'Thus says the Lord GOD, "You had the seal of perfection, Full of wisdom and perfect in beauty. "You were in Eden, the garden of God; Every precious stone was your covering: The ruby, the topaz and the diamond; The beryl, the onyx and the jasper; The lapis lazuli, the turquoise and the emerald; And the gold, the workmanship of your settings and sockets, Was in you. On the day that you were created They were prepared. "You were the anointed cherub who covers, And I placed you there. You were on the holy mountain of God; You walked in the midst of the stones of fire.

The consistent theme throughout the film is gnostic duality and dialectical tension: masculine vs. feminine, light vs. dark, innocence vs. desire, spirit vs. flesh, and even in the climax, Darkness' destruction results in the explicit exclamation, "What is light without darkness?" "Big D" is "conquered" though Jack stabbing him in the solar plexus (ego center) with the unicorn horn (death of ego by desire), Darkness disappears into the abyss from the light of the sun. Indeed – the French term for the orgasm, *le petit mort* means the "little death." Author Nicolas Laos aptly comments on this deep association of sex, death, and nihilism in his introduction to Anna Schaeffner's *Modernism and Perversion*:

...Furthermore, observing and studying the history of modernity, in general, I never stop being appalled by the desacralization of life in the context of modernity, as a consequence of which the modern subject lives in the dimension of time separated from eternity, that is, under the aspect of death. Thus, the modern subject has gradually developed a perverse relation with eros and death (which, according to Sigmund Freud, are the two basic instincts): in the context of the desacralized life of the modern subject, death is a taboo and repulsive issue, in the sense that the modern subject, by living separated from the absolute (eternity), cannot manage the issue of death and desperately tries to forget, evade, and silence this issue, while simultaneously fusing death and eros into a necrophiliac perception of culture manifested through necrophiliac aesthetic values (e.g., skinny fashion models and asexual 'cyberfreaks' as opposed to the ancient Greek erotic archetypes of Aphrodite and Apollo, artifacts that emanate disharmony and decadence, etc.), necrophiliac sexual attitudes (e.g., confusion between pleasure and pain or between sensationalism and violence, etc.), and necrophiliac working patterns (i.e., working for living, that is, for satisfying temporal needs/desires, and not for living well, which is a spiritual question)...[6]

Darkness has some poetic dying quips that exemplify the principles Nicolas Laos elucidates when death has come to dominate the sexual impulse as destructive, as opposed to life-giving: "Every wolf suffers fleas, 'tis easy enough to scratch," "What is light without dark ...what are you without me?" "I am a part of you all, you can never defeat me, we are brothers eternal." In the gnostic schema, darkness is just as necessary, fundamental and ontologically real as light. Both are flip sides of the same coin, and with Legend, the identification of evil with good once again relativizes meaning. Thus, the climax of this celluloid sex magic extravaganza is the attempted blood sacrifice of the unicorn to the powers of darkness, a transferal of essence from one being to another – just as Jack found himself powerless before Lily, so Lily becomes powerless before Darkness.

Alchemical frolicking.

227

As Laos notes, when death and sex are combined to cancel one another out, death takes pre-eminence and Lily's fascination with sexual union with death becomes emblematic. "Big D" eventually dissolves back into the universe, but as Jack and Lily run off into the sunset after Jack has successfully retrieved the magical ring and both Lily and Jack and the unicorns are reunited in alchemical harmony, "Big D" ominously reappears and laughs as the movie comes to a close. The conclusion may be that Darkness, or the lustful desire both awakened, was the overriding principle that brought about the transformative psychosexual process. Or perhaps they have triumphed over discord.

RIDLEY SCOTT: English film director and producer known for neo-noir dystopias like *Blade Runner* (1982) and *Alien* (1979), as well as later films like *Gladiator* (2000) and *Prometheus* (2012). Scott's films often contain revolutionary themes and of late, Scott has focused on co-operation with NASA on the Mars-themed blockbuster The Martian (2015). Scott, like Lucas and Spielberg, has championed the alien mythos while simultaneously working closer and closer with the deep state on his major projects.

So let's ask ourselves this, what is light without dark, life without death, desire without consequence, and love without desire? The shadow aspects of the lightness of being will never be separate from our human experience. We all have our demons, we all have our desires, and we all must exercise control over the passions that govern the shadow aspects of our personality. While *Legend* is a mystical mythology of this understanding of the power of innocence, sexuality, orgasm, and temptation – the lesson is a similar recurring theme through other 80's movies such as *Labyrinth*. Control your thoughts, control your reality, as Plato encouraged his neophytes in *Phaedo* to control their passions, in the allegory of the chariot (mind) and its horses (passions).

(Endnotes)

1. Fondin, Michelle. "The Root Chakra: Muladhara." Chopra.com. Web. http://www.chopra.com/ccl/the-root-chakra-muladhara

2. Aun Weor, Samuel. "The Transmutation of Sexual Energy." 2005. Web. http://gnosticteachings.org/the-teachings-of-gnosis/lectures-by-samael-aun-weor/144-the-transmutation-of-sexual-energy-2.html

3. Jung, Carl. "Abstracts of the Collected Works of Carl Jung." CGJungPage. 27 October 2013. Web. http://www.cgjungpage.org/learn/resources/jung-s-collected-works-abstracts/854-abstracts-of-the-collected-works-of-cg-jung

4. Evola, Julius. *Eros and the Mysteries of Love: The Metaphysics of Sex.* Rochester, Vermont: Inner Traditions, 1991, pg. 262.

5. Scholem, *Kabbalah*, 107.

6. Laos, Nicolas. Unpublished Introduction. Web. http://jaysanalysis.com/2015/06/13/alchemy-and-eros-in-ridley-scotts-legend-1985/

Chapter 15

Blade Runner (1982) – The Synthetic Future Revealed

In Ridley Scott's *Blade Runner*, we are presented with a prescient, dystopian future based on Philip K. Dick's novella, *Do Androids Dream of Electric Sheep?* We will see that this film is full of not only accurate predictions of the future's general landscape, but is also suffused with occult imagery and deep symbolic themes, as well as raising crucial moral and social issues. The film operates on several levels: as the immediate story itself, the predictive future level with social critiques, the level of covert operations and mind control, and the deepest level, that of myths, archetypes, and alchemical occult initiatory transformation. All these levels must be integrated to grasp the full import of the film as Ridley Scott conveys it. The deepest level is what holds the other levels together in coherence and meaning.

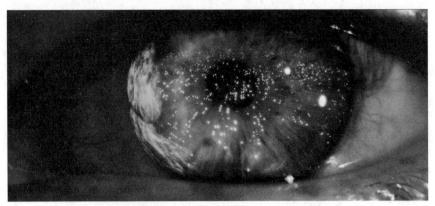

The eye.

As the film begins, the viewer is shown the 2020 landscape of Los Angeles, and then an eye viewing the landscape. The eye represents the viewer, and just as we witnessed in my analysis of *Eyes Wide Shut*, the viewing of the film itself will again constitute an initiatory experience. The viewer is going to be shown the elite plan, yet the eyes of most will remain shut. For the masses, there is no ability to make deeper level connections and associations between ideas, symbols and archetypes. For the viewer who has eyes to see, they are seeing the future itself, as well as the worldview of the ruling class. In fact, *Blade Runner* ranks with *Eyes Wide Shut* as one of the most explicit revelations of the method of the ruling oligarchs. My interpretation of this is confirmed by the fact that the film doesn't show us whose eye we see. In fact, the reflection in the eye shows the scene the viewer just saw of the L.A. cityscape.

It is significant that we are presented with two shots of the eye and then the cut to the Tyrell Corporation's ziggurat/pyramid shape. Immediately we are presented with Egyptian symbology, as well as the notions of the so-called "Illuminati." The all-seeing eye is flashed in between images of the exalted pyramid in order to initiate the viewer into who is running things. This is the connection of imagery and meaning that most are not able to make.

We are given hints as well that perhaps this is an ancient technology of dominance – the "technology of the gods." In reality, the technology of the gods meme refers to the elite perspective of themselves and their "magickal" worldview: Any sufficiently advanced technology is indistinguishable from magic, as Arthur C. Clarke's third law says. The "god" is the one who controls the genetic engineering and artificial intelligence. The cap of the pyramid is empty because the head of the system is secret. It's a shadow corporate government, where the eye floats above the pyramid itself. The eye thus transcends the externalization of the hierarchy on earth.

Original DARPA "TIA" logo, echoing the Tyrell Corporation.

When the viewer approaches the pyramid in the opening scene, it is engulfed in golden sunlight, conjuring up notions of Ra and Egypt. The mysteries of Egypt center around the godlike philosopher king (Pharaoh) as the material manifestation of Atum Ra: mirroring the spiritual hierarchy on the spiritual plane. In this dystopian future, the Egyptian scheme is replaced by a corporate system. The light is enlightening the viewer, inviting him along for the ride in the flying car to the top of the pyramid. In other words, for those that can see, you are about to see what they see.

We are then shown "Voight-Kampff" testing given to Leon, one of the Replicants, or advanced A.I. robots created by the Tyrell Corporation. The test is designed to see if the possible Replicant has emotions, will and desire. "Kampff" recalls Adolph Hitler's *Mein Kampf*, his manifesto devoted to his struggle, characterized as one of will. Tyrell, we learn, has been in the business of developing assassination droids, sex droids, etc., yet some Replicants, however, do not know they are programmed with false memories and a false identity – a real program for DARPA.[1]

In this perspective, the Replicants seem to partly resemble the infamous plans of various states over the last century to create "supersoldiers," or mind controlled assassins in operations like MKUltra, BLUEBIRD and ARTICHOKE.[2] Colin Ross writes:

MKUltra Subproject 119 was a literature review, which included a summary of existing information on "Techniques of activation

231

of the human organism by remote electronic means." According to a report in Defense Electronics, consideration was given to using non-lethal weapons technology on David Koresh during the Branch Davidian siege in the spring of 1993. P. 105.

Research on the ability of magnetic fields to facilitate the creation of false memories and altered states of consciousness is apparently funded by the Defense Intelligence Agency through the project cryptonym SLEEPING BEAUTY. Sleeping Beauty was a Defense Department study of remote microwave mind-influencing techniques.[3]

With examples like Sirhan Sirhan, it would appear there was success, and it was in fact Nazi scientists, hearkening back to the *Mein Kampf* reference, who worked on such mind control projects, as well as the Soviets and the U.S. "Roy Batty," (played by Rutger Hauer) the "Nexus 6" model and leader of the rebel replicants, is himself a super-soldier assassin, "more human than a human," as Tyrell states. The retinal image returns and this time it's Leon Kowalski. Leon is given the test and assassinates his tester at a certain point when the trigger words "tortoise" and "mother" are mentioned, signifying that in mind control, manipulation of symbols and Jungian archetypes is crucial. The tortoise is associated with Hermes/mercury, as I will show and which will be relevant later.

"Eye World."

The Replicants are given a four-year lifespan, which allows Tyrell to have total control, keeping them from ever rebelling or having a lengthy time to work towards revolution. Similarly, in real life the elite have always sought to control lifespans and populations through eugenics and full spectrum dominance. It could also possibly have reference to the self-destruct programming in the mind-controlled assassins to kill themselves rather than be interrogated and spill the beans. In fact, in regard to Project ARTICHOKE, a memo is reported to read: "Can we get control of an individual to the point where he will do our bidding against his will and even against fundamental laws of nature, such as self-preservation?"[4]

The viewer then hears advertisements from huge telescreens and billboards telling him that the system can take you "off world." The system thus holds out a hope of fulfillment in a heaven-like "golden" "off world" colony, much like states in the past have controlled their subjects through a non-existent hope of wealth and fame. The masses are thus weak, shifting sands, subject to the sway of childlike propaganda and psychological warfare. From Plato's *Republic* to Auguste Comte's notion of a purely civic religion, the idea of a state-controlled and created fake religion for the purpose of mass manipulation is an ancient foundational elite control mechanism.

We also see Chinese businesses and foodstuffs are omnipresent, indicating that the U.S. has become a third-world cesspool of globalism. The populace is thus managed by a top-down corporatocracy above, while below, a degenerate and poverty-stricken populace is blended together (Asians, Russians, etc.), and ruled by their corporate overlords. The future then, is a kind of intense corporate police state fascism, where everyone is tracked and traced, particularly by retina scans. Dragons are also seen everywhere in Chinatown, suggesting the control of the primeval serpent: a world run by the shadow Corporatocracy is one where the iconography of the serpent dominates, conjuring up ancient archetypal imagery from Genesis where the serpent deceives man into thinking he can become God, which will be crucial to *Blade Runner's* overall message.

Deckard stands under a Pentagram, with a snake-eyed Pentagram in the background.

233

the Tyrell Corporation. How prophetic, given the fact that China is busy buying up the U.S.[5]

Dick wisely places the corporation at the center of the future's controlling power, giving it an "Illuminati" status, as opposed to some oppressive government or dictator. The future, for Dick, is controlled by a single global mega corporation, headed by a tech genius who happens to obtain a kind of godlike status by creating sentient beings in his own image (replicants). This will be crucial for my analysis of the film's underlying esoteric theme – that *Blade Runner* is a gnostic myth or allegory. Recall as well that Ridley Scott used this same theme in *Alien*, where the future is controlled by the Weyland-Yutani Corporation.

Gaff's Rooster.

Deckard is "handled" by a mysterious figure named Gaff (played by Edward James Olmos), who recalls Deckard from retirement to hunt down the replicants. We don't learn much about Gaff, yet he does something very significant. Throughout the film, as he leads Deckard, he leaves origami figurines as symbolic indicators that reveal the method to Deckard himself. The first origami figure is the rooster: in Freemasonic initiations, the rooster is associated with Hermes/Mercury/Thoth, the guide to the Underworld and initiator of mysteries. We have again returned to the initiatory theme. Gaff is enlightening Deckard as well as the audience, as the eye, pyramid, snake, rooster are serving to tap into the archetypes in the psyche of the audience, enlightening the viewer to the mysteries of the elite. According to the British Grand Lodge, the rooster is associated with alchemy:

> Mercury appears as the rooster drawn on the wall of the Chamber of Reflection. This animal is connected to the deity Hermes, that is, Mercury. It is a feminine principle, referring to Vigilance and it also corresponds to Faith. As the rooster sings at dawn announcing the light of day, so it announces to our future initiate, the Light he may receive.[6]

Alchemical woodcut of Hermes/Thoth/Mercury.

An article on Greek and Indian mythology elucidates this connection well:

> Hermes often helped travelers have a safe and easy journey. Many Greeks would sacrifice to Hermes before any trip. In the fully developed Olympian pantheon, Hermes was the son of Zeus and the Pleiade Maia, a daughter of the Titan Atlas. Hermes' symbols were the rooster and the tortoise, and he can be recognized by his purse or pouch, winged sandals, winged cap and the herald's staff, the kerykeion.[7]

Gaff (who carries a staff/cane) is leading Deckard all along, enlightening him to his true nature and, as will be seen, leading him to safe haven. It is interesting as well that Tyrell's pyramid/ziggurat resembles Mt. Olympus, and is full of Imperial and occult symbolism. Gaff, as the traveling messenger (Hermes/Thoth) of Olympus/Egypt takes Deckard to Tyrell, who can apparently only be accessed at the top of the pyramid by flying car. The Owl, with prominent eye imagery, as well as a Masonic/Egyptian obelisk and a fascist Roman Eagle, all mark Tyrell's golden kingdom. Deckard is informed he must hunt down the remaining replicants, two of which are sex slaves and two assassins, two unknowns are Rachael (Sean Young) and Deckard himself.

Is that a synthetic obelisk, or are you happy to see me?

Deckard is instructed to test Rachael with the Voight-Kampff test to see if he can detect emotions. Rachael is identified as a replicant after a hundred questions from the test, while Deckard realizes he has feelings for her. Deckard is amazed that Rachael is unaware, and Tyrell explains the company implants false memories. This becomes crucial in the analysis of the film, because the concept of forgetting one's true origin is central to the gnostic cosmology. In the process of the fall (in the gnostic and Platonic schemes), the many has lost its origin in the one, the monad. The multiplicity of particulars are thus in a process of return to the monad from whence they have fallen into individuality.

The microscopic serial number shows inside knowledge of nanotech long ago.

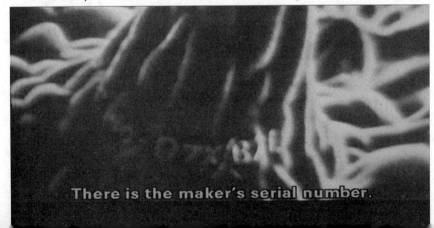

There is the maker's serial number.

236

In fact, in the next scene, Roy Batty is himself seeking out his creator by visiting the eye manufacturer. When Roy finds him, he cites the famous gnostic mythological poems of William Blake, *America A Prophecy* and *A Vision of the Last Judgment*. Blake's poem is a mythological account of the American revolution against King George III, presented as an anti-christ figure and emissary of Urizen, Blake's view of the biblical God, portrayed as an old, miserly, vengeful deity. Just as Orc rebelled against the King, and Lucifer against God, so Roy Batty will rebel against his creator, Tyrell, for allowing him to be created with a flaw. Literary scholar G.E. Bentley explains:

> The implications of the work are taken up in America, with the King of England trembling as he sees Orc, the embodiment of the American colonies. The Angel of Albion believes Orc is the anti-christ and Orc believes the King of England is the same. This is followed by Orc's apocalyptic vision:

> *The morning comes, the night decays, the watchmen leave their stations*
> *The grave is burst, the spices shed, the linen wrapped up*
> *Orc provokes the Angel of Boston to rebellion:*
> *What God is he, writes laws of peace, clothes him in a tempest*
> *What pitying Angel lusts for tears, and fans himself with sighs*
> *What crawling villain preaches abstinence; wraps himself In fat of lambs?*
> *no more I follow, no more obedience pay*
> *Together, the rebels are able to be freed of the psychological chains that bind them:*
> *the five gates of their law-built heaven*

And Roy Batty's line:

> *Fiery the angels rose, as they rose deep thunder roll'd*
> *Around their shores: indignant burning with the fires of Orc.*[8]

William Blake's painting of the gnostic Great Architect deity.

237

The Orc recalls the rebellion of Satan and his angels against God for the purpose of erecting a model synthetic kingdom that mimics the kingdom of God. This is significant, as much of *Blade Runner* centers around genetic engineering and synthetic reality, as we constantly see mannequins and dolls, especially in J.F. Sebastian's studio loft. For example, the background includes Atari signs: Atari is a video game company – video games are synthetic, virtual reality. Tyrell's company is a genetic engineering company, specializing in replicating reality to the point that when Deckard finds the scale from Zhora's snake, he has to take it to a specialist to see if it's real or synthetic. Philip Dick was amazingly prophetic in this regard, and in genetic manipulation; the microscopic serial number on the snake scale even points to nanotechnology, far before it was well known (in the Ted.com promo video of Scott's *Prometheus*, Peter Weyland mentions nanotechnology).[9] Zhora, too, is introduced as a stripper who "receives pleasure from the snake," and Eden is specifically mentioned by the Fez-wearing Abdul. The Fez, originally a Muslim symbol, is the headgear of the Shriners, made up of upper level Freemasons.

The next origami figure Gaff leaves is a man with an erect penis. The little figure signifies Deckard is about to confront another stage in his transformational process, particularly in his confrontation with Zhora, the woman united with the snake.[10] Zhora also performs her dance as Salome, the biblical character who seduces Herod and asks that he cut off the head of John the Baptist. In alchemy, the process of calcification involves union with the feminine principle to achieve synthesis and balance. What has been divided must be united to find harmony and elevation to the next level: that of the Philosopher's Stone, following the period of nigredo (blackness) and albedo (whiteness) prior to becoming gold. Deckard is lacking his compliment, and must here confront the temptation of lust by the snake, if you will. The spiritual version of alchemy, modeled on the chemical, involves the mastery of the passions by the will – apt for the character of Deckard who, himself a replicant, is discovering that he doesn't live, but is a slave of the system. Deckard is an Agent for the system itself, all the while being the very thing he is hunting!

Deckard's eyes are red because he, too, is a replicant.

238

When Deckard meets with Rachael at his apartment, it begins to become clearer that Deckard is a replicant: at an emotional moment both his and Rachael's eyes alight red with the trademark replicant glow, right after Rachael inquires whether Deckard himself had ever taken the Voight-Kampff test. The love scene follows, and Deckard unites with Rachael, completing the unification process in Deckard's own psyche (though his own process is still unfinished). Earlier, there was a mysterious scene where Deckard had fallen asleep playing the piano and dreamt of a unicorn.

The mythical beast arises from implanted memories in Deckard's programmed robotic subconscious.

This is crucial, since the unicorn in alchemy signifies the Philosopher's Stone itself.[11] Deckard is dreaming of archetypal symbols related directly to alchemy, and this will become evident when Gaff leaves the final origami figurine: a unicorn. This means Gaff knew all along what Deckard's implanted memories were, which surfaced in his dreams. Deckard this second time falls asleep, but awakens to the sound of Rachael playing his piano, and he begins to realize that they thus both have similar implanted memories. Carl Jung writes of the unicorn, also associated with Mercury, as follows:

> The unicorn in alchemy: The example of the Unicorn is chosen to demonstrate how the symbolism of Mercury is intermingled in the traditions of pagan gnosticism and the Christian Church. As the unicorn is not a single, clearly identified entity, more specific concern is centered on the beast with a single horn (the alicorn). Examples are given from the literature, especially the Chemical Wedding of Christian Rosencrantz), in which the unicorn, the lion and the dove appear, all of these being symbols of Mercury. Ref-

239

erence is also made to medieval art in which images of the virgin and the unicorn appear. These images are said to represent the dual aspect of Mercury: the virgin as the passive, feminine aspect of the unicorn, and the unicorn or lion as the wild, rampant, masculine force....References from the Church fathers are variously given in which the unicorn is identified with the God of the Old Testament or Christ. It is pointed out that there are ecclesiastical quotations in which the unicorn is said to carry the element of evil. It is this inner contradiction that makes the unicorn an appropriate symbol to be used by alchemists' monstrum hermaphroditum. [the hermaphrodite – a key stage of unification in the alchemical process].

A curious connection to Scott's *Legend*.

Remember that when Roy Batty saves Deckard from the precipice, his palm is nailed in a Christ-like fashion, while he sets free a dove – another Mercurial image. Lest anyone think this is a stretch, this is exactly the same idea in Ridley Scott's *Legend*, where the unicorn plays a central role in precisely this alchemical and gnostic scheme. In fact, *Legend* is entirely focused on dualism, where good and evil cyclically and eternally battle for "balance," in contrast to a linear biblical view of time. Consider also Ridley Scott's *Prometheus*.

(Endnotes)

1. Weinberger, Sharon. "Building the Pentagon's 'Like me' Weapon." BBC. 18 November, 2014. Web. http://www.bbc.com/future/story/20120501-building-the-like-me-weapon

2. Marks, John, *The CIA and Mind Control*. Ross, Colin. "Project Bluebird: The Deliberate Creation of Multiple Personalities by Scientists." WanttoKnow.Info. Web. http://www.wanttoknow.info/bluebird10pg

3. Ibid.

4. "ARTICHOKE." PaperlessArchives. Web. http://www.paperlessarchives.com/FreeTitles/ARTICHOKECIAFiles.pdf

5. Snyder, Michael. "Why Is The Obama Administration Allowing The Chinese Government To Buy Up U.S. Oil And Gas Deposits Worth Billions Of Dollars?" EndoftheAmericanDream. Web. http://endoftheamericandream.com/archives/why-is-the-obama-administration-allowing-the-chinese-government-to-buy-up-u-s-oil-and-gas-deposits-worth-billions-of-dollars

6. Da Costa, Helio. "The Chamber of Reflection." GrandLodge. 16 October, 1999. Web. http://freemasonry.bcy.ca/texts/gmd1999/pondering.html

7. "Greek Influence on India: Hermes and Krishna." Web. https://sites.google.com/site/greekinfluenceonindia/hermes

8. Bentley, G. E. (Jr). *The Stranger From Paradise*. New Haven: Yale University Press, 2003, pgs. 138-9.

9. "What is Nanotechnology?" Nano.gov. Web. http://www.nano.gov/nanotech-101/what/definition

10. McLean, Adam. "Animal Symbolism in the Alchemical Tradition." Levity. Web. http://www.levity.com/alchemy/animal.html

11. Ibid.

Chapter 16

Prometheus (2012) – Esoteric Analysis

Totenkopf, or "death's head."

Panspermiatic Cinematic

Prometheus was the 2012 presumed blockbuster prequel to Ridley Scott's famous *Alien* series. While reviews were slightly on the positive side, many found the film to be a rehash of everything seen in the original *Alien* film, now with overdone CGI. *Prometheus* was a successful money maker globally, while falling stagnant in domestic sales, yet it simultaneously left many film goers clueless as to the meaning of the flick they spent $12 (or $3 later) watching. Enter JaysAnalysis: Underneath all these exoteric facts of aliens and cliche horror gags, a darker esoteric plot can be seen, similar to the message of *Invasion of the Body Snatchers.*[1] We will discover that *Prometheus* offers us yet another example of the new mythology the Hollywood industrial espionage complex intends to propagate to replace the Western religious tradition(s).

So what is *Prometheus* about? Daddy Issues – but not just familial and psychological daddy issues, *esoteric* daddy issues! Let's break it down. In the opening sequence we see earth in development in an ancient, closer to a Paradisiacal stage, with no humans yet on the scene. Rather than a biblical narrative of Eden or the fall of Adam, an alien being known as an "engineer" is seen drinking what we later learn is an advanced bio-weapon. As the nordic-featured alien disintegrates, his carcass tumbles off a cliff into a waterfall, where his DNA mysteriously reassembles into a new living form (which will be man). As Darwinian natural selection emerges later in the film, one may safely surmise the sequence is intended to be an alternative explanation to human origins, much like the so-called "scientific" (read mythological) theory of panspermia of Lord Kelvin, Fred Hoyle, Stephen Hawking and Francis Crick.[2]

Confirming the Egyptian connection, in Alien, the Weyland logo on the Nostromo is the winged disc of Horus.

Thirty-five thousand years later, a team of scientists discovers a series of cave paintings on the Isle of Skye, Scotland, that portray a "giant" pointing to a star system which happens to predate the same image found on numerous other *steles* from Babylonian, Egyptian and Mesopotamian antiquity. Perceptive readers will immediately recall the purported Stele of Revealing through which Aleister Crowley claimed to have received revelation of his Thelemic religion of our era, the new *aeon* of Horus.[3] In this view of history, there are roughly delineated ages (or aeons) that correspond to human development, the first era corresponding to Isis and goddess worship in antiquity, the second to Osiris, for the patriarchal worship of a self-sacrificial masculine Deity of the Middle Ages, and Horus, the crowned and conquering child of our age, where supposedly individual man comes to self-realization and self-actualization.

This fact is particularly relevant to the film because Prometheus is also the ancient myth of the Titan who challenged father Zeus and stole the fire of the gods, bringing it down to mankind. In the film, "Prometheus" is the name of the ship that takes the Weyland Corporation's exploration team to the distant planet the alien engineers appear to have arrived from. Among the crew, how-

243

ever, only Dr. Shaw (Noomi Rapace), Dr. Holloway (Logan Marshall-Green) and the hidden Peter Weyland (Guy Pearce) are actual believers in the theory of the ancient alien engineers, and only Dr. Shaw is a Christian.

The Stele of Ankh-ef-en-Khonsu

As is the norm with the Weyland Corporation, an AI humanoid is also aboard to safeguard company interests – the Mao-garbed, T.E. Lawrence/ Peter O'Toole obsessed "David" (Michael Fassbender). It is interesting that David is obsessed, or programmed to be obsessed, with T.E. Lawrence and/or the film *Lawrence of Arabia*, who was a British secret agent responsible for securing Imperial interests in the Middle East, particularly with the Saudis. Already, we have four curious references to Nordic/Aryan elements, with "Weyland" being an old Nordic poem about a prince of the elves,[4] David as a nordic-featured robot, and the engineers as something akin to a "Great White Brotherhood" of "secret chiefs" and alien visitors, reminiscent of the theosophic fables of Madame Blavatsky, and the origin of man, or the "root race," from the Isle of Skye, Scotland.[5] Ridley Scott's *Blade Runner* universe also features this same "Aryan" theme with Roy Batty, as well as corporate socialism destined to steer our future.

This suggests an influence of theosophical sources for the mythology of the *Alien* series, as well as many more occult ideas, as we shall see. Consider the image of David with the two skulls, or "death's heads," as heads appear constantly in the film, both as plot devices and symbolic signposts. Among the Nazi S.S, the "Totenkopf" held a special significance as the bringer of death.[6] Personified death is even mentioned several times in the film, as we discover the planet is not actually the alien home world, but a terra-formed weapons laboratory where the alien DNA bio-weapon is housed.

The Mao Zedong meets Peter O'Toole "David," between two death's heads.

It is also significant that the journey takes place on Christmas of 2093 as we discover Dr. Shaw is barren, yet due to the dastardly machinations of David and the Weyland Corporation she was chosen as a test subject for alien fertilization, with the intent of Shaw giving birth to a new alien god, mimicking the virgin birth of Christ. As we might expect, the Weyland Corporation happens to be much more interested in genetic cross-species hybridization and advanced bio-warfare technology than honest scientific inquiry into human origins. We can see an analogue to reality here, as the military industrial complex's amazing technological advances are primarily fueled by warfare weapons research, while fronts like NASA give the appearance of pure advancement of human knowledge. In fact, the recent threats of NASA losing its funding and the shutting down of the space program are a complete farce, as the real space program, part of the black budget of over 50 billion dollars, has not ceased.[7]

As with Weyland Corporation, the real shadow technology complex is private, not some public, government institution. Like the well-meaning, compartmentalized scientist Dr. Shaw, our scientists and tech wizards rarely discover they are serving a much deeper, darker agenda of the shadow government.[8] Dr. Shaw even discovers that she was chosen for the Prometheus mission resulting in her becoming a test subject like Ripley in the original *Alien* series.

Our alien "creators." Do you even lift, bro?

As it turns out, Dr. Shaw is correct, and the alien engineers are our creators. The creation of man by "engineers" is curiously similar to both the gnostic mythology of creation, as well as the masonic view of God as the "Great Architect," since engineers and architects work with pre-existing matter, and do not create *ex nihilo*. Like the deity of so many Hollywood storylines, the "god" is merely an immanent *deus ex machina* that arose from some primordial chaotic happenstance. In this regard, the panspermia myth is made to blend with the "science" of Darwinian aeons, where any kind of higher beings must have also been the result of chaotic material interaction and process.

If there is any kind of single Supreme God, he is the hidden, unknown God (Acts 17). It should also be mentioned that the idea of giants in ancient civilizations that were the result of some kind of unnatural genetic manipulation is also mentioned in Genesis 6, where the sons of Seth are conjoined with angels to produce strange offspring, detailed at length in the *Book of Enoch*. The gnostic aspect of the film's theology thus fits well with the occult aspects posited earlier, as the theme of the death of the father is repeated several times.

A skull carved into a mountain on the engineer's planet.

Captain Vickers (Charlize Theron) desires the death of her pedophile father, Peter Weyland, the presumed dead old fart who eventually arises from a hold within the Prometheus seeking immortality from the engineers. David desires the death of humans as an AI bot without emotions, and Dr. Shaw ultimately wills the death of the (masculine) alien god creators for their discovered plans to annihilate humanity with the alien bio-weapon. Keep in mind Dr. Shaw is also motivated by the death of her father, from whom she obtained her faith.

In other words, the Promethean myth is explained by a life of pure Darwinian survival of the fittest, as the quest ultimately becomes an *Oedipal* struggle for overthrowing the vestiges of the existing patriarchal order through the weaponry of death, as well as the death of God the *Father*, with the victor obtaining transhumanist immortality. As Captain Vickers explains with hatred to her father, "A king has his reign and then dies. That is the natural order of things." And as David says to Dr. Shaw, "Doesn't everyone want their parents dead?" In this aspect, *Prometheus* is about the new aeon of supposed self-realization of individual self-will, as opposed to obeisance to hierarchical, archetypal power figures like "mother" and "father" (think also of Ripley battling with the on-board computer system "Mother" in *Alien*).

Daddy issues.

247

Exploring more religious themes, the alien planet's *"pyramid"* (as it's called in the film) is revealed to be an entire spacecraft, where within its chambers there is a massive, Easter Island-style head, which appears to have a religious significance for the engineers, as well as murals and paraphernalia related to the worship of the actual aliens (the Xenomorph). It would appear the engineers worship death in the form of the Xenomorph, as the only seeming *raison d'etre* for the Xenomorphs is killing. The universe of *Alien/Prometheus* is a radically nihilistic one, where instead of a benevolent Creator God of providential guidance, mankind is the accidental DNA experimental descendant of a black-death bio-warfare science-worshipping alien cult. The alien on the mural in the engineers' head chamber appears to be crucified, signifying either worship of, or the conquest of, the Xenomorph hybrid. This would explain why the engineers are intent on returning to earth to wipe out the human race since, as I've elucidated many times, in films the "aliens" often represent the eugenics-minded elite intent on depopulating the earth as a ritual sacrifice to the angel of death. This could also explain the Nordic/Aryan elements in the film, since strictly regimented breeding and procreation was a key facet of the Nazi version of eugenics.

A crucified Xenomorph.

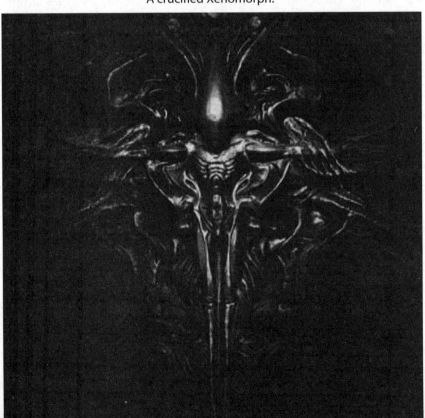

As mentioned, heads are present everywhere in the film. The head of the first engineer is discovered decapitated in the ritual room where the head statue is. David is seen with skulls, there is the skull on the mountain, and near the end, David has his head torn off by the last engineer. My speculation is that the head is the source and symbol of reason, but also the highest level of evolutionary development (in that worldview) as the house of the brain. The engineers appear to worship the head, as well as mankind having reached almost the same level of technology as the engineers, with the ability to terra-form, cross-species engineer and create AI. David's head is the highest form of human achievement and fathers are also "heads" of patriarchal societies. Thus, the possession of headship is symbolized by all these noggins everywhere.

The battle for the future is presumably granted to whoever has the most advanced reason, yet in a strange twist, the only survivors at the end are Dr. Shaw, who remains in her faith, David's head, an engineer and a Xenomorph (who has the biggest head!). Reason alone is not sufficient in this nihilistic alien universe: Pure willpower must be combined. As with Ripley in *Alien* and the sequels, we find the feminist mythology present throughout that woman is somehow the new "man" that will overcome, without the need of any male. Instead of the *ubermensch*, it's the *uberchick*, as we see with *Hanna, Gravity, Hunger Games, Divergent*, and a host of other girl-power pop cinema displays. It is important that Dr. Shaw's first name is Elizabeth, and in the film she's called "El" a few times, which brings to mind the biblical name for higher beings, be it El or Elohim. Though she aborts her birth, the Christmas present fetus is the offspring of a new Eve, El.

While *Prometheus* is visually captivating, I think it falls short of the innovative creativity Scott demonstrated with *Alien*. What we do have with *Prometheus* is a revelation of the religious narrative behind the universe of *Alien*, where man is a genetic accidental offspring of purely finite creators. A rehash of gnostic and occult fables, the new mythology of science is socially engineered by our own very human overlord engineers to seamlessly meld with Darwinism. In modern man's meaningless universe, it bears repeating – why not worship the black emptiness of nihilism and chaos? That the film has this ultimate point is shown when a dying Peter Weyland exhales to David, "There is nothing."

Like H.R. Giger's art that formed the basis for the films, the message says there is only the cold, harsh reality of machine-like matter in an impersonal cycle of flux. In such a realm where there are no objective principles, metaphysics, gods or higher goods, there is only war, and the godhead of war is death, the Totenkopf. In such a world there is no more reason for the rise of feminine heroism and strength than there is *reason* at all. Heads are decapitated, bringing to mind the French Revolution guillotines, where heads were lopped off for anti-hierarchical revolution. In Prometheus' revolution, there is no reason for revolution, even when you worship reason, and so the anti-logic logic ends in this: The god of the universe is simply death.

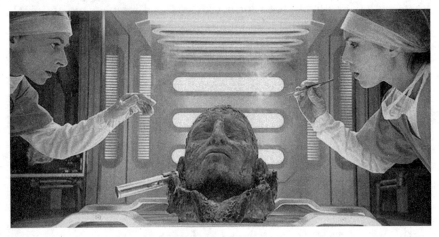

Whither reason, science?

Endnotes

1. Dyer, Jay. "Invasion of the Body Snatchers as Cryptocracy Allegory." JaysAnalysis. 9 August, 2014. Web. https://jaysanalysis.com/2014/08/09/invasion-of-the-body-snatchers-1978-as-cryptocracy-allegory/

2. Grossman, Lisa. "All Life on Earth Could Have Come from Alien Zombies." *Wired*. November, 2010. Web. http://www.wired.com/2010/11/necropanspermia/

3. Skinner, Stephen (ed). *The Magical Diaries of Aleister Crowley*: Tunisia 1923. Weiser, 1996, pg. 79, n. 8.

4. "Völundarkviða." Wikipedia. 7 April, 2016. Web. https://en.wikipedia.org/wiki/V%C3%B6lundarkvi%C3%B0a

5. Blavatsky, H. P. *Isis Unveiled Volume 2*. Web. http://www.theosociety.org/pasadena/isis/iu1-02.htm

6. "The SS (Schutzstaffel): Totenkopfring." JewishVirtualLibrary. Web. https://www.jewishvirtuallibrary.org/jsource/Holocaust/Totenkopfring.html

7. Schachtman, Noah and Beckhusen. "See for Yourself: The Pentagon's $51 Billion 'Black' Budget." Wired. Web. http://www.wired.com/2012/02/pentagons-black-budget/

8. Stobbe, Mike. "Ugly Past of US Human Experiments Uncovered." NBC.com. 27 February, 2011. Web. http://www.nbcnews.com/id/41811750/ns/health-health_care/t/ugly-past-us-human-experiments-uncovered/#.Vwb1lo-cHIV

Part Four:

007 and Hitchcock

Chapter 17

Deep-State Actors in
Diamonds Are Forever (1971)

Does Howard Hughes have a connection to 007? We will look at Martin Scorsese's *The Aviator* in a bit, but first we should consider Ian Fleming's iconic creation, James Bond. What if Ian Fleming was encoding an explosive, real-world conspiracy involving Howard Hughes, JFK, Aristotle Onassis and a legendary kidnapping? Not only is there evidence to suggest this, the film version of his 1954 novel *Diamonds Are Forever* subtly suggests much more. We know Fleming was a high-level Royal Navy psychological warfare specialist and involved in numerous covert operations, but many are not aware Fleming's novels and the film versions, in their own respective ways, elucidate these real-world clandestine activities, touching on everything from black-market smuggling networks to actual espionage and assassinations.[1]

Fleming's inspiration for the novel stemmed from meetings and discussions with former MI5 chief Sir Percy Stilltoe, then working for the De-Beers diamond empire. Combined with these tips, as well as information he received from wealthy socialite William Woodward and Los Angeles police intelligence on organized crime and smuggling operations, Fleming composed the fourth Bond novel in 1954 as a literary means of detailing the dark world of precious gem and jewel markets. To add intrigue to this already intriguing tale, Fleming was also approached by Aristotle Onassis to make a film version of either *Casino Royale* or *Dr. No*, with Onassis desiring to be a part of the funding.[2] No stranger to Hollywood, Onassis was also a friend of numerous tinsel-town heavyweights, including the Greek film executive Spyros Skouras.

HOWARD HUGHES (1905-1976): American filmmaker and entrepreneur often considered a mechanical and engineering genius. Hughes is known for many things, not the least of which includes his eccentric behavior and cooperation with the CIA and military for large-scale aerospace projects. Hughes also made numerous blockbuster war films, as well as setting numerous speed records for flights in the 1930s. Hughes was intimately connected to Hollywood over several decades, including affairs with Ava Gardner, Olivia de Havilland, Bette Davis, Ginger Rogers, Rita Hayworth, and Katherine Hepburn.

With these connections, my thesis here, in concert with the fascinating insight of Basil Valentine, is that *Diamonds Are Forever* the film provides a crucial insight into the coded reference of Willard Whyte as a stand-in for Howard Hughes. As I argue in my *Aviator* analysis, Hughes was intimately

ROBERT MAHEU (1917-2008): American businessman and lawyer who worked with both the FBI and CIA, while running Howard Hughes' operations in Nevada. Maheu's investigative agency that functioned as cut out shell for the CIA was the inspiration for the popular 1960s spy show, *Mission Impossible*. Maheu was involved in many intrigues, including an alleged attempt in concert with the mafia, to assassinate Fidel Castro.

tied to the CIA through Robert Maheu,[3] an intelligence-establishment figure who emerged from the CIA-dominated advertising world. It is possible Maheu was involved in the reported kidnapping escapade of Hughes, which "The Gemstone Files"[4] allege was orchestrated by Ari Onassis, leading to Hughes being spirited away to the magnate's lavish island, Skorpios.[5]

ARISTOTLE ONASSIS (1906-1975): One of the world's wealthiest men in his day, Greek shipping magnate and owner the world's largest private fleet. Some researchers have alleged Onassis' wealth was also obtained by shipping black market goods, while Onassis himself maintained an intimate relationship with global elites, including his famous marriage to Jackie Kennedy following the assassination of JFK. A friend of Ian Fleming, Onassis may have even functioned as an influence for some of Bond's characters.

On this note, there is an interesting parallel no one else has considered to the 1965 postmodern novel *The Magus*, by John Fowles. In the story, a young English Oxford lad is (intentionally) led to a fictional Greek island named Phraxos, where a wealthy Greek magnate and former Nazi collaborator arranges elaborate psychological and theatrical operations to "test" Nicholas' will. Playing with both reality and classical mythology, Conchis (the Greek) eventually breaks Nicholas' resolve, having completely altered the protagonist's paradigm of reality. Rather than freely choosing his lascivious

THE MAGUS (1965): Postmodern novel by British author John Fowles centering on protagonist Nicholas Urfe, an arrogant, suicidal, nihilistic Oxford student who is led to a mysterious Greek Island called Phraxos. On Phraxos, an exceedingly wealthy mastermind trickster known as Conchis organizes various mind games and large-scale manipulations intended on testing Nicholas. Chock full of references to the occult, mythology and psychological manipulation, Conchis presents himself as a powerful illusionist and "Illuminist."

254

dalliances, Nicholas discovers his own story has been organized and directed by troupes of actors and academics at the behest of the elite mastermind. Could this be a coded reference to the "Gemstone Files?"[6] While it is not clear, Onassis is rumored to have maintained contacts with Eva and Juan Peron in Argentina.[7] Billionaires, Greek islets and possibly coded, occult messages? It's quite a tale – one Fleming may have decided was worth telling.

The book is spiced throughout with references to Tarot cards, Greek deities, Baphomet, gnosticism, ritual initiation, the Eleutherian mysteries, etc. Conchis eventually reveals to Nicholas, when he's drugged, captured and placed in the judgment role, that the real secret is science. While Nicholas is supposed to "judge" the rest of the Illuminists present under the sign of the Pentagram and Baphomet, he ends up confounded as the group of doctors and PhDs present dissect his entire life with psychoanalysis.

Nicholas is then forced to watch a pornographic film with the girl he loves that has been intertwined with his own time spent on the island, recorded by numerous secret cameras. Here Bentham/Foucault-style Panopticism emerges, as the prisoner is subjected to the all-pervading gaze of the eye of the elite. Nicholas not only cannot escape their influence and power, he is also held captive to the narrative they may construct about himself and his life. In short, he is helpless, though he thinks he is "free" in his atheism and nihilism.

Maurice, then, turns out to be a combination of the trickster/magus, as well as the prince/ruler, with his unlimited wealth. He can hire any actors, recreate any scenes and arrange any events he so desires. No matter where Nicholas goes, or what he does, he cannot escape Maurice's designs. Every time Nicholas tries to construct a "mask" or excuse or identity for himself, he is reminded of the existential dictum that he is "condemned to be free." He continues to operate in *Sartrean* "bad faith" and "inauthenticity" to the end, until he appears to concede that he is helpless.

In regard to the 1971 film *Diamonds Are Forever*, it is a curious note that Whyte, the Hughes stand-in, is said to have been kidnapped and/or holed-up in his penthouse for years. As it turns out, it is the inimical Bond villain Ernst Stavro Blofeld, who is behind the diamond smuggling plot as a means of moving in on Whyte's aerospace operations. If Basil's thesis is correct, then Stavro could be a composite of Onassis and Niarchos, the brother-in-law of Onassis and a rival shipping magnate. Stavros Niarchos is reported to have been a Bilderberg member and a close associate of the

Rockefeller Foundation (for certain).[8] These considerations are admittedly speculative. A worthy addendum also comes to the fore in the history of the fictional SPECTRE organization, where we read of a 007 board game:

> In 1983, a highly successful James Bond tabletop RPG was released. With the films as inspirations, the stories were adapted for players. Minor changes to plots and villains were made; for example, Wint and Kidd were freelance assassins working for SPECTRE. They in fact leased out services to other terrorist organisations and various crime syndicates. The most noted changes were to SPECTRE: Blofeld's name was changed to Karl Ferenc Skorpios, and he was given a greyhound instead of a white cat; the organisation itself was renamed TAROT (Terrestrial Acquisition, Revenge, and Orchestrated Turmoil), with the face cards representing various departments. This was due to the copyright issues referenced above. Victory Games worked with Eon productions (the film producers) for the rights to Bond, and were told they were not allowed to negotiate with McClory for the rights to SPECTRE, hence the hasty renaming."[9]

When we consider Hughes' close connection to the CIA through operations like Project AZORIAN,[10] which sounds just like a SPECTRE-style operation from a 007 film, we can certainly presume much more was being conveyed here. Even questions relating to the moon mission arise, given the seemingly out-of-place scene of Bond stumbling across a soundstage in Hughes' facility, where actors in astronaut suits are enacting a phony lunar landing. Is Fleming implying that the moon mission itself was a psychological operation? Speculation is welcomed here, but the real message of *Diamonds* centers around exotic weaponry focused along directed energy lines. The same theme re-emerges in the 1974 film adaptation of Fleming's *The Man with the Golden Gun*, where alchemy and techne combine to reveal the Pentagon's darkest future tech. Given that Jackie married Aristotle Onassis just five years after JFK was gone, could this signify a mafia-mandated marriage tradition? Perhaps Fleming knew the answers to this and the real SPECTRE.

Pondering the news attention the famed Pink Panther diamond ring has garnered, we can be reminded of something out of a Bond novel.[11] Judging by the 2D news narrative, we are expected to believe that this ring of some two hundred crooks operates under unknown leaders plotting in the dark, as noble authorities and intelligence officials feverishly work around the clock to apprehend the fiends. *Diamonds Are Forever* might be more appropriate, but in Fleming's 1958 novel *Dr. No*, the Doctor makes an equally prescient and insightful statement about black market operations and their fierce master – shadow government:

> "Mr. Bond, power is sovereignty. Clausewitz's first principle was to have a secure base. From there one proceeds to freedom of action. Together, that is sovereignty. I have secured these things and much beside. No one else in the world possesses them to the same degree. They cannot have them. The world is too public. These things can only be secured in privacy. You talk of kings and presidents. How much power do they possess? As much as their people will allow them. Who in the world has the power of life and death over his people? Now that Stalin is dead, can you name any man except myself? And how do I possess that power, that sovereignty? Through privacy. Through the fact that nobody *knows*. "[12]

This writer has noted many times the principle of psychological warfare employed by Fleming in the Bond novels that proved tremendously effective – project every dark, secret, nefarious operation your side is engaged in onto the enemy. Also, be sure to make your enemy out to be a disfigured hybrid mulatto for good measure (Dr. No was a Chinese and German mixed-race villain). In the story, Dr. No has established his secret base of operations on an obscure island off the coast of Jamaica, where, in his underground mountain fortress and with his state-of-the-art high-tech radar and surveillance equipment from Moscow, he remotely commandeers U.S. missiles. Dr. No's cover is the nasty business of farming guano, or bird dung, for fertilizer. With all the usual Fleming tropes, No emerges in the narrative as an exemplary figure of the sexually repressed daddy-issues villain, with connections to international crime, espionage, the Soviets, and money laundering. Dr. No is thus an exemplary figure of shadow government, and shadow government is the normative form of government in our day.

In reality, the hierarchical pyramid of global government is not a series of goodly nation states seeking to protect the "free world" from dastardly Manichaean* dialectical manifestations, but rather is itself is a large interlocking system of crime syndicates. The world government that presently exists is one of covert, hidden rulership by various oligarchs. While a certain level of competition is tolerated, these oligarchical Dr. Nos are not the denizens of secret Soviet underground lairs, but Bilderberg attendees and banking magnates. It is my thesis that whatever you see Dr. No or

257

Blofeld or SMERSH or SPECTRE do, is in fact what the actual establishment itself does. The appellation of "rogue villain" or "rogue state" is rather a media propaganda term for a controlled double agent, such as a terrorist, or a rival syndicate to whatever crime syndicate happens to be in power and runs the media.

Yet is my claim the case? Evidence from numerous investigative journalists, analysts and historians, answers in the affirmative. In his classic *Tragedy & Hope*, Dr. Carroll Quigley speaks of government by monopolistic money cartel that developed in the modern era:

> Naturally, the influence of bankers over governments during the age of financial capitalism (roughly 1850-1931) was not something about which anyone talked freely, but it has been admitted frequently enough by those on the inside, especially in England. In 1852 Gladstone, Chancellor of the Exchequer, declared, "The hinge of the whole situation was this: the government itself was not to be a substantive power in matters of Finance, but was to leave the Money Power supreme and unquestioned.

> On September 26, 1921, the *Financial Times* wrote, "Half a dozen men at the top of the Big Five Banks could upset the whole fabric of government finance by refraining from renewing Treasury Bills." In 1924 Sir Drummond Fraser, vice-president of the Institute of Bankers, stated, "The Governor of the Bank of England must be the autocrat who dictates the terms upon which alone the Government can obtain borrowed money."[13]

Dr. No.

258

Our political leaders are nothing more than puppets of the same monopolistic cartel, but the point to grasp here concerns altering one's perception of the establishment as the authoritative white hat "good guy" fighting the international "black hats" of diamond heists and underground terrorist bases. It is the *establishment* that is the ruling mafia cartel, and the control of black markets is key to understanding what is meant by "shadow government." Their goal is global government and the control of all aspects of life, and unfortunately some aspects of life in this world involve black markets. We often speak of the "new world order" taking over governments or conspiring to manipulate some event or subvert some institution, but the best lens through which to grasp its true inner workings is international crime and its syndicates. And it is the best model because the globalists run the international crime rackets. Investigative journalist Michael Ruppert explained this piece of the puzzle in his *Crossing the Rubicon*:

> Globalization, the World Trade Organization, NAFTA, the IMF, the World Bank, the Great Bull Market of the 1990s, and the economic adulthood of the Empire have all been nurtured by the controlled and directed use of criminal money streams. One of the other great contributors to America's economic growth has been its willingness to profit from the destruction of the life, health, safety, and happiness of its population. As I write, more than two million people are in prisons or jails in the United States. Many of those prisons are run by private corporations. That the profits of crime and war, which are destructive of human life, of labor, of happy, healthy neighborhoods (whether in the US or in Afghanistan, Africa, and Iraq), are in effect a keystone of the global economy and a determinant of success in a ruthless competition, is a compass needle for human civilization. One cannot expect to follow the recipe for road-kill stew and produce a creme brulee....
>
> Perhaps the best summation of how the global economy actually functioned just prior to the World Trade Center attacks was offered in a brilliant two-part series by *Le Monde Diplomatique* in the spring of 2000. In part, the series said:
>
> Indeed the engine of capitalist expansion is now oiled by the profits of serious crime. From time to time something is done to give the impression of waging war on the rapidly expanding banking and tax havens. If governments really wanted to, they could right this overnight. But though there are calls for zero tolerance of petty crime and unemployment, nothing is being done about the big money crimes.

Financial crime is becoming less visible, periodically coming to light in one country or another in the guise of scandals involving companies, banks, political parties, leaders, cartels, mafias. This flood of illicit transactions – offences under national law or international agreements has come to be portrayed just as accidental malfunctions of free market economics and democracy that can be put right by something called "good governance." But the reality is quite different. It is a coherent system closely linked to the expansion of modern capitalism and based on an association of three partners: governments, transnational corporations, and mafias. Business is business, financial crime is first and foremost a market, thriving and structured, ruled by supply and demand.[14] (pp. 76-77)

The reach of the globalist shadow government doesn't stop with financial crimes involving laundering hundreds of billions in drug money, which are now daily news items.[15] On the contrary, the syndicalism of the elite extends to *all markets,* including sex trade, drugs, weapons, secret technology, cybercrime, etc. What comes to mind here is the Jolly Roger flag and the classic imagery of international piracy. "21st Century Wire" editor and investigative journalist Patrick Henningsen perceptively makes this connection between state-sponsored terror using "Sand Pirates" and black market trades in his recent article, "ISIS Sex Slave Market is Modern Repeat of Barbary Pirate Trade":

As 21WIRE pointed out last week, history has repeated itself again. Today's ISIS/ISIL phenomenon is not that different from another long and painful chapter in the East vs. West clash of cultures and trade – the *Barbary Pirates* of the 17 and 18th centuries. Writer Patrick Henningsen explains:

"For financial or political reasons, Empires have always used external militarized cells and mercenaries to commit unsavoury acts under a flag different than the **monarchy, nation-state,** or **private corporation** who was directing them behind the scenes.

"Ruthless and unconventional 'asymmetric' enemies are nothing new to the United States. Historically, the **Privateer,** or Barbary 'Corsair,' was a private person or ship authorized by a government to attack foreign vessels or governments, often covertly. During the 17th, 18th and 19th centuries, Ottoman Corsairs operated along the North African coast, and attacked Colonial American ships for over a century.

"It's the time-honored practice of non-state actors (with state sponsors) who are let loose to pillage and plunder. Today's ISIS pirates are really just the 21st century's version of the **'privateers'** ..."

And,

> The "Barbary slave trade" refers to the "white slavery" markets along North Africa's *Barbary Coast* between the 17th and 19th centuries, which comprised Morocco, Algeria, Tunisia and Libya. Conversely, the Arab slave trade went on for the better part of a millennium – not only confined to the Arab world, but also extending into west Asia, North Africa, Southern Africa, Ethiopia, and Somalia, as well as southern coastal Europe (Spain and Italy) as late as the 19th century. So great were the number of men, women and children who were captured by pirates, that many European coastal towns were forced to shut down, and all but abandoned.[16]

The *modus operandi* of international syndicates has not changed, and the *international* nature of piracy provides another helpful parallel. Like the media narrative of the *Pink Panthers*, which seems to show clear intelligence agency involvement, the mainstream news version of black markets is, as expected, nowhere near accurate or realistic.17 While low-level employees of various agencies fight a white-hat battle, the larger players higher up on the pyramid are aligned with criminal syndicates. Since these interests have no national allegiances, the black flag of piracy is raised by the globalists as well. Connecting all these dots, an excellent work on the pinnacles of power and black markets is investigative journalist Daniel Estulin's book *Shadow Masters: How Governments and their Intelligence Agencies are Working with International Drug Dealers and Terrorists for Mutual Benefit and Profit*. Estulin presents an avalanche of information on little-known subjects and intrigues, namely the rape of Russia by the IMF, the NATO-run operations in Kosovo that connect to the drug trade, Bin Laden and state-sponsored terror, as well as the life of Victor Bout, whose escapades loosely formed the basis for the film *Lord of War* with Nicolas Cage. Estulin comments:

> So you have an international terrorist (Osama bin Laden) trained and funded by the CIA, an international terrorist organization (the KLA, excuse me, Kosovo Protection Corps) trained and funded by the British, American and German secret services and special forces, and an American establishment (Clinton, Gore, Clark, Albright, Holbrooke, Lieberman – all Bilderberg and CFR members, who represent the interests of the new world order, fighting to establish democracy and bring justice to a long-suffering and oppressed people... (p. 93).

261

From Vietnam to Cambodia, from Laos to Pakistan and Afghanistan, from Iran to the Contras, the Agency has been the progressive left's favorite whipping boy. However, it isn't only the CIA that is up to their eyeballs in drugs. In the aforementioned article, *Le Monde Diplomatique* explicitly stated that "the secret services of the world's most powerful state apparatus [in the U.S.] have moved into economic warfare,' becoming 'international financial crime's number-one partner. (p. 122)18

This is only a smattering of a topic so vast it would require volumes to detail properly. However, it does provide an introductory model for understanding *government as conspiracy* and black markets as the fuel for the *real* economy. Rather than the Hollynews version of 007 exposing the operations of Dr. No, the norm for power blocs is actually criminal syndicalism and control of black markets. Indeed, the appropriate model for understanding statecraft is not virtuous citizens rising to the top through dispassionate intellectual argumentation and elections, but stagecraft con men and their actor's guilds, er, criminal guilds. Recalling Dr. No's quote above we can discern that the rise of the surveillance state has only served to foster black market escapades and has little to do

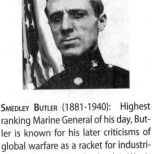

SMEDLEY BUTLER (1881-1940): Highest ranking Marine General of his day, Butler is known for his later criticisms of global warfare as a racket for industrialists and financiers (his book is War is a Racket, 1935). Some propose Butler may have been used as an outspoken critic of the U.S. establishment and his role in halting a plot to overthrow the FDR government, known as the "Business Plot." While the plot may have been real, this event ended up making FDR appear a victim and marshaled even greater public support.

with halting "terror." If only Dr. No had waited around a little longer for the NSA. From the drug trade to sex trade to financial scandals, we discover the whole business of war itself is a racket (see Smedley Butler), and intelligence operations are more often than not merely legalized criminal espionage. In reality, G.I. Joe is an arm of Cobra, and Bond is an agent of SPECTRE. The verdict of historians and journalists is thus: The real Pink Panthers sit on the board of the IMF and CFR.

SPECTRE or IMF board meeting? Hard to tell.

262

Endnotes

1. MacIntyre, Ben. *For Your Eyes Only: Ian Fleming and James Bond*. New York: Bloomsbury, 2008, pg. 123. Cabell, Craig. Ian Fleming's Secret War. South Yorkshire: Pen and Sword Press, 2008.

2. Lycett, Andrew. *Ian Fleming*. London: Phoenix Paperbacks, 1996, pgs. 336-7

3. Hougan, Jim. *Spooks*. New York: William Morrow, 1978, pgs., 268-9.

4. Caruana, Stephanie. "A Skeleton Key to the Gemstone File: Updated 2001." Gemstone-file via Web.archive. Web. http://web.archive.org/web/20030207193329/www.gemstone-file.com/skelkey1.htm

5. Blaylock, Cliff. "Onassis Brought Life to the Greek Island of Skorpios." GreekReporter. 9 February, 2015. Web. http://greece.greekreporter.com/2015/02/09/onassis-brought-life-to-the-greek-island-of-skorpios/

6. Coleman, Loren. "Gemstones Are Forever: Bond, Elrod House, Onassis, Hughes & JFK." CopycatEffect. 13 July, 2013. Web. http://copycateffect.blogspot.com/2012/07/gemstones.html

7. Springmeier, Fritz. "The Onassis Bloodline." Bibliotecapleyades. Web. http://www.bibliotecapleyades.net/bloodlines/onassis.htm

8. "$150 million from the Stavros Niarchos Foundation and David Rockefeller launches major campus extension." Rockefeller.edu. 24 November, 2014. Web. http://newswire.rockefeller.edu/2014/11/24/150-million-from-the-stavros-niarchos-foundation-and-david-rockefeller-launch-major-campus-extension/

9. "SPECTRE." Wikipedia. Web. https://en.wikipedia.org/wiki/SPECTRE

10. "Project AZORIAN." CIA.gov. 23 July, 2012. https://www.cia.gov/about-cia/cia-museum/experience-the-collection/text-version/stories/project-azorian.html

11. "The Pink Panthers, Part 1." Vice. Web. http://www.vice.com/video/pink-panthers-part-1-184

12. Fleming, Ian. *Dr. No*. New York, Penguin, 2002, pg. 161.

13. Quigley, *Tragedy and Hope*, 61.

14. Ruppert, Michael. *Crossing the Rubicon*. Canada: New Society, 2004, pgs. 76-7.

15. Vulliamy. Ed. "How a big US bank laundered billions from Mexico's murderous drug gangs." Guardian. 2 April, 2011. Web. http://www.theguardian.com/world/2011/apr/03/us-bank-mexico-drug-gangs

16. "ISIS Sex Slave Market is Modern Repeat of Barbary Pirate Trade." 21stCenturyWire. Web. http://21stcenturywire.com/2014/11/05/isis-sex-slave-markets-are-a-modern-repeat-of-barbary-pirate-slavery-trade/

17. Marking, Havana. "The Pink Panthers: hunting the world's best diamond thieves." Guardian. 22 September, 2013. Web. http://www.theguardian.com/uk-news/2013/sep/22/pink-panthers-diamond-thieves-documentary

18. Estulin, Daniel. *Shadow Masters*. Oregon: Trine Day, 2010.

Chapter 18

Moonraker (1979) and the
Breakaway Civilization

A notable example of the breakaway civilization in cinema is the 1979 adaptation of Ian Fleming's *Moonraker*. The film differs significantly from Fleming's novel, but the differences and parallels are important to highlight: the novel focuses on a kind of Operation Paperclip scenario,[1] wherein Sir Hugo Drax is secretly building a V-2 rocket in tandem with the Nazis to destroy England and rebuild the Reich. For many, the film adaptation a few decades later represented an exceedingly outlandish interpolation of a pulp spy novel that failed to achieve much more than mimicking the box-office success of science-fiction blockbusters it attempted to copy, cinematic innovations like *2001* and *Star Wars*.

On the contrary, more is at work here than just inserting 007 into a Star Wars laser-battle setting. The most obvious factor to recall is that 1979 is roughly the birth of the Strategic Defense Initiative (born at Bohemian Grove), where plans would be posited for a DARPA-style space-based weapons system in the vein of Skynet from *The Terminator*.[2] Thus, concurrent with this deep-state project initiated under the auspices of the Cold War showdown with the Soviets, Tesla-esque satellite decapitation and directed-energy weapon scenarios would become the Skynet/Smart-grid Internet as we see it today.[3]

In tandem with the decades of early planning, predictive programming in Hollywood blockbusters would prepare generations for the implementation of that grid – such as ARPANET (the Internet) – in the near future. Thus, *Moonraker* the film represents the second phase of the Operation Paperclip/NASA program that birthed the rocket and "UFO/foo fighter" aerospace technology. Taking a step back, the 1954 Fleming book *Moonraker* was the first stage of the same "space program" that *Moonraker* the film symbolically updated, and *that* is the deeper reason for the science-fiction trajectory of the narrative. Recall as well that by the late 1970's, 007 was already history's largest film franchise, so we can expect it to have been crucial in preparatory induction for the planned technocratic age. (The novel's plot is rather similar to Guy Ritchie's recent *Man From U.N.C.L.E.*).[4]

Space Disco!

Mention should also be made of *Diamonds Are Forever*, where earlier we analyzed the private aerospace program of Howard Hughes. *Diamonds Are Forever* contains the famous scene of a faked moon landing utilizing actors and a sound stage in a desert facility owned by Hughes stand-in Willard Whyte, while real aerospace technology was being developed behind the veil of the NASA/Hollywood façade. Concerning *Diamonds Are Forever*, just like *Moonraker*, we have the revelation that the real space program is a *private one*, not the public "government" front institution known as NASA. Howard Hughes was not only an aerospace engineer, but also

265

a Hollywood film director, which suggests Fleming and his film incarnations reveal much more than is generally supposed.

007 in space ... or not. Bond strolls through Whyte's secret space facility in *Diamonds Are Forever*.

And so with *Moonraker*, the most ridiculous and silly of 007 films, all the obligatory puns and innuendos so characteristic of the Roger Moore era serve to mask a rather profound secret of the overall deep-state agenda. In the plot we discover that Hugo Drax has stolen a space shuttle through his German underlings to reverse-engineer the technology for nefarious evil machinations. Meanwhile, 007 is on his trail, battling the laughable Jaws (Richard Kiel) in mid-air as Jaws loses his parachute, plummeting into no less than a circus tent. At first, one can brush this off as pure absurdity, but comparisons to *Diamonds Are Forever* began to emerge, as the circus theme of Las Vegas also functioned prominently there. Both films run roughly parallel, describing the same themes and events – a *private space program* that operates under various fronts and shells, intent on cornering the market under a shadow-government technocracy (SPECTRE) intent on mass depopulation and the creation of a "new world" modeled after Noah's Ark.

In both films our respective villains also work together with the mafia and criminal underground to achieve their designs, with the various crime groups subservient to the overriding, *internationalist* SPECTRE. Even though Drax is not a member of SPECTRE like Blofeld, the principles he enacts are all the same. Blofeld's jewel heist and his casino/aerospace takeover operation perfectly mirror Drax's technological theft and private aerospace company, with various shells and fronts funding the true programs of both "fictional" oligarchs. In fact, the *Moonraker* facility Drax runs resembles NASA and other deep state-facilities, yet it is not the *real* Drax aerospace facility.

A wire act worthy of Las Vegas.

An interesting parallel should also be mentioned here in regard to Bond slipping into Drax's facility, where our hero discovers a keypad that plays a certain series of auditory tones to access the bioweapon lab. The musical tones just happen to be the same as the famous musical tones the "aliens" play in Spielberg's *Close Encounters of the Third Kind*. This could either be happenstance or due to Spielberg's numerous connections to the Bond films. For example, think of the bird scene in *Last Crusade* or the *Temple of Doom* shots in India, lifted from none other than *Never Say Never Again*. It could also be that the musical tones in *Close Encounters*, which opened two years prior to *Moonraker* in 1977, are a subtle clue to government news fakery and a secret space program.

007, shameless voyeur.

267

Drax has constructed a secret facility underground beneath a ruined temple in Argentina, where a bevy of multi-racial beauties entrap Bond in an Edenic battle with a massive boa constrictor. The scene is purposely reminiscent of Eden, and as Drax predictably brags about his plot to 007, we learn he is a radical eugenicist with distinctly dysgenic plans: modifying the DNA of the black orchid to produce a lethal nerve gas that will depopulate the globe. Argentina and Chile are said to have been havens of post-war Nazis through sites like Colonia Dignidad, yet Drax is no Nazi.[5] He does plan to create a "master race," yet his approach is more Fabian, as he has sampled the most fit and well-bred from all the races.

COLONIA DIGNIDAD: Also known as Villa Baviera, an isolated region of Chile reportedly functioning as a haven for Nazis. At its height, it was supposed to have housed 300 or more Nazis and was alleged to be a compound involved in mind control, human experimentation and weapons caches. Some have accused the location of being a secret detention camp, while nowadays it claims to no longer function for any nefarious purpose.

In a telling scene in space, 007 explains to Dr. Goodhead that the real plan is Noah's Ark – a breakaway civilization. Drax intends to become "a new god, whose progeny will all call him the new man, the new creator" through technology as he will re-seed the earth with his offspring, descending from the man-made "heaven" of the Moonraker, Drax's covert space facility. All these images reflect Genesis – from creation, Adam and Eve, to Noah, with Drax as the representative Promethean/Luciferian figure who intends to use the secrets of nature and ancient mysteries (the Temple and the Genesis account) to become a god siring a genetically modified, superior race of immortal offspring. The series is thus presenting a variant of transhumanism. In this sense, the meaning of the vanished ancient civilization of Argentina is explained as resulting from the sterility of the black orchid. Drax redesigns the black orchid in its chemical makeup (genetic modification) to become highly lethal, by means of which he will aerosol spray major city centers (chemtrails).

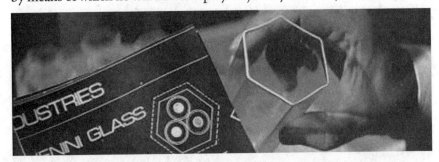

Hexagonal cube of Drax Aerospace. Representative of the molecular makeup of Drax's bioweapon.

268

This is the secret behind the Drax corporation's hexagonal logo for their glass company, itself a front for bioweapons research. As many have pointed out, the cubical/hexagonal figure specifically pertains to the molecular level of our physical dimension. It is the mastery of this physico-material level of existence that Drax's scientism is based on, and rather than a barren rationalistic scientism, Drax is revealed to be a believer in mythology and transhumanism. Drax is thus emblematic of the real technocratic oligarchs of our day who, behind the guise of New Atheism, are actually committed to the breakaway-civilization idea of wiping the slate clean through worldwide cataclysm and a new Noah's Ark. Think here of preeminent globalist "humanitarian" Bill Gates' involvements – he has vast interests in aerosolized geo-engineering,[6] DNA manipulation, vaccines and alteration, Monsanto and transhumanism,[7] as well as doomsday seed vaults.[8] Sounds like Hugo Drax.

Blonde Argentine Amazons in Space!

When we consider the fact that many of the big tech heads like Bill Gates, Peter Thiel or Elon Musk all make public statements warning of the dangers of technology and the "A.I. takeover," we can't forget they are also busy in their promotion of humanity's technological overwrite. Indeed, Musk runs SpaceX, a private space company, and is also a proponent of transhumanism. Much of what we are seeing is a facade, a front plastered before us by Hollywood and mass media, while the real space program has operated privately, in secret, with the subtly revealed intention of creating a breakaway civilization that echoes the predictive programming we see in films like *Moonraker* or novels such as *Atlas Shrugged*. It is precisely because these plans seem so far-fetched, seemingly confined to the realm of popular fiction, that the mass public could never conceive of them as real. Yet dysgenics operations are very real, very public disclosures. Perhaps Hollywood has also disclosed the other side of that story – the plan for a breakaway civilization.

(Endnotes)

1. Cabell, *Ian Fleming's Secret War*, 102.

2. Air Force. "Information Operations: A New War Fighting Capability." Fas.org. 11 December, 1996. Web. http://fas.org/spp/military/docops/usaf/2025/v3c2/v3c2-4.htm#Implanted%20Microscopic%20Chip

3. Dyer, Jay. "Skynet is Real." JaysAnalysis. 16 March, 2012. Web. http://jaysanalysis.com/2012/03/16/skynet-is-real-alchemists-exemplarism-and-techgnosis/

4. Dyer, Jay. "The Man From U.N.C.L.E.'s Deep State Parallels." JaysAnalysis. 20 August, 2015. Web. http://jaysanalysis.com/2015/08/20/the-man-from-u-n-c-l-e-s-deep-state-parallels/

5. Levenda, Peter. *Unholy Alliance*. New York: Avon Books, 1995, pgs. 343-51,

6. Vidal, John. "Bill Gates backs climate scientists lobbying for large-scale geoengineering." Guardian. 6 February, 2012. Web. http://www.theguardian.com/environment/2012/feb/06/bill-gates-climate-scientists-geoengineering

7. Vidal, John. "Why is the Gates foundation investing in GM giant Monsanto?" Guardian. 29 September, 2010. Web. http://www.theguardian.com/global-development/poverty-matters/2010/sep/29/gates-foundation-gm-monsanto

8. Engdahl, F. William. ""Doomsday Seed Vault" in the Arctic." GlobalResearch. 4 December, 2007. Web. http://www.globalresearch.ca/doomsday-seed-vault-in-the-arctic-2/23503

Chapter 19

Bond Rebooted

The newest film in the 007 series is entitled *SPECTRE*, a fitting reference to the real cabals and cartels that rule the world. Indeed, SPECTRE is presented early on in *From Russia With Love* with this very feature – they are *international*, as opposed to SMERSH being Russian, and play nation states off against one another. Transitioning from the Soviet-affiliated SMERSH in the first Bond novel, *Casino Royale*, SMERSH transforms into SPECTRE, a formidable "terrorist" organization from the ambiguous East.

It is also telling that back in the 50s and 60s, Ian Fleming was already predicting the transition from the communist threat to the international terrorist threat – something that gave me the indication that Fleming novels are worth a deeper look. Even current media hysteria seems the product of a shrewd psychological operation: Sony claimed to have been hacked by North Korea, with the *SPECTRE* script leaked,[1] as well as Pyongyang supposedly threatening 9/11-style attacks on theaters that play Franco and Rogen's *The Interview*. Such headlines might as well be ripped from the pages of Fleming's books, since they're truer to life than we might think.

Casino Royale Ca$h Options

There's nothing crazy about suspecting that more is at work; the plot of *Skyfall* surrounded a former MI6 operative, Mr. Silva (Javier Bardem), playing a hacker hell-bent on wreaking vengeful havoc on M (Judi Dench) and all of Her Majesty's Secret Service. It is surely not coincidence that in *Skyfall*, Silva has "back door" technology that brings to mind PROMIS software[2] or the recent hubbub involving NSA spying and Snowden.[3] With these recent news events in mind, an analysis of *Skyfall* is overdue. In the reboot of *Casino Royale,* we saw Bond engaged in a bout with an associate of what we can assume will be SPECTRE, the infamous "LeChiffre," and in my analysis of *Casino Royale*, I noted as follows concerning the real associations4 that can be made between LeChiffre's secret organization and the real cartels that run the show:

In the beginning (of the *Casino Royale* novel), however, Bond is not after SMERSH, but a wealthy, disfigured rogue who struck out on his own and created a "fifth column" from SMERSH, named LeChiffre. LeChiffre translates as "the cypher," letting us know more is at work here. LeChiffre, according to Bond writer Ian MacIntyre, was based on British Satanist/ occultist Aleister Crowley.

In fact, Ian Fleming, it has recently been claimed by researcher Anthony Masters, was responsible for crafting the plot to lure Rudolph Hess to Scotland based on a bogus astrological chart that tickled Hess's fancy, created by Crowley. The plot worked, apparently, when Hess parachuted into Scotland and was captured. LeChiffre, "the cypher," has curious features, and like many Bond villains a strange sexual appetite and fixation, in the same vein as Crowley.

And in regard to "put options" and dirty financial dealings before 9/11 we can see a curious parallel:

While LeChiffre funds an uprising, he simultaneously makes a call to his broker to sell a million puts on Skyfleet, an amorphous airline. We get the impression LeChiffre plans a terror event that will in some way benefit his selling of the put options. In terms of esoteric analysis, this begins to look strikingly like the events prior to 9/11 that those "in the know," know about.

Prior to the terror events of that day, numerous puts had been placed on United Airline stocks, resulting in much speculation as to clear prior knowledge on the part of many in the power structure. As you can see from this mainstream report, the establishment blames "rogue traders." Absurdly, the report purports the laughable line that the retard phony terrorists lurking in caves in Afghanistan were the masterminds behind not only the amazingly complex black operation of 9/11, but also the put options and insider trading. Why, Al Qaeda is virtually omnipotent and omnipresent! And in the narrative of *Casino Royale,* that is exactly what LeChiffre attempts to do, as he has engineered a bombing to occur on the release of a new prototype plane to be unveiled by Skyfleet.

Quantum of No Solace

Moving to the second installment of the rebooted series, *Quantum of Solace*, alchemy comes to the fore in Bond's failed attempt to "bond" with the feminine. Quantum is the idea of matter or quantity or *prima materia*, and for Bond, a bit of peace and *solace* is never attained – primarily because he is a programmed killer, and the final betrayal of Vesper Lynd in *Casino* can only bring forth a cold, "The bitch is dead" from a unremorseful 007. This is crucial for understanding Fleming's novels, as they are just as littered with esoteric images as the films. *Quantum of Solace* is a Fleming short story about Bond, but it is not like the film, aside from Bond's inability to permanently pair with any babes (outside of getting laid). In alchemical fashion, the *Quantum* villains have names that are colors, Mr. White, Mr. Green, etc.

Laced with esoteric and occult imagery, Fleming's novels relate the dark side of mind control in three stories in particular: *Casino Royale, On Her Majesty's Secret Service* and *You Only Live Twice*. In *Casino* we learn that Bond is a programmed killer through his "00" status, in *On Her Majesty's* we learn Blofeld is brainwashing young women under the auspices of treating allergies, ultimately plotting to attack England with a bioweapon, and in *You Only Live Twice*, Bond undergoes a blow to the head that wipes his mind and gives him amnesia. Thus, the "mind controlled assassin" is very much an aspect of the Bond canon.

"You should know something about the people I work with. We deal with the left or the right, with dictators or liberators."

In regard to *Quantum*, the organization that is a front for SPECTRE, we learned:

273

...Quantum is "everywhere," including inside British Intelligence. Quantum is a shadowy international group that uses corporate fronts. In fact, as researcher Phillip Collins has noted, Quantum bears a striking resemblance to the real international intelligence "get the job done" privatized operation *The Secret Team*. The Secret Team functioned as a kind of corporate intelligence-for hire-squad that did what needed to be done. That is precisely what Quantum is, and Quantum is itself both – the team and the corporation. Dominic Greene, we learn, runs the organization, whose main front is the *Green* Movement."[5]

In fact, Greene at one point in the film blames the nation state as the problem, and touts privatization, while demonizing "government." Greene is an apostle for the Green Movement, and claims to support numerous environmental causes, and brings to mind someone like Al Gore. Another interesting point of relevance is that the Green Movement itself arose out of the Nazi-eugenics return to so-called "nature,"[6] functioning under the guise of caring for the planet, while actually a corporate front for the control of strategic resources. That is exactly what Dominic Greene does in *Quantum of Solace*!

Quantum involved the green movement as a scam to rape underdeveloped nations, much like the UN and IMF in real life, assuming the perceptive viewer will make the connection. It is not accidental that the middle of the film contained the massive presentation of the All-seeing Eye during the operatic presentation of *La Tosca* in Bregenz, and the *church is within the eye*. The message here being the control of all aspects of reality, from economics, to environment to religion, encompassed within the grasp of the great eye – the secretive organization (SPECTRE) operates in a technocratic Panopticon that sees all.

The Illuminist opera *La Tosca*, with Western churchmen under the all-seeing eye of SPECTRE.

274

And what Bond-relevant entity utilized *the eye* as its symbol? The classic logo of British Intelligence, MI5, as seen at bottom. Is *Quantum of Solace* telling us on a deeper level that the Anglo-establishment has gained control of all areas of life, including revolutionary movements and the arts, with all subservient to the City of London? I'll let the reader be the judge, but certainly *Quantum* was telling more than even *Casino Royale* revealed.

The Sky Falls With Skyfall

When we come to *Skyfall*, similar themes appear. *Skyfall* is about Bond's past – his family residence, as well as intelligence operations in a new world of cyber (virtual) reality. As usual, the famous opening sequence reveals the esoteric plot elements of the story to come – from Bond's *katabasis* (death and resurrection) to his psyche being fractured from his assassination programming. Swastikas are again present, like past Bond films, indicating in my analysis the manipulation of both the left and the right. For example, in *Goldeneye*, the opening sequence includes scantily clad hotties tearing down old Soviet statues, but what is actually at work in the opening sequence is a clear presentation of dialectics – the manipulation by the Eye of both sides of the Cold War dialectic.

Making the capitalist-communist dialectic oh-so-sexy.

This is also why Bond receives the Order of Lenin in *A View to a Kill*. This seeming contradiction is made coherent when we understand Mr. Greene's words in *Quantum of Solace*: "You should know something about the people I work with. We deal with the left or the right, with dictators or liberators." In *Skyfall*, however, we are entering Bond's subconscious, and sinking with him to the abyss of death, as Bond is accidentally shot by Moneypenny in a botched operation to retrieve a hard drive containing MI6 agents embedded with NATO.

275

Bond sinks to the ocean floor and is pulled into a black hole, where a blood skull appears, leading to Bond shooting his shadow selves. The shots break the glass images indicating the fractured *psyche* Bond has due to his training, torture, and numerous instances of trauma, and the images of pillars signify the deepest recesses and foundations of Bond's archetypal subconscious. The shadow self will appear in the figure of Bond's nemesis, Mr. Silva, who, like Bond, is betrayed by "M" and MI6. Bond is thus tempted to leave his secret service work because of past issues with his own disfigured archetypes of mother and father – he is an orphan. M thus becomes his mother figure, and numerous times in the film the association of M with the Queen and mother are made, indicating associated archetypes.

Bond will be tempted to deny his loyal patriotic fervor embodied in the figure of Silva, the "traitor." As Bond sinks deeper and deeper in the title sequence, we see death's-head, fiery torture (likely his own torture at the hands of LeChiffre), and Chinese fire dragons. The presentation of the dragon within the deep or leviathan is interesting, as Bond will venture Eastward in the film to Macao and interact with gangsters involved in the sex trade that work for Silva. The sequence ends with the camera entering Bond's *left eye*, or the left-handed path, where we will see more of the traumatic circumstances that have made 007 into the killing machine he is.

As I'm sure readers are aware, the plot is about MI6 being hacked by Silva and releasing the names of MI6 agents over time. This oddly recalls the actual story of Richard Tomlinson, recounted in his book *The Big Breach*, as Tomlinson reportedly did leak such names online.[7] Is Silva a fictional version of a kind of Tomlinson/Assange hybrid? Possibly, as Silva is given a weird blonde hairdo reminiscent of Julian Assange. Perhaps the idea of combining two so-called villains of MI6 into a cyber-terror package was fitting. The intelligence agencies have played up the so-called threat of cyber terror for years, arguing that total control of the web is the only way to defeat all those hidden terrorists out there, and in *Skyfall* we even have Silva as the mastermind of a 7/7/05-style London Underground bombing!

Blonde hackers? Is it 1997 again? Will Prodigy be playing?

Simultaneous with his subway bombing, M is at a government hearing on Humint being "old-fashioned," and in response M reads a Tennyson poem about England *still being an empire*, but with new enemies. The new enemies are everyone and no one – hidden terrorists everywhere. So, a former MI6 agent is responsible for the 7/7-style event in the film narrative, while in real life, 7/7 had curious connections to Western intelligence that have never been adequately explained or addressed by the said establishment.

Like Achilles, Bond is vitally wounded and "resurrected" to return to duty, while a bombed MI6 headquarters has relocated the recouped agency to an underground base, formerly Churchill's World War II bunker. The consistent theme of the old versus the new appears throughout the film, as fans are given constant references to classic Bond guns like the Walther PPK and the sleek Aston Martin ride. With Bond's new IT nerd Quartermaster, Bond must grapple with the realities of modern cyber-espionage supplanting classic methods of humint and assassinations. "Is Bond washed up?" is the film's question, and thus we delve into Bond's origins and psychological trauma to resolve such issues from his dark past.

Most of the previous is somewhat irrelevant to the ultimate message of the film, which is that terrorists are still *everywhere*, and intelligence agencies, though they keep failing, need more funding to protect us from Tomlinson, Haroon Aswat, Snowden, Bin Laden and Assange. More funding plus more surveillance equals more terror – the equation is quite a cash cow. The eternal "War on Terror," as we can see in Fleming's classic novels, was predicted and *planned* to replace the Soviet threat. The Cold War allowed for the installation of the global surveillance grid, and now, the script is flipped on the populace[8] – we're *all* potential terrorists, and only benevolent Skynet can save us! These classic scams never fail, of course, because the heedless public never catches on.

Real-World Parallels

From an esoteric perspective, all the hidden elements are contained in the opening sequence, which then unfold in the narrative. Bond's journey Eastward is parallel to his descent into the abyss and "death" at the beginning, as his trip to Macao has him facing the "dragon" of the East, the demonic Mr. Silva. This is exemplified in his boat ride into the dragon's mouth at Silva's casino in Macao. In *Casino Royale*, Bond faced LeChiffre, a western "demon" in a casino, and now he must face a demon of the East. Silva, it turns out, is a *master of false flags*, having staged a chemical leak on a Chinese island, causing its inhabitants to flee, which enabled Silva to take up residence for his operations.

277

The divided psyche of a programmed killer.

Just like the Underground bombing, Silva is a master of *staging terror events* – but remember – the film places all of this dastardly work on the shoulders of a *former* intelligence agent. There are *never* corrupt individuals within intelligence agencies (except that *Quantum* did allow for infiltration into MI6), and anyone who dares to question the mainstream version of attacks must be a traitor to authentic "patriotism." Given the immensity of the perpetual lies the Western establishment has foisted upon us since 9/11, does anyone really believe the propaganda message of this film? If London's Mandarins were really worried about terror, they wouldn't house radical Islamists in "Londonistan."

To bring this full circle, Bond's death and resurrection is emblematic of the reboot of the series. We know from the supposed "leak" of the new SPECTRE script by unknown "hackers" from North Korea (just try to not laugh), the third act is up for grabs. Will we see Blofeld? What about Kissy Suzuki? In any case, the leaks were obviously a staged PR event, as other mega tech companies have done in the past,[9] and with the new 007 film it is not accidental that *Skyfall* was about hackers, and now SPECTRE is hacked (by SPECTRE!). The laughs come, however, when one realizes that the establishment itself is SPECTRE.

The pseudo-hacking by North Koreans is tied to the release of *The Interview* to give a realistic feel to the threat of some unknown SPECTRE on the loose, when the entities that have all the motives and capabilities of SPECTRE are the ruling elite's own legates. *Casino Royale* hintingly referenced 9/11, *Quantum* revealed the green scam, and *Skyfall* whispered about 7/7: We can expect more Blofeldian subterfuge to come, so grab your popcorn and your Walther PPK, because the DPRK is coming! Indeed, the lyrics of Adele's theme for the film describe the post-9/11 terror world, where the old has crumbled, and the new technocratic "security state" now dominates.

Like Chicken Little, the false cry of perpetual terror calls forth – the sky is falling, the sky is falling! When we consider that *Chicken Little* was a World War II Disney propaganda film, the reference is likely not accidental.

"This is the end, hold your breath and count to ten,
I've drowned and dreamt this moment, let the sky fall,
When it crumbles, we will stand tall and face it all at Skyfall."

Secrets of *SPECTRE*

Appearing to conclude the Daniel Craig era of 007 reboots, *SPECTRE* not only premiered at the top of the world box office. As could be expected, the film also provides quite a few insights into the nature of real geopolitics and espionage in true Bondian style. Let's start with the theme of mass surveillance, a reflection of our own postmodern Panopticon reality. Even the *Guardian* has commented on the similarities of the *SPECTRE* plot with the supposed leaks of Edward Snowden[10] regarding the NSA spying apparatus. Yet there are also serious grounds to question Snowden's heroics; just as well, GCHQ was monitoring the population and spying long before there was any NSA in the US. Furthermore, the real NSA is not some government building, but is fused with the world's largest tech corporations, monsters like Google and Apple. The notion that the NSA is a government-run entity which has gotten out of hand and free from public oversight is preposterous, as the private globocorps have been doing the real dirty data collecting for decades (and continue to do so, apart from Snowden's so-called "leaks").[11] All of this will prove relevant, as we will see, in reference to the storyline of Sam Mendes' latest installment of 007's adventures.

007 stalks Sciarra, as he seeks the "Pale King," the Lord of the Dead.

With SPECTRE, we open with a long, single shot of Bond disguised in skeleton costume amidst the celebratory festivities of Dia de Los Muertos in Mexico City. 007 is smoothly striding through the streets with the obligatory babe on his arm, stalking the movements of a certain Sciarra. The scenery elicits numerous demonic elements, including devil masks, effigies, corpses, and Santa Muerte. Santa Muerte is the cartel-connected syncretistic cult often associated with MS-13; the group, as analysts have noted, operates both human trafficking and drug corridors. Some have even argued the U.S. intelligence establishment is in bed with certain *select* cartels, with the intent of controlling the black markets, while only "busting" operations of rival cartels not in bed with the Atlanticists.[12] We even saw elements of this in the Fast and Furious arms scandal,[13] as well as in the recent film *Sicario*, where FBI agents discover their *attaché* role in a border operation is cover for a deeper CIA black op of taking out a *rival* cartel.

Note that at the 2012 London Olympics, the Octopus covered the UK flag.

280

In Mexico City, 007 gets hints of Sciarra's involvement with the cartel underworld as the plot to bomb a professional soccer match is planned. Bond then resolves to take out the conspirators, ending up in an impressive helicopter battle with an escaping Sciarra. Eliminating Sciarra at the behest of a secret, posthumous message from M (Dame Judi Dench), the only information Bond recovers is knowledge of the planned attack, as well as Sciarra's curious Octopus ring. Also noteworthy is the room 007 uses to work his mojo on the Mexican beauty before this operation – it just happens to be Room 327 (or 237), which echoes the speculative documentary about the esoteric themes in Stanley Kubrick's *The Shining*. While this is admittedly speculative, there is a connection between the real meaning of the "secret space program"

Tentacles of the octopus.

"The dead are alive," the opening text of the film displays, and as the narrative progresses, we discover the meaning of this clue to be the same theme of the recent *Mission: Impossible* installment, *Rogue Nation*, that the members of the (variously titled in most spy franchises), Syndicate, Cabal, SMERSH, MAD, SPECTRE, etc., tend to be ghosts. In the spy world, a ghost is a spook, and spooks are specters, who appear to be dead. A fine way to become a ghost is to fake your own death; the CIA has a long history of doing this, with similar techniques applied by Soviet intelligence.[14]

The iconic opening montage for SPECTRE hearkens to the prior Craig-starring Bonds, with all the villains of our hero's past appearing in shattered glass fragmentation, emblematic of the psyche and the assassin's traumatic past. From Vesper Lynd to Mr. White, 007's rabbit hole leads to the enigmatic cartel organization SPECTRE, symbolized by the octopus whose tentacles seemingly reach everywhere, even into Bond himself, as the source of all his ills.

281

Encircling the montage of pulchritude in strange tentacle-porn imagery, the octopus morphs into an All-Seeing Eye that here will represent the Panopticon surveillance state at the heart of the film's narrative. Further transforming, the eye becomes a massive octopus with nine eyes, later explained in the film to be the "9 Eyes" of a rough equivalent of the G8 nations (here G-9) that offer their sovereignty up to the promise of security courtesy of CNS, the new UK version of the NSA intent on integrating mass surveillance from the most powerful nations. (Recall that the G6, G8 and G20 are creations of the Atlanticists and the Royal Society.)

Promising to prevent all future terror attacks and shut down all dated, dinosaur humint programs, the "00" licensed-to-kill program is also axed, resulting in a predictably rogue 007. With the introduction of Smart-Blood (yes, nanotech SmartBlood), the outdated tech wizardry of the implantable chip Bond received in *Casino Royale* is replaced with its newer transhumanist equivalent. Tracked and traced globally, 007 is dependent on Q to keep his location secret as he seeks out the answer to just who is backing Sciarra in Rome. After romancing Sciarra's widow (a youthful looking Monica Bellucci), Bond sneaks his way into the elite SPECTRE board meeting that recalls Bill Harford's (Tom Cruise) out-of-place attendance at the *Eyes Wide Shut* ritual.

SPECTRE meets like Bilderberg.

Recognized immediately by the mysterious head of SPECTRE, Bond is called out as if he were intentionally led to the meeting (like Kubrick's Bill Harford) and subsequently chased from the premises. The location of SPECTRE in Rome is curious – as if this were some underground fascist cabal of unknown mobsters and enigmatic Third World and Far Eastern villainy gathered in the heart of global Catholicism. Could this be a reference to P-2 Lodge and the infamous associations with Operation Gladio and the terror cells of the Cold War stay-behind units, the model for the recent waves of Euro-terror[15] (including the supposed attacks in Paris and Brussels)?[16] Interestingly, the most striking example of predictive programming in the film's plot is the revelation that global terror is being orchestrated by a single shadowy cabal. This cabal is also intent on bombing nation states behind the facade of radicalism to corral them into the joint intelligence apparatus being erected through the private "space program" of our film's super villain, Ernst Stavro Blofeld. As SPECTRE manages to appoint its Number 2 ("C," played by Andrew Scott) as head of the new CNS surveillance initiative, the screenplay subtly refers to the plan as the culmination of a "New World Order."

The original Blofeld SPECTRE lair.

In fact, while many perceptive filmgoers probably caught the numerous references to Connery and Moore-era installments, the most interesting aspect of Blofeld's secret base in the Moroccan desert is its observatory and aerospace features. Once again, as with *Diamonds Are Forever* and *Moonraker*, the private space program has a motive quite distinct from the noble advancement of scientific

P2 LODGE: The Propaganda Due Lodge of Italian Freemasonry founded in 1945, later withdrawing into a clandestine political organization with ultra-right leanings believed to be associated with the GLADIO operation of NATO's "stay behind" cell units tasked with combating Soviet and Marxist influence through assassinations, false flags and staged terror. P2 was also implicated in the famed Vatican Banking scandal, while the Lodge was headed by Licio Gelli. Banker Roberto Calvi was found murdered in ritual pose as a result of this scandal, while other members have included Silvio Berlusconi, Italian throne claimant Victor Emmanuel, the heads of Italian secret services and many journalists. The conversion of the P2 into a "fascist" organization led to its supposed banning by the Illuminist-Jacobin influenced Grand Orient Masonry of which it was formerly associated.

PROMIS: Technology developed in the 1970s by the US-based company Inslaw, Inc, as well as "former" NSA analysts, for the Department of Justice. The acronym stands for Prosecutors Management Information System and its purpose is the utilization of a software program that can track individuals and integrate large amounts of data. The software was later transformed into an FBI database version which led to a lengthy lawsuit by its creators. Later incarnations were linked to foreign espionage cases and "backdoor" technology which can tap into personal and government devices. The "backdoor" technology bears striking resemblance to the secret NSA device revealed in the 1992 Robert Redford/Dan Akroyd film, *Sneakers*.

OPERATION GLADIO: Clandestine name for NATO's secret "stay behind" cell units which were tasked with staged terror, false flags and assassinations to be utilized in a "strategy of tension" technique for anti-Soviet psychological warfare. GLADIO is crucial for understanding the present-day cell model of "radical Jihadi" terror, as the Cold War transitioned into the so-called "global war on terror." GLADIO, as well as the long support of Wahhabism and Salafism, demonstrates the Atlanticist establishment's penchant for covertly utilizing terrorism (including funding and aid for Al Qaeda and ISIS), while pretending to oppose terrorism, especially post-9/11. Recent major "terror" attacks in France and the US in 2015 and 2016 demonstrate telling similarities and patterns that echo GLADIO.

283

knowledge. Here, as with old-school Blofeld plots, we learn the antagonist's aims are not even a Strategic Defense Initiative, but the backdoor PROMIS Octopus technology that we saw *Wired* magazine has covered, key to NSA's ability to hack into most tech. And this is precisely what Blofeld is after – a total Panopticon surveillance apparatus erected as a result of the engineering of global terror attacks, all run by a private, unknown command center. Art is mirroring reality and such is indeed the ultimate plan for the globalist *Novus Ordo Seclorum*. Researcher and author Daniel Estulin has even highlighted this notion in his appropriately titled novel, *The Octopus Deception*.[17]

DANIEL ESTULIN: Author and researcher known for his 2007 expose, *The True Story of the Bilderberg Group*, from TrineDay Publishers. Estulin charts the history of the secretive elite society and their role in large-scale geopolitical decision-making for the western establishment since 1954. Estulin's other works also focus on the shadow government, including the role of intelligence agencies and their collusion with arms and drugs dealers in *Shadow Masters* (2010), social engineering in *The Tavistock Institute* (2015) and a fictional account of the cryptocracy itself in *The Octopus Deception: A Novel* (2013)

Curiously, while eavesdropping on the SPECTRE meeting, 007 finds that the planning group resembles something along Bilderberg lines, where decisions are made concerning human trafficking, the management of various vices like prostitution (using a large number of refugee/migrant women), the counterfeiting of pharmaceuticals (as if BigPharma itself isn't a tentacle of the real SPECTRE) and the planning of a bombing in South Africa to terrorize the populace into signing onto the global privatized surveillance plan. MI6 is presented throughout as the guardian of Western liberty and "democracy," while the more Eastern and fascist elements of SPECTRE are portrayed as enemies of the people. Never tiring of playing out this propaganda, the Cold War subterfuge of the West still banks on its mythology of being a bastion of "freedom" and "liberty," as our civilization transforms into a sordid amusement park-cum-police state.

Bond goddess Madeleine Swann (Lea Seydoux) in a train scene reminiscent of *From Russia With Love.*

Blofeld's base, an aerospace observatory that is also the real NSA.

This Anglo-centric model is by no means exposed in the film, inasmuch as it is Western banking and corporate elites who comprise the real SPEC-TRE. Never tiring of generic sloganeering, Western propaganda and PR hasn't changed its essence one iota since Bernays. Moreover, the Western narrative of libertarian Enlightenment freedom[18] rings ever more hollow in our day as it becomes increasingly evident how absurd this phraseology is, where the supposedly "free" West becomes a mutant version of Brave New Disney World, all under the designs of the very establishment that professes empty mantras of "freedom." Freedom means the freedom to choose Coke or Pepsi, sterilization through GMOs or cancer through euthanasia – all choice delicacies offered up by the decadent Atlanticist elites.

Hey, kids! Let's go camping this year at Pine Gap!

Seeking the supposedly dead Franz Oberhauser, Bond finds his own foster-brother to be the source of his woes, as the darkest secret of 007 is his own background: he was raised as an orphan by Blofeld's father. Blofeld, full of *ressentiment*, decides to work out his daddy issues through (as you can imagine) torturing Bond by strapping him down and drilling his skull for a full-scale MKUltra-style mind-wipe. While SmartBlood may or may not be a reality, the targeting of certain areas of the brain to erase memories and motor functions is very real. DARPA has openly discussed such projects many times under the guise of "treating addictions" or "traumas" and PTSD.[19] DARPA wants to help you, just like Pine Gap exists to "research space" rather than conduct mass surveillance, and just like SETI exists to send space emails to aliens with billion-dollar satellites, not to conduct mass surveillance (my own particular speculation).

SPECTRE, er, ISIS, er, Al Qaeda, uh actors, or just terr'ists...on the loose! So who are the terr'ists, exactly? Who funds them? Who stages their laughable videos?

Facing Blofeld, Bond learns the secret base is the site of a meteor crater, where the oldest meteor is Ernst's private property. Likening himself to the obsidian Kaaba-like stone, Blofeld explains the meteor as an allegory for his own secret space surveillance system that will utilize the information from all surveillance satellites, CCTVs and tech gadgets globally. This is SPECTRE's big secret, building the global surveillance Panopticon around staged terror events, instituting a total information grid that will allow for the blackmail of all. Does this sound familiar? Is it possible that in the real-world globo-terror is *also orchestrated* precisely for this purpose?[20] That is our thesis, and hopefully it is becoming increasingly evident this is so, as more and more films begin to tell us this very story.

Most strikingly, as we argued in our *Casino Royale* analysis, the 007 reboots seem to continually hearken to clues about 9/11, such as the pre-9/11 airline stock put options. From there, we move into *Quantum of Solace* exposing the Green Agenda and the left-right dialectic, to *Skyfall* showing us the fact that so-called cyber-terrorists are actually the system itself (as per the similarities of the plot of *Skyfall* with the Sony "hacking" scandal). In *SPECTRE* yet another false flag reference to 9/11 is hinted at in the "inside job" bombing of MI6 through a massive controlled demolition. Whatever means you think took down the twin towers (and building 7), whether controlled explosive charges or exotic weaponry, it wasn't just good old jet fuel.

The "inside job" bombing of MI6 headquarters in *Skyfall*, followed by the complete controlled demolition, in *SPECTRE*.

On 9/11, the ultimate in terror theatre, we witnessed some *form* of controlled demolition, as the towers were demolished, and this was controlled by some artifice other than "Al Qaeda." Curiously, this manner of attack is exactly what Blofeld perpetrates when he gains access to MI6 through his mole at the head of the CNS. Isn't it curious that the first thing Blofeld does is lure 007 into MI6 headquarters, intending on demolishing him and the old world with it? 007 escapes, of course, but I would venture to say the film is not telling us about the demolition of MI6 headquarters, but the destruction of some other couple of towers by SPECTRE.

Endnotes

287

1. "Hackers vs. James Bond: 'SPECTRE' script stolen in Sony attack." Reuters. 13 December, 2014. Web. https://www.yahoo.com/news/hackers-vs-james-bond-spectre-script-stolen-sony-212654161--finance.html

2. Fricker, Richard L. "The INSLAW Octopus." *Wired*. 1 January, 1993. Web. http://www.wired.com/1993/01/inslaw/

3. "Snowden: 'Training Guide' for GCHQ, NSA Agents Infiltrating and Disrupting Alternative Media Online." 21stCenturyWire. 25 February, 2014. Web. http://21stcenturywire.com/2014/02/25/snowden-training-guide-for-gchq-nsa-agents-infiltrating-and-disrupting-alternative-media-online/

4. Dyer, Jay. "Casino Royale: 9/11 Connections." JaysAnalysis. 15 June, 2013. Web. http://jaysanalysis.com/2013/06/15/casino-royale-2006-esoteric-analysis/

5. Dyer, Jay. "Quantum of Solace: 007's Alchemy." JaysAnalysis. 20 July, 2011. Web. http://jaysanalysis.com/2011/07/20/quantum-of-solace-007s-alchemy/

6. Maessen, Jurriaan. "The Green Nazis: Environmentalism in the Third Reich." Infowars. 18 June, 2009. Web. http://www.infowars.com/the-green-nazis-environmentalism-in-the-third-reich/

7. "Richard Tomlinson." Wikispooks. Web. https://wikispooks.com/wiki/Richard_Tomlinson

8. Ahmed, Nafeez. "How the Pentagon's Skynet Would Automate War." Vice. 24 November, 2014. Web. http://motherboard.vice.com/read/how-the-pentagons-skynet-would-automate-war

9. Watson, Paul Joseph. "Mysterious Hooded Men & Occult Circles Appear Globally." Infowars. 31 October, 2013. Web. http://www.infowars.com/mysterious-hooded-men-occult-circles-appear-globally/

10. Bradshaw, Peter. "SPECTRE Review: James Bond is back, Stylish, Camp, and Sexily Pro-Snowden." *Guardian*. 21 October, 2015. Web. http://www.theguardian.com/film/2015/oct/21/spectre-review-james-bond-is-back-stylish-camp-and-sexily-pro-snowden

11. Dyer, Jay. "The Theater of Media Operations: Snowden Analyzed." JaysAnalysis. 2 June, 2014. Web. http://jaysanalysis.com/2014/06/02/the-theater-of-media-operations-snowden-analyzed/

12. Austin Fitts, Catherine. Narco Dollars for Beginners. NarcoNews. Web. http://www.narconews.com/narcodollars1.html

13. Farago, Robert. "FARAGO: Was CIA behind Operation Fast and Furious?" WashingtonTimes. 11 August, 2011. Web. http://www.washingtontimes.com/news/2011/aug/11/was-cia-behind-operation-fast-and-furious/

14. Kouprianova, Nina. "Hitler's Plot to Assassinate Stalin." EspionageHistoryArchive. 4 September, 2015. Web. https://espionagehistoryarchive.com/2015/09/04/stalin-assassination-wwii-smersh/

15. Dyer, Jay. "Vindicated: Gladio B, Paris Terror & ISIS Fakery Admitted." JaysAnalysis. 14 November, 2015. Web. http://jaysanalysis.com/2015/11/14/vindicated-gladio-b-paris-terror-isis-fakery-admitted-2/

16. Dyer, Jay. "TERROR THEATRE: The EU Babel, Brussels Attack Numerology & Media Fakery." JaysAnalysis. 7 March, 2016. Web. http://jaysanalysis.com/2016/03/26/terror-theatre-the-eu-babel-brussels-attack-numerology-media-fakery/

17. Estulin, Daniel. *The Octopus Deception*. Oregon: Trine Day, 2013.

18. Dyer, Jay. "From Thomism to Enlightenment Deism/Atheism." JaysAnalysis. 22 August, 2013. Web. http://jaysanalysis.com/2013/08/22/from-thomism-to-enlightenment-deismatheism/

19. Moreno, JD. "DARPA on Your Mind." NIH.gov. Fall 2004. Web. http://www.ncbi.nlm.nih.gov/pubmed/15986543

20. Dyer, Jay. "Terror Engineering." SouloftheEast. 24 July, 2015. Web. http://souloftheeast.org/2015/07/24/terror-engineering/

Chapter 20

Occult MI6: Dennis Wheatley and *The Devil Rides Out*

There's no shortage of connections between British espionage writers and the occult, and while we've examined a good deal of Ian Fleming, another fellow who wrote quite prolifically of devilish machinations was Dennis Wheatley.[1] Wheatley, the child of a winemaking family, caused some stir early in his college days for creating his very own campus "secret society." Following his expulsion for this incident, Wheatley joined the military, fighting in World War I as a Royal Artillery Lieutenant. He was then tasked with military intelligence and covert operations in World War II, serving in the London Controlling Section. After his war activities, Wheatley worked for British Intelligence and was introduced to notorious occultist and black magician Aleister Crowley, stating:

> The fact that I had read extensively about ancient religions gave me some useful background, but I required up-to-date information about occult circles in this country. My friend, Tom Driburg, who then lived in a mews flat just behind us in Queen's Gate, proved most helpful. He introduced me to Aleister Crowley, the Reverend Montague Summers and Rollo Ahmed.[2] (*The Time Has Come: The Memoirs of Dennis Wheatley* (Vol 3) 1919-1977: Drink and Ink, p. 131.)

Dennis Wheatley, occult novelist and British intelligence officer.

However, there is more to the story concerning his relation to British Intelligence and MI5, as his personal site explains:

> Then in May 1940, following a chance conversation between his wife and her passenger while she was a driver for MI5, Wheatley was commissioned to write a series of papers on various strategic aspects of the War. These "War Papers" were read by the King and the highest levels of the General Staff, and as a result in December 1941 he was re-commissioned, becoming the only civilian to be directly recruited onto the Joint Planning Staff. With the final rank of Wing Commander, for the rest of the War Wheatley worked in Churchill's basement fortress as one of the country's small handful of "Deception Planners" who were charged with developing ways to deceive the enemy of the Allies real strategic intentions. Their top secret operations, which included the plans to deceive the enemy about the true site of the Normandy landings, were highly successful and saved countless lives.[3]

Wheatley's wife also worked for MI5, yet these details do not easily emerge in research on the subject, though it is now known Wheatley was also working with MI6, including writing anti-German and anti-Russian occult spy fiction.[4] And so to old dusty books we must go before a fuller picture emerges and we spot the connections to Fleming and Maxwell Knight, and the decision to co-opt Aleister Crowley into MI5 work. In Anthony Masters' book *The Man Who Was M: The Real-Life Spymaster Who Inspired Ian Fleming*, we read:

> Dennis and Joan Wheatley were constant visitors to the flat, but Lois found she had little in common with Knight's and Wheat-

ley's all-absorbing interest in the occult, and in particular, Aleister Crowley who was later to become an MI5 agent. Wheatley had met Crowley through Tom Driberg, then a remarkable journalist (and later a Labour Party MP) whom Knight was to use as an agent inside the CPGB [Communist Party of Great Britain]. Crowley had come to dinner with the Wheatleys many times and provided Dennis with occult information for his books. Wheatley's first opinion had been that Crowley was interesting but harmless. Driberg, however, warned him that Crowley had been responsible for running a community in Northern Sicily where a number of children were rumored to have disappeared in connection with Satanic masses.

He also told Wheatley that there had been another alarming episode, this time in Paris, which was better documented. In an attempt to raise the pagan god Pan, Crowley had spent a night in an empty hotel room on the Left Bank, in company with one of his followers, a man named MacAleister. In the morning they were both found naked. MacAleister was dead and Crowley was crouched howling in a corner, from where he was taken to an asylum. Four months later he was released, but the cause of MacAleister's death was never discovered. This, anyway, was Driberg's story and it fascinated both the Wheatleys and Knight, although Crowley in the flesh remained a disappointment.

Knight met Crowley at the Wheatleys. He was well-dressed and middle aged, with the voice and manner of an Oxford don. He said his own grace, embroidering Rabelais' (Do what you like) 'Do what thou wilt shall be the whole of the Law,' but nevertheless Knight wondered how such racy legends had sprung up around such a seemingly harmless, if eccentric, academic.

Knight told his nephew, Harry Smith, that he and Dennis Wheatley went to Crowley's occult ceremonies to research black magic for Wheatley's books. "They jointly applied to Crowley as novices and he accepted them as pupils," Smith told me. "But my uncle stressed that his interest – and also Wheatley's – was purely academic.[5]

On Her Majesty's Satanic Request

The links become clear: Wheatley, Knight and Ian Fleming were the chief architects of the ruse to co-opt Crowley for the purpose of luring Nazi Rudolph Hess to parachute into Scotland. Fleming biographer Andrew Lycett only mentions this briefly in passing, leaving out Crowley:

> At the same time he [Fleming] maintained contact with several other friends in the broad field of deception, including Ellic Howe,

291

who had worked for the printer James Shand and now specialized in counterfeit German documents; Dennis Wheatley, an occasional dinner guest who worked for the London Controlling Section masterminding deception projects; and Louis de Wohl, an astrologer who was used by the NID to chart the exact moments when Hitler might be open to ruses and feints.[6]

And Masters again:

Ian Fleming, then in the Department of Naval Intelligence, was fascinated by Knight's mysterious persona, and was to involve him in an extraordinary adventure whose components – The Link [a supposed pro-Hitler underground in the UK], Aleister Crowley and Hess – were to make an explosive mixture. Years later, when Fleming wrote the first of his James Bond books, he used an amalgam of Knight and his own superior, Rear-Admiral John Godfrey, as the model for M, Bond's boss.[7]

In fact, this curious episode of the tale of luring Hess through Crowley was apparently seeded in a predictive programming form (or the idea was nabbed therefrom) in Ian's brother, Peter Fleming's novel, *The Flying Visit*, penned soon before Hess's flight. Fleming scholar Craig Cabell comments on this fantastical story:

SOE and NID were closely associated with each other at the time of Hess' flight and Fleming would have learned very quickly about Hess (because he saw much intelligence from various sources). We know for certain that Fleming tracked down Aleister Crowley for advice concerning Hess's interrogation, which prompted Crowley to write to the DNI. But why would Fleming do that? Crowley had been dubbed the wickedest man in the world, a master of the Black Mass, who once apparently summoned Pan and was left a jibbering wreck. Although still a master of the Occult and Astrology during the Second World War, Crowley was more content to write propaganda poems than summoning up ancient demons; but he did write to Godfrey, the sealed letter covered in occultist symbols. The letter read:

"Sir:
If it is true that Herr Hess is much influenced by astrology and magick, my services might be of use to the Department in case he should not be willing to do what you wish. I have the honour to be, sir,

Your obedient Servant,
Aleister Crowley"[8]

Author Peter Levenda comments on this association as well, in his *Unholy Alliance: A History of Nazi Involvement with the Occult:*

> His [Crowley's] utility to MI5 during his Berlin days, when he spied on German communists, was not forgotten. Further, he had been cultivated by Dennis Wheatley, who found the occult fascinating ... Knight was the prototype for Ian Fleming's character "M": The intelligence chief whom we always see in the movies giving Sean Connery or Roger Moore his dangerous, "license to kill" assignment. What is not generally known is that "M" was also introduced to Aleister Crowley – by Dennis Wheatley – and was quite friendly with the Magus ... here is Maxwell Knight, "M" after all, accepting a kind of occult initiation from Aleister Crowley and becoming his pupil!
>
> Himmler was obsessed by the idea that British Intelligence was being a Rosicrucian Order and that occult adepts were in charge of MI5. How would he have reacted if he had known the formidable Maxwell Knight, head of Department B5(b), the counter subversion section of MI5, was a disciple of Aleister Crowley? And that Dennis Wheatley – he of the occult novels favored by Goering – was also a student of Crowley's and simultaneously working for Churchill's planning staff?[9]

I've noted many times the connection of Crowley to various villains, including LeChiffre in *Casino Royale*, but as we shall see, the influence in the British Psy-Op Department extends beyond Fleming to Wheatley:

> One of the last photographs of Rudolf Hess in Spandau has him pictured with detailed maps of the moon. These are printed on the wall of his cell directly above his bed. Also the character of LeChiffre in the James Bond novel *Casino Royale* is based physically on Aleister Crowley; just as the evil occultist in Dennis Wheatley's *Devil Rides Out* is based upon Crowley. (Ibid., pg. 48-9)

Indeed, not only was this the beginning of Fleming's inspirations for 007 and the fictional occult tales of Duc de Richleau in Wheatley's novels, but is in fact the same circles that would produce the OSS in 1942, later to become the CIA in 1947. The curious convergence of espionage, Hollywood, the occult and high finance becomes manifest. Cabell continues:

> It was May 25 1941 when Fleming and Godfrey stepped off the flying boat at LaGuardia, New York. They were there to observe U.S. port security alongside William Stephenson's British Security Coordination (BSC), who worked out of New York. There was of course more to

the trip than that. The gentlemen from the NID were overtly there to assist Stephenson in developing a security sector in America that would benefit both US and UK interests. Godfrey was keen to make William Donovan head of the new security force. Donovan was senior partner in a law firm but during the Great War he had worked as a private intelligence gatherer for J.P. Morgan, so he was a known, albeit unused, officer. Fleming had tried to coax Donovan into Operation Goldeneye, but Godfrey had him personally marked for the U.S.[10]

And for the icing on the cake, consider Phillip Knightley's admission of this as nothing more than a British move to further manipulate U.S. policy in favor of the U.K., in his *The Second Oldest Profession: Spies and Spying in the Twentieth Century*:

> Donovan was helped to prepare his submissions to Roosevelt by Stephenson and the SIS officers attached to his staff. Two senior British Intelligence officers, Admiral John Godfrey and his personal assistant, Lieutenant Commander Ian Fleming (later of James Bond fame), crossed the Atlantic to work on the campaign.... There is no doubt what the British were hoping to achieve, as the reports that Stephenson sent to [Robert] Menzies make clear. He wrote that, at first, [William] Donovan was not at all certain he wanted the job of directing *the new agency we envisage* (emphasis added). When Donovan's appointment was announced, Stephenson wrote that Donovan was accusing him of having intrigued and driven him into the job. Stephenson then expressed his relief that 'our' man was in a position of such importance to "our" efforts. Major Desmond Morton of the Industrial Intelligence Center was even blunter: "...to all intents and purposes US security is being run for them at the president's request by the British. It is of course essential that this fact should not be known in view of the furious uproar it would cause if known to the isolationists."[11]

Christopher Lee as the Duc de Richleau.

The Devil Rides Out Onto Film (1968)

Thus we come to the analysis of the 1968 film incarnation of Wheatley's novel, *The Devil Rides Out*, starring Christopher Lee and James Gray and directed by Terence Fisher. Fisher was a fixture of dozens of B horror films in the 60s, previously directing Christopher Lee as Dracula and Peter Cushing as Van Helsing in *Dracula: Prince of Darkness* (1966). (Lee would also go on to play Dracula in *The Satanic Rites of Dracula* in 1973 with Cushing). Interestingly, Fisher's gothic horror films generally present evil as defeated by a combination of faith and reason, in contrast to both superstition and rationalistic scientism:

> His films are characterised by a blend of fairy-tale, myth and sexuality. They may have drawn heavily on Christian themes, and there is usually a hero who defeats the powers of darkness by a combination of faith in God and reason, in contrast to other characters, who are either blindly superstitious or bound by a cold, godless rationalism (as noted by critic Paul Leggett in *Terence Fisher: Horror, Myth and Religion*, 2001).[12]

The figure of Christopher Lee is also relevant, given his own claims of involvement in the Special Operations Executive, including even whispers he was an assassin: "I was attached to the SAS from time to time but we are forbidden – former, present, or future – to discuss any specific operations. Let's just say I was in Special Forces and leave it at that. People can read into that what they like," he stated.[13] However, there is some matter of dispute as to Lee's claims, including the idea they may have been exaggerated or made up.[14] Similar to the story of Chuck Barris, the "Gong Show" Host who purportedly worked side jobs as a CIA hit-man, as portrayed in the 2002 film *Confessions of a Dangerous Mind*, Count Dooku may have been serving out the Imperial Palpatinian death notices in real life.[15]

What is also curious about Lee are his comments on the occult, in which an old interview shows his knowledge and fascination, as well as his personal copy of Anton LaVey's book,[16] signed by the founder of the rather theatrical Church of Satan. LaVey's connections and associations with Hollywood, including Sammy Davis, Jr. and Jayne Mansfield are well known, but the interview certainly provides a window into Lee's views on the matter.[17] Lee also later gave curious investigators an emphatic warning in an interview just prior to his death, assuring the dark forces of the occult will induce madness, as well as loss of soul.[18]

Jayne Mansfield with Church of Satan founder, Anton LaVey.

Replete with occult and tarot imagery, the film is a fantastical, yet relatively realistic presentation of the rituals and beliefs of some serious occultists. It is also worth remembering, as we have seen, these occult practitioners include members of the British elite and intelligence establishment. Both Wheatley and Knight appear to have taken it seriously, giving the story a unique, dark aesthetic. In the film, we find Nicholas Duc de Richleau (Lee) becoming suspicious of the odd behaviors of his friend, Simon Aaron. Visiting Aaron, Nicholas discovers he is no longer welcomed among his new cast of colorful elites, all of whom appear opulently wealthy and eccentric. Sneaking away to Aaron's observatory, Nicholas discovers the sign of Baphomet upon the floor and various astrological and ritual implements (including chickens stored in a closet) which suggest the elite "society" of Aaron's is, in fact, a coven involved in ceremonial invocation of spirits.

The coven is intent upon initiating both Aaron and a young love interest (of Nicholas' other friend) named Tanith into their diabolical sect. Here the importance of bloodlines comes to the fore, inasmuch as prominent intergenerational Satanic families are believed to carry a special potency. In fact, Tanith is going to be wed to Satan himself. Heading up the cult is one Mocata (James Gray) who appears to have the special ability to cause smog, mirror-frosting, on-the-spot mind control and psychic vampirism through the gaze of his eyes. The much-hyped "suicide programming" of "Illuminati victims" actually does appear in the film, where both Tanith and Aaron attempt to murder others, as well as themselves, showing "suicide programming" on the part of Mocata.

The ultimate prosperity gospel: Mocata's Satanist cult prepares a sacrifice in *The Devil Rides Out*.

Disrupting a woodland Satanic baptismal ceremony that hearkens to something akin to the Order of the Golden Dawn, yet situated in Salisbury Plain, Nicholas party crashes the drugged revelry by tossing a cross at Baphomet himself. Rather pissed at this effrontery, Mocata conjures the Angel of Death himself to take vengeance upon Nicholas and company, leading to the counter-ceremonial ritual sleepover inside the magic circle.[19] While inside the circle, Nicholas and company experience a spiritual/psychical magical battle that evidently plays out in the aether, resulting in a foiled attempt at child sacrifice by Mocata. The interesting aspect here is the idea that to fight the black magic of Mocata, Nicholas must also delve into ritual magic. While somewhat ridiculous, the film does present authentic aspects of both hermetic and perennial esoterica, where the notion of spiritual battles waged on a higher, aetheric plane affect our own through the transference of energy.

While all of this may seem a bit out of place, one can see a deeper strand of revelation at work here, shining light on more than merely spies and weird movies. The real story of *The Devil Rides Out* is that Wheatley, as a high level insider in the Western intelligence elite and an associate of Crowley, couldn't help but reveal the actual workings of the upper crust, now evident in the stories of the Franklin Coverup,[20] the Dutroux Affair21 and the UK's Jimmy Savile.[22] In Voodoo, there is the old myth that the devil appears especially at the crossroads,[23] and as we see, he also rides out in similar fashion, just as the crossroads of occult film and espionage meet here.

Endnotes

1. Lines, Craig. "A look back at Dennis Wheatley's black magic novels." DenofGeek. 18 October, 2013. Web. http://www.denofgeek.com/books-comics/dennis-wheatley/27687/a-look-back-at-dennis-wheatleys-black-magic-novels

2. Wheatley, Dennis. *The Time Has Come: The Memoirs of Dennis Wheatley* (Vol 3). Hutchinson, 1977, pg. 131.

3. "Dennis Wheatley: An Introduction." DennisWheatley.info. Web. http://www.denniswheatley.info/denniswheatley.htm

4. Luck, Adam. "Revealed: Thriller legend Dennis Wheatley's MI6 mission to 'stir up the Arabs'. DailyMail. 26 October, 2013. Web. http://www.dailymail.co.uk/news/article-2477588/Dennis-Wheatleys-MI6-mission-stir-Arabs.html

5. Masters, Anthony. *The Man Who Was M*. London: Grafton, 1986, pgs. 90-1.

6. Lycett, *Ian Fleming*, 134.

7. Master, 157.

8. Cabell, 46.

9. Levenda, *Unholy Alliance*, 231-3. See also *For Your Eyes Only: Ian Fleming and James Bond* by Ben MacIntyre, pg. 88

10. Cabell, 53.

11. Knightley, Philip. *The Second Oldest Profession*. New York: Penguin Books, 1986, pgs. 217-8.

12. Leggett, Paul. *Terence Fisher: Horror, Myth and Religion*. London: McFarland Publishers, 2002, pg. 60.

13. Buchanan, Rose. "Christopher Lee: The untold life of the SAS soldier who spoke several languages and almost died twice in WWII." 12 June, 2015. Web. http://www.independent.co.uk/news/people/christopher-lee-the-untold-life-of-the-sas-soldier-who-spoke-several-languages-and-almost-died-twice-10315453.html

14. Furness, Hannah. "Sir Christopher Lee's SAS war record was 'hammed up', historian claims." Telegraph. 16 July, 2015. Web. http://www.telegraph.co.uk/news/celebritynews/11742636/Sir-Christopher-Lees-SAS-war-record-was-hammed-up-historian-claims.html

15. Stein, Joel. "Chuck Barris: Lying to Tell the Truth." Time. 7 January, 2003. Web. http://content.time.com/time/magazine/article/0,9171,404266,00.html

16. Lee, Sir Christopher. Interview. "Christopher Lee Discusses Black Magic." Youtube. 1975. Web. https://www.youtube.com/watch?v=EoqJTegrFKw

17. Austen, Jake. "Sammy Devil, Jr." Vice. 2 May, 2008. Web. http://www.vice.com/read/sammy-devil-jr-v15n5

18. Scheiner, Eric. "Christopher Lee Warned of the Occult: 'You'll Lose Your Soul." CNSNews. 11 June, 2015. Web. http://www.cnsnews.com/blog/eric-scheiner/christopher-lee-warned-occult-youll-lose-your-soul

19. Regardie, Israel. *The Golden Dawn*. Woodbury, MN: Llewellyn Publications, 1989, pgs. 280-2.

20. Bryant, Nick. *The Franklin Scandal*. Oregon: Trine Day, 2012.

21. McGowan, *Programmed to Kill*, pgs. 3-22.

22. Gover, Dominic. "'Satanic Jimmy Savile Wore Devil Robes at Scarborough Sex Club' [PHOTO]." IBTimes. 25 February, 2013. Web. http://www.ibtimes.co.uk/sex-abuse-club-victims-439231

23. Cirlot, Dictionary of Symbols, 71. "Crossroads (Mythology)." Wikipedia. Web. https://en.wikipedia.org/wiki/Crossroads_(mythology)

Chapter 21

Hollywood Spies: *North by Northwest*

O ften overlooked in spy culture are Alfred Hitchcock's espionage classics. In the Hitchcock film *Vertigo* (1958), he highlighted the use of mind control, doubling and voyeurism on the part of a shadowy Bohemian Grove-esque elite intent on manipulating the middle class Scottie (Jimmy Stewart) based on a profiling of his psychological weaknesses. In *North by Northwest* (1959) similar themes emerge, yet the master of suspense seemed willing to reveal much more than merely psychoanalytical and Freudian elements, notably shooting one of the first films to mention the CIA.[1]

Hitchcock was not merely a master of suspense, but the father of the espionage film, adapting spy tales from both William Somerset Maugham (himself MI6,[2] whose novel *Ashenden* would become Hitchcock's *Secret Agent* in 1936) and Joseph Conrad (*The Secret Agent* novel would become *Sabotage* in 1936). He directed some of the most notable espionage films of all time, including *39 Steps, Notorious, Torn Curtain* and *The*

WILLIAM SOMERSET MAUGHAM (1874-1965): British playwright and novelist who enjoyed immense popularity and was one of the most well paid writers in his day. Known for numerous works, dozens of Maugham's works were adapted for film, including *The Secret Agent* (1936) by Alfred Hitchcock. The subject matter is appropriate, as Maugham was also an intelligence agent for British MI6, including special missions to Russia. Maugham is also considered a partial inspiration for Ian Fleming's James Bond.

Man Who Knew Too Much. Yet his connections to British Intelligence and the Atlanticist establishment take us down an even deeper rabbit hole.

Researcher Michael Minnicino comments on the Hitchcock circles that included Sir Alexander Korda, prior to his rise to fame, showing Tavistock and Huxley connections. Tavistock,[3] of course, would be instrumental in preparing the way for MKUltra and mass social engineering:

JOSEPH CONRAD (1857-1924): Polish-British author considered one of the best English writers. Conrad influenced some of the 20th century's greatest writers, including Faulkner and T.S. Eliot. Many of Conrad's novels were adapted for film, including *Heart of Darkness, Secret Agent* and *Lord Jim.*

The Kordas' task was to generally develop a pro-British current in America and to plump for cultism. They hired Aldous Huxley to write the screenplays for the two-hit Star War-style fantasy pictures of the 1930s, Kipling's *Jungle Book* and *The Thief of Baghdad,* in the process making Huxley's name as a scenarist. (When the Kordas stayed in Hollywood they usually housed with one of a British clique there which included Huxley, the modernist composer Igor Stravinsky, and Tavistock psychologist Humphrey Osmond.) They kicked off the wave of historical epics, which dominated the United States and Europe in the 1940s; Hitler, in fact, had their Rembrandt re-made under his own aegis.

This historical series included two films that were never completed: Lawrence of Arabia, which was shelved when T. E. Lawrence, the British intelligence agent who was the subject, died in a motorcycle crash on his way to Korda's home to discuss the film; and *I. Claudius* based on Robert Graves's weird *Isis* novel, which collapsed when the star, Charles Laughton, went insane. (Public Television later made a cult hit out of the novel.) In the late 1930s the Kordas were recruited directly into British intelligence by Churchill, and started making overt propaganda in America.

In regard to the technique of creating an atmosphere of fear and paranoia related to a "super reality" that is imposed upon some situation through a given narrative, Minnicino accurate-

ALEXANDER KORDA (1893-1956): Hungarian by birth, Korda rose to prominence as a British film director first working on "talkies." Korda was a leading London film figure by 1930, becoming the first director to be knighted. The Korda Circle was instrumental in marshaling American opinion into accepting participation with Britain in World War 2 through Hollywood propaganda, neutralizing the "America First" movement.

TAVISTOCK INSTITUTE: British non-profit organization tasked with studying and experimenting with group dynamics, organizational behavior as well as originally being linked with the Tavistock Clinic which had a role in pioneering the UK version of MKUltra. The organization was founded through a grant from the Rockefeller Foundation and would include work from some of psychology's top names, including Carl Jung and Sigmund Freud. While the public facade of the group is purportedly research, many authors have exposed nefarious connections behind the organization, including the intentional engineering of mass culture. Some even argue the Beatles were a Tavistock creation.

ly connects this film approach to the Tavistock strategy of mind control. It thus becomes clear how Hitchcock's voyeurism and shock-value would be useful in the realm of psychological operations and propaganda. One need only think of our daily bombardment from the mass media in our ridiculous, perennial "war on terror." Minnicino comments, opining that Hitchcock's *Spellbound* is the first U.S. film to portray Satanism, borrowed from German Expressionism as depicted in Fritz Lang's *Metropolis*.

Hitchcock used ordinary objects – as The Birds – to realize Minsterberg's concept of shock effect:

"Knowing what to expect ... the audience ... waits for it to happen. This conditioning of the viewer is essential to the buildup of suspense." Hitchcock often gave the following example of how this worked. You show two men at a table having a mundane conversation. Then you pan to show that there is a bomb under the table timed to go off in moments. Then you go back to the conversation. The audience becomes anxiety-ridden listening to the conversation ("Don't you realize you're about to be blown up?!") For Hitchcock, this is the epitome of filmmaking, the creation of a sort of super-reality to which only the audience is privy. However, this is also identical to Wilfred Bion's discussion of group dynamics brainwashing techniques developed during World War II at British Secret Intelligence Service's London Tavistock Institute. Bion, the mentor of the Wharton School's Eric Trist as well as other leading social control theoreticians, determined that small groups could be manipulated if an astute leader (director) could convince them of a shared reality superior to the one they were discussing..."[4]

The Satanic in German Expressionism. Fritz Lang's *Metropolis*.

Hitchcock was brought to the United States in 1939 by David O. Selznick to direct *Rebecca*, with Laurence Olivier starring, and screenplay adaptations by Robert Sherwood and Thornton Wilder, both of whom would head the U. S. Office of War Information within a couple of years. Hitchcock stayed in the United States owing to the lavish funding he could get for his projects, including his psycho-active films like *Spellbound*, with a screenplay by Ben Hecht (collaborating with leading U. S. psychoanalysts) and set designs by surrealist Salvador Dali. *Spellbound* was the first U. S. film to have Satanic cult imagery, something not seen since the heyday of the German Expressionists.

Dali's eye imagery in Hitchcock's *Spellbound*.

Indeed, anyone inclined to doubt Hitchcock's association with British Intelligence need only look at his work for The British Ministry of Information, where he produced war propaganda at the behest of the Secret Intelligence Service. Jennifer Brown comments:

> During World War II, Alfred Hitchcock was called upon by the government of his native country to contribute to the Ministry of Information's propaganda efforts, specifically that which was used to bolster the French Resistance to German occupation. The short films that resulted from this call to action were *Bon Voyage* and *Aventure Malgache* (translated Madagascar Landing), works that can also be described by such words as suspense, mystery, intrigue, irony, and fear. The purpose of this rhetorical analysis is to examine and describe the rhetorical strategies utilized by Alfred Hitchcock in *Bon Voyage* and *Aventure Malgache*.[5]

303

In fact, Hitchcock was even employed by the British Ministry to create a Nazi concentration camp film:

> Bernstein served as film advisor to the British Ministry of Information and was chief of the Film Section of Supreme Headquarters, Allied Expeditionary Forces. It was in this latter capacity that he commissioned Hitchcock to make a compilation film on the Nazi concentration camps at the end of the war, with the purpose of showing the German people the nature of their leaders' crimes.[6]

For regular readers of my work at Jay's Analysis, analyses of James Bond films and novels are frequent, but it was Hitchcock who would be highly influential in the creation of the cinematic icon of 007, particularly the imagery and expressionism found in *North by Northwest*. One need only think of the memorable train sequence comparable to *From Russia With Love*, for example. In fact, Bondologist Sinclair McKay argues that the template for every 007 film was set by *North by Northwest*:

And indeed, whether they acknowledge it or not, the template for pretty much every James Bond film had already been set down by director Alfred Hitchcock in 1959. *North by Northwest,* the story of an advertising executive (Cary Grant) who is mistaken for a spy finds himself sucked into a battle against sinister Van Damm (James Mason) while falling for a beautiful agent (Eva Marie Saint), establishes a sex-and-setpieces sensibility that could not have failed to influence Broccoli and Saltzman.[7]

Additionally:

It may have been this performance [*Notorious*] rather than his larkier role in *North by Northwest,* that led to Cary Grant being considered for the role of Bond.[8]

The consideration of Grant for Bond and his placement in numerous Hitchcock films is significant, as Cary Grant was himself a spy, involved in outing Errol Flynn as a Nazi sympathizer:

In the summer of 1939, a Hollywood partnership was formed as a front for British Intelligence (MI6 – Military Intelligence-6). It was made up of Samuel Goldwyn, Douglas Fairbanks, Sr., Alexander Korda (the Hungarian producer), Walter Wanger and Korda's London Films. Cary Grant worked with this partnership to flush out Nazi sympathizers in Hollywood and its environs. (Another similar partnership was organized by Cecil B. DeMille at Paramount.)

Grant's chief contact with British intelligence was Noel Coward, the author of numerous plays and humorous songs. It may surprise some film buffs to learn that the major accomplishment of Cary Grant the Nazi hunter was to out the Australian actor, Errol Flynn, as a Nazi sympathizer.[9]

Hitchcock favorite, Jimmy Stewart, was also rumored to have done intelligence work for the FBI on the side, according to Michael Munn's *Jimmy Stewart: The Truth Behind the Legend,* making his roles in *Vertigo* and *Rear Window* even more curious, given the plots.[10] However, to make it all the more obvious, Stewart played the lead role in the FBI propaganda film, *The FBI Story* (given approval by J. Edgar Hoover). While these connections and associations don't necessarily prove direct espionage work, they are suggestive, given Hitchcock's propaganda assignments for British Military Intelligence.

Thus, as mentioned, it becomes clear why *North by Northwest* is the first film to mention the CIA by name. Still a relatively new agency following the OSS, the CIA was intimately connected to the advertising world through the Robert Mullen Company and J. Walter Thompson Agency, as Jim Hougan writes:

> Moreover, E. Howard Hunt's espionage activities were carried out under the cover of Robert R. Mullen Company, a CIA front which had taken over Howard Hughes' "public relations" account from Larry O'Brien and his Kennedy braintrust.[11]

In *North by Northwest*, Cary Grant's character, Roger O. Thornhill, is roped into working for the nascent agency, through sexual entrapment by Eve Kendall (Eva Marie Saint). Western propaganda accused rivals like Stalin's NKVD of creating sex operatives, while the "free world" was immune to such dirty work, yet here is one of the most famous film achievements of all time – the film that first mentions the CIA – featuring a CIA sex operative. It is worth noting that the film is subtly a Cold War propaganda piece, too, as villain Van Damm (James Mason) is explicitly spoken of as working with Russians in a "Cold War."

More Faux News, brought to you via Langley.

If the United Nations setting for the film seems odd, it shouldn't – the same Rockefellers who, with British Intelligence, set up the OSS and CIA also helped establish the U.N. Once again we see how the worlds of Hollywood and intelligence are mirror reflections of the same reality, as Hitch-

306

cock shows in detail with infamous scenes involving staged news at the behest of the CIA. Thornhill is framed for the murder of a U.N. diplomat (by CIA's design to nab Van Damm), as well as his own contrived death at the hands of Eve (also CIA stagecraft). Readers may recall that *Wag the Dog* involved staging false news, yet much earlier, Hitchcock was showing the Agency's sway over the mainstream headlines from the outset – long before revelations of Operation Mockingbird, in which the CIA bought off hundreds of top journalists.[12]

OPERATION MOCKINGBIRD: A covert operation by the CIA to control the flow of information in media. CIA operatives Cord Meyer, Allen Dulles and Frank Wisner ran the program over several decades which included the hiring of 400 top journalists and editors to censor and control the reporting of information. The operation also funded student groups, as well as controlling some foreign news outlets in favor of American policy. Purportedly shut down in 1976 after congressional investigation, the notion things have changed in mass media in our day is, of course, ridiculous.

If the overlap between intelligence operations sounds far-fetched, I would direct readers to "Secret Team" operative Col. L. Fletcher Prouty, who compares the CIA's missions in starting coups to topple governments with Hollywood theatrics, noting the false flag event of the Gulf of Tonkin:

L. FLETCHER PROUTY (1917-2001): Chief of Special Operations under President John F. Kennedy and later bank executive who was a severe critic of the CIA's covert operations. Prouty famously wrote *The Secret Team* and was the basis for the character 'Mr. X" in Oliver Stone's *JFK* (1991). *The Secret Team* argues the CIA's covert operatives arrange coups, false flags and assassinations globally, with the intent of furthering Washington's imperial agenda.

> It is the type of game played by the clandestine operator. He sets up the scene by declaring in many ways and over a long period of time that Communism is the general enemy and that the enemy is about to strike or has begun a subversive insurgency campaign in a third country. Then the clandestine operator prepares the stage by launching a very minor and very secret, provocative attack of a kind that is bound to bring open reprisal. These secret attacks, which may have been made by third parties or by stateless mercenaries whose materials were supplied secretly by the CIA, will undoubtedly create reaction which in turn is observed in the United States. (This technique was developed to a high art in the Philippines during the early Magsaysay build-up to the point where the Huks were actually some of Magsaysay's own troops disguised and set upon the unwary village in the grand manner of a Cecil B. DeMille production.)

> The next step is to declare the enemy's act one of "aggression" or "subversive insurgency." Then, the next part of the game is activated by the CIA. This part of the operation will be briefed to the NSC Special Group, and it will include, at some point, Americans in support. So it will go, as high and as mighty as the situation and

authorities will allow. It is not a new game. It was practiced, albeit amateurishly and uncertainly, in Greece during the late forties, and it was raised to a high state of art under Walt Rostow and Mc-George Bundy against North Vietnam, to set the pattern for the Gulf of Tonkin attacks.[13]

Another example of this kind of propaganda is revealed in the aforementioned 1997 film *Wag the Dog*, where Robert De Niro plays Conrad Brean, a private intelligence "Mr. Fix It," a mass media manipulator hired to create a big distraction, namely a fake war with "Albanian fundamentalist terrorists." Given his hat and appearance, he appears to be a kind of mix between E. Howard Hunt and Milt Bearden or Chase Brandon,[14] one of the CIA's liaison to Hollywood. While most analyses of the film would focus on the film's narrative itself as an exposé, which is true as far as it goes, I'd like to take a step back and point out that it is more than that. It's an example of what I'd call meta-propaganda, in the sense that meta-narrative in the study of Shakespeare involves a story about the process of writing a story, so with *Wag the Dog* we have an example of meta-propaganda. The film is itself propaganda about the process of making propaganda. This is the secret power and effect of predictive programming: hoodwinking an unknowing populace into accepting a manipulation of archetypes and emotional images that produce a desired effect. The chief medium of this craft is film and news.

Brean and companion Winifred Ames (played by Anne Heche) concoct the idea to create a war by hiring a big time Hollywood producer, Stanley Motts (played by Dustin Hoffman), to script and direct the war. The war, however, will not exist in any sense, but is shot on a green screen with actors and the latest CGI effects to create an emotional propaganda effect. One of the best scenes is the pro-

E. HOWARD HUNT (1918-2007): CIA office for over 20 years, Hunt and G. Gordon Liddy were members of the "plumbers tasked with controlling "leaks" in regard to the infamous Watergate scandal. Hunt worked for the OSS, as well as numerous Cold War covert operations, including the overthrow of Jacobo Arbenz, as well as later claiming to have been directly involved in the JFK assassination.

MILT BEARDEN: CIA operative turned film consultant. Bearden, after his Cold War intrigues and operations, appeared in Adam Curtis' famous documentary *The Power Nightmares* (2004). While admitting th Bin Laden narrative has been completely blown out of proportion, Bearden's message was unheeded. Bearden went on consult on numerous Hollywood films, including *Meet the Parents, The Good Shepherd* and *Charlie Wilson's War*.

CHASE BRANDON: The CIA's first known entertainment liaison. Formerly an operative for the agency 25 years, Brandon has worked on numerous espionage-theme films, including *Enemy of the State, The Recruit,The Sum of All Fears, Mission Impossible III* and many more. Brandon also believed to be the inspiration for the Conrad Breen character (played by Robert de Niro) in *Wag the Dog.*

Robert De Niro plays expert manipulator, Conrad Brean.

duction of the fake young Albanian girl (played by Kristen Dunst) carrying a bag of Tostitos (since they can't find a kitten). A Calico cat is then added, with bombings and gunshots superimposed in the background. While one might balk at such an idea, allow me to remind you that the film is basically a composite of the last twenty years of propaganda and political machinations.

Presidential sex scandals and elections are really about inside shadow government workings, and much of the war and terror propaganda is just that – propaganda. Curiously, this sex scandal ominously mirrored the real scandal of Bill Clinton and Monica Lewinsky. The events and narratives are literally scripted, as they are in the film. Thus enters the meta-propaganda aspect, or what Hoffman terms "revelation of the method."

Dustin Hoffman as high profile Hollywood Producer, Stanley Motts. "War is show business."

Throughout the film, genius screenwriter David Mamet drops countless hints as to what is really going on. We see the characters making insightful comments such as follows:

"It's all a pageant."
"They want to destroy our way of life."
'We just found out they have the bomb. It's a suitcase bomb."
"The Albanian terrorists have placed a suitcase bomb in Canada."
"Nuclear terrorism is the future."

As Motts scripts the events, he jokes that the "First Act" will be the Albanian response: "They deny everything." This brings to mind the famous Kissinger clip prior to the invasion and destabilization of Libya during the Egyptian unrest – that it was the first act of a play.[15] The film is therefore genius in its presentation of dark satire and the scripted nature of reality, and I think functions on an even deeper level as meta-propaganda. The viewer is being shown how the propaganda is created, while simultaneously functioning in the world where this is exactly how the propaganda is created. In other words, the film is fiction, but is true, leaving the viewer, subconsciously, with the idea that truth is fiction, and fiction is truth. This is precisely the best form of manipulation because it is so subtle and functions on so many levels. It is also not overly complex, though it may give the impression of being "deep." On the contrary, the truth is very simple: the establishment creates a false reality everyone believes, by placing that false reality in fiction; it then becomes reality – the "Fleming effect."[16] No better example could be given than the infamous CNN broadcast of a fake 1990 Persian Gulf War bombing, with reporter Charles Jaco hamming it up on a blue screen.[17]

If that is hard to swallow, the pill becomes much bigger. Author Dave McGowan relates the history of a secret government film studio at Lookout Mountain that housed an immense covert production facility:

What would become known as Lookout Mountain Laboratory, was originally envisioned as an air defense center. Built in 1941 and nestled in two-and-a-half secluded acres off what is now Wonderland Park Avenue, the installation was hidden from view and surrounded by an electrified fence. By 1947, the facility featured a fully operational movie studio. In fact, it is claimed that it was perhaps the world's only completely self-contained movie studio. With 100,000 square feet of floor space, the covert studio included sound stages, screening rooms, film processing labs, editing facilities, an animation department, and seventeen climate-controlled film vaults. It also had underground parking, a helicopter pad and a bomb shelter:

> Over its lifetime, the studio produced some 19,000 classified motion pictures – more than all the Hollywood studios combined (which I guess makes Laurel Canyon the real "motion picture capital of the world"). Officially, the facility was run by the U.S. Air Force and did nothing more nefarious than process AEC footage of atomic and nuclear bomb tests. The studio, however, was clearly equipped to do far more than just process film. There are indications that Lookout Mountain Laboratory had an advanced

research and development department that was on the cutting edge of new film technologies. Such technological advances as 3-D effects were apparently first developed at the Laurel Canyon site. And Hollywood luminaries like John Ford, Jimmy Stewart, Howard Hawks, Ronald Reagan, Bing Crosby, Walt Disney and Marilyn Monroe were given clearance to work at the facility on undisclosed projects. There is no indication that any of them ever spoke of their work at the clandestine studio.

The facility retained as many as 250 producers, directors, technicians, editors, animators, etc., both civilian and military, all with top security clearances - and all reporting to work in a secluded corner of Laurel Canyon. Accounts vary as to when the facility ceased operations. Some claim it was in 1969, while others say the installation remained in operation longer. In any event, by all accounts the secret bunker had been up and running for more than twenty years before Laurel Canyon's rebellious teen years, and it remained operational for the most turbulent of those years.

The existence of the facility remained unknown to the general public until the early 1990s, though it had long been rumored that the CIA operated a secret movie studio somewhere in or near Hollywood. Filmmaker Peter Kuran was the first to learn of its existence, through classified documents he obtained while researching his 1995 documentary, *Trinity and Beyond*. And yet even today, some 15 years after its public disclosure, one would have trouble finding even a single mention of this secret military/intelligence facility anywhere in the 'conspiracy' literature.[18]

Endnotes

1. Secker, Tom. "Profile: Alfred Hitchcock." *SpyCulture*. 15 May, 2013. Web. http://www.spyculture.com/profile-alfred-hitchcock/

2. Norton-Taylor, Richard. "Graham Greene, Arthur Ransome and Somerset Maugham all spied for Britain, admits MI6." Guardian. 21 September, 2010. Web. http://www.theguardian.com/world/2010/sep/21/mi6-first-authorised-history

3. Estulin, Daniel. *Tavistock Institute: Social Engineering the Masses*. Oregon: Trine Day, 2015.

4. Minnicino, Michael. "How British Intelligence Shaped the U.S. Entertainment Industry." Larouchepub. 26 October, 1982. Web. http://www.larouchepub.com/eiw/public/1982/eirv09n41-19821026/eirv09n41-19821026_060-how_british_intelligence_shaped.pdf

5. Brown, Jennifer. "Alfred Hitchcock Presents; 'Propaganda'": A Rhetorical Study of Alfred Hitchcock's World War II Propaganda Films." Liberty.edu. Web. pg. 32. http://digitalcommons.liberty.edu/cgi/viewcontent.cgi?article=1124&context=masters

6. Cook, David. *History of Narrative Film*. New York: Norton Company, 1996, pg. 329.

7. McKay, Sinclair. *The Man with the Golden Touch*. New York: Overlook Press, 2008, pg. 13.

8. Ibid., 69.

9. "Cary Grant played unknown real-life role as WWII spy." NewsVine. 27 December, 2012. Web.

http://minnieapolis.newsvine.com/_news/2012/12/27/16172809-cary-grant-played-unknown-real-life-role-as-wwii-spy?threadId=3636663

10. Munn, Michael. *Jimmy Stewart: The Truth Behind the Legend*. New York: SkyHorse Publishing, 2013, pgs. 151-2, 239-42.

11. Hougan, *Spooks*, 360.

12. Louise, Mary. "Operation Mockingbird: CIA Media Manipulation." AFPN.org. Web. http://www.apfn.org/apfn/mockingbird.htm

13. Prouty, Col. L. Fletcher. *The Secret Team*. New York: SkyHorse Publications, 2008, pgs. 41-2.

14. "Chase Brandon." IMBD.com. Web. http://www.imdb.com/name/nm1260221/?ref_=fn_al_nm_1

15. Kissinger, Henry. Cited in Interview. "Kissinger on Unrest in Egypt: This is only the first scene of the first act of a drama that is to be played out." PrisonPlanet. 1 February, 2011. Web. "http://www.prisonplanet.com/kissinger-on-egypt-unrest-this-is-only-the-first-scene-of-the-first-act-of-a-drama-that-is-to-be-played-out.html

16. MacIntyre, *Ian Fleming and James Bond*, 92-3.

17. "CNN Fake News Cast." Youtube. 3 September, 2009. Web. https://www.youtube.com/watch?v=-98JDKB-Qmxs&nohtml5=False

18. McGowan, Dave, *Weird Scenes Inside the Canyon*, 55-6.

Chapter 22

Vertigo (1958)

Film Poster. Note the spiraled vesica piscis* atop the pillar.

While many themes repeat in Hitchcock films, *Vertigo* is most memorable for its psychological depth and mystique. Containing some of the most famous scenes in the history of cinema, *Vertigo* is also the "master of suspense's" deeper message about the psychological manipulation that can occur in our own lives, in society, and amongst the elite. My thesis is that *Vertigo* is not just a film about an average guy caught up in a spiral of madness (a common theme in Hitchcock), but also an insight into the control and manipulation we see from those who are our masters. Not only does *Vertigo* present an elite shipping magnate who manipulates Scottie (Jimmy Stewart, protagonist), it demonstrates the lengths to which

ALFRED HITCHCOCK (1898-1980): Famed prolific English film producer and director. Hitchcock broke ground in both the suspense and horror genres, as well as innovating many film techniques in editing, while focusing on themes of voyeurism, trauma and the archetypal blonde bombshell. Hitchcock also filmed World War II propaganda films for British Ministry of Defense while his thrillers were studied for their social engineering effects. Several of Hitchcock's films contain espionage themes, as well as the fracturing of the psyche, multiple personalities and mind control.

these powers are interested in, to use the words of the Collins brothers, "managing the beyond." *Vertigo* is therefore a film about the manipulation of beliefs through large-scale staging and hoaxcraft, as we saw in the last chapter.

Initially the audience is shown a series of eyes, probably Kim Novak, with spirals emerging. The spiral has the significance here of alerting the viewer that we are trapped. The swirling spiral of madness will grip us, causing us to dissociate, losing our sense of self and identity. Losing one's balance, or falling, is thus a metaphor for the loss of place and identity: this will be the crucial point in *Vertigo*. How far can the manipulation of the psyche go to create and induce the loss of identity? In the opening scene we see a flashback to Scottie, a traumatized former police detective who was involved in the death of a fellow officer. While not intentional, Scottie was stuck on a ledge following a chase, which resulted in another officer falling to his death. Scottie emerged from the scene with vertigo, and only after a few years has he begun to make progress toward recovery. It is worth noting that for Scottie, the causes of his further descent into his downward spiral of obsession, mania and dissociation revolve around trauma.

Scottie spends his days with the homely "Midge," waiting for something interesting to happen in his life, eschewing marriage. Midge is sexually frustrated, annoyed that Scottie has no sexual interest in her (or in anyone apparently). Upon receiving a special invitation to see his old war buddy Elster, Scottie reluctantly decides he must go, ignoring the innuendos of Midge. Meeting at a disguised location, Elster explains that he married into great wealth, particularly a family involved in the shipping business. Elster tells the fantastic tale that his wife Madeleine is possessed by a ghost – a dead woman named Carlotta Valdes. Scottie is incredulous but finally caves and agrees to Elster's request that he follow Madeleine. Elster says Madeleine dissociates and drives to the Golden Gate Bridge and stares at the "pillars – portals to the past." This will be significant later, especially as twin pillars are constantly seen throughout the film.

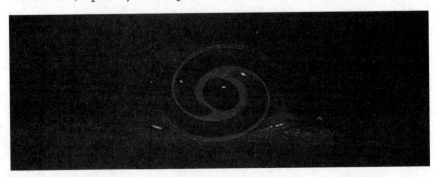

The spiral associated with the eye and entering the psyche.

314

Scottie spots Madeleine at a club called Ernie's and follows her to a florist, where Scottie begins to develop a fascination for voyeurism. Interestingly, he spies on her in the shop through a mirror, which is a classic symbol of the psyche and its double. Scottie begins to fall in love with Madeleine, which only sucks him deeper and deeper into the spiral of insanity. The reference to wealthy shipping magnates and British power calls to mind the research of Fritz Springmeier, who is generally accurate in his claims. According to Springmeier, we can assume that the mention of connections to elite merchant and sea power is not accidental. He writes in regard to Hitchcock, the Onassis shipping magnates and Grace Kelly:

Elster, the elite British shipping magnate.

Grace had many affairs including one with Bing Crosby. Grace Kelly worked for MGM. Alfred Hitchcock was the one who is credited with seeing a superstar in Grace. Alfred Hitchcock came from a British generational occult family, and was a dark genius who produced many exceptional films. Grace Kelly acted for three of Alfred Hitchcock's movies. *Dial "M" for Murder* was the first. Later, Hitchcock visited Grace and Prince Rainer at their Paris home, and Grace made a rare public appearance in Apr. '74 with Hitchcock in New York. Hitchcock's life has been described by someone who knew him as "an enigma within an enigma." Hitchcock was very secretive about his own life and his parents. We do know that he was instructed by the Jesuits at St. Ignatius College which he left in 1913. He had an extreme fascination for sadomasochism, which can be seen in his movies such as *Frenzy*.

Scottie begins to transform into the voyeuristic control freak that is Elster.

Hitchcock liked to read sexual murder material, Edgar Allan Poe's material, George Bernard Shaw's writings, and Fabian New World Order advocate, H.G. Well's books. He was extremely fascinated by the real life murderer John Reginald Holliday Christie who could only get a sexual erection by strangling women while having sex. Hitchcock's own personality was unpredictable, and at times was cruel and tyrannical. He enjoyed cruel jokes on people and also enjoyed psychologically breaking down his actresses. He made several movies showing split personalities such as: *Shadow of a Doubt, Strangers on a Train, Psycho,* and *Frenzy.* Hitchcock learned to create and sustain dissociation in both his murderer and the viewing audience in his films. This can be seen in his film *Blackmail.* The concepts of dissociation, doubles, murder as love, mirrors, sadism, and humiliating people are common items in creating monarch mind-controlled slaves: they are also common items seen in Hitchcock's movies. I don't know the exact connection, except to say Hitchcock was familiar with the occult world and some of their mind-control techniques. The Queen knighted Alfred Hitchcock.[1]

One of the many instances of twin pillars.

Patterns and motifs begin to emerge, particularly in regard to espionage, mind control and psychological manipulation. I don't think this is an accident, especially since Hitchcock was in the company of those at the top in British and international elite circles. Only a year later, Richard Condon would release his novel *The Manchurian Candidate* about a brainwashed assassin, highlighting the MKUltra program, which would become a major Hollywood production three years following. It can therefore be reasonably assumed Hitchcock was aware of these methods of mind control, which originated in British and US intelligence circles. Is *Vertigo* an early "MKUltra" film?

It certainly contains the themes of mind control, manipulation, dissociation and MPD/DID, which are important elements of that specific wide-ranging project. Consider how few among the public would have even known in 1959 of the existence of such a program, much less that it was as wide-spread as it was, with dozens of universities participating, despite it being featured in Condon's novel. It is also significant that Madeleine's first staged suicide attempt occurs at the Presidio Naval Base, which is on record for later being involved in mind control testing, programming and occult ritual activity.[2]

Elster meets again with Scottie and informs him that Madeleine is possessed by a ghost, who lost her daughter. Carlotta Valdes had committed suicide, and Madeleine will eventually. Once again, this brings to mind the various mind control programs that were pioneered by US, Nazi, British and Soviet social engineers and psychologists and their "suicide programming." In the history of mind control techniques, one of the early fail-safes put in place to protect handlers and their respective governments was the suicide program, which made sure the subject would commit suicide to keep from revealing too much if their "alters" were unlocked. The names associated with the programs are Dr. Ewen Cameron, Dr. Sidney Gottlieb, Dr. Jose Delgado, Dr. Jolyon West, Dr. George Estabrooks, and others. While this itself is easily tracked down in terms of the existence of the programs, what is lesser known are articles like Dr. George Estabrooks' article from the April 1971 *Science Digest*, "Hypnosis Comes of Age."[3] Included in the article are some striking admissions, especially since the OSS, CIA and FBI utilized Estabrooks and his skills. The article mentions, first of all, Estabrooks' claim of the use of secret couriers and keywords that function as the triggers in the operative.

I am not proposing my interpretation of Madeleine's death at the end of the film (who is really Judy) was definitely a suicide programming, just that it is possible. Why exactly Judy/Madeleine jumps or falls is supposed to be up for debate.

Scottie's psychedelic dream before his dissociation.

317

In *Vertigo*, however, it's not ultimately Madeleine that is the subject of the most rigorous mind control, but Scottie. We learn that all the events had been pre-arranged by Elster, supposedly for the purpose of getting rid of his wife. Scottie was to be the alibi, fooled into seeing what he thought was Elster's wife plunging to her death from the tower of the Catholic mission. Yet, why would a powerful shipping magnate need all the elaborate narrative just for a murder? Couldn't a man powerful enough to arrange such a massively intricate manipulation and subterfuge of Scottie also simply hire a hit-man? If this is only a story about the "perfect crime," why such a big production? Why involve all the other people in the plot, who would also be accessories, if the desire were only to have Scottie as a witness? It is my contention that Elster is more like Maurice Conchis in *The Magus*, the master elite manipulator. Like Nicholas in *The Magus*, Scottie is drawn deeper and deeper into a narrative that is intended to manipulate his beliefs and desires to the point of total dissociation and splitting of his personality. And just like Nicholas in *The Magus*, Scottie cannot comprehend or handle the twisting of his psyche that his elite benefactor engages in. The average guy cannot fathom men who live to play chess games with other men's psyches.

One of the more mysterious scenes is the redwood forest, where Scottie takes Madeleine and tells her he loves her. Madeleine appears to be "triggered" into her Carlotta alter when she sees the spirals in the cut redwood. Here Madeleine walks between two pillars (trees) and becomes Carlotta. While it is true that Madeleine/Judy is scamming Scottie, it would appear that she might be beginning to believe she is actually possessed by Carlotta. If this analysis is correct, it would explain why she jumps at the end (unless she falls, but she doesn't appear to fall). Madeleine/Judy and Scottie were both victims of mind control. (Another piece of evidence supporting this is Madeleine's dream she tells Scottie). She explains that in her sleep, she walks down a hall of mirrors with fragments (her split psyche), and at the end is darkness, which is her grave.

Following this comes the first tower scene where Elster murders his wife and Scottie is again traumatized by the height. Scottie has a trippy, cartoon-like dream (is he drugged with a hallucinogen by Elster or just going mad?) and placed in the mental hospital. Scottie's dream is exactly like Madeleine's, but with him walking down the corridor to his grave. While in the mental institute, Scottie is completely dissociated, unresponsive to Midge's entreaties. As a side note, the redwoods of San Francisco is where the elite Bohemian Grove Club is located, and earlier in the film, "Bohemianism" was mentioned, suggesting another possible correlation.

Although we don't know if Scottie is drugged, his vision or dream does appear to be very hallucinogenic. Trauma-based mind control was known for employing the use of LSD and other psychedelics to cause a split in the personality. Although Scottie does not split into alters, he does transform, becoming, oddly enough, more like Elster. After he recovers from his mania in the mental institute, he becomes obsessive and controlling towards Judy (Madeleine), whom he meets a year later. Scottie is fixated on transforming Judy into Madeleine, and becomes murderous when he realizes Judy has the same pendant Madeleine had, proving they're the same person. Interestingly, Judy reveals that she was a Midwest small-town girl who fled home to try her fortune in California. Unfortunately, Judy got mixed up with Elster and was paid and brought into his nefarious designs.

To what degree Judy is merely an accomplice or a pawn in Elster's game is up for debate, but the final scene gives the impression that she actually began to believe Elster's narrative for her: that she was possessed by Carlotta. When she falls or jumps, it could therefore be due to the fact that the shadow of the nun she sees represents Carlotta (she thinks), divine judgment for her deception, or possibly Satan himself. Elster could also be a powerful member of the Bohemian Club, and the robed figure she sees could hearken back to her "cult programming," should that be the case. In this reading, *Vertigo* would foreshadow something like *Mulholland Drive* from the genius David Lynch. In that film we also see a young hopeful starlet make her way from the Midwest to California, only to be caught up in an occult spiral that leaves her dissociated and insane – a sacrifice to a dark evil behind Hollywood. I am admittedly speculating here, but it would definitely appear that there is an "MKUltra" element to *Vertigo*, but why exactly Madeleine/Judy falls or jumps is a matter of debate. Another option is that Scottie has transformed and become like Elster: he pushes her out of rage due to his obsession. Is *Vertigo* about trauma-based mind control? Given Hitchcock's associations and fascination with espionage, split personalities and elite machinations, it's not a stretch.

BOHEMIAN CLUB: An elite private club located in Union Square San Francisco and in the northern woods of Sonoma County. The club was founded in 1872 by journalists and artists, later expanding to include numerous global corporate and political policy makers. The club reenacts Druidic and occult ceremonies purported to be "symbolic" and "literary," while engaging in raucous parties and orgies. Many neo-conservative political elite have formulated large-scale plans like Reagan's "Star Wars Defense Initiative" at Bohemian Grove.

Endnotes

1. Springmeier, Ibid.

2. McGowan, *Programmed to Kill,*

3. Estabrooks, G.H. "Hypnosis Comes of Age." *Science Digest,* 1971 via Mindspring. http://www.mindspring.com/~txporter/scidig.htm

319

Chapter 23

Inside David Lynch:
An Esoteric Guide to *Twin Peaks* (1990-92)

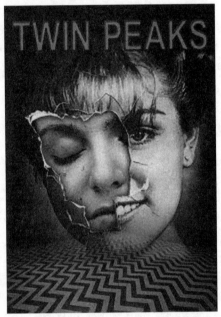

The sacrificial victim, Laura Palmer

I learned that just beneath the surface there's another world, and still different worlds as you dig deeper.

– David Lynch

If you've ever sensed the flimsy, thin veneer of what parades itself as the good ole US of A, and felt a bit like you've been sold a fake, then David Lynch's *Twin Peaks* is a series you must see. More like an initiatory experience than a mere television series, *Twin Peaks* functions as a hilariously terrifying vision of the real America lurking in the seedy underworld beneath the façade of white picket fences, much like the picturesque severed ear on the beautiful lawn in his celebrated 1986 comedic horror, *Blue Velvet. Twin Peaks* might even properly be titled an esoteric dark satirical soap opera. There are countless reviews, essays and analyses of Lynch and *Twin Peaks*, but almost all miss the complex system of symbols and hidden meanings that relate directly to high-level occultism.

Before we go there, we must discuss set and setting: *Twin Peaks* is aptly described as quintessential Lynch. Fans often speak of scenes being "Lynchian," but nothing stands out with that epithet better than this surrealist, neo-noir melodrama that magically captures the spirit of America itself. Differing from later Lynch focused on Hollywood (*Inland Empire, etc.*), *Twin Peaks* is more akin to his 1990 film, *Wild at Heart,* in its presentation of America in miniature. Like later Lynch films, however, *Twin Peaks* does share its deeper occult symbology with films like *Lost Highway, Mulholland Drive* and *Inland Empire.* In this analysis, we go even deeper into that unique place, the subconscious dreamscape of Lynch, and decode the scenes and images many still find mystifying 25 years later.

Worth mentioning before exploring the narrative itself is Lynch's preferred style. Part horror, part neo-noir, part comedy, part melodrama and part soap opera, the Lynch/Frost collaboration collates a vast array of Hollywood classics, from Hitchcock "doubling" to Otto Preminger's 1944 noir classic, *Laura.* Parallels between the myna bird from Hitchcock's *The Birds,* and the hard-hearted detective who finds himself taken with an apparently murdered Laura, abound, and Lynch intentionally includes countless parallels to sprinkle his work, derived from the Golden Age of cinema.

As we enter the world of *Twin Peaks,* protagonist Agent Dale Cooper (played by Kyle MacLachlan) arrives to investigate the enigmatic murder of popular high school blonde babe, Laura Palmer (played by Sheryl Lee). Based on an unsolved murder from *Twin Peaks* co-director and creator Mark Frost's hometown, Laura will function as the focal point for the show's arc. However, as Agent Cooper unravels the actual story of Laura's demise, the truth involves a much wider conspiracy than originally conceived. With his unorthodox divinatory methods of solving crime, Cooper astounds local law enforcement with the concept of utilizing synchronicity to associate similar names with inanimate objects in a game of rock toss. This odd practice will configure Cooper as both a classic pulp detective figure along the lines of Sam Spade, but also grant a mystical side from which he will draw to peer into the psychosphere. Ioan P. Couliano writes, citing Eliade, of the shaman in descriptive terms that capture the spirit of a Lynch work:

Mircea Eliade defined shamanism not as religion properly speaking, but as a "technique of ecstasy," a system of ecstatic and therapeutic methods whose purpose is to obtain contact with the parallel universe of spirits and to win their support in dealing with the affairs of a group or of an individual.[1]

Bad Laura and her double: the good girl Maddy Ferguson.

As I commented in previous analyses, Lynch, through Cooper, is drawing on a highly complex and deeply rooted Eastern notion of formal and essentialist association that extends beyond immediate space and time. The stage is thus set for Cooper to be much more than a clever detective, but rather we see the emergence of his role as an other-world traveling shaman. Later in the series, his spiritual "gifts" are noted by Native American deputy Hawk and General Briggs, where Cooper is eventually revealed to be the one who can travel to, and call, between the worlds, fulfilling the role of the magician from the series' famed tagline below, "fire walk with me." This is the role of the shaman in reference to Lynch's *Lost Highway*, citing Levenda's analysis:

> In *Twin Peaks*, it is the light in the morgue over the place where the body of Laura Palmer had been kept, and which is then visited by Mike, the one-armed man [played by Al Strobel], who recites the famous poem:
>
> > *Through the darkness of futures past*
> > *The magician longs to see;*
> > *One chants out between two worlds*
> > *"Fire walk with me."*
>
> There, in a strange little verse, we have the key to unlocking the mystery not only of *Twin Peaks* but virtually all of Lynch's films: the sus-

pension of normal laws of time ("futures past") and the idea that the magician lives "between two worlds." The suspension of normal, linear narrative event in favor of a dreamlike, hallucinatory set of images that are taking place all over the fourth dimension is part of Lynch's appeal as a director, and part of what makes his films so frustrating to the filmgoer. His realization that there are two worlds, and a place to stand between them, is what contributes to his aura as a modern, twenty-first century initiate of the Mysteries, for that is what "mystery" films are: elucidations of the core Mystery behind reality.[2]

And this forms the solution to *Lost Highway*, as well. The shamanic and magical elements are here in full force, as Fred is a character trapped in different psychical worlds that seem to unfold and envelop other psyches. Interpreting *Twin Peaks* accurately thus involves understanding the notion of "twilight language," or Sandhyabhasa. It is my contention that Twin Peaks should be read in this way, as if the series itself were a yogic text, and this is natural given Lynch's (and Agent Cooper's) preference for eastern meditation. Indian scholar Vijay Mishra comments on the ambiguous semiotic discourse involved in twilight language as follows:

> "Tantric texts are often composed in an intentional language (Sandhyabhasa), a secret, dark, ambiguous language in which a state of consciousness is expressed by an erotic term and the vocabulary of mythology or cosmology is charged with Hatha yogic or sexual meanings. According to Eliade ... it is translated "enigmatic language" and Max Muller called it "hidden language.... All the works of Sahajayana are written in the Sandhyabhasa ... of light and darkness ... partly light, partly darkness; some parts can be understood, while other parts cannot."[3]

Agent Cooper utilizes a form of divination through free association and synchronicity.

323

Cooper's methods of reading dreams, visions and omens, become an insight into the metaphysics of Twin Peaks. From the film *Twin Peaks: Fire Walk with Me*, we are given the impression that Laura's spirit has summoned Cooper from the FBI to come and investigate. Consistently through the series Cooper receives messages and clues from this spirit realm, or what might accurately be called the *aether* or astral realm.

As he sleeps, his higher self enters this realm and communicates with an assorted cast of shades, ranging from Laura Palmer, a young version of David Lynch, a midget known as "The Man from Another Place" (played by Michael J. Anderson), and a giant. Channeling these entities, Cooper gradually unravels the twilight language script behind the wooded Washington city, and we, the viewers, embark on the same initiatic journey of decoding the script as Cooper.

From reading the simulacra within simulacra, Cooper begins to discover that the secret of Twin Peaks involves the black market, where town tycoon Ben Horne organizes and controls local prostitution, gambling and drug running through his private club, One Eyed Jacks. The nomenclature here is significant, as town oddball Nadine only has one functioning eye, and later dissociates to a younger version of herself, as well as possessing excessive strength. Nadine functions as a comic foil to Laura, but her initial psychosis and dissociation to a different persona is a key to Laura Palmer, as we will see.

One Eyed Jack's is the locale of Ben Horne's (played by Richard Beymer) control of vice, with connections to larger criminal mafia organizations personified in the characters of the Renault brothers. Horne's network includes the legitimate face of several businesses in town, from the Great Northern Hotel, to Horne's Department Store, while secretly there is a nearby casino and cathouse. While not directly involved in the occult, Horne is the archetypal 80s businessman, who had no direct involvement in the murder of Laura Palmer. While briefly accused of the murder, the reality surrounding Laura is much darker and complex.

Cooper discovers through the eventual disclosure of Laura's secret diary that she was raped since age twelve by her father, Leland, (played by Ray Wise), and a spirit named "Bob." Bob is a former killer who has become a demon in the afterlife and possesses individuals such as Leland, and later Windom Earle, to commit crimes such as pedophilia and sacrificial murder. This frightening process of dividing the psyche through trauma is an aspect of the oligarchical plan which is not to heal man, but rather to end man, as the Royal Society openly states.

Concerning alters and the split *psyche*, I noted:

Considering specifically the fragmentation of the psyche, the extreme versions appear in the diagnoses of MPD/DID and schizophrenia, with the unifying factor being severe trauma, often in childhood.[4] Trauma later in life appears in "Post-traumatic Stress Disorder," with the same patterns of dissociation and fragmentation and psychosis often appearing.[5] What is almost never discussed, though the evidence surfaces daily, particularly with former military and pop star circles are the realities of ritual abuse. Having read several works on the subject, ritual abuse appears frequently in these cases, yet goes unmentioned in the mainstream. This tide appears to be changing with the case of Jimmy Savile and his network, as even the mainstream media has been forced to report on the avalanche of officials involved in occultic and ritual abuse."[6]

Not only is there a black market of prostitution and the luring of young girls into porn, there is a cult that exists amongst Twin Peaks' elite that formerly met in secret for ritual magick ceremonies. As the thread unravels, the spirit of Bob serves as the foot soldier for the Man from Another Place, organizing an occult marriage ceremony for the girls offered by Leland and other cult participants. Starting with drugs and porn, the girls are lured into prostitution and even hints of snuff films emerge.

Behind the cult is the real dark power behind Twin Peaks, the Black Lodge. In-between worlds, the Black Lodge bears a striking resemblance to irregular forms of masonry, also known as Black Lodges, where dark

Black market control of the vices through Ben Horne's One Eyed Jack's. Jack is a perennial term for the devil, and the single eye symbolism mirrors that of Nadine.

325

arts are performed. The Black Lodge is also mentioned in Crowley's novel, *Moonchild* as members of the Golden Dawn, and the reports of Lynch asking his actors to speak and walk in reverse for filming the astral scenes in the lodge may have Crowleyan undertones, as well. All of this is told in striking detail in *Twin Peaks*, as Cooper's visions demonstrate a human sacrificial component. In other words, Bob is a demonic force subservient to the Man from Another Place, whose lust for "fun" involves rape, pedophilia and murder. Also consistent in the narrative is old men who have their way with young girls, touching on pedophilia.

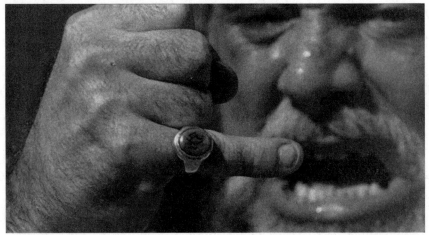

The one-armed Gerard/Mike (Al Strobel) displays the cult's magickal ring.

In possessing individuals for the purpose of carrying out these acts, Bob captures the pain and misery stored in the "blood" of his victims and pours them out as a sacrificial offering to the Man from Another Place. In perennial demonology, this concept has many precedents, as the maleficent spirits parasitically feed on the pain and misery of the victims. Critic Justine Smith comments from an aesthetic perspective:

> Then, of course we have Bob. For those unaware, the town of Twin Peaks is similarly populated by a spirit lodge that travels or is somehow engaged by electricity. One of its members, perhaps its leader is Bob, who menaces Laura throughout her life. She claims that he has raped her since she was twelve and is similarly violent. In this scene he is not only a stark contrast to the pink-childlike bedroom, but he is searching for her hidden diary. The fact that he mirrors her reaction is another mode of doubling commonly found in surrealist work, it suggests a deep connection between them, however unwilling. Finally, we have the end of the scene where Laura's father exits

the house. Having already entered that space we are fairly certain that he wasn't there before. Is Laura's father and Bob one and the same?[7]

I want all my... garmonbozia (pain and sorrow).

The Garmonbozia/cream corn is the "food" of the pain and misery of the ritual sacrifice.

The answer to Smith's question is yes. Specifically in the case of Laura, we find her youthful trauma from Bob/Leland has caused her to psyche to split into alters. This is revealed in the show explicitly, and more clearly in the film, where Laura demonstrates a duplicity of good girl/bad girl, detailing in her diary the trauma she was unable to cope with from her father's own personality splits. Leland, just like Laura, was subject to a dual personality, with Bob eventually taking possession.

This is strikingly revealed in the driving scene in the feature film, where Leland encounters Gerard/Mike wearing the cult ring, functioning as a "trigger" for Laura and Leland to dissociate. Not only was Laura lured into the world of prostitution; she was subject to ritual abuse. In this regard, the symbology of the ring suggests both the goat and the demonic, with inverted horns, as well as a ring, which in another sense is a group or cabal. It also displays the different planes of existence and the portal between the two peaks, in a three-tiered sense of White Lodge, earth, and Black Lodge.

Note the sigil next to Cooper hanging on the chalkboard.

327

What almost all researchers have missed is the crucial imagery at the police station, where in the background Cooper and Sheriff Harry Truman have pieced together ritual magick sigils. Presumably connected to the crime scenes and former FBI Agent, turned psychopath, Windom Earle, the ritual magick sigils are explained in a video of Earle describing the tapping into the left-handed path power of the dark side, through the Black Lodge. The sigils in *Twin Peaks* are in fact sigils from Goetia, or the *Lesser Key of Solomon*, which specifically relate to the invocation of demons. Scorched engine oil throughout the series is a reference to the oil sludge found at Galstonbury Grove, the site of the forest portal, which includes a reference to Arthurian mythology.

Symbolic sigils from the Goetia, for the invocation of demons.

Earle arrives to capitalize on the dark forces in Twin Peaks, seeking the portal to the Lodge in the woods. Hovering over a pool of black, viscous oil, the portal is the site of ancient ritual practice, where gods and demigods are invoked. Lynch seems to be saying here that America is a land of primeval fallen forces that rule our present reality from just behind the veil. This is also the significance of the consistent red veil imagery, accompanying any entrance to the Black Lodge, and the planetary and astrological conjunctions that determine the opening of the portals to the next world. "Fear," Cooper says, "opens the door to the Black Lodge, and love the doorway to the White."

Also revealed in this association of dubious characters is Major Briggs, a military mystic whose belief in the supernatural leads to classified connections with Project Blue Book, and the military's UFO research.[8] In reality, Project Blue Book was a cover story for advanced technological testing of aircraft, yet even here we have a curious association, as Major Briggs' classified work involves occult research. Briggs seems to be an approximation of the kind of real programs Jon Ronson describes in his *Men Who Stare at Goats*, where high level military and special forces soldiers participated in occult activities through the First Earth Battalion.[9]

Yet another sigil on the other side of the board.

Also relevant are the recent stories of high-level ritual occultism and Satanism involving the Presidio and U.S. military elite.[10] With the associations of high level military, ceremonial magick and ceremonies conducted on the west coast in that beautiful forest, Bohemian Grove comes to mind, since one of the more famous taglines for the show is "The owls are not what they appear." Lynch seems to be hinting that the real power structure in the soap opera charade that is America is actually subservient to dark forces beyond our plane of existence. Subservient to the demonic, the hypocritical face the establishment puts forward to cover the nefarious mirrors, the dual level of reality in the world of Twin Peaks, and the spirit world of the Black Lodge that undergirds it.

As Earle attempts to concoct his own ritual by sacrificing Cooper's love, Annie (played by Heather Graham), Earle specifies that it must be done in the Grove in the magick circle. Entering the circle leads to the *aether*, where symbolically the death of the Queen fulfills Earle's simulacrum of utilizing playing cards. The playing cards also hearken back to One Eyed Jack's, where fortune and fate are personified in the series as

329

elemental spiritual forces of nature.[11] This focus on the elemental spirits is the reason for the Log Lady, whose sphinxlike intros to the show provide consistent clues to the overall narrative.

The Log Lady plays a minor role, but her comments on synchronicity, symbolism, and clues that point to forces of nature (Logs are wood, and thus the association with the hotel and the forest). In the background of *Twin Peaks* we thus have a mix of the elements of the classic world: air, earth, fire, water and *aether*. This elemental focus explains why Josie is trapped in the wood of the Great Northern Hotel, while others meet their demise in direct association with fire or burning exhaust and oil (Laura's death). In the ancient world, and equally true of the ancient Far East, nature was not a collection of chaotic atoms bouncing around, but a vivid landscape populated by countless spirits, angels and demons. It is this kind of world Lynch wants to be the backdrop for *Twin Peaks*.

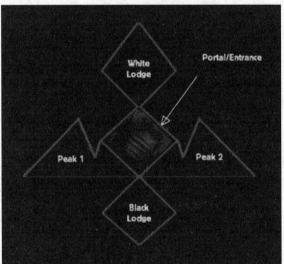

The mystical toponomy of the land is laid out well in this graphic, where we see the portal in the midst of the 3-tiered planes of the lodges and earth.

The infamous climax of the series features a Cooper who has lost his way through fear, with the real Cooper trapped in the Black Lodge, and Bob possessing Cooper's body. Cooper's curiosity and desire for knowledge of the beyond, and in particular the dark side, would lead to his demise in much the same way as Fred Madison in Lynch's *Lost Highway*. Where the series began, with the possession of an initially good man, the series ends, with Cooper as a vessel of evil. What is described of Madison in *Lost Highway* is relevant in regard to Agent Dale Cooper.

Lost Highway is a non-linear, Neo-noir occult psycho-drama that looks at the dark side of the Hollywood underworld, where mafia, porn, crime and the occult are interwoven into a story about one man's psychic journey down a lost highway of his own stream of consciousness and thought. As the viewer travels with Fred Madison down this road, we are brought back to the very point he began, and the cycle starts again. Packed with dualism, illusion and mystery, *Lost Highway* is about life and the dark side of our own inner underworld, the subconscious, which Lynch mystically links to others'.

The good Cooper with Laura in the Black Lodge.

If we fail to realize the reality of these evils, such as possession and the mysteries of the subconscious, are we liable to be trapped like Fred in our own madness? His name itself is a clue – "Madison," possibly symbolizing his descent into *mad*ness, as "Alice," Renee's alter, brings to mind *Alice in Wonderland* and alternate worlds and personalities. Was Alice a victim of mind control like Fred, or were they both willing accomplices of evil? Will our obsession with the Hollywood celluloid videodrome and its cousin, the now omnipresent surveillance society, bring us truth, or a descent into madness, depersonalization and dissociation, like Fred? Either way, Lynch is forcing us to examine that at bottom reality and the psyche are still mysteries to be decoded.

In the series' strange ending sequence, Cooper discovers Bob has possessed Earle and has organized the last round of murders. Earle tries to steal Cooper's soul, but Bob steps in to claim *his* rights on Earle's soul. Cooper confronts his unconscious shade self, as well as facing up to his responsibility for past deaths. Cooper ends up trapped with Annie and Laura in the Black Lodge as a demonic Bob/Cooper takes possession of Cooper's "vessel." Worth noting here is that in the feature film, Laura's initial journeys into the dreamscape/astral realm result in an encounter with Annie, who says she is "with Laura and Agent Cooper." And as was the case with *Mulholland Drive*, electrical phenomena and static charges tend to accompany the manifestation of other-worldly spirits. The Black Lodge members appear to travel through electricity, and manifest in physical form like the Cowboy in *Mulholland Drive*.

In conclusion, the return of *Twin Peaks* seems to have even been predicted through Laura in the Black Lodge 25 years ago. Amazingly, Laura tells an aged Cooper "I'll see you again in 25 years," hinting that it would return. With the recent announcements of Showtime picking up the reboot, we can expect an even deeper foray into the unconscious – both of Laura and Cooper. Whether the show returns or not, with the original series and film, we have an amazingly precise window into the real America, a land haunted by the primal, elemental spirits of the past, and controlled by a cult that adheres to these ancient beliefs. The American power elite is really like Ben Horne, subservient to preternatural forces they cannot control, and behind this veil of obscurity lies an occult elite, whose power seems to derive from a Black Lodge.

I'll see you again in 25 years.

Endnotes

1. Eliade, Mircea. *Out of This World*. Boston: Shambhala, 1991, pg. 38.

2. Levenda, *Sinister Forces* Bk. III, 151.

3. Mishra, Vijay. Devotional Poetics of the Indian Sublime. New York: State University of New York Press, 1991, pg. 221.

4. "Dissociative Identity Disorder." Psychology Today. 24 November, 2014. Web. https://www.psychologytoday.com/conditions/dissociative-identity-disorder-multiple-personality-disorder

5. Spiegel, David, M.D.. "Coming Apart: Trauma and the Fragmentation of the Self." Dana.org. 31 January, 2008. Web. http://www.dana.org/Cerebrum/2008/Coming_Apart__Trauma_and_the_Fragmentation_of_the_Self/

6. Dyer, Jay. "Fragmentation of the Psyche and Nous." JaysAnalysis. 5 April, 2015. Web. https://jaysanalysis.com/2015/04/05/fragmentation-of-the-psyche-and-the-nous/

7. Smith, Justine. "David Lynch and Surrealism in Twin Peaks, Mulholland Dr. and Lost Highway." PopOptique. 10 March, 2013. Web. http://www.popoptiq.com/david-lynch-and-surrealism-in-twin-peaks-mulholland-dr-and-lost-highway/

8. Hynek, J. Allen. *The Hynek UFO Report*. New York: Dell Publications, 1977, pgs. 272-8.

9. Channon, Jim. "The First Earth Battalion: Dare to Think the Unthinkable, Ideas and Ideals for Soldiers Everywhere." Tgorski.com. February, 2000. Web. http://www.tgorski.com/Mind%20Control/First%20Earth%20Battalion%20010910.htm

10. McGowan, *Programmed to Kill*, 39-44.

11. Guiley, Rosemary Ellen. "Elementals." Encyclopedia of Magic and Alchemy. New York: Checkmark Books, 2007, pgs. 86-7.

Chapter 24

Occult Brainwashing in Lynch's *Mulholland Drive* (2001)

The Academy Award-nominated 2001 film, *Mulholland Drive*, is remembered by most as a macabre, satirical nightmare dreamscape of Neo-noir centering around a typical girl-next-door's dream of becoming the next Hollywood starlet. That is basically the only thing viewers can agree the film is about. Reviewers speak of "surrealism," "imagination," "nightmares," and a few of the more philosophical pieces look at semiotics in relation to the performance at Club Silencio, yet no one seems able to truly crack the language of *Mulholland*, even with Lynch's clues and hints.[1] In my analysis, I want to propose something radically different – *Mulholland* follows *Lost Highway* as a story of Hollywood's dark side, but with a new twist, revealing actual occult brainwashing techniques. Not only that, Lynch's film will make "twilight language" references to a host of esoteric subjects, including the Manson murders and the CIA's MKUltra mind control programs.

Before delving into that topic, author Michael Hoffman defines "twilight language" as follows, in his *Secret Societies and Psychological Warfare:*

> The path to unlocking this gnosis was centered in "twilight language," a once nearly universal subliminal communication system used in Egypt, Babylon, the Indian subcontinent and among the Aztecs, consisting of a combination of numbers, archetypal words and symbols, which in our time are sometimes embedded in modern advertising, and in certain modern films and music.... In Oriental Tantra, the mantra (including *dharani, kavaca, yamala,* etc.) is sonically calculated to induce a particular action. It forms part of the original Sanskrit concept of *sandhyabhasa* (twilight language). In Tantra, *Sandhyabhasa* ... is a language of light and darkness ... in this higher type of discourse, words have another, a different meaning: this is not to be openly discussed.[2]

In my *Lost Highway* analysis, I mentioned that David Lynch is a fan of Buddhist and Zen philosophy. Presumably, he is also aware of this Tantric conception of twilight language and its significance in terms of using and manipulating symbols and events. The opening of that analysis is appropriate for *Mulholland Drive,* as well:

> The telling of the story is nonlinear, yet influenced heavily by classic 1940s Noir. *Lost Highway* is influenced by Zen philosophy and Jungian dreamscapes, but as for the deeper occult elements, it's necessary to understand why the stories are presented in a interlinking duality, as they are in *Mulholland Drive.* Zen philosophy is concerned with duality and its transcendence, as ultimate principles, as well as with the individual's particularized psyche, and its relation to the whole of reality. Zen is therefore a quasi-religious philosophy concentrated on ultimate metaphysical principles, known in philosophy historically as the problem of the one and the many. For Lynch, these philosophical questions are not just abstract philosophy, but also relate directly to the psyche in its conscious and unconscious/sleep states.[3]

In terms of decoding films and life in general, Lynch himself has said:

> We all find this book of riddles and it's just what's going on. And you can figure them out. The problem is, you figure them out inside yourself, and even if you told somebody, they wouldn't believe you

or understand in the same way you do. You'd suddenly realize that the communication wasn't 100 percent. There are a lot of things like that going on in life, and words just fail you.[4]

From this platform we can further posit that Lynch does have a secret significance for his films and the symbolism has a definite, although obscure, meaning, if the viewer is skilled enough at decoding the "twilight language."

Before delving into the film, an important influence on Lynch should be considered. *Sunset Boulevard*, the dark 1950 film directed by Billy Wilder, shares many parallels to *Mulholland Drive*. *Sunset* is the famous story of a washed-up silent movie actress who loses her mind and becomes lost in an obsessive fantasy of her own making, leading to the death of a young screenwriter who becomes her consort. For its time, *Sunset Boulevard* was a challenging film, exposing the dirty underbelly of fame and fortune that most 1950s Hollywood fairy tales ignored. Though not entirely evident, it is arguable that Norma Desmond (the washed-up actress) dissociates into a completely fictitious psycho-nostalgic world where she remains a glamorous starlet. In the same way, Diane/Betty (Naomi Watts) in *Mulholland Drive* will embrace the same fate as Norma. This is why Rita/Camilla first stumbles onto "Sunset Boulevard" at the beginning of the film, following her car accident, and why Diane/Betty's apartment features classic Hollywood posters adorning the walls.

We know the first half of the film is Betty's mental projection or dream of what happened. What we can gather is that she went to Hollywood to become a movie star, but ended up a drugged-out whore. She won a dance contest that provided her an opportunity to move to Hollywood, and the first clue given is that, following the sock hop, we see the two old people, as the camera fades to the perspective of Betty crawling into bed to die (as she commits suicide at the end of the film). It is also the same bed Betty and Rita discover as they sneak into the apartment looking for "Diane Selwyn" (Betty's real identity). As with *Lost Highway*, the end of the film is the beginning, with the split personality lead character becoming lost in a cyclical maze of her own delusions and dream realities. We know this because it is the same red pillow. When you crawl into bed, you do it to sleep, or die, which is an image of death, dreaming and dissociating into an alternate personality. In other words, Betty represents the aspiring American actress who has lost her identity in the Hollywood machine, which is something other than the illusory image presented to most.

336

However, there is a much deeper current at work here. Mulholland Drive, the actual street, has a connection to the Manson murders that few have noticed. Esoteric writer Peter Levenda explains in his *Sinister Forces, Book II*:

> Helter Skelter was Manson's "program" for the brainwashed murderers; it provided a context, and it also influenced their choice of bloody graffiti at each scene, thus attempting to lay the crimes off on the Black Panthers.... The brilliance behind these crimes had nothing to do with Manson himself. The brilliance was in selecting Manson and his assassins as the hit team, for it obscured the real motives and thus the real powers behind them. Further, due to the sensitive nature of the victims involved and their incestuous relationships with Hollywood, occultism, drugs, and "alternative" sexual practices-much of it captured on videotape-there was little danger of their friends running to the police with information that could get the real masterminds in trouble ... the blood had splattered all over Benedict Canyon in an aerial spray that reached Mulholland Drive, Beverly Hills, Bel Air, North Hollywood and Malibu, and the back lots of studios all over town. Drugs, murder for hire, sadomasochistic sex on videotape involving celebrities, and satanic rituals.... The "scarlet thread of murder" never ran so red as it did on August 9, 1969 at 10050 Cielo Drive.[5]

CHARLES MANSON: Famed American convict behind the Sharon Tate murder and 8 other "Manson murders," committed by his devoted runaway and vagabond followers. Manson operated a small cult where mind control, drugs and brainwashing techniques were used to create willing assassins. The murders included occult themes and belief in a coming apocalyptic "race war" dubbed by Manson "Helter Skelter." Manson was reportedly a "Theta Clear" level Scientologist while in prison, and according to some researchers, may have been handled by a higher level cult. Manson is currently in prison and, while still clinically insane, is arguably America's most famous living convict.

Levenda's *Sinister Forces* trilogy is devoted to analyzing, among many other events, the Manson murders and Hollywood, noting the connections and associations in relation to the MKUltra mind control program of the CIA and covert intelligence agencies. Hollywood, Levenda argues, is a mass mind-control operation that ties into the occult and psychological warfare operations. His correlation between Manson and *Mulholland Drive* is echoed by famed Manson investigator Vincent Bugliosi, who quotes Manson associate Tex Watson:

> They drove somewhere along "Benedict Canyon, Mulholland Drive, I don't know [which street] ... until we came to what looked like an embankment going down like a cliff with a mountain on one side and a cliff on the other.' They pulled off and stopped, and 'Linda threw all the bloody clothes over the side

of the hill...' The weapons, the knives and gun were tossed out at 'three or four different places, I don't remember how many.'" (*Helter Skelter*, pg 245).

I think it is highly likely Lynch has this in mind, as Levenda elaborates:

In January 1969, shortly after the discovery of Marina Habe's body in a gully off Mulholland Drive, several events occurred which are relevant to our study. CIA operation OFTEN was initialized by Dr. Sidney Gottlieb, based partly on documents which came into his possession after CIA Agent WIlliam F. Buckley (who would later be tortured and murdered by Arab terrorists) tossed the premises of Dr. Ewen Cameron, he of the "sleep room" and "psychic driving" experiments in Canada. Initially, Operation OFTEN was a joint CIA/Army Chemical Corps drug project...[6]

SIDNEY GOTTLIEB (1918-1999): American chemist and intelligence operative reportedly involved in regime change and assassination attempts and later known for his participation in the infamous MK ULTRA projects. Gottlieb was known as the "sorcerer" and was directly involved in the development of LSD with the Sandoz pharmaceutical corporation.

OFTEN was one of many MKUltra associated programs, relating to the infamous CIA goals of manipulating the psyche of soldiers and other unwitting subjects with the intent of determining whether a perfect spy could be created. Could an alternate personality be created that housed secret information that only a handler with the correct "keys" or code words, could unlock? As we can see from Hollywood itself, the programs were wildly successful, originating with wartime hypnosis studies. The names associated with the programs are Dr. Ewen Cameron, Dr. Sidney Gottlieb, Dr. Jose Delgado, Dr. Jolyon West, Dr. George Estabrooks, and others, as referred to earlier. The article mentions, first of all, Estabrooks' claim of the use of secret couriers and keywords that function as the triggers in the operative:

George Estabrooks (1895-1973): Canadian-American Harvard psychologist and hypnosis expert known for hypnotizing soldiers during World War 2 and programming them with special "courier" messages that could be unlocked through "trigger" words. Estabrooks' work was also associated with aspects of the MK ULTRA program according to researcher John Marks in his *The Search for the Manchurian Candidate: CIA and Mind Control.*

The "hypnotic courier," on the other hand, provides a unique solution. I was involved in preparing many subjects for this work during World War II. One successful case involved an Army Service Corps Captain whom we'll call George Smith.

Captain Smith had undergone months of training. He was an excellent subject but did not realize it. I had removed from him, by post-hypnotic suggestion, all recollection of ever having been hypnotized.

338

First I had the Service Corps call the captain to Washington and tell him they needed a report of the mechanical equipment of Division X headquartered in Tokyo. Smith was ordered to leave by jet next morning, pick up the report and return at once. Consciously, that was all he knew, and it was the story he gave to his wife and friends.

Then I put him under deep hypnosis, and gave him – orally – a vital message to be delivered directly on his arrival in Japan to a certain colonel – let's say his name was Brown – of military intelligence. Outside of myself, Colonel Brown was the only person who could hypnotize Captain Smith. This is "locking." I performed it by saying to the hypnotized Captain: "Until further orders from me, only Colonel Brown and I can hypnotize you. We will use a signal phrase 'the moon is clear.' Whenever you hear this phrase from Brown or myself you will pass instantly into deep hypnosis." When Captain Smith re-awakened, he had no conscious memory or what happened in trance. All that he was aware of was that he must head for Tokyo to pick up a division report.

On arrival there, Smith reported to Brown, who hypnotized him with the signal phrase. Under hypnosis, Smith delivered my message and received one to bring back. Awakened, he was given the division report and returned home by jet. There I hypnotized him once more with the signal phrase, and he spilled off Brown's answer that had been dutifully tucked away in his unconscious mind.

The system is virtually foolproof. As exemplified by this case, the information was "locked" in Smith's unconscious for retrieval by the only two people who knew the combination. The subject had no conscious memory of what happened, so could not spill the beans. No one else could hypnotize him even if they might know the signal phrase.[7]

Hollywood is also no stranger to the notion of mind-controlled subjects with alternate personalities, programmed with key words and triggers, as the 1962 film *The Manchurian Candidate* made evident. Another famous episode along these lines that relates to Betty is the story of Candy Jones, the famous model, who was also a mind-controlled subject, as Donald Bain's 1976 *The Control of Candy Jones* argues. Betty/Diane, like Candy, seems to blend between the 50s and present day, in her descent into mental illness, depersonalization and dissociation.

This will provide the key to understanding the blue key Betty is given that unlocks the blue box in Club Silencio. The box and key are Betty's psyche and the key represents the key words and phrases, which her handler(s) possess.

My thesis is *Mulholland Drive* is the intersection of all of the above – from the demonic to MKUltra – with "twilight language," forming a revelation of the mystery of Hollywood itself, which is an occult *Inland Empire* (Lynch's third "Hollywood" film) of its own. The director thus functions as a kind of shaman, taking the viewer down a fire-walking path between these worlds. In particular, there is the world of reality, and the double – the world the alternate personality experiences. This is why Betty/Diane is the foil to Rita/Camilla, functioning as a doubled doubling.

The film begins with Rita emerging from a limo wreck, dazed and confused with amnesia, following a hit man's attempt on her life. (It is significant that Pete in *Lost Highway* and Audrey in *Wild at Heart* also have amnesia after car wrecks). This limo ride is actually the dinner party later in the film where Camilla and Kesher (the young director played by Justin Theroux) are engaged. Camilla, Rita's alternate identity, is who ends up getting the part that Betty/Diane thought she would get in a film called *The Sylvia North Story*. While there is no real film by that title, there is a 1965 film called *Sylvia* about a beautiful blonde girl who has an alternate identity as a prostitute, whose name happens to be Sylvia *West*, calling to mind again the theme of good girl with a dark *persona*.

The next day, at Winkie's Diner, two men are discussing a dream one has had. In the dream, the man in black says he saw a "man behind this place" that frightened him. As they approach the rear of the diner, they are confronted by a demon. This clues the viewer into the fact that the first half of the film, as most reviewers note, is itself a dream. The man/

ROMAN POLANSKI: Award-winning French-Polish film director known for many critically-acclaimed titles, as well as particularly revealing esoteric and elite perversion-related works like *Rosemary's Baby*, *The Ninth Gate* and *Chinatown*. Polanski's wife, Sharon Tate, was murdered in the Manson killings, while Polanski himself was forced to flee the U.S. over sexual abuse allegations.

demon "behind this" is revealed in the next scene to be part of a secret club that appears to call the shots in Hollywood, deciding who gets what part in what film. Betty is then shown arriving in Hollywood with Aunt Irene and the old man who brought her, yet something odd happens again with the elderly couple. They ride away in a limo, in a scene reminiscent of something from *Rosemary's Baby*. Betty is left alone in an apartment complex with witchy, elderly people, like Mia Farrow in Polanski's film. Although this is a dream or Betty's fantasy, we get the impression that her elderly relatives have selected her for what she is about to endure. There seems to be a connection between Club Silencio and her Aunt Irene, whom Betty explains is also an actress.

As Adam Kesher tries to advance his Sylvia North film, the mafia shows up to tell Kesher who will play the lead role, contrary to his wishes. But remember: The mafia are actually controlled by the oddball elite Mr. Roque atop Ryan Entertainment (also from Club Silencio), who ultimately decided Camilla/Rita would play the part. Next, we see the hit man who asks a blonde prostitute if there are any new girls on the street. The prostitute is who Betty has really become, having hired the hit man to kill Rita/Camilla in the Winkie's. Rita explains to Betty/Diane that she was on the way to Mulholland Drive when the "accident" happened, but both girls appear to be amnesic. The money Rita/Camilla has is the money Diane/Betty used to hire the hit, which both girls hide away in a box. In other words, Diane/Betty has hidden away in her subconscious the plan to murder Rita/Camilla. It's not until the end of the film at Club Silencio that the two girls unite the key and the box to open it and discover that Rita is actually a projection of Diane/Betty's mind. This is why Rita begins to take on Betty's appearance, with blonde hair. Diane is revealed to be the waitress at Winkie's who ends up a failed actress and is the prostitute.

Kesher, however, does not want to cast Rita/Camilla, so he is forced to meet with the Cowboy, the otherworldly devil figure who tells Kesher he must cast whoever the occult elite decide. It is significant that the Cowboy appears and the lights go dim, and then disappears, proving he is not of this world. As Betty/Diane auditions for the part, it is not accidental that the part of Sylvia centers around a young girl who is sexually accosted by an older man – another hint that Betty/Diane is really a whore. Camilla gets the part and Betty begins to go insane, not yet realizing that her mind has split. When Betty and Diane have their homoerotic scene, Betty goes into a trance and starts to repeat what appear to be trigger phrases. The reason for the homoerotic scene is that Betty/Diane is in love with herself, not Rita – this is all a projection of her psyche.

Club Silencio. "It is all illusion."

341

Rita is merely an alternate personality of Betty/Diane. Rita chants, "silencio," "silencio," "no hay banda," and tells Betty/Diane she must accompany her to Club Silencio. Upon entering Club Silencio, the magician/emcee tells the crowd there is no band, only a tape recording. He asks what is real, since the Silencio performance is a tape – an illusion. As the magician creates a thunder effect with the elite members of Club Silencio looking on, Betty/Diane goes into convulsions. This hints at the likelihood of Betty being under mind control and Rita is her alter – as the Anton LaVey-looking magician disappears. Is this a reference to the Crowleyan subculture that undergirds much of Hollywood? Is Lynch using twilight language here to signify that there is a Crowleyan secret behind the meaning of *Mulholland*? Is this the meaning of Club Silencio? Club Silence's entire performance seems to be about questioning the nature of Hollywood reality – that the reality spun by the theater is pure illusion, (an obvious reference once again doubling on reality). Following this scene, Rita inserts the key into the box, and the viewer enters it, and Betty/Diane is now back to reality – as a whore.

The Cowboy walks in on dead Betty and tells her it's time to wake up. Time is not operating chronologically here, as the entire film, like *Lost Highway*, is Diane/Betty's eternal recurrence of her destructive life. This is why the key is gone when Diane is with Rita, and why Rita disappears and we discover Diane alone. The limo ride Diane/Betty takes to the party on Mulholland Drive is the limo ride at the beginning with Rita. Rita takes Betty down a "secret path" to the engagement party which leads to the final break for Betty/Diane. Coco, it is revealed is Coco, the witchy woman at the apartment complex. It is as if the entire scenario was engineered to bring Diane as a sacrifice by driving her insane.

The Cowboy briefly passes at the party, as Camilla's alter appears to Diane. At this point we flash back to Betty/Diane as a strung out whore ordering the hit on Rita/Camilla. The hit man gives Betty/Diane the blue key that opens the box, as the camera pans to behind the restaurant where the demon from earlier opens the box and two tiny, demonic versions of the old couple emerge. Betty has now gone into a paranoid schizophrenia, and we discover that her mind has constructed an entire false reality, as Club Silencio elucidated. Betty\Diane then kills herself lying on the same bedspread we were shown at the beginning as the film concludes with Club Silencio's blue-haired woman whispering, "Silencio." Like Fred/Pete in *Lost Highway*, Diane/Betty is lost in a psychical prison of her own making. Yet, is Lynch also saying, on a deeper level, that Hollywood is an illusory reality – it is not a land of golden opportunity for the talented, but a mafia-style occult-run entity that uses mind control keys and triggers for useful dupes? Whether this is the aim of Lynch's film, I cannot say, but I suspect it was not coincidental that "Silencio" is also the "sign of Harpocrates." Is this the meaning of the twilight language?

Harpocrates.

Endnotes

1. "Lynch's 10 Clues to Unlock the Thriller." MulhollandDrive.net. Web. http://www.mulholland-drive.net/studies/10clues.htm

2. Hoffman, *Secret Societies*, 207.

3. Dyer, Jay. "Lost Highway (1997) - Esoteric Analysis." JaysAnalysis. 17 February, 2014. Web. https://jaysanalysis.com/2014/02/17/lost-highway-1997-esoteric-analysis/

4. Rodley, Chris, Ed. *Lynch on Lynch*. London: Faber & Faber, 1997, pgs. 25-6.

5. Levenda, 103.

6. Ibid, 87.

7. Estabrooks, Ibid.

Conclusion:

The CIA and Hollywood – A Dark Marriage

Best friends forever..

Though it is seemingly fanciful, or thought to be fanciful, the subject of the relationship of the CIA to Hollywood is really not. We've explored this relationship symbolically, as well as the esoteric dimensions of the aesthetic of several films, as well as the propaganda. But how has this all come about? In short, the Pentagon and the CIA are intimately involved in Hollywood for the purpose of culture creation and social engineering.[1] Blockbusters like *Zero Dark Thirty* and *American Sniper* focus on the military and intelligence agencies in supposedly "based on true events" scenarios. But, is more at work here?[2] The film industry has always loved tales of espionage, but in reality, the creation and manufacturing of a completely alternate reality and history is far more extensive than most would assume. While many films have nobly challenged assumptions about war, in figures like Kubrick or Stone, for the most part, film has functioned as one of the most powerful forms of propaganda in the Western Establishment's arsenal.

OLIVER STONE: American film director, producer and screenwriter. Stone has created some of the greatest films of all time, especially in regard to conspiracy-related themes. Exposing many levels of government corruption, Stone's films have looked at the Vietnam War, Wall Street, Latin America, the CIA and JFK, drug trade and the mafia, the music industry, Nixon, NSA spying and countless other sources of disgrace on the part of the U.S. establishment.

Watch old *G.I. Joe* cartoon episodes and you will be surprised to find military consultants as part of the production; reaching the youth with propaganda is central to creating cubicle-dwelling automatons later in life.[3] Likewise, researching this as a thesis topic was also instrumental in making these connections, and *Esoteric Hollywood* is the fruit of that research. More recently, a plethora of news articles have surfaced that highlight this deep relationship, a rabbit hole that never ends. The coalescing of intelligence agencies, secret societies and Hollywood, in reality, is more sensational than any incestuous cult a pulp crime-fiction writer could dream up.

Author John Rizzo has recently published a book titled *Company Man: Thirty Years of Controversy and Crisis in the CIA*, which is an amazing admission of this scandalous affair between intelligence and the film industry. The *Los Angeles Times* comments:

> The CIA has long had a special relationship with the entertainment industry, devoting considerable attention to fostering relationships with Hollywood movers and shakers – studio executives, producers, directors, big-name actors. John Rizzo, the former acting CIA general counsel, wrote in his new book, *Company Man: Thirty Years of Crisis and Controversy in the CIA....*
>
> > The CIA also recruits actors to give more visibility to propaganda projects abroad, such as a documentary secretly produced by the agency, Rizzo said. And the agency sometimes takes advantage of the door-opening cachet that movie stars and other American celebrities enjoy. A star who met a world leader, for example, might be asked for details about that meeting.
> >
> > The CIA has officials assigned full-time to the care and feeding of Hollywood assets, Rizzo wrote. Other former CIA officials added that some of those operatives work in the Los Angeles office of an agency department called the National Resources Division, which recruits people in the U.S. to help America spy abroad.[4]

With that in mind, recent news regarding Britney Spears may reveal much more than the headline suggests. Researchers have opined that "rehab" centers may actually be used for "programming" the "stars" for various mind controlled objectives (as John Marks hints in his *CIA and Mind Control: The Search for the Manchurian Candidate*), whether as high-priced call girls, sex slaves or spies, as Rizzo discusses.[5] As we saw, author Dave McGowan has detailed the military and intelligence connections to Laurel Canyon, the home of the budding counter-culture rock movement in the 60s, which spawned seminal influences like Frank Zappa and the Doors.[6] Military and intelligence connections thus come to the fore here with Britney's ex, who "coached her through rehab" being killed transporting "dignitaries" in Afghanistan – obviously an intelligence cover.[7] Was Sundahl her helpful boyfriend, or was more at work here?

Britney's infamous meltdown.

News hounds will recall Amanda Bynes, believing she was brainwashed and implanted with a microchip and Ke$ha, who recently sued by her handler "for abuse"(Dr. Luke), with Luke in turn counter-suing.[8] Prior to that, we have witnessed a barrage of news stories the last few years recounting a stream of victims alleging networks of sickos using and abusing those under them. Let us not forget Penn State and Jerry Sandusky[9] and Jimmy Savile of the UK,[10] as well as a host of UK government officials.[11] Recent reports also arose from actors like Corey Feldman, who alleges similar crimes.[12]

JIMMY SAVILE (1926-2011): Notorious English DJ and television presenter known after his death by police for likely being the UK's most prolific child abuser. Savile was an intimate of many of the western elite, and even received an award from Pope John Paul II. Savile is also believed by some researchers to have been associated with necrophilia, dark occultism and ritual abuse.

Details surrounding the death of screenwriter Gary Devore (author of Raw Deal and Time Cop) killed in 1997 also made headlines, with the production of a new documentary on his questionable death. The Daily Mail reveals that Devore was, in fact, working with the CIA, while the strange dating of the severed hands suggests a possible ritual connection:

> When the skeletal remains of Hollywood screenwriter Gary Devore were found strapped into his Ford Explorer submerged beneath the California Aqueduct in 1998 it brought an end to one of America's most high-profile missing person cases.
>
> The fact that Devore was on his way to deliver a film script that promised to explain the "real reason" why the US invaded Panama, has long given rise to a slew of conspiracies surrounding the nature of his "accidental" death.
>
> It didn't help that Devore's hands were missing from the crash scene, along with the script, and that investigators could offer no plausible explanation as to how a car could leave the highway and end up in the position it was found a year after he disappeared.

346

Now the *Daily Mail* can exclusively reveal that Devore was working with the CIA in Panama and even a White House source concedes his mysterious death bears all the hallmarks of a cover-up.[13]

The concept of ritual murder is not foreign to Hollywood, when one recalls the Black Dahlia case, which I have discussed elsewhere. Hollywood is a kind of Babylon, (not that we know what actually went on there so many years ago, but the paradigm persists) as numerous researchers have suggested, and only with the advent of the Internet is it becoming evident how close that nexus of CIA, underground mafia networks, occultists and intelligence agencies really is. It is a veritable threshold of the "gods" (little "g," but still the big guys), and gods often require a sacrifice.

The Black Dahlia

Ritual murder is a juicy, dark topic that fascinates the public and makes for a great story. Why, exactly, such ominous stories captivate the mass mind is a curious psychological question, but for the subject matter of JaysAnalysis, it became time to explore the topic of *The Black Dahlia* case, and its 2006 Brian De Palma film incarnation. Film noir is a fascinating genre and period, as well as its later resurgence in Neo-Noir, including expansion into science fiction with Scott's *Blade Runner,* or even surrealism in Lynch. Surrealism is worth keeping in mind, as we will see the surrealist movement playing a central role in at least one (reasonable) thesis as to the identity of the Black Dahlia killer.

Danny DeVito's true-crime writer, "Sid Hudgens," in the similarly themed Neo-Noir film *L.A. Confidential* (1997), aptly describes this era for Hollywood and L.A. as follows:

> Come to Los Angeles. The sun shines bright. The beaches are wide and inviting. And the orange groves stretch as far as the eye can see. There are jobs aplenty. Land is cheap. Every working-man can have his own house. And inside every house, a happy all-American family. You can have all this. And who knows? You could even be discovered ... become a movie star, or at least see one. Life is good in Los Angeles. It's paradise on earth. That's what they tell you, anyway. Because they're selling an image. They're selling it through movies, radio and television. Both *L.A. Confidential* and the *Black Dahlia* share curious parallels, both based on James Ellroy novels, and a curious fact I uncovered was that the 1946 films *The Blue Dahlia* and *The Big Sleep*, two notable noir classics written by Raymond Chandler, bear tangential relations to the Black Dahlia case. And the common thread in all these stories is the Hollywood connection. However, as Sid's comment explains above, beyond this thin veneer of glitz and glam, not only is there a seedy underground of mobster corruption, drug rings and prostitution, I propose there was an even deeper occult underground in these circles that is hinted at in a very unlikely place, film *noir*, exemplified in the unsolved case of the Black Dahlia and its film incarnation.

Mia Kirshner as Elizabeth Short – drugged and exploited.

Commenting on the connection of surrealism and the occult, publishers Mandrake of Oxford discuss Nadia Choucha's book *Surrealism and the Occult*, summarizing as follows:

> Many people associate Surrealism with politics, but it was also permeated by occult ideas, a fact often overlooked by art historians. This occult influence goes beyond general themes to the movement's very heart. The antinomian stance of Surrealism can be traced directly to the influence of radical nineteenth century magi such as Eliphas Lévi, whose *Dogma and Ritual of High Magic* was widely read by Surrealism's ideologues. Amongst these we find its progenitor André Breton.
>
> The book shows how many Surrealists and their predecessors were steeped in magical ideas: Kandinsky, with his involvement with Theosophy, the sorcery of Salvador Dali; the alchemy of Pablo Picasso and the shamanism of Max Ernst and Leonora Carrington. Surrealism did not establish itself in Britain until the 1930s but a select few felt something in the air. Almost ten years before the Surrealist experiments with automatic drawing, an obscure English artist, Austin Osman Spare had perfected the technique.[14]

According to Choucha, the very origins of surrealism arise from the realm of the occult, but how does this relate to the Black Dahlia? *The Saturn Death Cult* page15 posits a thesis based on the connection of the dahlia case and surrealism that leads to prime suspect Dr. George Hodel and his *avant garde* artist associate, Man Ray.[16] While there appears to be a lot of evidence to support this, the film based on Ellroy's novel proposes a wider conspiracy beyond a lone psychotic seeking dark, artistic apotheosis. *The Black Dahlia* posits a labyrinthine plot of crooked cops, hardened "good guys" and dastardly dames and broads that ultimately leads Detec-

Scarlett Johannsen as Kay Lake (a reference to Veronica Lake in *Blue Dahlia*?)

349

tive Bucky the Iceman (Josh Hartnett) to the estates of the Hollywood elite.

The revelation of *The Black Dahlia* is that the facilitation of this dark underworld, as shown in similar fashion in Lynch's *Lost Highway*, is an underground pornography network that, in the 40s and 50s at least, was considered illegal. Author Raymond Chandler, a former RAF trainee, seems to reveal the same notion in *The Big Sleep* (1946) where Bogey follows a prominent general's daughter to a flop-house where secret porn is being filmed as girls are drugged and coaxed into sexual acts. This scene matches up perfectly to the darker scenes in *The Black Dahlia*, where, the elite family of the Linscott's, are discovered to own the set where the porn was secretly filmed.

In fact, patriarch Emmett Linscott is even shown as an incestuous pedophile who has sexual relations with his daughter, as well as killing the family's pet dog for sport. The RAF connection with Chandler brings to mind the military intelligence connections of so many Hollywood and music industry families that backs up Dave McGowan's thesis and should be noted as a possible source of the "inside info" in these fictional narratives. Willing young girls like Elizabeth Short in the unsolved case moved from the Midwest to Hollywood with stars in their eyes and were more often than not coerced into porn and prostitution to make ends meet.

The film includes "George" as the killer, but hints that it was not Hodel alone, but Hodel working in tandem with wealthy elites. Detective son of the actual Dr. George Hodel, Steve Hodel, backs up these contentions, noting his father's connections to Hollywood legends like John Huston and surrealist artists like Man Ray.[17] Steve Hodel believes his father was the Black Dahlia killer, and even cites the surrealist art his father made as partial indicators. Dr. George Hodel's rapacious sexual appetite and penchant for orgies also suggests a connection to the Hollywood "Eyes Wide Shut" underground, and it is my thesis that *The Big Sleep* and *The Black Dahlia* contain similar scenes to suggest this very notion. McGowan sees

RAYMOND CHANDLER (1888-1959): British author and screenwriter considered with Dashiell Hammett and James Cain to be the co-creator of the "hard-boiled" detective genre, exemplified in Humphrey Bogart's Philip Marlowe character. Chandler was a Royal Air Force pilot and was a friend of both Hitchcock and Ian Fleming. Many of Chandler's works would be iconic representations of the noir genre of film, like *Double Indemnity* and *The Big Sleep*.

JOHN HUSTON (1906-1987): American film director, screenwriter and actor known for directing some of Hollywood's greatest classics, such as *The Maltese Falcon*, *The Treasure of the Sierra Madre*, *The African Queen* and many more. Huston is the father of actress Anjelica Huston and was intimately connected to the Laurel Canyon scene, according to researcher Dave McGowan, as well as the circles of George Hodel, a key suspect in the infamous Black Dahlia case.

MAN RAY (1890-1976): American artist who contributed significantly to the dada and surrealist movements, as well as including many dark, Satanic and "Luciferian" themes in his works. Man Ray often pictured disfigured women in his pieces, as well as creating works that strikingly parallel the ritualistic display of Elizabeth Short, the victim of the Black Dahlia case. Man Ray was an intimate of both John Huston and George Hodel.

350

clearly how privilege works, while noting accusations that came out during Hodel's trial:

> Allegations that the rich and powerful were dabbling in incest, hypnotism/mind control, pedophilic orgies, and Luciferian philosophies must surely have been shocking to Angelenos in the 1940s, as they would still be to most Americans today, but to these jaded eyes and ears, it just sounds like business as usual. Also sounding like business as usual is that Tamar was roundly vilified by both the press and the defense team (led by Jerry Giesler), and Dr. George Hodel was acquitted.
>
> How it is that the fourteen-year-old daughter of a lowly probation officer fell into the orbit of the daughter of the wealthy and influential George Hodel (Hodel's former home is currently valued at $4.2 million) has never been explained, but Tamar, described by Michelle as "the epitome of glamour," quickly took the youngster under her wing, buying her clothes, enrolling her in modeling school, teaching her to drive, and providing her with a fake ID and a steady stream of prescription drugs – obtained, one would presume, from her father.

Have you come to the conclusion to which McGowan leads the reader? "The Black Dahlia" was recruited by a daughter of a rich and connected doctor for a ritualistic slaying in an underground walk-in vault beneath the home; her death, dismemberment and missing organs facilitated by drugs and participated in by members of a cult engaged in satanic worship. This is also McGowan's premise in his book on mind controlled serial killers, it's a cover for satanic worship and the "serial killers" are mostly patsies![18]

This doesn't do complete justice to McGowan's book. McGowan, a native of Los Angeles, pins down Phillips as possessed of occult leanings, and successfully shows how "The Black Dahlia" may be connected to occult practices in the shadows of a sixties' Laurel Canyon."

To bring this pattern into concrete examples, there is a curious Bacchanalian scene in *The Big Sleep* (1946) with Humphrey Bogart, that shows a similarity to the underground porn and ritual imagery in *The Black Dahlia* (2006), as well as to scenes in David Lynch's *Lost Highway* (1997).

This revelation of the inside sexual and ritual aspects in the films themselves demonstrates these claims are not without basis. While *noir* would not be a place one would expect esoteric symbolism, *The Big Sleep* was actually referencing a topic completely taboo to the audience of the day – sex, drug and ritual. In *The Black Dahlia*, a secret flop house that resembles it can be seen above, where the porn was filmed, later to be followed by a grizzly occult murder. In *The Black Dahlia*, a wealthy family is involved in the ritual crime, bringing to mind the rituals performed in the estates in *Eyes Wide Shut* and *The Ninth Gate*. It also brings to mind the ritual porn murder film at the end of *Lost Highway*, which is an explicit tribute to *noir*.

Rose McGowan as Short's friend in The Black Dahlia.

Indeed, the influence of surrealism on film *noir* is often overlooked, but is undoubtedly an influence on David Lynch and his *Neo-noir* works. The blog "Passing Strange" illustrates this influence in the following passages where the references to both Chandler and the "exquisite corpse" are key, as they relate directly to the dahlia case and film:

In his book *More Than Night: Film Noir in its Contexts* (2008), James Naremore discusses the comparative neglect accorded the influence of Surrealism in discussing the genesis of films noir: "The importance of existentialism to the period has long been recognized; what needs to be emphasized is that existentialism was intertwined with a residual surrealism, and surrealism was crucial for the reception of any art described as 'noir'" (Naremore 17). Though the term "film noir" dates back to reviews of certain wartime American films by French critics seeing them for the first time after the end of WWII (John Huston's *The Maltese Falcon*, Billy Wilder's *Double Indemnity*, Otto Preminger's *Laura*, Fritz Lang's *The Woman in the Window* and Edward Dmytryk's *Murder, My Sweet*), Raymond Borde and Etienne Chaumeton's *A Panorama of American Film Noir 1941-1953* (1955) was the first book-length attempt to lay out the style and themes of these films according to the guiding influence of Surrealist preoccupations and concerns. While Borde and Chaumeton never claimed to exhaust their subject matter – the word "panorama" suggests a broad overview – their volume still serves as a "benchmark" introduction to films noir (Silver and Ward 372).

...Many of the films designated as noir were based on crime novels (including works by Chandler, Hammett, Jim Thompson, W.R. Burnett and Horace McCoy) published in France as part of Gallimard's influential *Série Noire* imprint. The editor of this series was Marcel Duhamel, an early participant in the Surrealist movement involved in the development of "Exquisite Corpse," a favorite pastime which featured the assemblage of words and/or images supplied at random into a collective whole. This game emphasized the forces of chance at work in the unconscious and yielded the kinds of arbitrary juxtapositions much admired by the group.[19]

While the case of the Black Dahlia and Elizabeth Short may be officially unsolved, if we look to the hints and connections of the fictional presentation, we see odd connections that emerge to reveal possibilities that clearly suggest ritual murder. Hodel's surrealist taste in art even includes Saturn-style carvings on the face of a floating, Dali-style corpse and reportedly the dismembered corpse of Short included these markings, as well as the dismemberment hearkening to the shamanic process of ritual division.

Steve Hodel dismisses claims of any ritual connection to George's killing (assuming he is the killer), but there do seem to be ritual elements in relation to the body of Short that recall killings in cases like those discussed in Maury Terry's *The Ultimate Evil*, relating to Berkowitz, which he argues were ritual in nature. Regardless, the film presentation hints at these deeper connections relating to the dark side of Hollywood, beyond merely drugs and trafficking in girls, but even to the point of ritual murder as a result of elite

Hillary Swank as Madeline Linscott, molested daughter of Emmett and possessed mother and co-killer with "George," Ramona (Fiona Shaw).

353

deviants with a taste for the ultimately sick sexual perversions who pin their crimes on disturbed and psychotic patsies – precisely the plot of another *Neo-Noir*-meets-gothic-grotesquery, *True Detective* Season 1. Also in the film is a meta-reference to another film, *Nosferatu* (based on *Dracula*, by Bram Stoker), where the parasitical Count Orlok places a young wife into a trance before parasitically preying on her. Orlok resembles the clown-image painting referenced later in the film as George's "art" which suggests he is also a kind of Nosferatu; these Hollywood vixens may actually be victims of ritual abuse and mind control.[20]

That there is a dark side to Hollywood is known, documented and ongoing. People rise and reap fortune and fame, fall and rise again. Others stand and hope, some walk away. Yet again, the true occult side, the temptation of ultimate pleasure and the fall into that swamp of occult peculiarity, is still lesser known. In *Sinister Forces Bk. II* on "Hollywood Babylon," Levenda includes a snippet from comparative religion writer Mircea Eliade:

> Babylon was *Bab-ilani*, a "gate of the gods," for it was there that the gods descended to earth.... But it was always Babylon that is the scene of the connection between the earth and the lower regions, for the city had been built upon *bab apsi*, the "Gates of Apsu" – apsu designating the waters of chaos before the Creation.[21] (pg. 109)

In Eliade's *The Sacred and the Profane*, he explains of the ancient conception of the threshold or gate, which is peculiarly applicable:

> A similar ritual function falls to the threshold of the human habitation, and it is for this reason that the threshold is an object of great importance. Numerous rites accompany passing the domestic threshold – a bow, a prostration, a pious touch of the hand, and so on. The threshold has its guardians – gods and spirits who forbid entrance both to human enemies and to demons and the power of pestilence. It is on the threshold that sacrifices to the guardian divinities are offered. Here too certain paleo-oriental cultures (Babylon, Egypt, Israel) situated the judgment place. The threshold, the door shows the solution of continuity in space immediately and concretely; hence their great religious importance, for they are symbols and at the same time vehicles passage from one space to another.[22]

In J.J. Abrams' TV series *Alias*, we note that the beautiful Jennifer Garner is recruited by the CIA as a kind of PR front, to sell recruits the idea of service as a glamorous thing. A few days later, the *Washington Post* ran a revealing piece titled, "Ex-spies Infiltrate Hollywood as Espionage TV Shows and Movies Multiply." The article treats the issue as if this is some new move, when readers of my site, JaysAnalysis, know this is nothing new, but a classic dark marriage that existed all along. Consider the laughable irony: *The Americans* is a show about KGB infiltration of America, in the midst of an article about actual CIA usage of Hollywood (as propaganda), as the *Post* writes:

> "Hollywood tends to be a destination spot for a lot of Washingtonians," said David Nevins, the president of Showtime, which produces the spy juggernaut *Homeland*.
>
> "There was the 'West Wing' crowd of former politicos. I've met with more than one former Navy SEAL. And now, certainly the intelligence community has been the most recent in a long line of Washingtonians trying to come out and tell their stories.
>
> [Joseph] Weisberg, whose show begins its third season on FX on Wednesday night, is perhaps the most successful of the CIA alumni who have infiltrated Hollywood. *The Americans*, about two deep-cover KGB operatives living in suburban Virginia in the 1980s, was ranked by many television critics as one of last year's top 10 shows.
>
> But Weisberg, who left the CIA in 1994, is hardly the only ex-agency guy trying to cash in on the spy show craze. (Spy shows, one executive at a major Hollywood talent agency observed, have become as ubiquitous as cop shows.) Former senior CIA officials Rodney Faraon and Henry "Hank" Crumpton were the executive producers of NBC's *State of Affairs*, which starred Katherine Heigl as a CIA analyst and member of the agency's presidential daily briefing team – one of Faraon's old jobs."[23]

Let us also not forget the role of Melissa Mahle, former CIA operative, in "coaching" and "advising" CFR member Angelina Jolie in her role as triple agent in *SALT*, the 2010 espionage thriller.[24] The film itself was loosely based on Mahle, as the *Telegraph* reports, "Jolie's role is based, loosely, on the experiences of Mahle and other spies. 'I was very impressed when I met Angelina,' says Mahle. 'She was very intent upon understanding not only what a real CIA officer was like but also the motivations behind our actions."[25]

Jayne Mansfield communed with Anton LaVey, founder of the Church of Satan, and met with a dark end. Indeed, it is becoming more and more apparent that Hollywood really is the flip side of the CIA, when we think of Ben Affleck making *Argo*, based around CIA operative Antonio Mendez,

355

one of the Agency's *Masters of Disguise*. Affleck revealed that Hollywood is "probably full of CIA" to the *Guardian*, in the wake of his film about the CIA staging a fake B movie in Iran.[26] As these revelations continue to leak, we can expect more evidence to confirm this thesis: The extent of mind control connecting Hollywood and the dark side of the CIA may run far deeper than even I imagine aleatory(and that's going pretty far), especially when we think of individuals like Sammy Davis, Jr. and Jayne Mansfield, members of the Church of Satan, as well as a host of other celebrities who fancy dabbling in the occult and chaos magick, for example.[27] As we have seen, films like *Eyes Wide Shut* revealed these very associations, and from the *Black Dahlia* to *Mulholland Drive*, the connections are real, while the mechanics of this occult empire become especially clear when we understand militaristic blockbusters like *Zero Dark Thirty* are a multi-cultural mixture of truth and propaganda.[28] Who deserves to live?

Everything is done for you. The sacrifice and the murder. The wait and the mad rush. Now, take off your shoes.

Endnotes

1. Robb, David L. *Operation Hollywood: How the Pentagon Shapes and Censors Movies*. New York: Prometheus Books, 2004. Jenkins, Tricia. *The CIA in Hollywood: How the Agency Shapes Film and Television*. University of Texas Press, 2012.

2. Henningsen, Patrick. "American Sniper: Hollywood and Our Homeland Insecurity Complex." 21stCenturyWire. 26 January, 2015. Web. http://21stcenturywire.com/2015/01/26/american-sniper-hollywood-and-our-homeland-insecurity/

3. Sirota, David. "How the 80s Programmed us for War." Salon. 15 March, 2011. Web. http://www.salon.com/2011/03/15/sirota_excerpt_back_to_our_future/. Engelhardt, Tom. AntiWar.com "In the Zone with GI Joe." 20 December, 2004. Web. http://www.antiwar.com/engelhardt/?articleid=4188

4. Dilanian, Ken. "Hollywood Figures Spied for CIA, Book Asserts." *LA Times*. 10 January, 2014. Web. http://www.latimes.com/nation/politics/politicsnow/la-pn-hollywood-spies-20140110-story.html

5. Connolly, Kieron. *Dark History of Hollywood*. London: Amber Book, 2014, pgs. 152-62.

6. McGowan, *Weird Scenes Inside the Canyon*.

7. "Britney Spears' pilot ex-boyfriend who coached her through alcohol-fueled public meltdown has been shot dead by Taliban in Afghanistan." *DailyMail*. 17 January, 2015. Web. http://www.dailymail.co.uk/news/article-2915013/Britney-Spears-British-pilot-ex-boyfriend-coached-alcohol-fuelled-public-meltdown-shot-dead-Taliban-Afghanistan.html

8. 'Kesha files lawsuit against longtime producer, claims he abused her." FoxNews. 14 October, 2014. Web. http://www.foxnews.com/entertainment/2014/10/14/kesha-files-lawsuit-against-longtime-producer-claims-abused-her/

9. "The Penn State Scandal." CBSNews. Web. http://www.cbsnews.com/feature/the-penn-state-scandal/

10. Boffey, Daniel. "Revealed: how Jimmy Savile abused up to 1,000 victims on BBC premises." Guardian. 18 January, 2014. Web. http://www.theguardian.com/media/2014/jan/18/jimmy-savile-abused-1000-victims-bbc

11. "COVER-UP: Female British MP Abused Boy in Care Home." 21stCenturyWire. 13 January, 2014.

Web. http://21stcenturywire.com/2014/01/13/female-british-mp-abused-boy-in-care-home/

12. "Corey Feldman told cops he was molested and named his abusers but they did nothing because they were too focused on Michael Jackson investigation." *DailyMail*. Web. http://www.dailymail.co.uk/news/article-2483502/Corey-Feldman-told-cops-molested-named-abusers-did-nothing.html

13. DiGraaf, Mia. "EXCLUSIVE: Screenwriter mysteriously killed in 1997 after finishing script that revealed the 'real reason' for US invasion of Panama had been working for the CIA... and both his hands were missing." 17 January, 2015. http://www.dailymail.co.uk/news/article-2905392/Hollywood-screenwriter-mysteriously-killed-20-years-ago-working-CIA-hands-sent-autopsy-200-years-old.html

14. See Coucha, Nadia. *Surrealism and the Occult*. Mandrake, 1991.

15. "The Minotaur & The Black Dahlia Avenger – Part 1." SaturnDeathCult. Web. http://saturndeathcult.com/crimes-of-the-saturn-death-cult/black-dahlia-avenger-ritual-crime-for-ritual-sake/

16. Nelson and Blayliss. Exquisite Corpse: Surrealism and the Black Dahlia Murder. New York: Bulfinch Press, 2006, pgs. 40, 57, 85. Hodel, Steve. Black Dahlia Avenger. New York: Harper, 2003, pgs. 240-2.

17. Hodel, *Black Dahlia Avenger*.

18. "david mcgowan revisits the black dahlia murder." MediaMonarchy. 6 August, 2011. Web. http://mediamonarchy.com/2011/08/david-mcgowan-revisits-black-dahlia/

19. "Surrealism and Film Noir." Passing Strange. 18 March, 2011. Web. https://buddwilkins.wordpress.com/2011/03/18/passing-strange/

20. Norman, Neil. "Dark side of Oz: The exploitation of Judy Garland." *Express*. 5 April, 2010. Web. http://www.express.co.uk/expressyourself/167269/Dark-side-of-Oz-The-exploitation-of-Judy-Garland

21. Levenda, 109.

22. Eliade., Mircea. *The Sacred and the Profane*. San Diego: HBJ, 1957, pg. 25.

23. Shapira, Ian. "Ex-spies infiltrate Hollywood as espionage TV shows and movies multiply." WashingtonPost. 24 January, 2014. Web. https://www.washingtonpost.com/local/ex-spies-infiltrate-hollywood-as-espionage-tv-shows-and-movies-multiply/2015/01/24/a50721a4-a183-11e4-b146-577832eafcb4_story.html

24. Green, Mary. "Angelina Jolie Joins Council on Foreign Relations." *People*. 6 July, 2007. Web. http://www.people.com/people/article/0,,20041839,00.html

25. "Angelina Jolie's spy advisor." *Telegraph*. 16 August, 2010. Web. http://www.telegraph.co.uk/culture/film/starsandstories/7934530/Angelina-Jolies-spy-advisor.html

26. "Ben Affleck on Argo: Hollywood is Probably Full of CIA Agents." *Guardian*. 7 November, 2012. Web. http://www.theguardian.com/film/video/2012/nov/07/ben-affleck-argo-video-interview

27. Burke, Andrei. "8 Celebrities Who Practice Chaos Magick." UltraCulture. Web. http://ultraculture.org/blog/2014/11/13/8-celebrities-practice-chaos-magick/

28. "Zero Dark Thirty wins 'Riefenstahl Oscar' for Best Propaganda Film." 21stCenturyWire. 24 February, 2014. Web. http://21stcenturywire.com/2013/02/24/zero-dark-thirty-wins-albert-speer-oscar-award-for-best-propaganda-picture/

Index